SCIENCE OF TODAY
AND
THE PROBLEMS OF GENESIS

SCIENCE OF TODAY
AND
THE PROBLEMS OF GENESIS

By

FR. PATRICK O'CONNELL, B.D.

A Study of the "Six Days" of Creation,
The Origin of Man and
The Deluge and Antiquity of Man
Based on Science and Sacred Scripture

A VINDICATION OF THE PAPAL ENCYCLICALS AND RULINGS OF THE CHURCH ON THESE QUESTIONS

"And he said: Let us make man to our image and likeness: and let him have dominion over the fishes of the sea, and the fowls of the air, and the beasts, and the whole earth, and every creeping creature that moveth upon the earth. And God created man to his own image: to the image of God he created him: male and female he created them." —Genesis 1:26-27

TAN BOOKS AND PUBLISHERS, INC.
Rockford, Illinois 61105

Nihil Obstat: Joannes McCormack
Censor Deputatus
April 14, 1959

Imprimatur: ✠ Joannes Kyne
Episcopus Midensis
April 16, 1959

Library of Congress Catalog Card No.: 90-71913

ISBN: 0-89555-438-0

Printed and bound in the United States of America.

TAN BOOKS AND PUBLISHERS, INC.
P.O. Box 424
Rockford, Illinois 61105

1993

Dedicated by the author and his brother to the memory of their dear Parents

CONTENTS

Part I
The Six Days of Creation

Part II
The Origin of Man

Part III
The Biblical Account of the Deluge

Part IV
The Antiquity of Man

PREFACE—PARTS I AND II

Serious doubt exists among some Catholics about what exactly the Church binds them to believe and what is a matter for free discussion in the account of the creation of the world and of man, found in the first two chapters of *Genesis*.

Great doubt still exists among them about what are the most recent conclusions of science on the problems dealt with in these two chapters. The doubt about the teaching of the Church is not the fault of the Holy See, for definite answers have been given by the Council of Trent to all doubts raised up to then, and since then, the teaching of the Church on these subjects has been officially explained in a number of Encyclicals, the first of which was *Providentissimus Deus* issued by Pope Leo XIII on December 18, 1893.

The real origin of these doubts was the acceptance as established facts of what are mere theories, and a consequent straining both of the words of Holy Scripture and of the directions given by the Authorities of the Church for their interpretation, in order to make them fit in with these imaginary scientific conclusions.

The object of this book is to give the scientific conclusions about the Six Days of Creation and the origin of man arrived at during the past few years, but not yet generally known, and to show that these conclusions are in agreement with the Mosaic account of Creation, and are a vindication of the Papal Encyclicals issued for its interpretation.

The author's original intention was to deal only with the question of the origin of man, but as the increasing demand of modern exegetes for greater freedom to depart from the literal meaning of *Genesis* on the question of the origin of Adam and Eve was based in part at least on the assumption that the account of creation found in *Genesis*—with light before the sun existed and vegetation before there was either light or heat—does not correspond with objective reality, he judged it best to show first that modern science has found answers to these apparent difficulties, and that the biblical account given in the time of Moses does actually correspond with objective reality.

With regard to the origin of man, the account given in *Genesis* interpreted according to the rules laid down by the Holy See, combined with the latest discoveries in the domain of paleontology, enable us to come to the very definite conclusion that man's body was not evolved from a lower animal. In the case of other living things, however, while it has been known from remotest antiquity that there is a principle of diversity in living things which causes the offspring to differ from their parents and from one another, and that this principle of diversity has produced new breeds or varieties, modern scientists have not so far been able to determine with certainty how far these mutations have resulted in new species or new genera in the course of the millions of years during which the animal and vegetable kingdoms have existed, or to say what was the number of the species or genera created by God at the beginning or in the course of the ages. There is, however, sufficient scientific evidence available to show that the theory of evolution in its extreme form is untenable.

This work consists of four parts: the Six Days of Creation, the Origin of Man, the Deluge and the Antiquity of Man.

The views expressed in this book are the result of a study of the problems involved that goes back to my college days 50 years ago, a study which has been kept up since. The exacting duties of missionary life in China delayed the publication of this book until the continuation of work there became impossible.

For the composition of this book the principal works in French and English including the most recent on the subjects dealt with have been consulted, and in addition, the principal books in Italian, Spanish and German. A full list of these books is given at the end of this book.

Just about the time that this work was completed, letters on behalf of three of the Sacred Congregations—the Congregations of the Holy Office, of Seminaries and Universities, and of Religious—were sent to all Ordinaries, Rectors of Ecclesiastical Faculties and Superiors General of Religious Institutes, warning them that the use of a book entitled, *Introduction a la Bible t.* I[er], *Introduction generale, Ancien Testament* was forbidden either as a textbook or a book of reference in all seminaries and Catholic universities of the world. A criticism of this book indicating some of the reasons why the use of this book was forbidden was published subsequently in the Vatican paper, *L'Osservatore Romano.*

As these documents indicate clearly that the various directives of the Holy See, as found in Papal Encyclicals and the decrees of the Biblical Commission, for the interpretation of the first 11 chapters of *Genesis* (with which the present work is concerned) have not been modified, we give the letters of the Sacred Congregations and the criticism of the book in question after this preface.

The author wishes to convey his thanks to three friends who wish to remain anonymous, who have cooperated with him in the production of this work: to a well-known author who read the manuscripts and offered valuable suggestions; and to two theologians who read and checked the whole work.

We tender our thanks to Messrs. Hollis and Carter Ltd., 25, Ashley Place, London, for permission to quote from *Is Evolution Proved? A Debate between Douglas Dewar and H. S. Shelton;* to Rev. Desmond Murray, O.P., F.R.E.S. for permission to quote from *Species Revalued,* published by Blackfriars, London; to Messrs. George Allen and Unwin, Ltd., London for permission to quote from Sir S. Zuckerman's chapter in *Evolution as a Process;* to the Macmillan Company, Fifth Avenue, New York; to the editors of B.A.C., Madrid for permission to translate and publish the chapter on *The Origin of Man* by Sr. Sagües, S.J. in Vol. II of *Sacrae Theologiae Summa;* to Joseph F. Wagner, Inc., New York City, for permission to quote from *The Theory of Evolution Judged by Reason and Faith* by Cardinal Ernesto Ruffini, and to other publishers from whose books we have taken short quotations.

If this book helps to conserve the traditional veneration for the Saint of the Old Testament who received the Law on Mount Sinai and witnessed to Christ on Mount Thabor, and to lighten the heavy task of modern biblical exegetes, the author will regard his labors as well recompensed.

LETTERS FROM THE SACRED CONGREGATION OF SEMINARIES AND UNIVERSITIES

Addressed to the Ordinaries of Dioceses and Rectors of Ecclesiastical Faculties

It is a well-known fact that the Church takes great care to ensure that students for the priesthood should get a solid training in Biblical studies.

This Sacred Congregation has examined the volume entitled *Introduction a la Bible t.* Ier, *Introduction Générale, Ancien Testament* (Ed. Desclée *et cie.*, 1957), and has judged it to be absolutely unsuitable [for seminaries and universities] because it fails to satisfy the requirements of sound pedagogy and of the method appropriate for biblical studies, and for other reasons as well.

All people concerned are therefore hereby warned that this work is not to be used either as a textbook for class or as a book of reference.

Given at Rome, in the Palace of Saint Callista, April 21, 1958.

J. Cardinal Pizzardo, Prefect; C. Confalonieri, Archev. de Nicopolis Secretary

Letter from the Sacred Congregation of Religious To the Superiors General of Religious

Rome
May 12, 1958

Very Rev. Father,

The Supreme Congregation of the Holy Office has entrusted this Sacred Congregation with the task of transmitting the following communication to the Superior Generals of Religious Institutes:

> This Supreme Congregation has submitted for examination the Volume entitled *Introduction a la Bible t.* Ier, *Introduction Générale, Ancien Testament*.

> On February 26 of this year the Eminent Fathers [of the Sacred Congregation of the Holy Office] have ordered us to warn Ordinaries and Superior Generals of Religious Institutes, that for reasons of method and pedagogy, they are not to accept the aforementioned book *Introduction a la Bible* to be used either as a textbook or a book of reference in their schools of theology.
>
> Ar. Larrona
> Secretary

The following is a criticism of *L'Introduction a la Bible,* with an indication of why its use was forbidden in seminaries and universities by the Sacred Congregation of Seminaries and Universities which was published in *L'Osservatore Romano* on July 2, 1958.

An Introduction to the Bible and an Opportune Document

The Sacred Congregation of Seminaries and Universities in a recent circular addressed to Ordinaries and Rectors of Ecclesiastical Faculties begins by recalling how important it is for the Church that the young clergy get a strict and solid biblical training and then issues the following declaration and order.

Here follows the text of the "letter of the Sacred Congregation of Religious forbidding the use of *L'Introduction a la Bible* in all Seminaries and Universities either as a textbook or a book of reference." *L'Osservatore Romano* then continues:

> In this volume of nearly 900 pages, a quarter of which is devoted to the general introduction and three quarters to the special introduction of the Books of the Old Testament, there are wanting above all that order, clarity and solidity, that are perhaps all the more necessary in a work of this kind which, although it does not claim to be a fundamental textbook, is nevertheless intended (as indicated in the Preface) to initiate priests, students and educated lay people into the scientific study of Holy Scripture: that is to say, intended for readers many of whom are not properly on their guard and are at grips with a subject which is certainly neither easy nor simple, without the aid of oral explanation by an enlightened master.
>
> To construct a book—and especially a book of this kind—in

great part on hypotheses, opinions and inductions, which are without solid proof and need to be verified, for the purpose of substituting it for the [traditional] works which, though not perfect and complete in all points, have nevertheless in their favour the experience and approbation of centuries, does not seem to be a scientific method of proceeding.

We could fill pages and pages with phrases, remarks and explanations taken from this book to show how fragile this new edifice is. Should not certain problems, out of respect for the Church and the regulations laid down by her, be more fitly and usefully studied in a more appropriate place, that is to say in studies destined only for a small body of specialists trained to deal with these difficult matters? There are people who think so, for they fear that otherwise the results, far from being an advantage of faith and science, may perhaps only lead to scepticism and confusion.

The eleven authors [nine contributors and two editors] who have collaborated in this work know and cite the Pontifical documents; they are not ignorant of the imposing tradition which comes down from the illustrious St. Jerome to the most weighty and most universally recognized scholars of different tongues, including the learned and eloquent Bossuet. But whoever reads these pages with an open mind free from prejudice, with that "full charity" of which the Encyclical *Divino afflante* speaks, is immediately disillusioned by a style, which, while readable, is not adapted to precise and accurate work. In it one does not feel oneself to be in the current of the royal stream of biblical science which is able and happy to receive into its bosom new legitimate and pacific tributaries. No! frankness which is on a par with our respect for good intentions compels us to remark that we feel ourselves being borne by another current; this work is an attempt, both surprising and disturbing, to introduce into the very bosom of the Church as definite truths, theories and systems which are still being debated and are by no means unshakable.

In this present article in which a full discussion of this work is neither possible nor opportune, may we be permitted to make some remarks, in keeping with the main theme of this article, which indeed might be multiplied.

For the Pentateuch, the theory of the four sources [of Wellhausen] which is comparatively recent, not being yet a century old, dominates the whole exegesis, as if it were a kind of

> fundamental article of faith, and the role which this theory assigns to Moses is not "the great part" assigned to him by the Biblical Commission ten years ago in the letter to Cardinal Suhard, to which the authors are fond of referring—in which letter, by the way, is found the observation that non-Catholic scholars find an explanation of certain peculiarities of editing not in the diversity of documents but elsewhere. (Ench. Bibl. 880).

The author of the criticism in *L'Osservatore Romano* then recommends the reading of an article by Fr. Bea, S.J., in *La Civilta Cattolica* of April 17, 1948, in which emphasis is laid on the advantages of the historico-traditional method of exegesis; and of another article by Fr. Leon-Dufour, S.J., in *Recherches de science religieuse* of April-June 1958 on the question of the fluctuations in various theories of exegesis since the first World War.

He then calls attention to certain passages in pages 27-30 of *Introduction a la Bible* dealing with the question of inspiration where the theory propounded is likely to cause alarm to those who hold the traditional view. The article in *L'Osservatore Romano* then continues:

> The ideal of the biblical exegete—which stands out resplendent in the Encyclical *Divino afflante*—who is filled with respect for the Church, furnished with all the scientific instruments, acting in the sphere which belongs to him, not impeded, but urged on and exhorted by the Church to seek a solution of difficult and unusual problems, to descend boldly so to speak in his bathysphere to the depths of a sea still unexplored and full of dangers in his endeavour to find a happy solution at the same time in accordance with the teaching of the Church and the certain conclusions of profane sciences—this ideal, we say, does not disconcert either the scientist or the devout believer, but appeals to every Christian, whether specialist or not.
>
> In this book *(L'Introduction a la Bible)* there is a question of a procedure which is completely different. There is question of remaking the principles of biblical exegesis from the very foundation after nineteen centuries of Christianity, as if up to the present nothing had been done in this matter. It is a procedure which is based on mere affirmations that are left unproven and on ignoring the precious confirmations of the traditional

opinions, afforded by the profane sciences—confirmations which are every day increasing in volume and importance, especially those which come from the sciences of archaeology and history. Our authors devote much space to the question of "literary forms," which is very much spoken of today and used in a form of fashionable propaganda, but which very few study deeply.

But can one say that in this facile introduction (which would not have been made too cumbersome by a moderate use of source references) the authors discuss these "literary forms and editorial processes" with that modesty and discretion recommended by the Church, and that they attain the ends which she desires?

"Let the biblical exegete," says the Encyclical *Divino afflante,* "make prudent use of that help, in order to prove that Holy Scripture is free from all error."

And truly, if there is any study which should be *edifying* in the most profound etymological sense of that word, it is that of biblical exegesis. The contrary [is true of this book in question]; we have to express the sentiment which we have experienced all the time during the reading of this volume, a sentiment experienced also by others, that it seems to us to be more *corrosive* than *constructive*. The making of this avowal does not mean that we fail to recognize the active good-will and uprightness of the many authors of this book, but we beg leave to ask them just another question, which will be the last: What Christian or what human being would be able to draw sustenance and comfort from their "synthesis of the Pentateuch" which they compress into two pages at the end of their lengthy treatise?

There come to our minds those noble and holy words in which the children of Israel confessed, when contracting powerful alliances, that they had no need of them since the Holy Books sufficed for their strength and comfort—*Habentes solatio Sanctos Libros.*

If there ever were times when consolation was needed it is certainly the times in which we live; times of prodigious and terrifying atomic experiments and cruel anguish, times also when attempts are being made to reduce the contents of the Bible to nothingness.

But at this time the Divine Book remains our only and our last consolation.

INTRODUCTORY

False scientific theories about the origin of the world and the origin of man have led to errors in the interpretation of the first chapters of *Genesis,* and these in turn have led to misrepresentations of Papal Encyclicals written to correct these errors. When erroneous interpretations of passages of Sacred Scripture have been a long time in possession, there is a tendency among commentators who have adopted these erroneous interpretations to regard attempts to state the true interpretation as acts of aggression, which they think themselves justified in condemning. The theory of Laplace with regard to the origin of our earth, now proved to be false, which flatly contradicted the Mosaic account, was so long in possession and was so widely adopted by commentators that attempts to defend the Mosaic account were denounced as an error to which the name "concordism" was given, and the Encyclical *Providentissimus Deus* issued by Pope Leo XIII, in 1893, to condemn the too great liberty taken by some commentators was represented and is still being represented as a charter of liberty that frees them from all restrictions. (See *Darwinism and Catholic Thought* by Canon Dorlodot, pp. 32 *et seq.*). The statement from St. Augustine incorporated in this Encyclical which says: *"The Holy Ghost, who spoke by them, did not intend to teach men these things (that is to say, the essential nature of the things of the visible universe), things in no way profitable unto salvation"* has been quoted repeatedly out of its context in favor of the view that we are not to look for objective truth in the Mosaic account of Creation and that full liberty is given in this Encyclical to depart from it. We give therefore for the benefit of our readers the whole passage in which this statement occurs in order that they may see that it has not the meaning which is frequently attributed to it. The following is the passage:

In the second place, we have to contend against those who, making an evil use of physical science, minutely scrutinise the sacred book in order to detect the writers in a mistake, and to take occasion to vilify its contents. Attacks of this kind, bearing as they do on matters of sensible experience, are peculiarly dangerous to the masses, and also to the young who are beginning their literary studies; for the young, if they lose their reverence for the Holy Scripture on one or more points, are easily led to give up believing in it altogether. It need not be pointed out how the nature of science, just as it is admirably adapted to show forth the glory of the Great Creator, provided it is taught as it should be, so if it is perversely imparted to the youthful intelligence, it may prove most fatal in destroying the principles of true morality. Hence to the professor of Sacred Scripture a knowledge of natural science will be of great assistance in detecting such attacks on the sacred books and in refuting them. There can never, indeed, be any real discrepancy between the theologian and the physicist, as long as each confines himself within his own lines, and both are careful, as St. Augustine warns us, *"not to make rash assertions, or assert what is not known as known."* If dissension should arise between them, here is the rule also laid down by St. Augustine for the theologian: "Whatever scientists can really demonstrate to be true of physical nature, we must show to be capable of reconciliation with our Scriptures; and whatever they assert in their treatises which is contrary to these Scriptures of ours, that is, to Catholic faith, we must either prove it as well as we can to be false, or at all events we must, without the smallest hesitation, believe it to be so."

To understand how just is the rule here formulated, we must remember, first, that the sacred writers or, to speak more accurately, *"the Holy Ghost, who spoke by them, did not intend to teach men these things (that is to say, the essential nature of the things of the visible universe), things in no way profitable unto salvation."* Hence they did not seek to penetrate the secrets of nature, but rather described and dealt with things in more or less figurative language, or in terms which were commonly used at the time, and which in many instances are in daily use at this day, even by the most eminent men of science. Ordinary speech primarily and properly described what came under the senses; and somewhat in the same way the sacred writers—as the Angelic Doctor also reminds us—went by what sensibly appeared, or put down what God, speaking to men, signified in a way men could understand and were accustomed to.

The Catholic interpreter, although he should show that those facts of natural science which investigators affirm to be now quite certain are not contrary to the scripture rightly explained, must, nevertheless always bear in mind that *much which has been considered to have been proved as certain has afterwards been called into question and rejected.*

It may also happen that the sense of a passage remains ambiguous, and in this case good hermeneutical methods will greatly assist in clearing up the obscurity. *But it is absolutely wrong and forbidden either to narrow inspiration to certain parts of Holy Scripture or to admit that the sacred writer has erred. For the system of those who, in order to rid themselves of these difficulties, do not hesitate to concede that divine inspiration regards the things of faith and morals, and nothing beyond, because (as they wrongly think) in a question of the truth or falsehood of a passage we should consider the reason and purpose which He had in mind when saying it—this system cannot be tolerated.*

For all the books which the Church receives as sacred and canonical are written wholly and entirely, with all their parts, at the dictation of the Holy Ghost; and so far is it from being possible that any error can co-exist with inspiration, that inspiration not only is essentially incompatible with error, but excludes and rejects, as absolutely and necessarily as it is possible, that God Himself, the Supreme Truth can utter that which is not true.

Pope Benedict XV

On September 15, 1920, Pope Benedict XV issued the Encyclical *Spiritus Paraclitus* in which he repeats and elaborates the above statement of Pope Leo XIII. The following quotation is taken from this Encyclical:

But although these words of our predecessor Pope Leo XIII leave no room for doubt or dispute, it grieves us to find that not only men outside, but even children of the Catholic Church—nay, what is a peculiar sorrow to us, even clerics and professors of sacred learning—who in their own conceit either openly repudiate or at least attack in secret the Church's teaching on this point. . . *But we remind them that they will only come to miserable grief if they neglect our predecessor's injunctions and overstep the limits set by the Fathers.*

1. No Distinction of Primary and Secondary Elements:

Yet no one can pretend that certain recent writers really adhere to these limitations. For while conceding that inspiration extends to every phrase—and, indeed, to every single word of Scripture—yet, by endeavouring to distinguish between what they style the primary or religious and the secondary or profane element in the Bible, they claim that the effect of inspiration—namely, absolute truth and immunity from error—are to be restricted to that primary or religious element. Their notion is that only what concerns religion is intended and taught by God in Scripture, and that all the rest—things concerning "profane knowledge" the garments in which Divine truth is presented—God merely permits, and even leaves to the individual author's greater or less knowledge. Small wonder, then, that in their view a considerable number of things occur in the Bible touching physical science, history and the like, which cannot be reconciled with modern progress in science!

Some even maintain that these views do not conflict with what our predecessor laid down since—so they claim—he said that the sacred writers spoke in accordance with the external—and thus deceptive appearance of things in nature. But the Pontiff's own words show that this is a rash and false deduction. For sound philosophy teaches that the senses can never be deceived as regards their own proper and immediate object.

Moreover, our predecessor, sweeping aside all such distinctions between what these critics are pleased to call primary and secondary elements, says in no ambiguous fashion that "those who fancy that when it is a question of truth of certain expressions we have not got to consider so much what God said as why He said it," are very far indeed from the truth. He also teaches that Divine Inspiration extends to every part of the Bible without the slightest exception, and that no error can occur in the inspired text: "It would be wholly impious to limit inspiration to certain portions only of Scripture or to concede that the sacred authors themselves could have erred."

2. *No Distinction of Relative and Absolute Truth*

Those too, who hold that the historical portions of Scripture do not rest on the absolute truth of facts but merely on what they are pleased to term their relative truth, namely, what people then commonly thought, are, no less than the aforementioned critics, out of harmony with the Church's teaching which is endorsed by the testimony of St. Jerome and other Fathers.

Pope Pius XII

The following quotation from the Encyclical *Divino Afflante Spiritu* issued by His Holiness Pope Pius XII should remove all doubt about the meaning of the passage we have just quoted from *Providentissimus Deus*.

The Vatican Council, in order to condemn false doctrines on inspiration, declared that the reason for which these same books are to be held by the Church as sacred and canonical is not that, having been composed by human industry they have been subsequently approved by her authority, nor merely that they contain certain revelation without error, but because, being written under the inspiration of the Holy Ghost, they have God as their author, and as such have been delivered to the Church herself.

Later on, this solemn definition of Catholic doctrine, which claims for these books in their entirety and with all their parts a divine authority such as must enjoy immunity from any error whatsoever, *was contradicted by certain Catholic writers who dared to restrict the truth of Sacred Scripture to matters of faith and morals alone, and to consider the remainder, touching matters of the physical or historical order as "obiter dicta"* and having (according to them) *no connection whatever with faith. These errors found their merited condemnation in the Encyclical "Providentissmum Deus,"* published on November 18, 1893 by our Predecessor of immortal memory, Leo XIII, who in the same letter issued very wise ordinances and directions for the safeguarding of biblical studies.

Pope Pius XII refers again to this question in his Encyclical *Humani Generis* issued in 1950. In this Encyclical he condemns the misuse of a Letter sent to Cardinal Suhard, Archbishop of Paris in 1948 by the Secretary of the Biblical Commission, in the following terms:

> In particular one must deplore a certain too free interpretation of the historical books of the Old Testament. Those who favour this system, in order to defend their cause, mistakenly refer to the Letter which was sent not long ago to the Archbishop of Paris, Cardinal Suhard, by the Pontifical Commission on Biblical Studies. This letter in fact clearly points out that the first eleven chapters of *Genesis*, although properly speaking are not in line with the historical methods used by the best Greek and Latin writers or by competent authorities of our own time, do nevertheless belong to history in the true sense which however must be studied and examined by biblical scholars.
>
> They not only set forth the principal truths which are fundamental for our salvation, but also give a popular description of the origin of the human race and the chosen people.

This letter to Cardinal Suhard, the misuse of which was condemned by Pope Pius XII, actually reaffirmed all that had been stated in the responses of the Biblical Commission of 1909, and embodied the following quotations from the Encyclical *Divino Afflante Spiritu* of 1943.

> The Catholic commentator must grapple with the problems so far unsolved, not only to repel the attacks of opponents, but also in the effort to find an explanation which will be faithfully consonant with the teaching of the Church, particularly with the traditional doctrine of the inerrancy of Scripture, while being at the same time in due conformity with the *certain* conclusions of profane scientists. (Extract from the Letter to Cardinal Suhard, January 16, 1948).

Conclusions from Above Quotations

The first conclusion to be drawn is that neither the Pope or any of the Congregations speaking in his name has ever made any statement that could be construed as giving permission to anyone to treat those parts of Scripture "touching matters of the physical or historical order as *obiter dicta* and having no connection whatever with faith."

The second conclusion is that the words of St. Augustine incorporated in the Encyclical *Providentissimus Deus,* so often misquoted, must be interpreted in the light of the very definite statements of both Pope Leo XIII and Pope Pius XII, that inspiration extends to matters in the Bible touching the physical and historical orders. The context in which the words of St. Augustine were quoted make this clear. Hostile critics were casting ridicule on the simple Mosaic account of Creation because it did not give details such as modern science has discovered. Pope Leo XIII inserted the quotation from St. Augustine to show that it is not the purpose of Sacred Scripture to teach men the essential nature of the visible universe, but at the same time he made it clear that no Catholic is free to regard the portion of the Mosaic account which touches matters of the physical or historical order as mere *obiter dicta.*

Now that modern science has proved conclusively that the Laplace theory is scientifically impossible and that the Mosaic account can be defended, no one can accuse the Holy See of accepting what was merely a theory for a scientific conclusion and of changing the interpretation of Scripture to suit it.

The statement of St. Augustine quoted in the Encyclical *Providentissimus Deus* that "the Holy Ghost (who inspired the sacred writers) did not intend to teach men the essential nature of the visible universe," and the statement in the same Encyclical which is quoted in the Encyclical *Divino Afflante Spiritu* of Pope Pius XII condemning those "who dare to restrict the truth of Sacred Scripture to matters of faith and morals, and to consider what touches matters of the physical and historical order as *obiter dicta* having no connection with faith," are not contradictory.

The first statement may be taken to mean that we are not to look to Scripture for knowledge of such things as the chemical composition of the sun or the length of the geological periods, while the second statement indicates that the account of the Creation found in the Bible which is given in terms commonly used at the time of Moses corresponds with the reality.

Did Moses Receive a Special Revelation About the Origin Of the World and the Origin of Man?

The decrees of the Council of Trent and Vatican declare that the books of the Old and New Testaments "contain revelation without error," that "they were written under the inspiration of the Holy Ghost and have God as their Author"; the passages from the two Encyclicals just quoted bind us to accept as true and as corresponding to objective reality, not only everything in the Bible that concerns faith and morals, but also what touches the physical and historical orders.

Now there are matters touching the physical order related in the first chapters of *Genesis* about which Moses could have had no knowledge from natural sources. His account of Creation is quite detailed and definite. As it stands the order is: God first created Heaven and earth; next He created light; next He divided the waters; next He made the dry land appear and gathered the waters into the seas; next He created the plants of the vegetable kingdom; next He formed the sun and the stars; next He created fishes, birds and animals in the order given; and last of all He created man.

The traditional belief both before and after Christ was that the Mosaic account corresponded with reality, which supposes that he must have got his knowledge from revelation. The Babylonian account of Creation gives practically no details and could have been of no help.

When the science of geology revealed the order of Creation, it was seen that the Mosaic order was accurate as far as geology was concerned, but that the common interpretation of the word *day* would have to be changed. There were, however, difficulties against the Mosaic order from astronomy that seemed to be unanswerable: How could there be light and vegetation before the creation of the sun? Then came the Laplace theory which ignored the Mosaic account, and the theory of evolution which rejected special creation.

Most Catholic commentators adhered to the view that the Mosaic account represented the objective reality and explained the difficulties as well as they could. Commentators, however, like Canon Dorlodot of Louvain University, who accepted the theory of evolution, appealed to the statement of St. Augustine that the Holy Ghost (who inspired the sacred writers) did not intend to teach men the nature of the visible universe, for justification of their view that we are not to look to the Bible for information about the order of Creation or even about the origin of man's body and referred to "concordism" as if it were an error condemned by the Church.

Last of all, science of our own day has come, this time not with theories, but with scientific conclusions, which enable us to defend the whole Mosaic account in the order given by Moses. The Laplace theory is gone, never to return; our earth was never part of the sun; "Let light be made" refers to the creation of the fiery nebulae, the source of light; the earth was once flat, without mountains, and covered with water; the earth was formed before the sun; the rest of the Mosaic order of Creation is confirmed by what geology has disclosed; the argument laboriously built up from paleontology against the special creation of man has collapsed.

To explain how Moses could have written an account of Creation so vastly superior, not only from a religious, but from a scientific point of view, to all the accounts of learned pagan nations, and even to accounts put forward within the last hundred years to replace it, we must return to the view that Moses was not only inspired by the Holy Ghost so that his account would contain no error against faith and morals, but that in addition he had received sufficient information by revelation about the facts of Creation to make the account worthy of its Author, the Holy Ghost, and to command the respect of true scientists of all ages.

To explain the unwavering stand of the Popes on the inerrancy of Scripture, even on matters touching the physical order, against formidable objections, we must have recourse to the doctrine of papal infallibility.

While we are not to look to the Bible for information "about the essential nature of the visible universe," it is reasonable to expect that Moses should have received from God sufficient information about the facts of Creation to guard him against making erroneous statements in an account of Creation of which the Holy Ghost is the Author.

There are on record some well-authenticated cases of visions and private revelations in which information about facts of the physical order not available from any natural source has been supplied to the recipients.

If, then, there is question only of private visions or private revelation, we find that information about the facts of the physical order was supplied so as to make the account true and accurate, should we not *a fortiori* expect to find in the very first page of the Bible an account in accordance with the actual facts, even though that involves the revelation of facts of the physical order?[1]

1. See *New Light on the Passion of Our Divine Lord* by Rev. Patrick O'Connell, published by Messrs. Gill & Son, Dublin.

PREFACE AND INTRODUCTION TO THE SECOND EDITION OF *SCIENCE OF TODAY AND THE PROBLEMS OF GENESIS*

By Rev. Patrick O'Connell

The first English edition of this book, which was published in 1959, was well-received everywhere—in Ireland and Great Britain, in North and South America, in Africa and India. In the interval since 1959 a French edition was published in France and an Italian edition in Italy, in both of which editions an account of two unsuccessful attempts to find two more "missing links" was added. The Italian edition was presented to His Holiness Pope Paul VI, who graciously sent the author a letter of thanks and his apostolic blessing. Copies of the Italian edition were sent to all the Italian Cardinals while Vatican Council II was in session. It was reviewed in *L'Osservatore Romano,* the organ of the Vatican, on July 11, 1964. The following is an English translation of this review in which a synopsis of the Author's refutation of the two main arguments for the theories of human evolution and polygenesis is given:

A review of the Italian translation of the portions of *Science of Today and the Problems of Genesis* which deal with the origin and early history of man, that appeared in *L'Osseravatore Romano* of July 11, 1964:

Patrick O'Connell: *Origine e preistoria dell 'Homo. Edizione Alzani Pinerola,* p. 179, L'1250.

The thesis of this book is that Palaeontology furnishes us with an irrefutable argument in favour of the traditional teaching of the Church, that no genetic link between man and beast exists but that the body of man was specially formed by God [from inanimate matter]. The book is therefore in perfect agreement with the teaching of *Humani Generis* [an Encyclical issued by Pope Pius XII in 1950].

The work is the result of fifty years reading and study. The Author shows that the biological arguments in favour of [human] evolution used in books by modern evolutionists, even in Italy, have been discarded by leading scientists, and even by atheists, such as the late Sir Julian Huxley, and that their most important argument, which is based on the fossils of creatures, claimed to be partly human, has collapsed completely. In particular, the Author shows that the famous "missing links"—the Neanderthal Man, the Java Man, the Peking Man (which Fr. Teilhard de Chardin uses as one of his principal arguments for his fantastic theories), the Australopithecine fossils and even the Oreopithecus of Baccinello—were in fact all cases of deception and fraud. The remaining "missing links," when not counterfeited artificially, belong to apes and monkeys and not to man.

This is a book which will be read from beginning to end with unabated interest, coming as it does after a stream of books with extravagant claims by evolutionists which have appeared and continue to appear on this subject, especially the books by Catholic authors which are full of gratuitous assumptions and wild speculations. These the Author [analyses] and justly condemns.

Since the first edition of this work was published, Vatican Council II has been held and has concluded its deliberations, and many books on the problems dealt with in this work have appeared, but neither the decrees passed by Vatican Council II nor the books that have appeared in the interval render necessary any changes or modifications in the solutions given in the first edition. With regard to Vatican Council II, the first edition of this book may be said to have been present, since it was in the hands of His Holiness Pope Paul VI, of all the Italian Cardinals and of many others present in the Council, and it was favorably reviewed in *L'Osservatore Romano* while the Council was in session.

The reasons why the books dealing with the problems of *Genesis* which have appeared in the interval have made no change necessary are: 1) Because the book was written at a most opportune time, just when sufficient scientific information became available, which made possible definite solutions of the four main problems of *Genesis*. When Pope Pius XII issued the encyclical *Humani Generis* in 1950, he was able to say that the theory of evolution of man had not been proved, but the claims made by evolutionists that the fossils of a number of intermediate forms had been found, though not proved to demonstration, had not been disproved. In 1953, however, with the forced admission by evolutionists that the "Piltdown Man" was a case of forgery, the collapse of the only direct argument for evolution, which is the existence of a series of intermediate forms between man and beast, began. By the time this book was ready for publication, the collapse was complete: Sufficient evidence had become available to show that every case of "missing link" put forward by evolutionists since the time of Darwin was a case of either fraud or error. 2) Because the present writer has had an advantage which the authors of recent books did not enjoy—the advantage of being able to consult the books of the beginning of the century (most of which are out of print) and the books published since then as they appeared. 3) Because all the principal books in English, French, German, Spanish and Italian with information on the problems of *Genesis* by astronomers, geologists, paleontologists and archaeologists were consulted by the author, who was the first to apply the most recent discoveries by astronomers to the solution of the problems of the first two verses of the Bible and to show that these verses really contained accurate scientific information which must have been supplied to Moses by the Holy Spirit, who is the Author of the Bible.

In the few years that have elapsed since the publication of the first edition of this book, the tactics employed by Catholic evolutionists have changed: formerly these men were satisfied with claiming that the evolution of man's body from a lower animal was nearly certain, and that the theory of human evolution was in complete accord with the teaching of the Catholic Church; now most of them claim that the evolution of man's body is a fact which theologians must recognize, and that its acceptance involves the acceptance also of the theory of polygenism and the necessity of changing the teaching of the Catholic Church on the unity of the human race and the doctrine of Original Sin.

In the accounts given in the books by those authors who are responsible for introducing the theory of polygenism into the Catholic Church, and thereby undermining the teaching of the Church on Original Sin, the reader will note that they, one and all, show complete ignorance of the findings of paleontology on the fossil remains of man (which constitute the only direct evidence for the theory of evolution or polygenism) so that it may be said that ignorance of contemporary science is the hall-mark of the Catholic advocates of the theories of human evolution and polygenism.

In this work there is no attempt at that form of concordism which is ruled out by the directives of the Holy See for the interpretation of Sacred Scripture, which consists in straining the meaning of Papal Encyclicals and other directives to make their meaning fit in with such unproven theories as evolution and polygenism, firstly, because this work deals mainly with science and not biblical exegesis, and secondly because it gives accepted scientific conclusions and not mere theories.

Quotations are given from decrees of Councils and Papal Encyclicals in order to show that the Holy See has never retreated from the position that the Bible contains no error of any kind. The same cannot be said of some of the writers on biblical problems whose works were dealt with in the first edition of this book or of writers of books which have since appeared. They have been frightened by mere phantoms, they have mistaken fantasies of atheists like Darwin and Haeckel for scientific conclusions and have run away from the impregnable positions marked out by the Vicars of Christ, to land in a morass of errors against both science and revelation.

A copy of a little book entitled *Original Sin in the Light of Present-Day Science,* recently published by the author, is being given along with copies of this new edition. This little book contains: 1) a brief summary of the parts of *Science of Today and the Problems of Genesis* which deal with the origin and early history of man; 2) an account of two new attempts to find "missing links"; and 3) a refutation of claims made recently by neo-Modernist writers, that modern scientific discoveries support their contention that the biblical account of Adam and Eve, Cain and Abel and the Deluge are only myths without historical foundation, borrowed from the Babylonians and that, accordingly, the teaching of the Church on the unity of the human race and Original Sin needs to be modified.

As these unfounded claims of the neo-Modernists, which are based on ignorance of the real findings of science have, unfortunately, been accepted by many Catholics and are even found in catechisms of Christian doctrine such as *A New Dutch Catechism,* I have decided to publish a new edition of this larger work in which a full refutation of these claims is given. In it readers will find the first and so far the only true solutions of the four major problems of *Genesis,* with a new and original solution of the Galileo case which vindicates the decisions of Popes Paul V and Urban VIII. This solution is based on discoveries made by astronomers in recent years about the composition and movements of the sun. The Bible says that the sun and moon stood still, but says nothing about whether the earth revolves around the sun or vice versa; the question whether the earth revolves around the sun or vice versa was therefore irrelevant. Galileo's main contention was that the sun is immovable and could not therefore be said to stand still. Modern science has proved that the sun is not immovable; that it is the only source of power for the whole solar system; God could therefore suspend the activity of the sun and with it the motions of the sun and moon and all the planets and thus prolong the length of the day in a manner worthy of Almighty God, which would not interfere with the order and harmony of the universe.

This new edition of *Science of Today and the Problems of Genesis* is humbly offered as a contribution toward the defense of the teaching of the Church on such fundamental issues as the unity of the human race, the doctrine of Original Sin and the inerrancy of Sacred Scripture as defined in the Councils of Trent, Vatican I and Vatican II.

Patrick O'Connell

August 15, 1968

DECREE OF VATICAN COUNCIL II ON THE DIVINE INSPIRATION AND INTERPRETATION OF SACRED SCRIPTURE (Chapter III)

Sacred Scripture: Its Divine Inspiration and Interpretation—The Meaning of Divine Inspiration

Those divinely revealed realities which are contained and presented in Sacred Scripture have been committed to writing under inspiration of the Holy Spirit. For holy Mother Church, relying on the belief of the Apostles [see *John.* 20:31; *2 Tim.* 3:16; *2 Pet.* 1:19-20; 3:15-16] holds that the books of both the Old and New Testaments in their entirety, with all their parts, are sacred and canonical because, written under the inspiration of the Holy Spirit, they have God as their author and have been handed on as such to the Church herself. In composing the sacred books God chose men, and while employed by Him they made use of their powers and abilities, so that with Him acting in them and through them, they, as true authors, consigned to writing everything and only those things which He wanted.

Therefore since everything asserted by the inspired authors or sacred writers must be held to be asserted by the Holy Spirit, it follows that the books of Scripture must be acknowledged as teaching solidly, faithfully and without error that truth which God wanted put into the sacred writings for the sake of our salvation. Therefore all Scripture is divinely inspired and has its use for teaching the truth and refuting error, for reformation of manners and discipline in right living, so the man who belongs to God may be efficient and equipped for good work of every kind. [*2 Tim.* 3:16-17, Greek text].

The Interpretation of Sacred Scripture

[12] However, since God speaks in Sacred Scripture through men in human fashion, the interpreter of Sacred Scripture, in order to see clearly what God wanted to communicate to us should carefully investigate what meaning the Sacred writers

really intended, and what God wanted to manifest by means of their words.

To search out the intentions of the sacred writers, attention should be given, among other things, to "literary forms." For truth is set forth and expressed differently in texts which are variously historical, prophetic, poetic, or of other forms of discourse. The interpreter must investigate what meaning the sacred writer intended to express and actually expressed in particular circumstances by using contemporary literary forms in accordance with the situation of his own time and culture. For the correct understanding of what the sacred author wanted to assert, due attention must be paid to the customary and characteristic styles of feeling, speaking and narrating which prevailed at the time of the sacred writer, and to the patterns men normally employed at that period in their everyday dealings with one another.

But, since Holy Scripture must be read and interpreted in the same spirit in which it was written, no less serious attention must be given to the content and unity of the whole of Scripture if the meaning of the sacred texts is to be correctly worked out. The living tradition of the whole Church must be taken into account, along with the harmony which exists between elements of the Faith. It is the task of exegetes to work according to these rules toward a better understanding and explanation of the meaning of Sacred Scripture, so that through preparatory study the judgment of the Church may mature. For all of what has been said about the way of interpreting Scripture is subject finally to the judgment of the Church, which carries out the divine commission and ministry of guarding and interpreting the word of God.

[13] In Sacred Scripture, therefore, while the truth and holiness of God always remains intact, the marvelous "condescension" of eternal wisdom is clearly shown, "that we may learn the gentle kindness of God, which words cannot express, and how far He has gone in adapting His language with thoughtful concern for our weak human nature." For the words of God, expressed in human language, have been made like human discourse, just as the Word of the eternal Father, when He took to Himself the flesh of human weakness, was in every way like men.

The portion of the decree on Revelation which deals with

the Divine Inspiration and Interpretation of Sacred Scripture is taken in part at least from the Encyclical *Divino Afflante Spiritu* of Pope Pius XII, which was issued in 1943, and which deals with the same subject in greater detail. The Encyclical therefore provides the best commentary that we have on the above decree.

I

THE MEANING OF DIVINE INSPIRATION

In *Divino Afflante Spiritu,* we read:

> In more recent times, however since the divine origin and the correct interpretation of the Sacred Writings have been very specially called in question, the Church has with even greater zeal and care, undertaken their defense and protection. The Sacred Council of Trent ordained by solemn decree that "the entire books with all their parts, as they have been wont to be read in the Catholic Church and are contained in the old vulgate Latin edition, are to be held sacred and canonical." In our own time the Vatican Council, with the object of condemning false doctrines regarding inspiration, declared that these same books were to be regarded by the Church as sacred and canonical "not because, having been composed by human industry, they were afterwards approved by her authority, not merely because they contain revelation without error, but because, having been written under the inspiration of the Holy Spirit, they have God for their author, and as such were handed down to the Church herself." When, subsequently, some Catholic writers, in spite of this solemn definition of Catholic doctrine, by which such divine authority is claimed for the "entire books with all their parts" as to secure freedom from any error whatsoever, ventured to restrict the truth of Sacred Scriptures solely to matters of faith and morals, and to regard other matters, whether in the domain of physical science or history, as *"obiter dicta"* and—as they contended—in no wise connected with faith. Our Predecessor of immortal memory, Leo XIII, in the Encyclical Letter *Providentissimus Deus,* published on November 18th in the year 1893, justly and rightly condemned these errors and safeguarded the studies of the Divine Books by most wise precepts and rules.

II

THE INTERPRETATION OF SACRED SCRIPTURE

In the Decree of Vatican Council II, we read:

> The interpreter of Sacred Scripture, in order to see clearly what God wanted to communicate to us, should carefully investigate what meaning the sacred writers really intended and what God wanted to manifest by means of their words.
>
> To search out the intentions of the sacred writers, attention *among other things* should be given to literary forms.

The decree does not specify what the "other things" are, but in *Divino Afflante Spiritu* we read the following:

> Let the interpreter then with all care and without neglecting any light derived from recent research, endeavor to determine the peculiar character and circumstances of the sacred writer, the age in which he lived, the sources written or oral to which he had recourse and the forms of expression he employed.
>
> [34] Thus can he better understand who was the inspired author, and what he wishes to express by his writings. There is no one indeed but knows that the supreme rule of interpretation is *to discover and define what the writer intended to express,* as St. Athanasius excellently observes: "Here, as indeed is expedient in all other passages of Sacred Scriptures, it should be noted, on what occasion the Apostle spoke; we should carefully and faithfully observe to whom and why he wrote, lest being ignorant of these points, or confounding one with another, we miss the real meaning of the author."

IMPORTANCE OF MODE OF WRITING

> [35] What is the literal sense of a passage is not always as obvious in the speeches and writings of the ancient authors, of the East, as it is in the works of our own time. For what they wished to be expressed is not to be determined by the rules of grammar and philology alone, nor solely by the context; the interpreter must, as it were go back, wholly in spirit to those remote centuries of the East and with the aid of history, archaeology, ethnology, and other sciences, accurately determine what modes of writing, so to speak, the authors of the ancient period would be likely to use, and in fact did use.

STUDIES OF BIBLICAL ANTIQUITIES

[40] Let those who cultivate biblical studies turn their attention with all due diligence toward this point and let them neglect none of these discoveries whether in the domain of archaeology or in ancient history or literature, which serve to make better known the mentality of the ancient writers, as well as their manner and art of reasoning, narrating and writing. In this connection Catholic laymen should consider that they will not only further profane science, but moreover will render a conspicuous service to the Christian cause if they devote themselves with all due diligence and application to the exploration and investigation of the monuments of antiquity and contribute, according to their abilities, to the solution of questions hitherto obscure.

In the above quotations from the Encyclical *Divino Afflante Spiritu* we find specified what the "other things" are to which the interpreter of Sacred Scripture should pay attention. The encyclical says:

> What they [the sacred writers] wished to express is not to be determined by the rules of grammar and philology alone, or solely by the context; the interpreter must as it were, go back wholly in spirit to those remote centuries of the East and with the aid of history, archaeology, ethnology, and other sciences, accurately determine what the model of writing, so to speak, the authors of that ancient period would be likely to use, and in fact did use.

The words "for the sake of our salvation" from the Decree of Vatican Council II on the interpretation of Sacred Scripture has been given a restrictive meaning by some commentators. The following is the complete sentence in which the words occur:

> Therefore since everything asserted by the inspired authors of Sacred Scripture must be held to be asserted by the Holy Spirit, it follows that the books of Scriptures must be acknowledged as teaching solidly, faithfully and without error the truth which God wanted put into the sacred teachings for the sake of our salvation.

In an article in *The Bible Today,* March 1968, Fr. Moriarity, S.J., interprets these words as follows:

> The formula of Vatican II. . .specifies the aspect under which all of the Bible may be said to communicate truth without error. This formal specification means that we must always assess the truth of Scripture from the view-point of its salvific function.

The following is the principal reason which he gives for restricting the inspiration and inerrancy of the Bible to those parts which have what he calls a "salvific function."

> Now it could be seen all too clearly [from the findings of archaeology and linguistic studies] that the Bible did not measure up to the exacting standards of modern historiography. Often as not, the biblical chronologies could not be squared with known dating sequences.

The Bible cannot be carved up into parts that have "a salvific function" and parts that have not. The whole Bible and all its parts is the work of the Holy Spirit, and it is the Holy Spirit who has guided the sacred authors in the choice of the contents of the Bible, including all information concerning the physical universe and history. Many exegetes wrongly assume that the Holy Spirit has furnished the sacred authors with no information about matters of science and history. The contemporary Italian astronomer, Joseph Armellini, has stated in an article in *Studium*:

"The Mosaic cosmogony is in perfect accord, indeed in amazing accord with the conclusions which modern astronomical cosmogony has reached."

In addition, the findings of the archaeologists based on nearly a century of excavations in Egypt, Palestine, Mesopotamia, etc., have confirmed the accuracy of the Mosaic account of the Deluge and the early history of man; and recent discoveries have shown that the older chronological system of Petrie, which is in agreement with the biblical chronology, is the right system, and that the system known as "the short chronology" adopted by Fr. Moriarity and some other biblical exegetes, but by no means by all, cannot now be defended against the new objections raised against it. The only way in which Moses could have obtained most of the information contained in the first eleven chapters of the Bible, which has been verified by astronomers, geologists, paleontologists and archaeologists, is by revelation, for in the time of Moses there was no natural means available for obtaining the information.

The knowledge that the information about the physical universe and early history contained in the Bible has been verified in our own time increases our veneration for the Bible and makes it easier for men to accept the spiritual truths and spiritual lessons conveyed along with it. If, as Modernists would have us believe, it could be proved that the very first chapters of the Bible, pronounced by the Church to be the inspired word of God, contained only Babylonian myths used by Moses to convey spiritual lessons, respect for the Bible would soon decline. Fortunately, modern science has come to the aid of the Magisterium of the Church and has brought forward conclusive evidence in confirmation of its decisions on the interpretation of the Bible.

DEFINITE SOLUTIONS SOUGHT

Finally, Catholic commentators are urged, in the Encyclical, to find solutions of the age-old problems of *Genesis* which will be in full accord with the doctrine of the Church and satisfy the indubitable conclusions of profane sciences.

> But this state of things is no reason why the Catholic commentator, inspired by an active and ardent love of his subject and sincerely devoted to Holy Mother Church, should in any way be deterred from grappling again and again with difficult problems, hitherto unsolved, not only that he may refute the objections of the adversaries, but also may attempt to find a satisfactory solution, which will be in full accord with the doctrine of the Church, in particular with the traditional teaching regarding the inerrancy of Sacred Scriptures, and which will at the same time satisfy the indubitable conclusions of profane sciences.

A glance at the headings and sub-headings of this work will convince the reader that advice given in *Divino Afflante*

Spiritu and included in the phrase "among other things" of the Decree of Vatican Council II has been faithfully adhered to in the composition of this work and hence the Decree in question does not make any change necessary.

A BRIEF ANALYSIS OF THE PRINCIPAL BOOKS ON THE ORIGIN AND EARLY HISTORY OF MAN WHICH HAVE APPEARED SINCE THE FIRST EDITION OF THIS BOOK WAS PUBLISHED.

GERMANY

"Das Stammesgeschichtliche Werden der Organismen und des Menschen"

This book is the work of four German Jesuit Fathers who give their personal views and make no claim to speak for the German Jesuits. It is dedicated to the memory of Charles Darwin, who, Fr. Haas, the Editor, says in the Preface, has a right to the gratitude and even to the veneration of mankind. On this point many Catholics and non-Catholics would profoundly disagree with Fr. Haas, for from the very beginning, Darwin's theory has been used to undermine Christianity and to promote atheism, and, at the present time, the theory, in spite of the unanswerable objections which modern science has raised against it, is being used as one of the chief arguments for polygenism.

As the title indicates, the book purports to give the history of the theory of evolution and of the various authors who wrote about it. The index of authors consulted contains the names of more than 400 writers, almost all of whom are evolutionists, and although the authors of this book favor the theory of evolution they do not mention the name of their French confrere, Fr. Teilhard de Chardin, among these 400 names.

This book begins with an attempt to answer Darwin's own objections against his theory of evolution, which he gives in Chapter X of *The Origin of Species,* but to which no answer could be given at the time he wrote.

These objections are: 1) Millions of fossils of no less than

5,000 different species of the invertebrates have been found in the rocks of the Cambrian Period all over the world. These fossils belong to perfectly formed living creatures and appear suddenly, without any indication of having been evolved. No undisputed fossils have been found in the sedimentary rocks beneath the Cambrian rocks to show the process of evolution. 3) No links between the invertebrates and the vertebrates have been found, nor have any links been found between the various species of the vertebrates.

In his attempt to answer the first difficulty, Fr. Lotze, the author of this section of the book, gives the usual claim of evolutionists (which has been denied) that some fossils have been found in the pre-Cambrian rocks, but admits that they are rare and doubtful. He then says that tests by the radio-active method have found indications of the presence of organic matter in rocks nearly three billion years old. He admits that the claim cannot be proved.

The claim is absurd: 1) because the radio-active method cannot be used to test the age of organic matter; to test the age of organic matter, the method used is the carbon 14 method, which gives results only for matter less than 40,000 years old; 2) organic matter, even if really found in rocky formations, cannot be presumed to be the same age as the rocks, because during the hundreds of millions of years that have elapsed since the Cambrian Period the surface of the earth has been churned up to a depth of several miles, and 3) three billion years ago the earth was not sufficiently cooled down to make possible the growth of plants from which the organic matter could be produced, for the earth was still warm enough to produce tropical vegetation at the Poles as late as the Pliocene Period.

In the second part of the book the origin of the vertebrates is discussed. Have any genuine intermediate forms been found in the fossil record to show that the vertebrates have been evolved from the invertebrates of the Cambrian Period? The answer is that no such intermediate forms have been found, neither have fossils of intermediate forms of vertebrates been found to show that one species has been evolved from another; Darwin's theory of the Origin of Species remains an unproven theory.

The third part deals with the origin of man and is written by Fr. Overhage, S.J., the co-author with Fr. Rahner, S.J. of a recent book entitled *Hominization.* This section is devoted chiefly to an account of the fossil remains of man. According to Darwin, Huxley, Douglas Dewar and practically all evolutionists and anti-evolutionists, the case for the evolution of either animal or man stands or falls by the fossil record. Since the time of Darwin, claims have been made periodically for the discovery of intermediate forms between man and beast (usually called "missing links"). Fr. Overhage gives a full list of these alleged intermediate forms or "missing links." He deals with the Neanderthal Man in great detail. More than 200 different fossils of the Neanderthal Man have been found up to date, according to Fr. Overhage, and during the century since Darwin, the Neanderthal Man has been used as the chief evidence for the evolution of man. Pictures and statues of the Neanderthal Man representing him as a creature more like an ape than a man, with savage countenance and head bent forward like the ape's, are still found in nearly all the museums of the world, and pictures of the same kind are inserted into most schoolbooks. However, Fr. Overhage, on page 258, in effect admits that all this has been a gross misrepresentation of the historic Neanderthal Man; that the Neanderthal Man was a man like ourselves. He quotes Sir Wilfred Le Gros Clark as saying in *The Fossil Evidence of Human Evolution* that the Neanderthal Man should be classified in the *Homo Sapiens* class, which means that he is a member of the human race, in all respects like ourselves, and that all that has been said of him, and is still being said of him, is just propaganda for Darwin's theory, without any foundation of fact.

Fr. Overhage gives a full list of the other "missing links": he tells his readers what evolutionists say about them, and leaves them under the impression that they are genuine, whereas not even one case of "missing link" out of all that Fr. Overhage mentions, has any real scientific evidence to support its claim.

Fr. Overhage discusses the question of polygenism, and leaves the reader under the impression that there is scientific support for the theory. The only direct evidence for either evolution or polygenism is the existence of the fossils of intermediate forms, and, as already stated, not one certain case has been found. Though the title of the book indicates that it is an historical account of the theory of evolution, from the evidence which Fr. Overhage gives in favor of the "missing links" (with the exception of the Neanderthal Man) the ordinary reader would conclude that they are all genuine, which is not true, for there is strong evidence to the contrary. Since not one of them has been proved, each and every case is merely a hypothetical "missing link," and since the teaching of the Church on polygenism is involved, a mere hypothesis or theory cannot be used as evidence, as Pope Pius XII warned Catholic writers in his encyclical *Humani Generis.*

FRANCE

L'Origine et Destin de la Vie
by Fr. Bergounioux, O.F.M., 1962
Professor in the Catholic Institute of Toulouse, France

Fr. Bergounioux, the author of this book of 350 pages, has been a life-long supporter of Darwin's theory of evolution and a member of the County Begouen Circle, which is to a great extent responsible for introducing the theory into the Catholic Church. As professor of the Catholic Institute of Toulouse he has had the opportunity of consulting all the most recent works on evolution and the origin of man. Among these is a work in eight volumes of a thousand pages each which was composed by various authors under the direction of Jean Piveteau, Professor at the Sorbonne University. Fr. Bergounioux gives us the following items of information from this work:

> 1) At the beginning of the Primary Period, 500 million years ago, the seas contained a multitude of living beings from the microscopic algae to the most complicated marine invertebrates. At this epoch, all the classes now known were represented, and among them, a number that have never disappeared. The

vertebrates, which did not appear until the Silurian Period (more than 100 million years later) were not represented among them. (*op. cit.* p. 119).

2) There is no possibility of establishing any link between the invertebrates and the vertebrates.

Biology is therefore unable to tell us whether there is any relation between the different groups. Paleontology alone could furnish us with information in this domain. We shall see (in the course of the book by Fr. Bergounioux) that Paleontology also is unable to solve this problem which is of primary importance. (*ibid,* p. 81).

3) There exist no intermediate fossils between terrestrial and aerial forms (between animals and birds). Certain people have put forward theories about primitive forms of birds *(pro-avis)* which are of no other interest except to show the fertility of the imagination of Paleontologists.

These admissions, which a life-long adherent to Darwin's theory of evolution sees himself obliged to make in his old age after reading Professor Piviteau's monumental work, amount to a confession that the two main arguments for evolution have collapsed.

The position taken by evolutionists, Catholic and non-Catholic, is that the evolution of species is a fact and that man cannot be regarded to be an exception. Contemporary science says most emphatically that there is now no evidence to show that species were the result of evolution; Darwin's own objections given in Chapter X of *The Origin of Species* have not been answered. Therefore the position of evolutionists, both Catholic and non-Catholic, with regard to the evolution of species in general and of man is untenable.

Fr. Teilhard de Chardin

Books Dealing with His Writings of a Scientific Nature

1) The first attempt at an evaluation of the scientific merits of Fr. Teilhard's writings was made by the present writer in the first edition of this book. This evaluation which readers will find on p. 74, and in the chapter on the Peking Man, pp. 124-158, was based on the results of exhaustive research

on the fossil remains of man, on the Ice Age and on the discoveries made by geologists and archaeologists during the present century, which was done in preparation for the writing of this book. The views which I then expressed have been confirmed by practically all the scientists of international reputation who have discussed the scientific merits of his works since then.

2) Gaylord Simpson

Gaylord Simpson of Harvard University refused to recognize Fr. Teilhard's principal work *The Phenomenon of Man* as a work of science. Simpson had met Fr. Teilhard and was on such friendly terms with him that Fr. Teilhard named him as one of his literary executors. Though Simpson had no love for the Catholic Church, he would at least have abstained from condemning Fr. Teilhard's principal work if he could have done so without loss of reputation, just as Marcellin Boule would have kept silent about the Peking Man if it had been possible. Simpson's verdict on Fr. Teilhard is clear—that he cannot be classed among scientists.

3) Sir Julian Huxley

In his introduction to the English translation of *The Phenomenon of Man* Sir Julian tells us that he met Fr. Teilhard in Paris in 1946 and that he had carried on a constant correspondence with him until his death in 1955. He tells us also that he and Fr. Teilhard had been pursuing parallel roads since they were young men and he claimed that in his own book *Scientific Humanism* he had anticipated the title of Fr. Teilhard's *The Phenomenon of Man.* Nevertheless, he makes no mention of any contribution that Teilhard had made toward the advancement of science except the discovery of the Peking Man. It is not true that it was Fr. Teilhard who discovered the Peking Man and, as will be shown in the chapter on The Peking Man (pp. 124-158), the Peking Man was a case of fraud, like the Piltdown Man, in both of which Fr. Teilhard was involved.

4) Dr. W. R. Thompson, F.R.S.

Dr. Thompson in an article to the periodical *Search* to whom the editor refers as "one of our best English-speaking scientists" says that Teilhard is neither scientific nor orthodox. Thompson quotes Professor Simpson as saying of Fr. Teilhard's *Phenomenon of Man* that "it should not be taken either as a scientific treatise or a derivation of religious conclusions from scientific premises."

5) Dr. Louis Bounoure, **Professor of Biology in Strasburg University**

Professor Bounoure, in his book *Recherche d'une Doctrine de Vie* analyzes Fr. Teilhard's works and points out the numerous errors in the various branches of science that they contain. He says that Teilhard has no claim to be called a scientist, and that the errors his works contain are a danger to the Faith.

6) Dr. Maurice Vernet

Dr. Vernet, who is also an authority on biology, in his book entitled *La Grande Illusion de Teilhard de Chardin,* besides pointing out Fr. Teilhard's ignorance of biology, deals with the philosophical errors in his works.

7) Miss Hilda Graef, who does not claim to be a scientist, has carried out considerable research on Fr. Teilhard. She cannot accept his science—but puts him among the mystics in her book entitled *The Mystics of Our Time.* She quotes him as writing in January 1936 that *"in his opinion missionaries made a great mistake in admitting, contrary to all biology, the equality of the races. . .Creatures so different from ourselves could not be converted unless one first transforms them on the human plane."* This may explain why Fr. Teilhard, who spent over 20 years in China, never made any attempt to convert the Chinese.

BELGIUM

Un Siecle d'anthropologie prehistorique: Compatibilité ou Monogenism? by Fr. Boné, S.J. Louvain.

(A series of articles in the June, July-August, 1962 issues of *La Nouvelle Revue Theologique* of Louvain).

As the title indicates, Fr. Boné in these articles discusses the question whether monogenism (the descent of the human race from a single pair of ancestors) is compatible with the scientific discoveries of the last century concerning the origin of man. The conclusion which he gives at the end of his last article is that monogenism is not compatible with these discoveries; however he admits the possibility of special Divine intervention in favor of monogenism, over-ruling what he calls "the laws of nature" as found in the theory of neo-Darwinism.

The importance of these articles of Fr. Boné lies in the fact that they are quoted by the principal advocates of the theory of polygenism in various countries and that Fr. Boné himself refers his readers to them in his article on evolution in the new edition of *The Catholic Encyclopedia*.

Fr. Boné gives as proofs of his alleged law of nature which, if not prevented by Divine intervention, will result in the simultaneous evolution of an indefinite number of ancestors of the human race: 1) the alleged discovery at various times during the past century of the fossils of intermediate forms between man and beast (usually called "missing links") and 2) the alleged discovery by evolutionists that mutations in the genes of the genetic cells, guided by a force called Natural Selection, will in the course of time cause a whole group or species to change into a new and different species.

Now in the course of this book evidence will be produced from the works of scientists of international reputation to show 1) that each and every fossil of alleged intermediate form or "missing link" has been found (usually after having been used for many years as evidence for the theory of human evolution) to have been either the fossil of a brute beast without any of the special human characteristics, or the fossil of a man like ourselves with all the special characteristics of man; 2) evidence will be produced from the writings of eminent biologists such as Dr. W. R. Thompson, F.R.S., former Director of the Commonwealth Institute of Biological Control at Ottawa, Canada, and Professor Bounoure, of Strasburg University, France, to show that the theory known as neo-Darwinism is totally devoid of scientific foundation.

Fr. Boné gives a complete list of all the "missing links" put forward during the century, beginning with the Neanderthal Man and ending with the fossils of extinct species of monkeys discovered in the Siwalik hills in India. Fr. Boné is not justified in putting the Neanderthal Man in the class of "hominids," or creatures supposed to be still in the process of evolution, for by 1962, when this article was written, it was acknowledged by such authorities as Sir Wilfred le Gros Clark of Oxford, Drs. Boule and Vallois of France and Fr. Overhage, S.J. of Germany that the Neanderthal Man belongs to the *homo sapiens* class and is a perfect man like ourselves; nor is he justified in representing even one of the fossils on his list as the fossil of a real intermediate form, for evidence to the contrary can be produced against each and every one of them. Fr. Boné can produce no evidence in favor of his theory of polygenism except two unproven theories or hypotheses: the hypothesis that real "missing links" exist, and the neo-Darwin hypothesis.

In the Encyclical *Humani Generis* of Pope Pius XII the use of mere hypotheses is forbidden in cases where the teaching of the Church is involved.

This encyclical says: [Clearly proved facts of science may be taken into account]:

> but caution must be used when there is rather question of hypotheses, having some sort of scientific foundation, in which doctrine contained in Sacred Scripture or in Tradition is involved. If such conjectural opinions are directly or indirectly opposed to the doctrine revealed by God, then the demand that they be recognized can in no way be admitted.

The Bible and the Origin of Man by Fr. Jean de Fraine, S.J., Louvain. English Edition, New York, 1962.

Fr. de Fraine, who is a Doctor of Sacred Scripture, is quoted by Fr. North, S.J. in *Teilhard and the Creation of the Human Soul* as holding the opinion that Adam in the Bible stands for a "corporate personality" (*op. cit.* p. 54), and by Fr. Francoeur on page 175 of *Perspectives in Evolution* as expressing the same opinion—which was rejected by His Holiness Pope Paul VI in the instructions to the Commission appointed to study the question of Original Sin.

In the course of his book, the late Fr. de Fraine stated on page 11: "Science considers man as a living organism showing a physical descent from other animal species of a somewhat similar nature."

On page 12 he says: "Science tells us that the age of man amounts to at least 50,000 years," and that "Fr. Boné S.J. of Louvain speaks of some 500,000 years."

On page 49, speaking of the formation of Eve from Adam he says: "By retaining the figurative meaning of symbolic details we easily explain the fact that the woman was taken from the man not as a material fact, but rather as a spiritual reality."

On the question of polygenism, on page 68 he speaks of "monophyletic polygenesis (the descent of the human race from many different ancestors evolved from one group or species of animals) as the most widely held scientific hypothesis," and on page 81 he says: "It seems that the restrictions of freedom [placed by Pope Pius XII] on the subject of polygenesis is not necessarily irrevocable."

From the above quotations it appears that Fr. de Fraine believes that modern science requires people to accept the evolution of the human race from lower animals, the evolution of Eve also and to accept as "most probable" that this evolution was the evolution of a whole group or "phylum."

In his short introduction, Fr. de Fraine gives us what he believes to be the scientific basis for all the above statements. On page vii, he writes: "The discovery of a fossil man from the Gibraltar skull (1848) to Zinjanthropus (August 1959) puts back the appearance of the first man."

On page viii he writes:

> The difficulties in this area [of believing in the unity of the human race] have been considerably increased by the simultaneous presence of the Neanderthal Man and *Homo Sapiens* and especially of the more recent discoveries in South Africa. . . . In presence of these scientific data a conscientious Catholic cannot help wondering: What relation is there between these scientific findings and the teachings of faith contained in the inspired books?
>
> . . . There can be no doubt that these ancient and rather naive conceptions [that Adam and Eve were directly created by God, etc.] are in conflict with the data of scientific prehistory.

From the above quotation it is perfectly clear that Fr. de Fraine is under the erroneous impression that each and every one of the "missing links" put forward by evolutionists, from the Neanderthal Man in the time of Darwin to the late Dr. Leakey's Zinjanthropus in 1959, is a genuine case of an intermediate form or genetic link between man and beast, whereas each and every one of these is a case either of fraud or error, as will be proved in this book.

Fr. de Fraine has at least the merit of telling his readers on what scientific evidence he bases his erroneous conclusions, but other prominent Catholic writers, among whom are Fr. Bruce Vawter, D.S.S. (in *God's Story of Creation*) and Fr. McKenzie (in *The Two-edged Sword*) gives us the same conclusions in the name of science without any attempt at proof of the claims made.

Bible: Word of God in Words of Men
by Fr. Jean Levie, S.J., Louvain

In this book Fr. Levie claims that the views which he expresses on such questions as the extent of the Deluge are based upon the most recent scientific discoveries; this claim is indicated by the headings of the chapters and by reference to recent books such as *Digging up Jericho* by Dr. Kathleen Kenyon. In dealing with the extent of the Deluge he gives the conclusion arrived at by Sir Leonard Woolley (which was based on excavations at Ur more than 30 years ago) what was really only a guess, namely, that the flood which destroyed the ancient city of Ur (which he believed to have been the Deluge) was confined to Mesopotamia and he (Fr. Levie) continues, saying that biblical exegetes are justified in taking this alleged fact into account (when dealing with the extent of the Deluge). Now in the present book readers will find abundant evidence drawn from the results obtained from excavations carried out in the Middle East and other places during the past 30 years which shows that the flood that destroyed Ur also destroyed Jericho and reached the high Plateau of Iran and the shores of the Arctic Ocean. The scientific evidence on which Fr. Levie bases his exegesis is definitely out of date.

Another of the defects of Fr. Levie's book is that instead of giving the text of the Encyclical *Divino Afflante Spiritu* of Pope Pius XII as it was issued (which would have been useful to his readers), he rewrote it and gave his own version, doubtless because the rewritten version would fit in better with his views than the original would.

AMERICA

Perspectives in Evolution, by Rev. Robert T. Francoeur, 1965

The title of Fr. Francoeur's book is misleading, for the principal subjects discussed in the book are the theory of polygenism (which he thinks modern scientific discoveries support) and the modifications that would be needed in the traditional teaching of the Catholic Church on the doctrine of Original Sin if the theory of polygenism should be proved. He quotes Fr. Boné, S.J. and Fr. Teilhard de Chardin, S.J. among his authorities; his arguments in favor of the theory of polygenism are substantially the same as those used by Fr. Boné and are open to the same objections.

(Further information about this book will be found in Original Sin in the Light of Present-Day Science *by the present author).*

The Wisdom of Evolution
by Fr. Raymond J. Nogar, O.P., 1963

Fr. Nogar begins his book with a letter of introduction from Professor Theodosius Dobzhansky, an atheist and an extreme evolutionist, who however begs to disagree with some of Fr. Nogar's conclusions that concern religion. As the title of the book indicates, Fr. Nogar defends the theory of evolution even as applied to explain the origin of man. His arguments for evolution are much the same as those given by Fr. Francoeur and could be used in support of the theory of polygenism. Like Fr. Francoeur, he says that the invertebrates were evolved, though he is aware that the evidence from the Cambrian rocks is against him; as evidence of the evolution of man he gives the usual list of "missing links" in which he includes those rejected by the great authorities on fossils, such as Professor Marcellin Boule of France.

Fr. Nogar's chief authority is Professor Simpson of Harvard University, whose opinion on Fr. Teilhard de Chardin's works he adopts. Simpson corresponded with Fr. Teilhard when he was alive and was appointed by him as one of his literary executors. Simpson, like Sir Julian Huxley, another of Fr. Teilhard's literary executors, is a militant atheist who never misses an opportunity to cast ridicule on Catholic beliefs. He says of Fr. Teilhard's chief work, *The Phenomenon of Man,* that it is not a scientific work.

The hidden forces of evolution as described by Fr. Nogar (for the existence of which he gives no proof) tend of their nature to produce a plurality of human ancestors if not prevented by special miracle. If a plurality of ancestors is admitted, the teaching of the Catholic Church is undermined. In the course of his book Fr. Nogar represents human evolution as an established fact, although this is forbidden in the encyclical *Humani Generis*. By a mere statement of the teaching of the Church on Original Sin, which he gives and accepts, he cannot free himself from the charge of undermining the belief of the faithful by giving the subtle but fallacious arguments of men like Dobzhansky and Simpson.

Fr. Nogar, like Fr. Boné, S.J., who favors the theory of polygenism, contributes an article to the new edition of *The Catholic Encyclopedia* on evolution. It is unfortunate that the high standard of scholarship which was maintained in the first edition of this great work should be lowered by the inclusion of articles from men who did not take the trouble to carry out sufficient research on a subject in which the teaching of the Church on fundamental doctrines is involved.

Key Problems of Genesis by Alfred Lapple

This is a translation from the German of Alfred Lapple's book which was first published at Munich and subsequently translated into English and published at Cork under its original title, *The Bible In The Changing World: The Problem of Genesis*.

For Lapple, the main problem of *Genesis* is the origin of man, and the solution that he adopts is that the evolution of man from a lower animal may now be regarded as an established fact. On page 47 he quotes Huerzeler (who rediscovered the fossils of the mythical *Oreopithecus* in a coal mine in Italy) with approval, who said:

> Evolution, rejected by religious zealots in their first shock as the work of the devil, is the magnificent fundamental principle of the plan of creation...

In proof of his thesis, Lapple gives the whole litany of "missing links," in which he includes the Neanderthal Man, and dates them from 100,000 years for the Neanderthal Man to 600,000 years for the Australopithecinae. For Lapple (like the other neo-Modernists) it follows that the biblical accounts of the formation of Eve is to be interpreted symbolically, as is also the biblical account of the Fall and punishment of sinful man, for on page 84 he writes:

> It has become increasingly clear that not only the Paradise narrative, but also the accounts of the Fall and Punishment of sinful man are symbolic compositions.

On the question of polygenism (plurality of human First

Parents) he adopts the extreme view of Herbert Haag that the biblical account would seem to favor polygenism rather than monogenism. For arguments to defend polygenism, practically all who hold the theory appeal to the supposed existence of the fossils of "missing links," and to mutations in the genes guided by Natural Selection; very few would go so far as to say that it can be deduced from the biblical account.

These are just a few of the errors contained in the book; to give a full list would require a book as long as the author's, for there are errors on almost every page.

The problems of *Genesis* may be divided up according to the domains under which they come: astronomy, geology, paleontology and archaeology. Experts in these various sciences (most of whom are atheists) have studied the problems of *Genesis* that belong to their domains and have recorded their findings in books. Any Catholic who presumes to speak in the name of science on any of these problems should first consult the books by experts before daring to contradict the biblical account as interpreted according to the directives of the Magisterium of the Church. Alfred Lapple does not appear to have heard of the existence of such books and certainly did not consult them.

I give just one example. The case of evolution, whether of species in general or of man in particular, stands or falls by the fossil record. There is a standard work of reference on fossils by two French authors named Boule and Vallois, both of whom are atheists and evolutionists who would be most eager to claim the existence of a real "missing link" if such could be found. The title of the book is *Les Hommes Fossiles*. The first edition of this book was published in 1923 and the last in 1952. In the last edition of the book a full account is given of all claims to have found fossils of forms intermediate between man and beast ("missing links"), since the time of Darwin with references to the principal books dealing with them. Not even one case out of all the claims put forward had been proved, while all the principal ones were definitely rejected. Boule and Vallois were atheists and evolutionists, but they had a world-wide reputation, and they gave the facts as they found them in order to protect their reputations and to defend atheism from the charge of having recourse to fraud and deception to support it. Marcellin Boule went all the way to China to examine the fossils of the Peking Man and scornfully rejected them as providing evidence for evolution; Fr. Teilhard de Chardin, S.J. who was in China at the time (as was the present author), accepted them against the opinion of the greatest expert of the time and is hailed by his admirers as a great authority on paleontology!

Lapple's book on *Key Problems of Genesis* may be regarded as a typical neo-Modernist production. The position of the Modernists and the neo-Modernists is that the Bible is a wonderful book with beautiful moral lessons, that the doctrines of the Catholic Church are helpful and inspiring, but that neither the Bible nor the Catholic Church rests on any scientific foundation, and that the doctrines contained in both need to be changed "with the changing world." Lapple quotes the responses of the Biblical Commission and the Encyclicals of the Popes on the questions at issue and thus puts the unwary reader off his guard, but like all the Modernists, old and new, he wants the evolution of man as an established fact, he wants Eve symbolically formed from Adam, and the symbolism extended to "the Paradise narrative and the accounts of the Fall and the Punishment of sin"; he wants all the "missing links," even the ones that have long been rejected by atheists. He is not alone among Catholic writers in clinging to discredited "missing links"; Fr. Karl Rahner, S.J. in his chapter in *The Evolving World and Theology* (*Concilium,* No. 26) appeals to the alleged existence of a race of "pre-hominids" as justification for his warning to the Magisterium of the Church against condemning the theory of polygenism!

In many, if not most, of the Universities and Major Seminaries of America the student, in this age of supposed enlightenment, is left under the erroneous impression that creatures called "hominids" (half-man half-beast) have actually existed and that fossils of them have been found, whereas the truth is that if all the professors of the Universities and Seminaries of America who deal with these subjects were mobilized, there would not be found one among them able to defend the existence of even one creature less than man and more than beast. The gap between man and beast cannot be bridged by scientific evidence; propagandists attempt to bridge it by fraud and deceit.

At the time of Darwin, the theory of evolution was adopted by atheists as a weapon against the Bible and against Christianity, and they gradually gained control of the Press. Now the control has been extended even to Catholic publishers. Catholics opposed to evolution will search the catalogs of the principal Catholic publishers in vain for a book that gives the case against evolution. If a Catholic author has a book that gives the arguments from science against evolution he must pay for the printing of it himself and publish it as well as he can. It is a most unsatisfactory situation that publishers should be able to dictate the views to be held on such questions as the origin of the human race in which the teaching of the Church is involved.

Part I

The Six Days of Creation

Chapter 1

THE FIRST DAY OF CREATION

The Origin of the Universe

Very remarkable progress has been made in the science of astronomy in our time, due largely to the installation of giant telescopes on Mt. Wilson and Mt. Palomar in the U.S.A. and at Jodrell Bank in England. Fred Hoyle in *The Nature of the Universe*[1] says: "Just as a blazing fire to a penny candle, so is the observational progress achieved in the last few decades to the work that came before it." In particular, the Laplace Theory (that our earth originally formed part of the sun), which for more than a century was regarded as an almost established fact and was used to interpret (or rather to contradict) the Mosaic account of Creation, has been proved to be scientifically impossible. That knowledge does not appear to have yet reached some biblical exegetes, for in very recent books on the first chapters of Genesis we find the Laplace Theory still regarded as a possible hypothesis.

The theory that the earth originally formed part of the sun was first advanced by French astronomer Marquis Pierre Simon de Laplace in 1796. This theory of Laplace must not be confounded with the Nebular Theory; it was merely an application of it that has been proved to be erroneous. The Nebular Theory was first propounded by Sir Isaac Newton in a letter to Bentley written in 1692 in the following words:

> If the matter of our sun, planets and all the matter of the universe were evenly scattered throughout the heavens and every particle had an innate gravity toward the rest, and the whole space through which the matter was scattered were finite, then the matter on the outside of the space would tend toward the

1. By permission of the publisher, Sir Basil Blackwell, Oxford, 1953.

> matter on the inside and a great spherical mass would be formed.
>
> But if the matter was evenly disposed through infinite space, it would never convene into one mass, but some of it would convene into one mass and some into another, and so make an infinite number of great masses scattered at great distances from each other throughout infinite space. *And thus might the sun and the fixed stars be formed supposing the matter to be of a lucid nature.*

In 1755, Kant attempted to develop Newton's theory and wrongly supposed that the atoms, on coming together, would generate rotary motion. Laplace avoided Kant's error and postulated the existence of the nebulae endowed with rotary motion, but he fell into another error by applying the theory to explain the origin of the earth and the planets. According to his theory, the sun was formerly a great mass of nebulae rotating in space and gradually condensing. As it condensed, some of the matter around the equatorial region failed to keep contact with the mass and was thrown out into space by the centrifugal force, and from this matter the earth and the planets were formed. The theory was modified in the present century because it was found that the centrifugal force would not be capable of throwing the huge masses to a hundredth part of the distance that the earth and planets are from the sun. The modified form was proposed by two Americans, Moulton and Chamberlain, and amended subsequently by two Englishmen, Jeffreys and Jeans. The amended theory supposes that a giant star passed near the sun, and by force of attraction tore huge masses from it and carried them to various distances, where they were recaptured by the attraction of the sun and commenced to revolve around it. (See *The Story of Science,* David Dietz, Cleveland, p. 121). Both the Laplace Theory and this later one are based on a discovery made by means of the spectroscope, that most of the chemical elements of the earth are found in the sun. Actually, 61 out of 92 chemical elements found in the composition of our earth have been identified in the sun; the remaining 31 have not yet at least been identified in it.

Now, more modern examination made with perfected

instruments has shown that although 61 of the elements are common to the sun and earth, they are not in the same proportion. These 61 elements common to the earth and the sun are in such a diluted form in the sun that they form only one percent of the mass of the sun.

In *The Nature of the Universe* (pp. 72 and 73), Hoyle writes:

> Apart from hydrogen and helium (the dominant elements in the sun) all the other elements are extremely rare all over the universe. In the sun they only amount to one percent of the total mass. Contrast this with the earth and the other planets where hydrogen and helium only make about the same contribution as highly complex atoms like iron, silicon, magnesium and aluminum. This contrast brings out two important points. First, we see that the material torn from the sun would not be at all suitable for the formation of the planets as we know them. The composition would be hopelessly wrong. And our second point is that it is the sun that is normal and the earth that is a freak. The interstellar gas and most of the stars are composed of material like the sun and not like the earth.

It is therefore absolutely certain that our earth never formed part of the sun and that both the Laplace Theory and its modifications are scientifically impossible.

A further theory which is devoid of probability has been proposed to replace them. It is that the sun had originally formed part of a binary system and that the second star exploded, driving the lighter material away into space and leaving the heavier elements behind. Now why postulate such a theory, or indeed why should the Laplace Theory have ever been seriously considered to explain the wonderful order and harmony of the solar system with its nine planets and thirty-one moons? This order and harmony certainly demand the intervention of Almighty God, and now that the Laplace Theory has been disproved, why should we accept another theory that supposes that God created or formed another sun greater than ours, only to explode it, send part of it into space and use what remained to form our earth and planets? It is true that some modern astronomers believe that such explosions have taken place in the past, but there is no evidence that anything like our complex solar system was ever formed out of the debris.

Leaving that fantastic theory aside, let us use the scientific conclusion established that the earth never formed part of the sun to help us to explain the opening verses of *Genesis:* "In the beginning God created heaven, and earth. And the earth was void and empty, and darkness was upon the face of the deep; and the spirit of God moved over the waters. And God said: Be light made. And light was made."

The discovery that the earth never formed part of the sun makes it possible to explain the Mosaic account as it stands, without doing violence to the text. We can begin by rejecting the explanation given by some modern exegetes, like Fr. Charles Hauret, that the first two verses are merely a preamble giving a summary of the work of Creation. The Mosaic account says: *In the beginning God created heaven and earth.* Most theologians hold as a probable opinion that Heaven in this first verse refers to the Heaven of the blessed, and that in the creation of Heaven, the creation of the angels is included. Both good and bad angels are referred to in the first three chapters of Genesis, which give an account of Creation. It would be strange if there were no mention of Heaven and the angels in the inspired account of Creation.

Next, the Mosaic account says that God created the earth and that it was void and empty and in darkness. If we adhere to the Mosaic account, the earth here can refer to no more than the earth itself and the planets, which are made of similar material and are dark bodies. All the materials on the earth capable of producing heat and light are the result of vegetation which absorbs and stores up the energy of the sun. In the Mosaic account, vegetation was not created till the third day, so therefore the earth at its creation was not only in darkness, but it had nothing capable of producing light.

Now there is no intrinsic reason for supposing that all the material of the universe was created simultaneously. There is therefore no scientific reason for denying or altering the Mosaic account which says that the earth appeared first in time.

Atheists postulate a universe that has evolved blindly from eternal matter without any divine intervention. Modern science has proved, however, that the actual materials that compose the universe must have had a beginning. Many non-Catholics, especially evolutionists, restrict God's intervention to one initial act, but Catholics know, or should know, that there is constant divine intervention; that divine intervention is necessary for the conservation of the universe; that it was necessary for the creation of vegetable and sentient life, for the creation of each human soul; that there has been special divine intervention in the Incarnation and Redemption and in the miracles of both the Old and the New Testaments.

That the creation of the earth, which was to be the scene of the Incarnation and Redemption, should have been due to a separate and special divine intervention, as Moses says, should be regarded as most fitting.

The Creation of the Material For the Sun and Stars

The reference to the darkness that covered the earth prepares us for the statement: *"And God said: Be light made. And light was made."* For the interpretation of this verse I shall quote first the statement of a scientist, Sir Bertram Windle, made at the beginning of this century, and then the statement of His Holiness, Pope Pius XII which embodies the latest discoveries of science.

Commenting on this verse in *The Church and Science,* Sir Bertram Windle says:

> In the first place it may be pointed out once more that the whole account of Creation centres round this earth of ours and is not necessarily or reasonably to be expected to contain a minute narrative of the universe and its formation. The statement as to the darkness in the previous verse certainly and admittedly relates to the condition of the earth. It would appear that the statement as to the light does the same, and that it gives us to understand that the next stage was the letting in of the light on the previously dark earth, which would occur when a condensation and precipitation of the dense vapours surrounding the earth had taken place.
>
> But where was this light derived from, since we are told

that the sun and the moon and the stars were not yet in existence? This is a very remarkable point and one which bears out the accuracy of the Biblical account in a very striking and unexpected manner. At the time that it was written and for many hundred years after, no one knew anything about the Nebular Theory, and it might have been argued that it was patently absurd to suppose that light could have existed before the existence of those bodies from which we now receive it. The Nebular Theory, however, clears up this difficulty, for it teaches that our solar system, which is all that the biblical account is concerned with, at the period in question, was composed of whirling and as yet imperfectly condensed masses of nebular substance. In the case of the sun, on account of its size, the condensation would take longer than in the case of the earth. It would be still incorrect to speak of it as a *sun,* but it was a source of light as were any other nebular masses which might have been in existence.

It is certainly remarkable, as far as we have got, that the Biblical account and that of science present no contradictions. That is what we, believers in revelation, would expect. . . .

The Holy Father Pope Pius XII gave the same explanation of the verse: *"And God said: Let light be made"* in an address which he delivered to the Pontifical Academy of Science on November 22, 1951, from which we take the following:

> With the same clear and critical look with which the mind examines and passes judgment on facts, it perceives and recognizes the work of creative omnipotence, whose power set in motion by the mighty *"Fiat"* pronounced thousands of millions of years ago by the Creating Spirit. . .called into existence with a gesture of generous love matter bursting with energy. *In fact it would seem that present-day science, with one sweeping step across millions of centuries, has succeeded in bearing witness to that primordial* "Fiat lux" *(Let light be made) uttered at the moment when, along with matter, there burst forth from nothing a sea of light and radiation while particles of chemical elements split and formed into millions of galaxies.*

The Holy Father, in the same address to the Pontifical Academy of Sciences, comments on the words, *In the beginning,* as follows:

> The examination of the various spiral nebulae, especially as carried out by Edwin U. Hubble at the Mt. Wilson Observatory, has led to the significant conclusion, *presented with all due reservations,*[1] that these distant systems of galaxies tend to move away from one another with such velocity that in the space of 1,300 million years the distance between such spiral nebulae is doubled. If we look back into the past at the time required for this process of the "expanding universe" it follows that from one to ten thousand million years ago, the matter of the spiral nebulae was compressed into a relatively restricted space at the time the cosmic processes had their beginning.

The Holy Father then goes on to point out that we should learn from this remarkable vindication of the biblical account of Creation in time to conceive a great reverence and esteem for the Sacred Scriptures:

> Although these figures seem astounding, nevertheless, even in the simplest of the faithful, they bring no new or different concept from the one they learned in the opening words of Genesis: *"In the beginning"* that is to say, at the beginning of things in time. The figures we have quoted clothe these words in a concrete and almost mathematical expression, while from them there springs forth a new source of consolation for those who share the esteem of the Apostle (St. Paul) for that divinely inspired Scripture which is always useful for teaching, for reproving, for correcting, for instructing. (*2 Tim.* 3:16).

This interpretation of the Mosaic account of the Creation of Heaven and earth, and especially of the verse, "God said: Be light made," which has the approval of His Holiness Pius XII, is in accordance with the directions of the Holy See for the interpretation of the first three chapters of Genesis given by the Biblical Commission on June 30, 1909. The Commission asked and answered the following questions:

> . . .2. Whether we may—in spite of the character and historic form of the book of Genesis, of the close connection of the

---

1. There is another modern theory, called the theory of *continuous creation,* which also requires a beginning and demands the action of a Creator.

first three chapters with one another and with those which follow, of the manifold testimony of the Scriptures both of the Old and New Testaments, of the almost unanimous opinion of the Fathers, and of the traditional view which (transmitted also by the Jewish peoples) has always been held by the Church—teach that the three aforesaid chapters do not contain the narrative of things which actually happened, a narrative which corresponds to objective truth and historic truth.

Answer: In the negative.

(b) Whether we may teach that these chapters contain fables derived from mythologies and cosmologies, but purified from all polytheistic error and accommodated to monotheistic teaching by the sacred author, or that they contain allegories and symbols destitute of any foundation in objective reality but presented under the garb of history for the purpose of inculcating religious and philosophical truth; or finally that they contain legends partly historical and partly fictitious, freely handled for the instruction and edification of souls.

Answer: In the negative.

. . .5. Whether all and each of the parts, namely the single words and phrases, in these chapters must always and of necessity be interpreted in a literal sense so that it is never lawful to deviate from it, even when expressions are manifestly used figuratively, that is metaphorically or anthropomorphically, and when reason forbids to hold, or necessity impels us to depart from, the literal sense.

Answer: In the negative.

. . .8. Whether the word 'Yom' (day), which is used in the first chapter of Genesis to describe and distinguish six days, may be taken in the strict sense of the natural day, or in a less strict sense as signifying a certain space of time; and whether free discussion is permitted to interpreters.

Answer: In the affirmative.

As a matter of fact, we find the word "day" used frequently in Scripture, and indeed in ordinary conversation, in the less strict sense. We read in Job: "Are thy days as the days of man, and are thy years as the times of men?" (*Job* 10:5); and in the Second Epistle of St. Peter: "One day with the Lord is as a thousand years, and a thousand years as one day." At the same time it is remarkable that special reference is made in the responses of the Biblical Commission to the interpretation of the word "day," while no specific reference is made to other difficulties such as light before the sun.

Finally, some modern French writers point out that a Babylonian account of Creation existed hundreds of years before the Mosaic account was written, which bears striking similarity to the Mosaic account and that the Mosaic account may have been borrowed from it.

It is true that there is a Babylonian account (which was not committed to writing until about 5,000 years after the Flood), that it is older than the Mosaic account and that it bears some resemblance to it, but the differences between the two accounts, even apart from the religious setting, are so great that the Mosaic account could not have been derived from it.

In the first place, this is not a modern difficulty at all. A Babylonian version of Creation and the Deluge was published by George Smith in 1876. The members of the Biblical Commission were aware of the existence of that version when they were issuing their decree in 1909 to the effect that it is not permissible to teach that the first three chapters of Genesis "contain fables derived from mythologies and cosmologies belonging to other nations, purified from all polytheistic error and accommodated to monotheistic teaching by the sacred author."

This Babylonian account that has come down to us is comparatively recent in Babylonian history; it does not even go back to the time of Abraham, for it was written about 1850 B.C., before the end of the First Dynasty. It is a very confused and incomplete account. It says that before the Creation took place there was war between Marduc, the Creator, and Tiamat, the female principle of evil, and that when she had been conquered, Marduc created the sun, moon and stars. No account is given of the creation of plants and animals, and there is no possibility of reconciling this version of Creation with the findings of modern science.

It is probable that a revelation of the origin of the world and all it contains was made to Adam and that it was preserved by the descendants of Seth down to the time of Noe, and by the descendants of Noe down to the time of Abraham, and was transmitted by him to his descendants.

The Mosaic account, which was written as much, if not more, for modern times as for the time of Moses has been shown by most recent discoveries to be so closely in agreement with modern science that we are justified in concluding that Moses was not only guided by inspiration and preserved from all doctrinal errors when recording it, but that he had a special revelation.

Chapter 2

THE WORK OF THE SECOND DAY

The Biblical Account of The Work of the Second Day

And God said: Let there be a firmament made amidst the waters: and let it divide the waters from the waters. And God made a firmament, and divided the waters that were under the firmament, from those that were above the firmament, and it was so. And God called the firmament, Heaven; and evening and morning were the second day. God also said: Let the waters that are under the heaven, be gathered together into one place: and let the dry land appear. And it was so done. And God called the dry land, Earth; and the gathering together of the waters, he called Seas. And God saw that it was good.
—*Gen.* 1:6-10

The work of the second day was a work of *dividing* all the water now on our earth, whether in the oceans, lakes and rivers, or in the clouds, into two parts: the part that remained on the earth, and the part that ascended and formed the clouds. There was a further division on the third day: the division of the earth into dry land and water.

This biblical account supposes that the waters now in the oceans and the clouds were originally together on the surface of the earth before the division was made. This would happen only if all the water was in the form of vapor that hung like a mantle over the earth. The biblical account asserts: 1) that the water was divided, 2) that some remained on the surface of the earth, and some ascended in the form of clouds, 3) that the whole surface of the earth was covered with water (which required that there should be no mountains at the time); and 4) that the work of division continued on into the third day, when the water was gathered into seas and the dry land appeared.

Now that Mosaic account, simple as it appears, is quite detailed, and all the details are fully confirmed by the findings of modern science. It is most remarkable that such an accurate description of the early history of our earth should have been given by Moses at a time when the surface of the earth was just the same as in our own day, with its high mountains and fathomless oceans. Such a description could not have been guessed at the time, and even now it would require a good knowledge of modern science to give as accurate an account.

What Modern Science Says About The Early Conditions of the Earth

We have seen that the Laplace Theory that the earth was once a fiery mass thrown off from the sun has been exploded. The further theory, that the interior of the earth is a molten mass of matter which occasionally erupts and that only the crust of the earth has condensed, has also been disproved. Modern science has been able to find a balance in which to weigh our earth and measure its density by means of the force of attraction of the sun and the planets. It has succeeded in proving that not only is the interior of the earth solid, but that its density at the center is several times greater than that at the surface.

David Dietz in *The Story of Science* (p. 23) says that the old idea (based on the Laplace Theory) that the earth had a molten interior has been abandoned for the reason that the earth as a whole is five and a half times as dense as water. The surface rocks are only two and three quarter times as dense as water, so that the interior of the earth must be more than twice as dense and heavy as the rocks on the surface; that is to say that it must be as dense and heavy as solid iron. Geologists are now agreed that volcanic eruptions are only surface disturbances, about ten miles deep.

Though scientists have been able to weigh the earth and calculate the density of the interior accurately, they have only been able to examine its surface. However, they have established that the surface of the earth was subjected to intense heat. We have seen that astronomers now regard it as practically certain that the material of which the sun is composed was originally scattered out over an immense space, whirling round and gradually condensing. The earth must have been in that space immersed in the nebulae: this would account for the traces of fire on the surface of the earth, and for the fact that the water in our oceans was once in the form of vapor that hung over the earth. Besides, scientists have established that 61 of the 92 chemical elements found on the surface of the earth are found also in the sun. These elements common to both the sun and the earth are principally the metals, and form only a small proportion of the surface of the earth. It is at least a possible hypothesis that these might have been condensed from the nebulae in which the earth was immersed, and deposited on the surface of the earth before the nebulae receded to form the sun. This hypothesis would explain the presence of a certain number of elements on the earth's surface found in the sun and would account for the luxurious vegetation that existed at the poles in past ages.

In the next place, geologists have established with certainty that originally there were no mountains on the earth, and that the earth was completely covered with water. If readers will consult geological tables in any work on geology they will find that even after dry land had appeared, the surface of the earth was alternately submerged and raised up, and that what are now high mountains were formerly under water. Geologists have been able to place in the proper geological period the formation of all the great mountain ranges of the world. They say that the mountain building did not commence until the carboniferous period, when the coal beds were formed; that the Rocky Mountains in North America and the Andes in South America were formed in the Cretaceous Period, and that the Alps and Himalayas were not formed until the Tertiary Period.

Modern science and the Bible agree, therefore, in stating: 1) that all the waters in the oceans and the clouds were once united, that is, that they were once in the form of a mighty pall of vapor that hung over the surface of the earth; 2) that they were separated, part being changed into water and covering the whole surface of the earth, and part receding from the earth and forming clouds; and 3) that the surface of the earth was flat and that there were no mountains.

What Is Meant by the Word 'Firmament'?

It may be freely admitted that the meaning of the word is somewhat obscure; the Hebrew language, like some other oriental languages such as Chinese, is deficient in abstract terms. We must look to the context to find the meaning. A very good explanation is given in the note on the sixth verse, Chapter One of Genesis, in the Douay version of the Bible, an explanation which has been accepted and quoted by Professor Windle in *The Church and Science.* It is: "*A firmament.* By this name is here understood the whole space between the earth and the highest stars, the lower part of which divideth the waters that are upon the earth from those that are above in the clouds."

A very different explanation is given by some modern writers such as Fr. Charles Hauret, who would have us believe that by "firmament" Moses meant a solid structure over the earth supported at the extremities by pillars, and that a supply of water was stored on the top of this structure, which was let down through trap-doors to the earth in the form of rain.

In the first place it is to be noticed that the Mosaic account of the separating of the waters on the surface of the earth into two portions—the portion which remained on the earth and the portion that formed the clouds, and the subsequent collection of the water on the surface of the earth into oceans—is extraordinarily accurate. *The question of what he meant by the word "firmament" is only a detail.* The theory that by "firmament" Moses meant a solid structure is absurd and is by no means a modern explanation. It is based on the false assumption that the Mosaic account of Creation does not correspond with reality, but merely embodies the crude notion of the time. But the notions of the time were not so crude as some modern writers represent them. The astronomers of the time knew quite a lot about the heavens. They had no telescopes, it is true, but they made their observations through hollow tubes which were directed toward the heavenly bodies and fixed, so that when a planet or a star moved, the motion would be revealed, for the tube would be no longer opposite it. The inhabitants of Central and South America had an accurate solar calendar with the Gregorian correction hundreds of years before Christ. Moses of course had seen water boil and the steam ascending, he knew that water evaporates under the influence of heat and goes up to the clouds, he knew that the clouds require no support, that they are mobile and are driven by the winds, and that when it rains the water comes from the clouds. He knew also that the heavenly bodies are not fixed and immovable, for the planets got their name of "wanderers" from the ancients, and that the various constellations have their seasons for rising and setting. The definition then of "firmament" as a fixed structure supported by pillars cannot be justified.

This explanation of the word "firmament" was probably suggested by the language used by Moses to describe the Deluge. He says: "All the fountains of the great deep were broken up, and the flood gates of heaven were opened. And the rain fell on the earth forty days and forty nights." (*Gen.* 7:11-12). The "great deep" evidently refers to the ocean, and so in the Mosaic account the Flood was not caused by rain alone, but from the water from the ocean that invaded the land. The opening of the floodgates of heaven is but figurative language to indicate the rain was unusually heavy. It may be remarked in passing that the Mosaic description of the flood as a tremendous catastrophe caused not only by torrential rains, but by an incursion of the sea, also renders untenable the theories of some modern writers that the Deluge was merely a local affair, like the floods that occur periodically in China and other countries when great rivers overflow their banks. In the case of all floods of which there is record, except the Deluge, while the destruction of property is considerable, the loss of life is comparatively small—whereas in the Deluge the whole population, except Noe and his family, was wiped out. Our Divine Lord, by using the Deluge as an example to describe the destruction that will take place at the end of the world, confirms the view that the Deluge was a disaster of immense magnitude and bears out the Mosaic description.

Chapter 3

THE WORK OF THE THIRD DAY

The Origin of the Vegetable Kingdom

In the Mosaic account we read: *And God said: Let the earth bring forth the green herb, and such as may seed, and the fruit tree yielding fruit after its kind.*

Moses was aware of course that the ground teemed with various kinds of living things, from the lowly worm that seemed to feed on earth, and yet he puts vegetable life first. In this he is upheld by modern science. Just as the earth itself, before vegetation was created by God, contained nothing capable of producing heat and light, so it contained nothing capable of supporting sentient life. Even the worm does not feed on earth but on decayed vegetation: and not to speak of the worm, the one-celled amoeba, the simplest form of life, feeds on vegetable matter, absorbs oxygen and gives off carbon dioxide.

And not only is vegetation necessary to provide the food for all forms of sentient life, but it is necessary also to provide the oxygen in the atmosphere without which sentient life would be impossible; it is necessary also to remove the carbon dioxide which sentient beings give off. Sentient beings absorb oxygen from the atmosphere and give off carbon dioxide, which is poisonous for them, and which if not removed can cause their extermination; vegetable plants absorb that carbon dioxide which is necessary for their life, and give off oxygen instead. And so by a wonderful arrangement of divine Providence the two kingdoms are interdependent on each other for their existence, but the vegetable kingdom is first, for all kinds of sentient life are dependent on it: 1) for their food, 2) for oxygen, 3) to remove the poisonous carbon dioxide from the atmosphere. Dare anyone say that it is but a lucky guess on the part of its inspired writer to put the vegetable kingdom before the animal, or to deny that the order here revealed provides an argument for design?

The Mosaic account of the origin of vegetable life is short and concise, but it is scientifically accurate, not only in putting vegetable life before sentient, but also in the order which it gives for the appearance of the different forms of vegetable life. It distinguishes between vegetable plants propagated without seed, those propagated by seed, and fruit trees with seed. Here again modern science supports the Mosaic order. The first fossil remains to be found are the algae or seaweed which appeared in the early Cambrian period. Seed-bearing plants and fruit trees did not appear till the Mesozoic age (the Triassic, Jurassic and Cretaceous periods). It is true that sentient life appeared in the meantime, but it was necessary that vegetable life should continue to develop in advance to support it.

Can the Appearance of Vegetable Life Be Explained by Spontaneous Generation?

It used to be believed that the tiny green plants that grow on the surface of stagnant water or in rain-water tanks were due to spontaneous generation, but modern science has shown that this is not so. These tiny plants consist of one cell of protoplasm, and are propagated, like the amoeba, by a division of this cell into two, and not by spontaneous generation. The question of spontaneous generation will be more fully discussed in the chapter on the origin of sentient life.

Note: In the Mosaic account it is clearly stated that vegetable forms of life appeared on the earth before animal forms: that primitive forms appeared first and only later on seed-bearing plants, but it is neither stated or implied that no animal forms of life appeared on the earth before the creation of the seed-bearing plants. Moses rightly places the creation of vegetable life before the creation of animal life, and then completes his account of its creation before dealing with the creation of the more complex forms of animal life ending with men. The fact that he places the creation of vegetable life on the third day does not necessarily mean that its creation was completed on the third day.

Chapter 4

THE WORK OF THE FOURTH DAY

The following is the Mosaic account [*Gen.* 1:14-16]:

> 14. *And God said: Let there be lights made in the firmament of heaven, to divide the day and the night, and let them be for signs, and for seasons, and for days and years:*
> 15. *to shine in the firmament of heaven, and to give light upon the earth. And it was so done.*
> 16. *And God made two great lights: a greater light to rule the day; and a lesser light to rule the night: and the stars.*

It has already been observed that the Mosaic order in which the formation of the sun is put after that of the earth is in agreement with the most recent findings of modern science. It is perhaps still more remarkable that Moses should attribute the formation of the stars to the same period.

Modern scientists are now practically agreed that the sun and stars were formed from nebulae, and that their formation took millions of years. The Nebular Theory which was proposed by Newton three centuries ago is now no longer a mere theory but is accepted by practically all astronomers, and is based on the observation of nebulae still in the process of condensation. Formerly, it was only at the eclipse of the sun that observations could be made; now the spectro-heliographs make it possible to take photographs at all times, and the spectrohelioscope makes it possible to observe the sun without the aid of photographs.

The result of modern observation shows that the sun is an immense globe of material in continuous combustion, the heat and energy derived from which is millions of times greater than that which could be derived from an equal mass of the best coal. Fred Hoyle in *The Nature of the Universe* (p. 29) says that if the sun were made out of a mixture of oxygen and the best coal, the immense mass would be reduced to ashes in only two or three thousand years, at the present rate of consumption of energy in the sun, while it is calculated that the present supply of combustible material in the sun will continue giving out heat and energy at the present rate for ten thousand million years, and that after that period when life on earth would cease as the result of accelerated combustion, the sun would still have material to last another forty thousand million years!

Astronomers have not only been able to observe that this mighty globe of incandescent gases is turning on its axis but have calculated that a revolution takes 24.6 days at the sun's equator, and strange to say 34 days at the poles.

What is it that keeps this great globe rotating at a regular rate and at the same time radiating heat and light? If the uninitiated were allowed to give their opinion, they would probably say that the source of energy is a continuous series of atomic explosions taking place in the sun. But such is not the case. The orderly process of rotating at a regular rate and giving out heat and light in constant quantities is not accomplished by the violent method of fission of the atoms, but by combination. Pope Pius XII in his address to the Pontifical Academy of Sciences (Nov. 22, 1951) gives the most recent findings of science on the subject.

He says:

> In the centre of our sun, according to Bethe, and in the midst of a temperature which goes as high as twenty million degrees, there takes place a chain reaction returning on itself in which four-hydrogen nuclei combine to form one nucleus of helium. The energy thus liberated comes to compensate for the loss involved in the radiation of the sun itself.

This radiation cools down the outer surface of the sun from 20 million degrees to about 10 thousand. Were it not for this outer blanket around the sun, the whole earth would be vaporized in a few minutes.

This activity within the sun has gone on on a colossal scale for hundreds of millions of years with absolute precision and regularity. Its outer surface has been kept at a regular temperature suited to the inhabitants of our earth. Regular activity on a much more colossal scale has been going on in the hundreds of millions of stars for hundreds of millions of years. All the material for the countless millions of stars sufficient to last for thousands of millions of years came into being when the words "Let light be made" were uttered by God.

What would our earth be like without sun? David Dietz in *The Story of Science* answers the question as follows: "Were the sun to go out, the earth would be plunged in darkness, relieved only by the feeble light of the stars, for the moon, of course, shines only by reflected sunlight. Within a few days, the temperature would be so low that all plant and animal life would be frozen to death. Before many days, the oceans would be frozen solid, and soon after, the atmosphere itself would freeze, forming first a layer of liquid air upon the surface of the earth, and then a layer of solid air."

Such must have been the original condition of the earth, or the materials for it, in the supposition that it was created before the nebulae.

With regard to the moon, it may be presumed that the material for it was created at the same time as that of the earth, but its formation is attributed to the same day as that of the sun, for it could not perform its function of reflecting the light of the sun until the nebulae from which the sun was formed had been sufficiently condensed.

Science of Today and the Case of Galileo

The condemnation of Galileo by the Congregation of the Holy Office in 1616 under Pope Paul V, and again in 1633 under Pope Urban VIII, has been used ever since by the enemies of the Catholic Church as an argument against papal infallibility and a proof that the Catholic Church is opposed to the progress of science. As the result of continued misrepresentation, the case is even now misunderstood both inside and outside the Catholic Church. For instance, Mr. F. Hoyle in *The Nature of the Universe,* published as late as 1953, writes: "The conflict between the Copernican theory and the Roman Catholic Church is well known, especially the part played by Galileo." Mr. Hoyle gives no explanation of the part played by Galileo, but on the same page (p. 14) he goes on to tell of the further information about the movements of the heavenly bodies added to that furnished by Copernicus: he mentions the name of Kepler, the contemporary of Galileo, who showed that the planets revolved not in the form of circles but of elipses, and of Newton who explained in terms of gravitation the details of the planetary motions, but he attributes nothing to Galileo.

The fact that the earth moves round the sun was not discovered or proved by Galileo. The theory goes back to the time of the Greek astronomer Pythagoras (580-500 B.C.); it was probably known to the early inhabitants of Central America, who had an accurate solar calendar, the same as that corrected by Pope Gregory XIII; it may have even gone back to the time of Adam, for a knowledge of the work of Creation may have been imparted to him before the Fall. Whatever about that, the credit of the discovery in modern times of the movement of the earth and planets around the sun belongs to a Catholic priest from Poland named Copernicus, who published his book on the subject in 1543, entitled *De Revolutionibus Orbium Caelestium.* Cardinal Nicholas of Cusa advocated the same theory, and neither he nor Copernicus encountered any opposition from the Holy See.

The question at issue between Galileo and the Holy See was not the truth of the theory of Copernicus, but the interpretation of the passage in Chapter X of Josue, which says that "the sun and the moon stood still." Galileo was not content with affirming the truth of the Copernican Theory, but he declared that the sun was immovable, and that therefore the Bible contained an error. This is proved by a letter written by the learned Cardinal Robert Bellarmine (now canonized), who was a member of the Congregation of the Holy Office at the time, to Foscarini, Galileo's friend. In this letter the

Cardinal states that "There would be no objection on the part of the Congregation to putting forward the system of Copernicus as the best explanation of the celestial phenomena provided no reference was made to the apparent conflict with the Bible." In the actual text of the condemnation the very first words are that the Congregation declares heretical the *teaching of Galileo that the sun is immovable.*

Modern Science Vindicates the Congregation

Since the time of Galileo great strides have been made in astronomy due to the improvements made in the telescope that was invented at the time of Galileo by the Dutch optician, Lippershey, and to the invention of the spectroscope, the spectroheliograph and the helioscope. Formerly, it was only possible to observe the sun at times of eclipses of the sun, but since the invention of the helioscope, it is now possible to make observations at all times. By the aid of these instruments it has been proved conclusively that the *sun is not immovable,* but rotates on its axis. In the second place, it has been ascertained that there is continuous activity in every part of the sun which consists in the transforming of hydrogen into helium. In the third place, it has been observed that the time that the sun (which is a gaseous body) takes to rotate on its axis varies from 24.6 days at the central section to 34 days at the poles.

It is to be noted that the shortest time for a rotation (24.6 days) is at the section in the center, where the greatest distance has to be traveled (nearly three million miles) but where the mass is greatest and the energy generated greatest (which is in proportion to the mass); and that the speed decreased for each section from the center to the poles in proportion to the decrease of the mass, until at the poles, where the distance to be traveled is very small, and the mass and internal energy proportionately small, it takes 34 days for a rotation. What is it that causes the great difference in the speed at which the sun rotates at the central section and at the poles?

We leave the solution of that problem to the astronomers.

It is, however, a possible theory that the decrease in the speed at which the sun rotates for each section from the center to the poles is connected with the decrease in the amount of energy generated in each section from the center to the poles. It is true that the planet Jupiter takes five minutes longer to rotate on its axis at the poles than at the central section, but as it has no source of internal energy, this theory could not be used to explain the small difference.

It is also a possible theory that the immense energy that is being continuously generated in the sun affects the motion of the planets, which are inert bodies having no internal source of energy, the only source of energy for the solar system being in the sun.

The behavior of the sun-spots which appear and disappear on the sun's surface in a regular cycle tends to confirm the theory that the rotation of the sun on its axis is affected by the internal activity, and that the earth and planets are also affected by it. These sun-spots are immense openings in the surface of the sun, sometimes as wide as 50,000 miles, from which gases issue in a spiral motion. These sun-spots exercise influence upon the earth by causing magnetic storms and displays of aurora borealis. The astronomer, Hale, demonstrated that the sun-spots were magnets of immense power.

Applying the foregoing considerations to the explanation of the miracle recorded in Chapter 10 of *Josue* which says that "the sun and moon stood still," we can draw the following conclusions:

1) It is quite certain that the sun is not immovable, as Galileo held, for it has internal motion, motion round its axis and motion in space.

2) It is possible to explain the prolongation of daylight by a suspension of the activity of the sun, which would bring the whole solar system to a standstill. Galileo, who knew nothing about the different movements of the sun, thought that the only way to explain the miracle of prolonging the daylight was to attribute it solely to a stopping of the rotation of the earth. That would most certainly require the exercise of God's almighty power, but it would appear to interfere with the order

and harmony of the solar system. God could just as easily have exercised His power by suspending the activity of the whole system at its source in the sun as at any particular point, and it would seem more worthy of Him, for it was He who by His almighty *Fiat* brought the whole system into being and fixed the laws which govern it.

It should be easy for Catholics in our time to accept this solution of the difficulty, especially as it vindicates the justice of the decision made twice by the Congregation of the Holy Office and approved by Popes of the time. It is a fact to be noted that the condemnation of Galileo was never withdrawn. The question of the infallibility of the Pope was not at issue in the conflict with Galileo, but there is the question of who was right.

The learned St. Robert Bellarmine who, we may presume, was the chief adviser of the Congregation, knew as much about the Copernican theory as Galileo and was therefore well aware of the objection it raised against the traditional interpretation of Chapter 10 of *Josue*, to which the science of the time provided no answer; but, being a man of God, he stood by the doctrine of the inerrancy of Scripture and preferred to suffer misrepresentation rather than yield. He was but following the rule laid down by St. Augustine already quoted: "Whatever scientists assert in their treatises which is contradictory to these Scriptures of ours, that is, to Catholic faith, we must either prove it as well as we can to be false, or at all events, we must without the smallest hesitation believe it to be so."[1]

---

1. Some people think that there is a similarity between the miracle recorded in *Josue* 10 and the miracle of the sun at Fatima in which Our Lady showed her power over the motions of the sun.

Chapter 5

THE WORK OF THE FIFTH AND SIXTH DAYS UP TO THE CREATION OF MAN

The Mosaic Account

God also said: Let the waters bring forth the creeping creature having life, and the fowl that may fly over the earth under the firmament of heaven. And God created the great whales, and every living and moving creature, which the waters brought forth, according to their kinds, and every winged fowl according to its kind. And God saw that it was good. And he blessed them, saying: Increase and multiply, and fill the waters of the sea: and let the birds be multiplied upon the earth. And evening and morning were the fifth day. And God said: Let the earth bring forth the living creature in its kind, cattle and creeping things, and beasts of the earth, according to their kinds. And it was so done. And God made the beasts of the earth according to their kinds, and cattle, and everything that creepeth on the earth after its kind. And God saw that it was good. —*Gen.* 1:20-25

It does not come within the scope of the present book, the principal object of which is to deal with the origin of man, to discuss in detail all the questions which arise from the above account given in the Bible. Three questions however which have a bearing on the following chapters, will be here discussed. They are: 1) whether the order given in the Mosaic account of the appearance of the various forms of sentient life agrees with the order disclosed by geology; 2) whether sentient life could have arisen by spontaneous generation; and 3) whether the various forms of sentient life now found in the world can be traced back to a few primitive forms, or whether the various species of at least the genera, were specially created by God at various times according as the earth was fit to receive them.

In most books dealing with geology, paleontology and biology, geological timetables are found which give the geological eras and periods during which the various forms of plants and animals first appeared. Now whether the various forms of animal life, the fossils of which first appear at various geological periods, were specially created, or had developed or evolved from previously existing forms, the order found in the geological strata agrees with the Mosaic order.

As will be seen from the geological timetable[1] here given, the geological order, which is the same as the Mosaic, is as follows: First of all, plant life, next, various forms of invertebrates in the sea, then fishes, then winged insects, then land invertebrates, then the great Saurian reptiles, then birds, then mammals, and last of all man.

The Mosaic account cannot therefore be dismissed as merely a record of the crude ideas of the people who lived at the time it was composed. No such account is found in the literatures of any of the ancient peoples of the world, whether Sumerians, Babylonians, Egyptians, Chinese, Indians, Greeks or Romans. The sciences of geology and biology were unknown in the time of Moses, and yet he wrote confidently and with considerable detail, as if he knew both. The Holy Spirit, who used Moses as His human instrument and who is the real Author, as all Catholics are bound to believe, inspired Moses to write both the account and the order as much, if not more, for the people of modern times when the hidden record of Creation had been disclosed to light, as for the people of the time of Moses, who had no suspicion that such a record existed.

The three estimates[2] for the number of millions of years of the different geological eras are taken from different modern textbooks, the smallest being from a textbook of the London University. There is a fourth modern estimate which is five times greater than the first. These estimates are not for

---

1 and 2. See next page for geological timetable.

ERA	PERIOD	RECESSION OF WATER GLACIAL PERIOD	RISE OF MOUNTAINS	FLORA	FAUNA	LENGTH OF PERIOD IN MILLIONS OF YEARS	THICKNESS IN FEET OF THE GEOLOGICAL STRATA
QUATERNARY	PLEISTOCENE				MAN	1½	600
Tertiary or Cenozoic	Pleistocene Miocene Oligocene Eocene	Retreat of ocean Warm climate	Rise of Alps and Himalaya Mountains	Seed-bearing plants and trees.	Mam-mals	59, 10, 3	12,000
Secondary or Mesozoic	Cretaceous Jurassic Triassic	Swamp deposits Much of land under water.	Rise of Rocky and Andes Mountains		Great Saurian Reptiles Birds	110, 15, 9	18,000
Primary or Paleozoic	Permian Carboni-ferous Devonian Silurian Ordovician Cambrian	Continents under water. Much of continents under water.	Coal deposits. Rise of mountains.	Ferns and primi-tive pines.	Land Inverte-brates. Winged insects. Fishes Marine inverte-brates.	330, 74½, 18	90,000
Azoic						550, ? 30	?

the age of the world, but for the length of the various geological eras beginning at the time when the earth was partly free from water and when deposits began to be made. Before the earth's crust hardened there were alternate depressions and elevations, so that what had been at one time under the sea became elevated, and vice versa. The portions of the earth above water were eroded by torrential rains, and the material eroded was deposited in the ocean; the ocean in its turn was elevated and became dry land subject to erosion. The various strata deposited in the ocean in early times, which are now dry land, are not all found in any one place but are scattered over the world. They are recognized by the fossilized flora and fauna which they contain. The various estimates for the length of the various eras are based on the thickness of the geological strata. These calculations are based on the double assumption that the earth was 93 millions of miles distant from the sun when the deposits began to be made in the Azoic Era, and that the rate of depositing was uniform. We have seen, however, that according to the most modern theory, the earth began its existence in the nebulae, which took millions of years to recede and condense. As a result of the great heat to which the earth would have been subjected if it were immersed in the nebulae, the rate of evaporation, consequent rainfall and depositing of eroded material in the early geological eras must have been many times greater than it would have been if the earth was 93 millions of miles distant from the source of heat.

No attempt has so far been made to construct a new geological timetable based on the most modern theory of the origin of the universe.

The estimating of the age of the world since it was created is an entirely different question. Of the age of the world, nothing more than a guess can be given, based on a theory which may not be applicable to the early condition of the earth. This question will be discussed in greater detail in the chapter on "The Antiquity of Man." (Part IV).

A glance at the geological timetable will be sufficient to convince the reader of the extraordinary accuracy of the Mosaic account. The following points should be specially noticed. The earth was originally flat and without mountains, as the Mosaic account requires. The recession of the water took a long time. Moses put the appearance of dry land in the second period; when he says that the dry land appeared, his statement need not be interpreted to mean that all the present dry land became free from water. The rise of the mountains corresponded with the cooling and attraction of the earth's surface. That process continued during several geological periods and was not completed till the time of the rise of the Alps and Himalayas in the Tertiary Era. If the earth had been 93 millions of miles from the source of heat all during this time, it is hard to see how the process of cooling could have taken so long. The glacial period that occurred after the final contraction of the earth prepared it for the coming of man. The close correspondence of the Mosaic account of the appearance of vegetable and the various forms of sentient life has already been noted.

Chapter 6

SPONTANEOUS GENERATION

All believers in God accept the doctrine that He created the world and everything in it out of nothing, and that all forms of life owe their origin to Him. For them, the question at issue with regard to spontaneous generation is whether God endowed the inanimate matter of the world with the power of producing living things, of both vegetable and animal kingdoms, in certain circumstances. It was the common belief of all, both pagans and Christians down to the seventeenth century, that spontaneous generation was a fact; pagans regarded it as a natural result of decay and corruption, while Christians who attempted to explain it attributed it to power given by God. It was believed in Egypt that mice issued from the mud of the Nile; Virgil wrote that the dead bodies of cattle produced bees; Shakespeare wrote in Hamlet that the sun breeds maggots in dead dogs, and in the Middle Ages it was believed that barnacle geese arose from the decaying timber of ships, and the question was even discussed by theologians whether the meat of the barnacle goose could be eaten on Friday! Pope Innocent III decided in 1215 that barnacle should be regarded as flesh meat.

In 1668, Francesco Redi from Italy proved by experiment that maggots could not be generated by rotting meat. His experiment consisted in putting meat in two jars, one of which he covered with fine muslin, while the other was left open; maggots soon appeared in the jar left open, but none appeared in the other.

The belief that bacteria could arise spontaneously persisted down to the time of Louis Pasteur (1822-1895), who proved by an experiment somewhat similar to that of Francesco Redi that such was not possible. For his experiment he used a flask with a long neck curving downwards. Into this he poured liquid which he had boiled. The curved neck prevented germs floating in the air from entering into the flask while it allowed pure air to enter. He did the same thing with another flask, which he left open on top. Germs were soon found in the flask left open on top, while none appeared in the one with the curved neck, even after the lapse of many days. He continued his experiments and found that germs could be destroyed in liquids such as milk without bringing them to the boiling point and thus destroying much of their nutritive value. In this lecture which he delivered at the Sorbonne in 1864, he explained his experiment and concluded his address with these words: "Never will the doctrine of spontaneous generation recover from this simple experiment."

However, atheists still continued to cherish the delusion that spontaneous generation was still possible. In 1868, four years after Pasteur's lecture at the Sorbonne, Huxley publicly claimed to have discovered that a primitive form of life is actually generated spontaneously in the depths of the sea. He got some mud that had been dredged from the ocean and examined it with a microscope, and thought he discovered that it moved. He named the substance *Bathybius Haeckeli* after Ernest Haeckel, the German rationalist. He lived under the delusion for eight years until it was proved conclusively that the movements that he observed in the mud could be produced by treating it with alcohol. Huxley admitted his error and withdrew his claim.

The question of whether the origin of life in the world can be explained by spontaneous generation has been raised again by two recent Catholic writers: Fr. Charles Hauret of Strasburg in his book *Origines* (Paris 1953) and by Dr. Messenger in *Evolution and Theology* (London, 1931). Fr. Hauret quotes *L'Homme et l'Univers,* a Brussels publication, as saying that students in some of the Continental universities are being told that living cells will soon be produced in the laboratory. He adds his own comment that in view of the progress made in the domain of chemistry in modern times, such does not seem impossible, but that Catholics need not be alarmed, for if such should happen they could attribute it to a power with which God endowed matter at its creation. There is no doubt about the intense propaganda in favor of atheistic evolution in universities, as in other bodies which influence public opinion, but it is not true to say that experiments are being carried out by scientists to produce living cells. Such is recognized to be in practice impossible even by the most extreme atheists. Not to speak of attempting to construct the complex substance known as protoplasm and endowing it with life, no attempt is being made or contemplated to restore life to any living organism once life has been pronounced to be extinct, even when a perfectly healthy organism has died by suffocation and is intact and still warm. Propaganda in favor of atheistic evolution carried on insidiously through schoolbooks, museums, the press and radio is certainly a danger to be dreaded; it is doing untold harm and ought to be combated by every means possible, but the prospect of producing living cells in the laboratory is a possibility so remote that it need not be considered.

Dr. Messenger does not contemplate the possibility of living cells being produced in the laboratory. His idea of spontaneous generation is the production of life from inanimate matter, not by virtue of any innate power possessed by inanimate matter, but by virtue of the command of God. Commenting on the words of Genesis:

> And God said: "Let the waters bring forth the creeping creature having life. . . ." and "Let the earth bring forth the living creature of its kind. . . ." he writes: "We conclude that Holy Scripture, according to its plain and obvious sense, definitely teaches the origin of all living things from inorganic matter, by what may well be called 'spontaneous generation.' " The plain and obvious sense of the words quoted is that all living things were produced from inanimate matter by the command of God, and that cannot be called "spontaneous generation" even by a stretch of the imagination.

The real question at issue, which Dr. Messenger is trying to explain, is how the divine decree of creating the various kinds of living things was translated into action. Did the animals issue forth from the earth visibly, as the Egyptians supposed the mice to issue from the mud of the Nile? That is a useless speculation. God gave the order, and living things came into being; that is all anyone will ever know until he is allowed to gaze on the Divine Essence in the beatific vision and see the source of God's activity.

It is the teaching of the Church that God from all eternity saw the present universe in its minutest details, even the number of hairs on each one's head and all the free acts of angels and men; that He decreed to create it in time and to intervene in the operation of the universe in various circumstances and at various times: In the miracles worked by the prophets of the Old Testament, the Incarnation, the miracles of Christ and His saints down to our own days. The most satisfactory interpretation of the Mosaic account of Creation and, as we shall see, the one most in accord with the findings of modern science, is that life began in time by the command of God; that the first form of life was of a primitive kind such as suited the conditions of the earth at the time; that God intervened at various times to produce other forms of life, according as the earth was prepared to receive them, and that when everything was ready for man, he was specially created.

As already stated, Dr. Messenger was a believer in the theory of evolution. Fr. Lattey S.J., who wrote the preface for Dr. Messenger's book, *Evolution and Theology,* says:

> The author would not (I fancy) repudiate the title of Catholic evolutionist, the former word always implying an ample submission to the government and teaching authority of the Holy See. For myself, I am not aware of any serious support given in Scripture or Tradition to the idea that Adam's body was formed from a strictly animal body or from a series of such bodies; and Dr. Messenger himself points out that in his opinion "Scripture yields only a negative result; that is to say, Scripture neither teaches nor disproves the doctrine of the evolution of the human body." (p. 275). He also remarks that "science cannot as yet bring forth any convincing evidence on the point."

As we shall see in a later chapter, Scripture as interpreted by the Holy See is not quite neutral on the question of the origin of the human body. The Catholic Church binds all to believe that Eve's body was formed from that of Adam, it *allows* Catholic scholars to investigate the question whether Adam's body might have been formed from animate matter, but *forbids* them to teach definitely that it was.

There is no evidence that Dr. Messenger investigated the question of evolution independently; he accepted the conclusions of others, such as his friend Canon Dorlodot of Louvain University, and then proceeded to search Scripture and the writings of Fathers and theologians for evidence that the theory of evolution was either taught or tolerated in these writings.

Chapter 7

THE ORIGIN OF THE VARIOUS SPECIES OF LIVING THINGS NOW IN THE WORLD

To solve any problem the first thing necessary is to get a clear idea of the problem to be solved in order to see whether it is simple or complex, and if complex, to see into what component parts it may be divided. The present problem is very complex, for the animal and vegetable kingdoms contain between them a little under a million and a half, and some say more than a million and a half different species. These species, numerous though they are, have each their distinctive features which they retain because they rarely interbreed with other species even of the same genus, and when they do, their offspring are almost always infertile. In the case of the species of the animal kingdom, of which there are more than 600,000, each, besides differing in structure, has its own peculiar habits and instincts.

For the purpose of classification, scientists divide living things into various categories according to the degree of similarity and differences between them. These divisions are into Kingdoms (animal and vegetable); Phyla (of which there are four for the vegetable, 11 for the animal, and four doubtful); Classes (mammals, insects, etc.); Orders (primates, carnivores, etc.); Families (siminidae, felidae, etc.); Genera (human, simian, feline, etc.); Species (man, gorilla, dog, housefly, etc.); and lastly, varieties of breeds. As we ascend the scale, the difference increases and the difficulty of one being formed from the other becomes accentuated.

Of the 11 phyla or ultimate categories into which the animal kingdom is divided, 10 have no backbone and are called the invertebrates; the remaining phylum, which has a backbone or a notochord, is called the "phylum chordatum." In this latter phylum are included men, horses, cattle, dogs, cats, rabbits, rats, mice etc., and in addition birds, frogs, reptiles, fishes; in all about 46,000 species. To describe adequately these 600,000 or 700,000 different species of the animal kingdom, each with its own distinctive structure, habits and instincts, several large volumes would be required. Then the countless millions of individual members of which each species is composed all differ among one another, and have each distinguishing characteristics not only in themselves but in all their parts, so that no two leaves of a tree are exactly alike. In spite of this great variety and the great differences, the animal and vegetable kingdom form a harmonious whole, and have continued to perpetuate themselves and at the same time to retain their essential distinctive features for millions of years.

This order and harmony in endless variety is one of the traditional arguments for the existence of an all-wise, omnipotent God.

Darwin in *The Origin of Species* endeavored to find an answer to this argument. In almost every page of this book, which has become the bible of atheists, he gives examples of the complexity of structure, great variety and marvelous instincts of the various forms of life, and as he describes each new wonder, he keeps on implying: "You must not attribute this to the power of God; it all began by chance, and has evolved according to the principles of natural selection, struggle for existence and survival of the fittest." Having implied his weary, blasphemous view in almost every page attributing the evident work of a benign Creator to principles that have been proved to be wholly incapable of producing the results, in the last paragraph of the book, apparently conscious of the absurdity of his claims, he tolerates the idea that a Creator might have started the elaborate scheme, provided that it be admitted that it evolved on Darwinian principles. This paragraph reads as follows:

> It is interesting to contemplate a tangled bank, clothed with many plants of many kinds, with birds singing in the bushes, with various insects flitting about, with worms crawling through

> the damp earth, and to reflect that these elaborately constructed forms, so different from each other and dependent on each other in so complex a manner, have all been produced by laws acting around us. These laws, taken in the largest sense, being Growth with Reproduction; Inheritance which is almost implied in reproduction; Variability from the indirect and direct action of the conditions of life, and from use and disuse; a Ratio of increase so high as to lead to a Struggle for Life, and as a consequence to Natural Selection entailing Divergence of Character and Extinction of less-improved forms. Thus, from the war of nature, from famine and death, the most exalted object which we are capable of conceiving, namely, the production of the higher animals, directly follows.
>
> There is a grandeur in this view of life, with its several powers, having been originally breathed by the Creator into a few forms or into one; and that, whilst this planet had gone cycling on according to the fixed Law of Gravity, from so simple a beginning, endless forms and most wonderful have been and are being evolved.

Soon after this "bible of atheists" was published, Darwin renounced belief in a Creator and became an atheist, so that his whole system, which is a tissue of absurdities, is based on a supreme absurdity.

Some Catholic evolutionists quote Darwin's last sentence in favor of their view that theistic evolution gives a grander idea of the power and wisdom of God than special Creation. St. Paul, however, says: "The foolishness of God is wiser than men; and the weakness of God is stronger than men." (*1 Cor.* 1:25). If we want to get an idea of what method of Creation is most in accord with the wisdom and power of God, we look first to the inspired account of Creation recorded in the first chapters of *Genesis,* and for confirmation of that account we look to the record of Creation written in the rocks.

What Science Says About the Origin of Species

To what branch of science are we to turn for an explanation of the origin of species? No branch alone can give the answer. The zoologist enumerates and classifies the animals; the entomologist does the same for the insects; the ornithologist studies the birds; it takes a whole army of botanists to examine and classify the 800,000 species of the vegetable kingdom; the morphologist studies the external appearance, the anatomist analyzes the internal structure; the physiologist studies the activities; the ecologist deals with the natural surroundings of plants and animals.

The experts in various departments usually give their findings in technical language, and the man-in-the-street and even the busy professional man have to depend on writers of popular books for a digest of the findings of the experts. The demand in countries where the majority of the population is pagan or semi-pagan is for books that give the evolutionists' solution, and besides, most of the popularizers are pagan or semi-pagan, and hence it is not to be wondered at that most of the books by so-called biologists speak as if the evolution of the million and a half species of the vegetable and animal kingdoms from a single living cell that originated by spontaneous generation were an established fact; whereas there is no scientific basis for the theory in its extreme form. The writing of popular books on the origin of living things and the composition of textbooks for the schools are not left to chance. Atheistic evolution is the official creed of Freemasons, whose books such as *Signs and Symbols of Primordial Man* by Churchward (which I have before me) tell the members that Freemasonry goes back to the first man, and that he was evolved from an ape. It is the official creed also of all communists and atheists, and it is a necessary basis for atheism. Books on the origin of living things written by Freemasons, communists and atheists all teach the extreme form of evolution, not as a theory, but as an established fact. As the majority of people in England and the U.S.A. practice no religion and are practical atheists, it is natural that the majority of books on the origin of living things cater to their views, especially since there are powerful and wealthy atheistic societies which will ensure a ready circulation for books that teach the evolutionary theory, and which will do all they can to injure the circulation of books that oppose it. The fact that most books on the subject in question teach evolution is commonly used by atheists as an argument that it must be true. The argument is put in various forms; the following quotation from *Evolution for John* by Henshaw Ward will serve as an example of what is found in many books: "Every reputable modern scientist believes in evolution as a matter of course. It is now an integral part of all general education and culture. To suppose that it may one day be abandoned is to live in intellectual barbarism."

No Catholic writer who happens to believe in some form of evolution should descend to using such a form of argument to defend his view, especially when there is a question of the origin of man, firstly, because the statement is false, for several of the best scientists of our time give weighty reasons to show that evolution in the common meaning of the word is biologically impossible and is contradicted by the geological record; and secondly, because such a form of argument is opposed to the spirit, if not to the letter of the Pope's teaching in *Humani Generis,* in which he says:

> Some however rashly transgress this liberty of discussion, when they act as if the origin of the human body from pre-existing and living matter were already completely certain and proved by facts which have been discovered up to now and by reasoning on these facts, and as if there were nothing in the sources of divine revelation which demand the greatest moderation and caution on this question.

The Direct Evidence on the Manner In Which Species of Living Things Have Been Formed

THE FIRST SOURCE OF EVIDENCE

The various branches of biology can catalogue, analyze and compare the various species of living things. Biologists can give an opinion on the question of whether it is biologically possible that one species may have evolved from another, or one genus from another, and even on this point there are fundamental differences of opinion among the greatest experts, but no biologist as such can give direct evidence on the question whether any species, not to speak of any phylum, has been evolved from another.

There are two direct sources of evidence on the origin of species. The first is the everyday observation of the behavior of plants and animals in the world. The gardener knows that new varieties of vegetables and flowers can be developed and are developed, but he does not try to improve his apple trees by crossing them with pear trees. The stock breeder knows that breeds can be improved and that new breeds can be developed, but he does not call this process evolution, nor does he try to improve the breed of cattle by crossing them with horses. In practice, neither the gardener or stock breeder, nor the expert botanist or biologist has any dreams of being able to change one species into another, not to speak of changing one genus into another. When a new breed of cattle, sheep, pigs or dogs has been developed successfully, the breeder does not call the process evolution, nor does he become so elated over his success as to try to change a cow into a horse.

THE SECOND SOURCE OF EVIDENCE

The second direct source of evidence about the origin of the various species comes from the fossils found in the various geological strata. The estimates of the time that has elapsed since the first living things appeared in the world vary from 30 million years to 500 million years. If we merely knew that 500 million years had elapsed, and had no record of the living things that existed during that time, we would be prepared to admit that great changes took place during that long period, judging by what can now be effected in the improvement of breeds of animals, etc.; and evolutionists would most probably claim that the discovery that such a period had elapsed should alone be sufficient to prove their theory.

However, the actual record of the rocks provides three formidable objections, for which no evolutionist has yet given a satisfactory solution, nor does there appear to be any prospect that solutions will be found. These objections are:

1) Varied and abundant fossils of animal life appear suddenly in the Cambrian rocks. These are fossils of living things of highly developed and complex structure. In the opinion of most geologists, the stratum below the Cambrian contains no fossils at all; the very most that is claimed is that some trace of fossils has been found in the stratum beneath the Cambrian.

2) Fossils of new types of animal life appear suddenly at various times during the geological periods, for which no link with previous living things can be discovered.

3) Judging by the length of time that the geological record shows to be necessary to transform one species into another, 500,000 years or even five times that time would be altogether inadequate to transform one genus into another, not to speak of transforming one phylum into another.

Charles Darwin States the Difficulties

Darwin's statement of the difficulties which the fossil record provides against his theory is found in Chapter 10 of *The Origin of Species.* Among the subheadings of the chapter are: *Intermediate Varieties Absent in any Single Formation; Sudden Appearances of Groups of Allied Species; Sudden Appearance of Groups of Allied Species in the Lowest Known Fossiliferous Strata.*

Let us take the last-mentioned difficulty first. Darwin states it as follows:

> There is another and allied difficulty, which is much more serious. *I allude to the manner in which species belonging to the main divisions of the animal kingdom suddenly appear in the lowest known fossiliferous rocks. . . .Some of the most ancient animals, as the Nautilus, Lingula, etc., do not differ much from living species;* and it cannot in our theory be supposed that these old species were the progenitors of all the species belonging to the same groups which have subsequently appeared, for they are not in any degree intermediate in character.
>
> Consequently, if the theory be true it is indisputable that before the lowest Cambrian stratum was deposited long periods elapsed, as long as, or probably far longer than, the whole

> interval from the Cambrian Age to the present day; and that during these vast periods the world swarmed with living creatures. Here we encounter a formidable objection; for it seems doubtful whether the earth, in a fit state for the habitation of living creatures, has lasted long enough. Sir W. Thompson concludes that the consolidation of the crust of the earth can hardly have occurred less than 20 or more than 400 million years ago, but probably not less than 98 or more than 200 million years. These wide limits show how very doubtful the data are; and other elements may have hereafter to be introduced into the problem. *Mr. Croll estimates that about 60 million years have elapsed since the Cambrian period, but this, judging from the small amount of organic changes since the commencement of the glacial epoch, appears a very short time for the many and great mutations of life which have certainly occurred since the Cambrian formation; and the previous 140 million years can hardly be considered as sufficient for the development of the varied forms of life which already existed during the Cambrian period.*

In that quotation from Darwin are contained the first and third objections mentioned above. He states the second objection as follows:

> The abrupt manner in which whole groups of species appear in certain formations has been urged by several paleontologists—for instance, by Agassiz, Pictet and Sedgwick—as a fatal objection to the belief of the transmutation of species. If numerous species, belonging to the same genera or families, have really started into life at once, the fact would be fatal to the theory of evolution through natural selection. For the development by this means of a group of forms, all of which are descended from some one progenitor, must have been an extremely slow process; and the progenitors must have lived long before their modified descendants.
>
> But we continually overrate the perfection of the geological record, and falsely infer, because certain genera or families have not been found beneath a certain stage, that they did not exist before that stage.
>
> *In all cases positive paleontological evidence may be implicitly trusted; negative evidence is worthless, as experience has so often shown.*

In these two passages Darwin admits:

1) that varied species belonging to the main divisions of the animal kingdom suddenly appear in the lowest known fossiliferous rocks, some of which still exist practically unchanged;

2) that during the time that has elapsed since the Cambrian Period, whole groups of species appear in an abrupt manner;

3) that the time available for the evolution of the species found in the Cambrian Period (in the unfounded hypothesis that such evolution took place), is altogether inadequate, as is also inadequate the time that has elapsed since the Cambrian Period to explain the evolution of the various forms of animal life found in the world at the present day.

The only evidence he can give for his system is negative evidence, which he admits is useless. In other words, Darwin admits that the positive evidence from paleontology available in his time proved that his theory of evolution was impossible.

The Evidence of Modern Authority

It is now a hundred years ago since Darwin published *The Origin of Species.* During that time very considerable progress has been made in the various branches of science which deal with the origin of living things, and very many books have been written on the subject. If the reader wishes to get in convenient form what are regarded as the most cogent arguments in favor of evolution drawn from the books that have appeared during the century, and a most convincing reply, he will find them in *Is Evolution Proved? an Argument between Douglas Dewar and H. S. Shelton*[1] conducted by letter, with Arnold Lunn as chairman and editor. The letters, in which every aspect of the question of evolution is discussed, were published by Hollis and Carter, London, in 1947.

About Mr. Shelton, the blurb of the book says: "Mr. H. S. Shelton, the champion of evolution, has contributed numerous papers to scientific and philosophical journals, and is the author of two books on education, including one on The Theory and Practice of General Science."

1. Published by Messrs. Hollis and Carter, London.

Of Mr. Dewar it says:

> Mr. Douglas Dewar F. Z. S., who is the author of a number of scientific books, has made a special study of birds, and it was his investigations as an ornithologist that led him to reject successively Darwinism, mutationism and finally the whole concept of organic evolution.

While Mr. Dewar was a specialist in ornithology, he was also one of the greatest all-around living authorities of modern times on all the aspects of the problem of evolution.

The general verdict of unbiased readers was that Dewar triumphantly answered all the arguments put forward in favor of evolution by Darwin, Huxley, Spencer etc., as recapitulated by Shelton. The book made many converts from evolution, especially among the intellectuals.

I take the following quotation from Dewar's chapter on "The Geological Record" to show what answer modern geology gives to the three objections against Darwin's theory quoted above:

> The theory of evolution must stand or fall by the evidence of the fossils. These furnish the only direct evidence. If this be against the theory, no amount of indirect evidence can avail...
>
> Fossils are the remains of, or of impressions made by animals and plants in the rocks. If an animal having a skeleton, shell, or other hard parts, be buried or covered by sediment after death before the hard parts have had time to decompose, they are likely to be preserved as fossils...
>
> One of the most formidable objections to the evolution theory is the fact that no fossil has been discovered of an animal intermediate between creatures having a very peculiar skeleton, such as bats, whales, dugongs, seals, frogs, turtles, pterodactyls, ichtyosauruses, etc., and the supposed ordinary quadrupedal animals, from which, according to the theory, they have been evolved. If this theory be true, these intermediate forms must have existed in immense numbers in the past. Darwin devoted a whole chapter of *The Origin of Species* in an attempt to meet this difficulty. The best he could do was to express his belief that the fossil record is "incomparably less perfect" than is usually supposed. And, so far as I am aware,

no later evolutionist has been able to improve on Darwin's effort. . .

The *Fossil Record* is far more complete than Darwin supposed it to be, and than his followers admit.

Every genus of animal having a skeleton or hard parts has left a fossil remains.

The following conclusions arrived at by Dewar after a lifetime of personal investigation and a close study of all the literature on the subject show that no solution has been found for the difficulties which Darwin himself stated against his theory.

1) A great and abundant marine fauna appears on the scene with startling abruptness at the beginning of the Cambrian Period.

Many of the Pre-Cambrian rocks which immediately precede the Cambrian rocks and underlie them are rocks in which fossils could equally well have been deposited, but not a single undisputed fossil has been found in them.

Suddenly in the Cambrian Period we find the sea full of highly organised types. We find nothing which suggests slow evolution. We find no experiment in the production of new types, no experiments, for instance, in shell making. The first shells are fully developed. We find these earliest animals as sharply differentiated into Species, Genera, Families, Orders and Phyla as they are today.

2) Every type of new animal appears suddenly in the geological record, endowed with all the attributes by which it is characterised. The changes it undergoes afterwards are comparatively insignificant. Sometimes, however, a group of animals about to become extinct undergoes considerable changes of a pathological nature before it disappears from the scene.

3) So far it has been found impossible to produce a series of fossils showing that one Family has gradually become converted into another Family, or an Order, Class or Phylum into another.

4) While it is open to doubt whether or not the geological record furnishes good evidence of one genus having been converted into another, it certainly shows *a*) that a large number of genera have persisted unchanged during long periods; *b*) in the cases where the record enables us to trace far back into the past two or more genera of a Family, their lines, instead of converging until they meet in a common ancestor, seem to follow a parallel course.

> 5) While the record indicates that some species have changed into other species, it also suggests that some species are exceedingly stable and have persisted during an immense period of time.

Mr. Dewar then takes up each of these five points, develops it and gives numerous examples to prove it.

With regard to Darwin's difficulty that "A period of 60 million years (since the Cambrian Period), judging from the small amount of organic changes since the commencement of the glacial epoch, appears a very short time for the many and great mutations which have certainly occurred since the Cambrian formation, and the previous 140 million years can hardly be considered as sufficient for the development of the varied forms of life which already existed during the Cambrian Period," Dewar writes as follows:

> According to the latest views, the earth has not been in existence for more than 3,000 million years, and it is open to doubt if the earth has been habitable for half that period.
>
> This time element is all-important, and in considering it I have taken care not to overstate the case against evolution; my figures are almost certainly too low.
>
> The lowest estimate of the time taken for the evolution of a new Species is 500,000 years. As the differences between two Genera of a Family are at least tenfold greater than those between two Species of a Genus, the minimum time needed for the evolution of a Genus is 500,000 x 10, or 5 million years. As the differences separating two Families of an Order are ten times as great as those that separate two Genera of a Family, 50 million years are needed for the evolution of a Family; and for similar reasons the evolution of an Order needs 500 million years, that of a Class 5,000 million years, and that of a Phylum 50,000 million years.

Admission of an Extreme Evolutionist

Apply the above to the case of a man, and you will find the difficulty of finding a genetic link between man and any animal, magnified several fold. All modern evolutionists now admit that man was not and could not have been descended from any of the great apes: the gorilla, the chimpanzee, the orangutan, the gibbon or from any of the monkey tribe; Leakey in his *Adam's Ancestors* makes the following admission:

> Each of these genera (gorilla, etc.) have certain characteristics in which they resemble man more than the others do, but also other characteristics in which they differ more from man. None of them could ever be regarded as representing a close cousin of man, nor could any of them qualify as representative of a stage of evolution through which man had passed in his gradual rise to his present position.
>
> (*Adam's Ancestors,* Fourth ed., 1953, p. 159).

So, therefore, according to the evolutionists themselves in the case of the supposed evolution of man there is no longer question of merely transforming or evolving one Species from another, or even one Genus from another; it is a question of transforming one Family into another, a process for which there is no geological evidence whatever.

Chapter 8

TESTIMONY OF BIOLOGISTS

When we speak of the testimony of a scientist, for instance a biologist, we mean of a specialist who has devoted his life to original investigation and who has made some original contribution to science; we do not mean a mere propagandist. Real scientists who make original investigations are rare, and as a rule, will not descend to mere propaganda. Among such we find several whose investigations compelled them to abandon the theory of evolution and admit special creation; while we do not find the contrary. Among those were the great French authority Vialleton, who lived in the first half of the present century, and Douglas Dewar, who died in 1956. Mr. Dewar writes as follows of Vialleton:

> Vialleton was a great zoologist. For forty years he worked at embryology, and he devoted himself in his latter years to the study of the limbs and girdles of backboned animals, and as a result of his labours in connection with these, he wrote *Membres et Ceintures des Vertébrés Tetrapodes,* published in 1924. As in my case, he, when a young man, accepted evolution, and his work in the laboratory and the museum, and mine in the field, led him and me to reject the theory. His last book *L'Origine des Etres Vivants: L'Illusion Transformiste,* published in 1929, from which I have just quoted, went through 17 editions within two years of publication, and has done much to cause many French biologists to reject what the French call correctly *Le transformisme* and we English incorrectly call Evolutionism. (*Is Evolution Proved?* p. 110).

Testimony of a Living Authority

The Rev. Desmond Murray O.P. is an authority on the science of biology; he has devoted much of his life to the study of the origin of living things and has written several books and articles on the results of his investigation. His latest book, published in 1955, is entitled *Species Revalued, A Biological Study of Species.* I take the following quotation from it:

> The theories put forward by evolutionists would lead us to expect to find that the earliest forms of life were simple and undifferentiated. This expectation is not realised, for the fossil record shows that the first organisms formed a complexus of fully developed and completely differentiated types. Thus, most of the phyla or divisions of the animal kingdom are represented. (See Raymond, *Prehistoric Life,* Harvard, 1939).
>
> The division Arthropoda, which includes the classes *Crustacea, Arachnida, Myriopoda,* and *Insecta* is represented not by an undifferentiated arthropod, embodying the features common to the four classes, but by members of each class. The Trilobites consist of two orders, which by the end of the Cambrian period included over 100 genera and 1,000 species (Duggan op. cit.). Therefore from the Cambrian epoch the living world has consisted of many different forms of life organised to a well-ordered hierarchical system. The diversity of organic life and its divisions into clearly defined groups is a characteristic of life as soon as evidence of it appears in the strata; there is no evidence that this diversity is the result of a process of gradual evolution.

Mr. Philip G. Fothergill, author of *Historical Aspects of Organic Evolution,* criticized Fr. Murray's book in a review of it published in the 1965 July-August issue of *Blackfriars* and again in a letter to *The Catholic Herald* of June 8 of the same year. He did not, however, deal with the main theme of the book or attempt to deny the truth of the above quotation. Mr. Fothergill defends the theory of evolution in season and out of season, and in his letter to *The Catholic Herald* expresses concern about the effect that Fr. Murray's book may have on the reputation of Catholic biologists among non-Catholics. A much more important question is the harm which propaganda for the theory of evolution, especially when applied to the origin of man, is capable of doing inside the Catholic Church.

Dr. W. R. Thompson, F.R.S., Director of the Commonwealth Institute of Biological Control, who was invited by the Publishers of Everyman's Library to write the preface to the 1956 edition of Darwin's *Origin of Species,* refers in it to the injury that Darwin's writings have done to religion and morality and quotes Sir Arthur Keith as saying that Darwinism is a "basal doctrine in the rationalist liturgy." (p. 22).

Fr. Desmond Murray deals with this question in greater detail in his chapter on "Science and Religion" in *Species Revalued,* as the following quotations will show:

> The words of Prof. Sedgwick of Cambridge came true: "It (Darwin's theory) is," he said, "a dish of rank materialism cleverly cooked and served up, merely to make us independent of the Creator." And again, "Humanity would suffer a damage that might brutalise it and sink the human race into a lower grade of degradation, than any into which it has fallen since its records tell us of its history.". . .
>
> Darwin opened the way to the journalist, the popular writer, the political propagandist, to all who resented disciplined thought; now they could have revenge for the inferiority of feelings it has brought upon them, and the pseudo-scientists have not been slow to follow the lead. Herbert Spencer gives forth the wildest speculations in an attempt to provide a new scientific philosophy of life, as he was pleased to call it. To many contemporaries of Darwin, on the other hand, it was very humiliating that man, hitherto looked upon as so noble and so wise a creature, should now be looked upon as one who had sprung from the ape. Darwin had discovered, so his theory worked out to its logical conclusion held, that man had not been created by the God of the universe, but was the mere descendant of a gibbering animal. The natural consequence was that sin was no longer a punishable act, it was a relic of the beast, which had not yet been thrown off in the course of evolution. His mind was also unreliable, just because it had been derived from an animal.
>
> Evolutionary theories also engendered pride. "Man may be excused," Darwin said, "for feeling some pride at having risen, though not through his own exertions, to the very summit of the organic scale, and the fact of his having risen, may give him hopes for a still higher destiny in the distant future." *(The Descent of Man.)*

All this has in a great measure led to Agnostic and Atheistic beliefs of the present day; at first faith in the Old Testament was shattered, then the miracles of the New Testament were supposedly explained away by the new theories, Christian Faith was undermined and finally, people were left wondering whether the great Christian truths were of Divine revelation, as happened with Darwin himself.

Perhaps the worst of all is that the minds of the young have been singed with doubt. Men and women without Christian faith, but tainted with Agnosticism, have for generations been teaching in the school, in the college and in the university; the harm done is immeasurable. The author of the *Origin of Species* did not foresee these consequences, nor did he intend them, yet he cannot altogether be exonerated from blame— "The works of man follow him." It is true that he was a kindly man and did not carry his theories into practice; for this reason his memory has been long preserved from criticism. At the end he was morbid and self-critical to an extreme, he was unhappy about himself and became ill.

Up to his own day the argument from design in Nature had reigned supreme, then with a suddenness the end came; "The foundations of this great deep were broken up by the power of one man and never in the history of thought, has a change been effected of a comparable order of magnitude"—so wrote Romanes (*Nature,* 1881). At one moment he thought he could do without design, the next his reason told him that the evidence for design by a personal God was overwhelming. To the last he was ever seeking an escape from religion but was never able to find it. Either every detail in nature must be designed or else there was no design at all. His letters show a resolution not to follow his thoughts to their logical conclusion. He had treated the sacred subject of man's body and man's mind without reference to religion; no wonder then that his writings produced a sense of liberation in the minds of many of his contemporaries. There were others too who wanted to escape, and they were pleased to know how this might be accomplished. From Darwin's day onwards to the present, many who took up the study of science did so with the same desire to escape from religion. The very mention of God in connection with scientific work is often taboo. (*Species Revalued,* pp. 153-156).

Catholic propagandists for the theory of evolution will say that it is the materialistic interpretation of it that is having evil effects on public opinion and behavior. To this we can reply by saying, 1) that there is no difference between the type of propaganda used by Catholic advocates of the theory and that used by atheists; in fact, as we shall see later on, forms of propaganda for the theory are found in recent books and articles by Catholic evolutionists which have been discarded by atheists as being out of date; 2) not only is there no scientific proof for the theory as defined by Darwin or his modern followers, but the theory is in contradiction with the findings of modern science. Why then attempt to introduce a theory among Catholics which is devoid of scientific proof and which has wrought havoc outside the Catholic Church?

Brief Account of the Development Of the Theory of Evolution

The following brief account of the development of the modern theory of evolution, which is based chiefly on *The History of Evolution (Evolution: Geschichte Ihrer Probleme und Erkenntnisse,* by Walter Zimmermann, published at Munich in 1954), shows that the teaching of the theory of evolution has resulted in the spread of atheism.

The author divides his history into four periods: the first period extends from the earliest times up to the beginning of the 16th century; the second, from the 16th century (the Reformation period) up to the time of the French Revolution; the third, from the time of the French Revolution up to the death of Charles Darwin; and the fourth, from the time of Darwin to the present day.

During the first period we have the Grecian and Roman philosophers. None of these contemplated or discussed evolution in the modern sense of transmutation of one species unto another. Aristotle investigated the problem of species; he gave minute and accurate descriptions of 500 different species and taught that these species were fixed. Although he shared the belief of his time that some forms of living things arise by spontaneous generation, he limited them to those lower forms that arise from the corruption of living things, and denied that the origin of life could be explained by spontaneous generation.

Next, we have the intellectuals of the Alexandrian School. The first of these was Philo the Jew, who lived at the same time as Our Divine Lord. He endeavored to reconcile the teaching of Plato with that of Moses and, in order to do so, he had recourse to an allegorical interpretation of Moses. He taught the simultaneous Creation of the universe and said that the Six Days are to be interpreted figuratively, as is shown in the following quotation: "When Moses said that God completed His work on the sixth day, there is question not of an interval of time but of a perfect number containing six units, three qualities and two trinities." Philo was the first to juggle with the Mosaic order of Creation; modern attempts to reconcile the Mosaic order with defunct scientific theories such as that of Laplace have been no more successful.

St. Ephrem of Edessa rejected the doctrine of simultaneous Creation in the following words:

> Let no one presume to look for allegories in the work of the Six Days. It is not permitted to affirm that those things were created instantly which the Scripture informs us appeared successively and on separate and distinct days, or that the words of Scripture are names that do not designate things, or that designate things other than the words express.

However, St. Ephrem interpreted the first verse of *Genesis* in the sense that God created *ex nihilo* the elementary matter from which the material universe—earth, sun, moon and stars—was subsequently formed.

St. John Chrysostom said that God could, but did not, create all things simultaneously.

St. Basil of Caesarea said that all things named by Moses have a real existence and that the Six Days are days of 24 hours.

His younger brother, St. Gregory of Nyssa, proposed a *via media.* He accepted the Alexandrian doctrine of simultaneous

Creation, but rejected the symbolic explanation of *Genesis* as taught by Philo the Jew.

St. Augustine followed the *via media* of St. Gregory of Nyssa. In *De Genesi ad Litteram* he wrote:

> It is more than probable that the seven days of Genesis were entirely different in their duration from those which now mark the succession of the time. . . .The seventh day had no evening; it means therefore a period of time, the other six are likewise. (*De Genesi ad Litteram,* lib. IV, cap. 18).

Like St. Gregory of Nyssa, St. Augustine held that God first created matter *ex nihilo* in an elementary state. On this He imposed laws according to which all things were formed.

When endeavoring to interpret what St. Augustine wrote about the work of the Six Days it must be remembered that he, like all those of his time and for centuries after, was under the erroneous impression that some living things arise from spontaneous generation, for he speaks of mice issuing from the mud of the Nile. The science of geology was unknown at his time, and neither the telescope nor the spectroscope had been invented. With regard to the different interpretations of *Genesis* he wrote: "Let each one choose according to the best of his power; only let him not fail to remember that he is a man searching as far as may be into the works of God."

St. Augustine therefore merely put forward a theory which he would most certainly have been ready to abandon or modify in the light of scientific discoveries after his time. The idea that one species could be transformed into another never even dawned upon him.

The teaching of the Scholastics on the origin of man is given in convenient form by Dr. Messenger in *Evolution and Theology,* Chapters 15 and 16, from which we take the two following quotations:

In his *Summa Theologica,* St. Albert the Great writes:

> It was neither suitable nor possible that the body of the first man should have been made otherwise than by God, as we are taught by the writings of the Saints and the Catholic Faith. . . .For man, even according to his body, is in some way

> the image of God, and therefore it obviously belongs to the same power to make man according to the soul and according to the body. (p. 206).

St. Thomas writes in question 91 of the first part of *Summa Theologica:* "I repeat that the formation of the first human body could not have been through some created *virtus*, but must have been immediately by God."

The second period was the period of the Renaissance Movement and Reformation. During the early part of this period those belonging to the various sects that broke away from the Catholic Church adhered to the biblical account of Creation, but as time went on there was a gradual drift toward a rationalistic interpretation. During the period, considerable progress was made in the various sciences: biology, medicine, paleontology. To it belong Ray and Linnaeus, who between them arrived at a method of classifying living things; Buffon, who prepared the way for Lamarck's theory of evolution; Bacon, who developed the inductive method of reasoning; the philosophers Leibnitz, Descartes and Kant, and finally Cuvier, to whom Zimmermann pays the compliment of being versed in all the sciences of his time. Cuvier defended the fixity of species and said that the Mosaic account of Creation harmonized with the deductions we have been able to make from the discoveries of geology, zoology and other sciences of our time.

The beginning of the third period, during which the theory of evolution, as it is now known, was formulated coincided with the period of the French Revolution and the rise of atheism. As formulated by Lamarck, the theory supposed the creation of God of a number of rudimentary organisms which evolved according to a divine plan and under the guidance of God into the present species. His theory had been suggested by his friend Buffon and then developed.

Lamarck's theory of evolution, though still held in a modified form by a small number, was soon supplanted all over the world, even in France itself, by the theory of Charles Darwin already referred to. Darwin mentions the name of

God in the last sentence of *The Origin of Species,* but never again. Since that time Darwinism has been associated with atheism, and has been used, as Sir Arthur Keith remarks, "as the basal doctrine of the rationalist liturgy." Haeckel, the German rationalist, eagerly adopted the system and, in his endeavor to popularize it, faked a series of photographs of what he alleged to be the development of the human fetus, and continued to use them even after they had been proved to be faked. In England the theory was adopted by Herbert Spencer, Thomas Huxley and other rationalists. In all probability the widespread adoption of the theory in almost every country in the world was due to the efforts of Freemasons and communists. At the time that Karl Marx was elaborating his system of communism, he joined the Freemasons at Paris. For the framework of his system he adopted a combination of the theories of Haeckel and Darwin. Besides, it is a well-known fact that the theory of Darwin, especially that part of it which says that man is descended either from the ape, or from the remote ancestor of the ape, is taught to the children in all communist schools, not as a theory, but as an established fact.

The theories of both Lamarck and Darwin were used not only to explain the origin of species in general, but of man in particular; in fact the only use that a number of so-called scientists saw in either of the theories was to afford proof that man was not specially created, but evolved from a brute beast. As there was no real proof, recourse was had to fraud.

Dr. W. R. Thompson refers to this fact in his introduction to *The Origin of Species,* in which he says that "the success of Darwinism was accompanied by a decline in scientific integrity." He gives as examples the case of the Piltdown skull, in which an ape's jawbone was substituted for the original human one, and the case of the Java Man, in which a battered skullcap of a gibbon was represented as belonging to a creature half-man, half-ape, in order to provide an argument for Darwin's theory that man was descended from an ape.

Dr. Thompson might have added many more examples of

fraud. For example, he might have referred to the Australopithecinae fossils, put forward by Drs. Dart and Broom as evidence of evolution, which were proved to be just fossils of ordinary apes by Professor Zuckerman in his chapter in *Evolutions as a Process,* edited by Dr. Julian Huxley, A. C. Hardy and E. B. Ford. (1954).

It is true to say, therefore, that this formulative period of the theory of evolution was barren of any practical results except to afford a basis for rationalism, a framework for communism, and to provide an incentive for the introduction of fraud and superstition into scientific investigation, when no genuine proof could be found for the theory.

The fourth period might be summed up as a practical acknowledgment of the bankruptcy of Darwin's theory by fitting the real scientific results achieved by Fr. Mendel into it and claiming that they belonged to it, in order to save the theory from devastating, modern criticism. It is like the attempt to save the corpse of Lenin from disintegration by fitting into it parts of other men's bodies.

In his introduction to *The Origin of Species* already referred to, Dr. W. R. Thompson recognizes the barrenness of Darwin's system, the injury it did to the progress of science and the fact that Mendelism owes nothing to it, and therefore does not belong to it.

In his article in *The Catholic Encyclopedia* (Vol. X), Sir Bertram Windle produces evidence to show that Fr. Mendel's experiments have in fact exploded the main points of Darwin's theory. In it he writes:

> Bateson (in *Mendel's Principles of Heredity*) claims that "his experiments are worthy to rank among those which laid the foundations of the atomic laws of chemistry"; and Lock, that his discovery "was of an importance little inferior to those of a Newton or a Dalton." Punnett also states that, owing to Mendel's labours, "the position of the biologist of today is much the same as that of a chemist of a century ago, when Dalton enunciated the law of constant proportions." . . .T. H. Morgan does not hesitate to say that Mendel's laws give the final *coup de grâce* to the doctrine of Natural Selection. (*op. cit.* p. 182).

With regard to the claim made by evolutionists that the origin of the various species now existing in the world can be explained by the science of genetics (which, as is admitted by all biologists, is but a development of Mendelism), Douglas Dewar writes in *Man a Special Creation* as follows:

> Modern experimental work indicates that variations in organisms appear in consequence of 1) the duplication or multiplication of the chromosomes that occur in the cell nucleus, 2) in the translocation or displacement of parts of chromosomes, 3) the loss of chromosomes or parts of chromosomes, 4) gene mutations, which appear to be the result of the rearrangement of the molecules that make up the gene, or the action of inhibitors or stimulators of the genes, 5) loss of genes, 6) cross-breeding varieties.
>
> All the above causes are simply a shuffling or rearrangement of parts of the chromosomes or of genes. Such rearrangements may be expected to yield a considerable amount of variation, but clearly must be within the type. . . .
>
> . . . If a species be defined as a freely interbreeding community, no new animal species has yet been bred by any experimenter. This is very remarkable in view of the fact that breeding experiments lasting over some 30 years have been made with the vinegar fly, *Drosophila melanogaster.* This produces about 25 generations in a year, hence some 900 successive generations of this species have been bred in the laboratory in the unsuccessful attempt to convert it into another type. This corresponds to about 30,000 years of human existence. *There appears to exist no mechanism whereby a new type of organism can arise from an existing one.* This explains why all breeds of dogs, pigeons, etc., despite their great diversity are still dogs, pigeons, etc.
>
> That it is impossible to change a dog or a pigeon into anything else but a dog or a pigeon is evident from such facts as the following which are taken from the work of Dr. Hurst, already quoted: "1) The gene is the sole basis of hereditary transmissions. 2) In every case that has been investigated more than one pair of genes are concerned in the development of each character. . . .Genetical experiments show that in the simplest case, at least four pairs of genes are concerned in the organisation and development of the wild agouti coat colour

of rabbits, and many other genes are also concerned."

The rearrangement of the molecules that make up one or more of the genes that regulate the colour of the rabbits' fur is likely to effect some change in that colour, but even if there be a simultaneous arrangement of the molecules of all such genes, the effect on the animal's coat is confined to the colour; all such changes are necessarily within narrow limits, and this applies equally to the genes that regulate other parts of the rabbit, and those of all other animals.

Take a simple one-celled organism, such as the amoeba—shuffle *ad infinitum* the constituent molecules of all the genes that control organisation of the amoeba, and what can the result be other than a modified amoeba?

In view of the discoveries in genetics made during the past 35 years, those who have a legal training marvel how any geneticist can believe that the great variety of animals that now exist are offspring of some ancestor far more simple than an amoeba . . .

Admission of Difficulties Against Evolution Made by Evolutionists

Sir Julian Huxley is one of the recognized exponents of the modern theory of evolution. He sets himself the formidable task of explaining the origin of the universe and all the phenomena that occur in it without admitting the existence of a personal God. In addition, he inherits belief in some form at least of Darwin's theory and attempts to defend it. He is a scientist, however, and as a scientist freely admits scientific conclusions difficult to reconcile with the theory, which some Catholic propagandists for the theory either deny or pretend to be ignorant of. His views on evolution were expressed in a series of radio broadcasts for the B.B.C. and were published in book form in 1952 under the title *Evolution in Action*. Both his own views and those of the chief modern exponents of the theory were given in greater detail in a book entitled *Evolution as a Process* published in 1954. There is a large measure of agreement between Sir Julian Huxley and both Fr. Murray O.P. and Douglas Dewar about actual scientific facts observed during the past half century, although he differs from them in explaining them. For instance, he agrees with Fr. Murray that species have been found that have remained unchanged for such a long period as 300 million years, and some of the examples he gives are the same as those given by Fr. Murray. He agrees with Fr. Mendel that modifications of species (which he claims ultimately lead to the formation of new species, but of which there is no proof) are due primarily not to an external agency but to an internal principle. He admits also that mutations which occur due to what he calls occasional failure of the genes to reproduce themselves accurately, would of themselves never result in any improvement of the species, not to speak of forming a new species, without the help of another agency which he calls "*Natural Selection.*" On page 5 of *Evolution as a Process*,[1] he quotes the calculations made by H. J. Muller which show that mutations alone occurring at random could never produce a new species.

On pages 8 to 12 he admits that a general, continuous improvement of organisms is not in accordance with the facts, and that in practice the process of evolution is finished. On page 8, he writes:

> Extinction is a commoner fate than continuance, and stability more frequent than transformation and advance; creatures of obviously lower grades or organisation flourish side by side with higher forms; many types have persisted essentially unchanged for tens or even hundreds of millions of years.

On page 11 he says:

> Indeed it would appear that by the Pliocene, the possibilities of improving the predominantly physical aspects of living machinery—its mechanical and chemical efficiency—had been exhausted. Put rather crudely, purely physiological properties had reached the limit of specialisation; the only road out of the evolutionary impasse was by way of brain and mind.

On page 12 he admits that man is pre-eminent among all creatures, and that if he disappeared he could not be replaced.

Sir J. Huxley admits with Darwin, Douglas Dewar and Fr.

1. Published by Allen and Unwin, London, 1954.

Murray that the first fossils that appeared belonged to organisms already highly organized, and has no solution for the difficulty, except to demand with Darwin a long period during which evolution was in operation but of which there is no record. The period he puts at 1,500 million years.

He admits also the sudden appearance of new species at various epochs, particularly toward the end of the Ice Age, during which the great Saurian reptiles all perished, and were replaced by the myriad species of mammals with which the world is now populated, and which, according to Dr. Huxley's admission, could not have been evolved from the Saurian reptiles because the latter were too highly specialized.

By the last admission quoted above, Sir. J. Huxley puts out of court completely the theory that man could have been evolved from any of the species of apes or monkeys, and puts the evolution of man back to the time when the lemurs first appeared. But even these were too highly specialized, and then even supposing that some animal had evolved physically in the direction of man, besides the physiological difficulties of acquiring upright gait, brain of human proportions, etc., there was the insuperable difficulty of taking the step toward concept-formation, language, and a tool-making psycho-social mode of existence.

Another Biological Impossibility— The Mammals Could Not Have Been Evolved From the Saurian Reptiles

Before the various species of mammals that now inhabit the earth made their appearance, the great Saurian reptiles held undisputed sway for millions of years. These monsters disappeared completely and in their place came the various species of mammals. In the book *Is Evolution Proved?* already referred to, Douglas Dewar proves that it would have been biologically impossible to transform these Saurian reptiles into mammals. He says:

> Such a transformation would involve, in addition to a number of physiological changes, and changes in the soft parts

of the body, fundamental skeletal changes. I will here deal with only the changes involved in the lower jaw, and the ear. These are: 1) In every reptile, past and present, each half of the lower jaw is composed of six bones, in all mammals it is made up of only one bone. 2) In every reptile the lower jaw articulates with the skull, not directly as in all mammals, but through the intervention of a bone, known as the quadrate. 3) In all reptiles the drum of the ear is connected with the tympanum by a single rod-like bone, called the columella; in all mammals this connection is by a series of three bones—the stapes, malleus and incus, so-called because they are shaped respectively like a stirrup, a hammer and an anvil. 4) In the mammalian ear there is a very complicated organ—the organ of Corti, that does not occur in the ear of any reptile. The most striking feature of this is its 10,000 rods or pillars (into which run some 20,000 nerve fibers) set in two rows on a base; each rod in a row leans towards its opposite number in the other row, so that their swollen ends or heads meet, the convex head of one fitting into a concavity in the head of its opposite rod. Thus a tunnel composed of some 4,000 arches is formed. Sound waves cause these rods to vibrate.

I maintain that the above changes cannot possibly have been effected gradually and, in consequence, the theory that a reptile ever became gradually converted into a mammal is untenable.

The above changes relate only to the skeletal parts of the head and jaw and are insignificant in comparison with the transformations supposed to have taken place in other parts of the body. Let me mention some of these. In addition to the change in the third eyelid, already noticed, the muscle that focuses the eye lost its stripes, and the blood supply of the iris became greatly modified. The mode of locomotion became revolutionised, the thorax became reorganised, the hip bone underwent changes, and the ankle joint shifted to the root of the toes from its original position between the two rows of ankle bones. The whole breathing apparatus was remodelled, which involved the origin of a new organ—the diaphragm. The transformists who do not believe that this structure can have been developed gradually, deem the mammals to be derived directly from amphibia. A mechanism developed for keeping the temperature of the blood constant, the left aorta was scrapped and the red blood-corpuscles lost their nuclei. The integument became changed beyond recognition; the scales disappeared and their place was taken by new structure—hairs; the skin acquired two extra layers; and three new types of gland sprang into being—the sebaceous, the sweat and the mammary glands. In the wall of the intestine the longitudinal muscles changed places with the circular ones. The chemical changes that take place within the body changed so that the waste products became mainly urea instead of uric acid. In effect the reptile became transformed into an entirely different kind of animal—a new class of animal.[1]

Conclusions of the Chapter

Our first conclusion is that spontaneous generation may be safely dismissed as an explanation of how life first appeared on the earth, and that there is not the remotest possibility that a living cell will ever be produced in the laboratory.

Our next conclusion is that *a*) as the fossils that appeared in the earliest geological stratum belonged to highly complicated and specialized organisms, *b*) that as organisms have continued unchanged for hundreds of millions of years, and *c*) that as fossils of multitudes of new organisms unconnected with that have gone before them have appeared suddenly on the earth just at times when it was in a fit state to receive them, the account given in Genesis best explains these facts that science has discovered.

Our third conclusion is that the problems of what were the original forms of the various species (with the exception of man) and how far the principle of diversity implanted in them by God at the beginning may have changed some of them in the course of the millions of years of their existence, remain to be solved.

Our final conclusion is that the theory of evolution, especially as propounded by Darwin, has produced nothing of benefit to the human race; that on the contrary it has been a potent factor in promoting atheism and communism; that the grafting of Mendelism into the theory is an admission that

1. *Is Evolution Proved?* published by Hollis and Carter, London, 1947, pp. 164 and 329.

it is devoid of scientific foundation; and that efforts to introduce the theory (especially the part of it which says that man is genetically connected with the brute beast) into the Catholic community are calculated to produce results among Catholics similar to those which have been produced outside the Catholic Church.

APPENDIX TO PART I

Since the above was written, we have received from Joseph F. Wagner, Inc., New York City, a copy of *The Theory of Evolution Judged by Reason and Faith,* by His Eminence Cardinal Ernesto Ruffini, a former Professor of Scripture in the Propaganda University at Rome, and now a Cardinal member of the Pontifical Biblical Commission. In this book, which is a translation of *La Teoria della Evolutione secondo la Scienza e la Fede* published at Rome, His Eminence examines and refutes all the arguments which have been put forward in favor of the theory of evolution by Darwin and his modern followers. He shows that evolutionists have failed to give any solid proof, not only for the origin of the present species of living things from one or few primitive forms, but even for the evolution of one species from another. In the few cases in which an attempt has been made to give real evidence for evolution, as in the case of the horse, it is a question of evolution within the family.

With regard to the origin of man, His Eminence rejects completely the theory that man's body was evolved from a lower animal, and gives evidence to show that such a theory is incompatible with the teaching of the Church.

The following quotation is taken from Chapter 2 of this book:

> Palaeontology has failed, up to date, not only to bring to light any certain or seriously probable document or proof that furnishes any support for the hypothesis of the transformation of the species, but it presents us with two positive testimonies to the contrary: 1) a great number of forms—and not the meanest in the order of organic perfection—suddenly appeared together; 2) the successive appearance of beings is not continuous, but irregular.

Let us now consider facts.

First of all, let us examine the case of the invertebrates. It is true that these appear before the vertebrates, but not, however, in the manner imagined by the evolutionistic theory. This supposes that the invertebrates have arisen one from the other, "type by type," class by class, "order by order," by way of intermediary gradations, and forms that are uncertain or unsettled, on the contrary when they do appear, the invertebrates appear all together—coelenterates, worms, mollusks, crustaceans, echinoderms; and we meet in each of these groups further subdivisions that are definite and distinguishable one from the other. The form of various "types" and minor groups, whenever it appears for the first time, is already as complete and finished as possible. In reality, from past ages till now, none of these types has undergone any important change.

As regards the vertebrates, while taking account of the scarcity of palaeontological documents, it is undeniable that they have not all appeared simultaneously, but successively. But this succession is not gradual, as the evolutionists suppose, namely, in the sense that from the primitive, relatively simple forms there has been a passing to complex forms by means of very slight changes. When the first forms of vertebrates appear they are quite definable and classifiable: the first amphibians have already specific limbs, in no way similar to the fins of fish, and the first mammal has a mandible (jawbone) formed of one piece and not of different parts as in other vertebrates.

The Cardinal then discusses the claim of evolutionists that intermediary forms have been discovered.

We enumerate some of the forms held to be intermediary.

The most famous is the Archaeopteryx.

This type of "primitive bird" was discovered in 1861 in the lithographic schists of the Upper Jurassic of Solenhofen in Bavaria. From many aspects it is a bird, but from others it is a reptile: it has the teeth and very long tail of the reptile with 21 vertebraes (in other birds 6 vertebrae as well as the pygostyle).

In reality, the Archaeopteryx is not an intermediary form, that is, a reptile in a state of transformation. It is only a way of speaking to place it between the reptiles and the birds. Apart from the tail it has nothing of the nature of the reptile. In all other respects it is a bird. It had feathers and it was a warm-blooded animal; as such, it would have had all the anatomical and physiological characteristics of birds: even the teeth are those proper to all birds of the cretaceous period. If it shows any affinity with the reptiles, this affinity is not greater than that which associates reptiles and birds in the one group of the Sauropsida.

* * *

Another palaeontological argument in favour of the theory of evolution is taken from the existence of continuous series of forms.

One of the most famous series is that of the horse.

He then gives Marsh's account of the evolution of the horse from a small creature with five toes, which is usually quoted in books by evolutionists, and adds the following comment:

Anyone examining the forms that represent this succession is very impressed by the gradual steps of the transformation, and might judge in favor of the evolutionistic theory; but, in reality, things are not just as clear as the forms or figures seem to suggest.

First of all, the order of such a series cannot be considered as certain; in fact, although they studied the same material, Cope, Matthews and Osborn were not able to agree completely in their interpretation of it. Moreover, there are some naturalists who deny that there is any probative value in the series.

The Six Days of Creation

With regard to the Six Days of Creation, Cardinal Ruffini writes:

Therefore, the Mosaic cosmogony is truly historical, both in relating the creation of the universe from nothing, and in faithfully recounting the formation of all things as God has deigned to manifest it to man. (p. 86).

And in a footnote he adds:

In this matter we willingly refer the reader to the scientific study of the illustrious astronomer, Joseph Armellini, who, setting the biblical concordance on a new base, shows how the Mosaic cosmogony is "in perfect accord, indeed in amazing accord with the conclusions which modern astronomical cosmogony has reached." (*Cosmogonia modernae e cosmogonia Mosaica* in *Studium.* Vol. 42, 1946, 152-156).

Part II
The Origin of Man

Part II

THE ORIGIN OF MAN

Introductory

Part II of the book, for which Part I is meant to serve as an introduction, deals with the origin of man.

The question of the origin of man, whether considered from a religious or a scientific viewpoint, is on an altogether different footing from the question of the origin of species in general. In discussing the question of the origin of man, whether from a religious or a scientific angle, all Catholic writers are strictly bound to heed the warning contained in the Encyclical *Humani Generis* of Pope Pius XII, in which he says:

> Some (Catholic writers) however, rashly transgress the liberty of discussion granted when they act as if the origin of the human body from preexisting and living matter were already completely certain and proved by facts. . . .and as if there were nothing in the sources of divine revelation which demands the greatest moderation and caution in this question.

Most of the books on the various scientific aspects of the origin of man are by non-Catholics, and many, if not most of these are by men hostile to the Catholic religion who not only ignore the teaching of the Catholic Church, but use the theory of the genetic connection of man with animal as an argument against Catholic teaching, particularly against the doctrine that teaches that all men are descended from Adam and Eve, and that Eve has been formed from Adam. Some Catholic writers who accept the theory of the evolution of man from the brute beast quote the arguments given by atheists for the evolution of Eve as well as Adam, and for the plurality of ancestors of the human race, without making any attempt to refute these arguments, except to say that these opinions have been condemned by the Church, thus leaving their readers under the erroneous impression that no scientific answer to the difficulty had been found.

In this book a separate chapter will be devoted to the teaching of the Church on the origin of Adam, the origin of Eve, and the unity of the human race.

The most recent discoveries in the domain of paleontology enable us to give scientific answers to the objections raised against the teaching of the Church about the unity of the human race and the formation of Eve from Adam. They also confirm the traditional opinion still held by practically all Catholics, that there is no genetic connection between man and the brute beast, but that he was specially created by God directly from inanimate matter.

How Far Has the Catholic Church Been Affected by the Man-From-Ape Theory?

It may be said that at the beginning of the present century, the Catholic Church in Ireland, England and America was not affected at all by the teaching of Lamarck, Darwin and their followers. The arguments put forward for the ape or lemur origin of man had been refuted, and Catholics were satisfied that they had nothing to fear from them.

During the half century that has passed, the clergy, with the exception of the late Dr. Messenger and perhaps one or two more, kept aloof from the propaganda in favor of the theory of human evolution, and even Dr. Messenger was very guarded in his statements on the question and has been misquoted.

Convert laymen like Chesterton, who might be expected to have imbibed the theory of human evolution in their youth, were among the staunchest opponents of the theory, and most loyally carried out the wishes of the Popes, that Catholics, while they were free to carry out scientific investigations about the origin of man, were forbidden to teach the man-from-ape theory as an already established fact.

It was not until recently that serious doubts have arisen in the minds of some Catholics about the teaching of the Catholic Church and the conclusions of science about the origin of man. These doubts have arisen partly from the teaching of the theory of evolution in English grammar schools which many Catholic children have no option but to attend, partly from a few propagandists within the Church, but principally from the writings of Catholic propagandists from the continent.

The Propaganda on the Continent In Favor of the Man-From-Ape Theory

The development of the theory of evolution on the continent coincided with the period of the growth of Freemasonry, the preparations for the French Revolution, the Rationalist movement and the rise of communism. An extreme form of the theory was adopted by Freemasons, Rationalists and communists alike.

This was a period of persecution for the Catholic Church, especially in France, when bishops and priests were engaged in a struggle for existence. Every means, from open persecution to the publication of indecent literature, was employed by the enemies of the Church to undermine its influence, and propaganda for the theory of evolution, which was then and still is the official creed of Freemasonry, was not neglected.

The theory as propounded by Rationalists and Freemasons was, of course, incompatible with the teaching of the Catholic Church.

At this critical time a small group of intellectuals which included a few priests, led by Count Begouen of Toulouse, set themselves the task of explaining to those willing to listen to them that there was no contradiction between the theory of Darwin about the ape origin of man, properly understood, and the teaching of the Catholic Church. They did not, however, stop at that, but became ardent propagandists for the theory of Darwin, not only about the origin of living things in general, but about the ape origin of man. The history of this propaganda, with an account of the methods used, has been given by the son of this Count Begouen, who succeeded to the title, in a book published by him at Paris in 1945 and entitled *Quelque Souvenirs sur le Mouvement des Idées Transformistes dans les Milieux Catholiques.* In this book he tells us that his own father, who was a believer in Darwin's theory about the ape origin of man, was the chief propagandist; that he himself inherited his father's views and was continuing the propaganda in Catholic circles, that his father's house in Toulouse was a meeting place for believers in Darwin's theory, and that among those who gathered there were "Catholics, Free-thinkers, Evolutionists and supporters of the theory of spontaneous generation against Pasteur." We may presume that the Freemasons did not neglect the opportunity offered to them to carry on insidious propaganda inside the Catholic Church. Count Begouen further tells us that he was in communication with all the prominent Catholic evolutionists in France and Belgium. He singles out for special mention the late Fr. Teilhard de Chardin S.J. (who was connected with the cases of the Piltdown Man and Peking Man) and Canon Dorlodot of the University of Louvain who, he says, attended the centenary celebrations in England for Charles Darwin.

Fr. Teilhard de Chardin enjoyed a great reputation as an authority on paleontology up to the time of the discovery of the Piltdown forgery a few years before his death, and his articles were accepted in high-class reviews like *Études,* a Jesuit publication. The extreme views that he expressed on the Neanderthal Man, the Java Man and the Peking Man, and his fantastic estimate for the age of man in the world have all been exploded. Whatever of his reputation as an authority on paleontology had survived the discovery of the Piltdown forgery, was destroyed by the collecting of his articles published in various magazines during his life and their republication in book form by an international committee of extreme evolutionists which included such men as Sir Julian Huxley, Sir Wilfred Le Gros Clark and G. H. R. von Köenigswald. Further details about Fr. Teilhard's writings will be given in the chapter dealing with the case of the Peking Man.

Canon Dorlodot

Of all the members of the Count Begouen circle, Canon Dorlodot was the one who did the most effective propaganda in favor of Darwin's theory inside the Catholic Church. As Professor of the University of Louvain and Director of the Geological Section, he was in a particularly favorable position to do so. As already mentioned, he attended the centenary celebrations in honor of the birth of Charles Darwin held in Cambridge in 1909, and delivered an oration in which he said "that Darwin completed the work of Isaac Newton." He was severely criticized in Belgium for having attended the celebrations in honor of Darwin, and in defense of his action he delivered a series of lectures at the University on *Darwinism and Catholic Thought.* These were published in book form in Belgium and were afterwards translated by Dr. Messenger and published in 1922.

The following is a specimen of Canon Dorlodot's reasoning: The Biblical Commission had not expressly condemned Darwin's theory of the origin of man; from that fact he makes the following deduction:

> If the Commission has abstained from including in its enumeration a point, the historical and doctrinal character of which has led to great discussion in modern times, it is clear that the silence of the Commission on the matter is voluntary, and in consequence, any Catholic writer who dared afterwards to censure an opinion which the Pontifical Commissions decided to leave open, would be guilty of grave irreverence to the Holy See, and of a grave sin of calumny against the authors or defenders of this opinion, not to mention the scandal which might follow, if, as a result of his rash conduct, men of science should be estranged from religion, or the church exposed to unjust attack. (Dr. Messenger's translation, p. 21).

From the context, the evident meaning of the above quotation is that Canon Dorlodot holds these priests who criticized him for advocating the man-from-ape theory of Darwin to be guilty of grave sin, and that he bases his accusation on the fact that the theory of human evolution was not expressly condemned by the Biblical Commission. The accusation is fantastic; the mere statement of it is sufficient refutation. The Church has always given permission for scientific investigation, but has never permitted anyone to teach as an established fact that man's body is derived from an animal.

The Encyclical *Humani Generis* of Pope Pius XII contains a severe censure on all those who ignore (or pervert) the meaning of Papal pronouncements. It says:

> Nor must it be thought that what is expounded in Encyclical Letters does not of itself demand consent, since in writing such letters the Popes do not exercise the supreme power of their Teaching Authority; for these matters are taught with the ordinary teaching authority, of which it is true to say: "He who heareth you, heareth me," (*Luke* 10:16), and generally what is expounded and inculcated in Encyclical Letters already for other reasons belongs to Catholic doctrine.

Canon Dorlodot quotes the statement of St. Augustine incorporated in *Providentissimus Deus* already referred to, and misinterprets it, attributing to it the meaning that exegetes are not only free to ignore those parts of the Mosaic account of Creation which refer to the physical order, but that it is an error which he calls "concordism" even to attempt to harmonize the Mosiac account with the findings of modern science. Having given himself the widest liberty, he then proceeds to give us his own version of what the Mosaic account means. His account is based on two theories, one of which, that of Laplace, has been exploded, and the other, that of Darwin about the ape origin of man, in the light of the most recent findings, lacks even a scientific foundation.

He appeals again to St. Augustine and also to St. Gregory of Nyssa for justification of his own teaching of the theory of evolution. He ignores the facts, however, that neither St. Augustine nor St. Gregory of Nyssa had even an idea of the theory of evolution in the modern sense, and that their explanations of how the divine decree of Creation was translated into fact was based on the false assumption that spontaneous generation was not only possible but had actually occurred.

Dr. Messenger

It was through Dr. Messenger, who studied under Canon Dorlodot at Louvain, that the views of the latter found their way into these countries. He first published a translation of Canon Dorlodot's *Darwinism and Catholic Thought* in 1922, and in 1931 he published his own *Evolution and Theology,* which was followed by *Theology and Evolution* in 1949. In these books, Dr. Messenger assumes that the theory of evolution is now practically an established fact. In his foreword (p. xxii) he states that he has no intention of discussing the scientific aspect of evolution in general, or even of man; and on the same page he states that the data of Revelation need to be supplemented by the data of natural science. He gives very little indication of the reasons on which his belief in the theory of evolution is based. He allows the statement in the preface (which is by Fr. Lattey, S.J.), that he is "a Catholic evolutionist" to stand without correction, and on page 274 he says:

> We consider that the *scientific* evidence, consisting as it does of so many converging lines, is sufficient to give a fairly high degree of certitude concerning the fact of, at any rate, some evolution. . . .

and on page 275 he adds:

> From a scientific point of view, there is so far no *conclusive* evidence that man is evolved. There are certain facts that seem to point that way, but we think we may safely regard the theory as a working hypothesis, or better still, as an inference.

He does not tell us what are "the converging lines that give a fairly high degree of certitude of evolution in general 'or of' the facts that seem to point to the evolution of man."

However, the following quotations from Dr. Messenger's *Evolution and Theology* show that he is in complete agreement with what is stated in the encyclical *Humani Generis* 1) about the special creation of the human soul, 2) about the unity of the human race, and 3) about the formation of the body of Eve from that of Adam. On page 276 of *Evolution and Theology* Dr. Messenger writes:

> We must emphasize that in the light of modern theological knowledge a Catholic must admit more than one Divine intervention in the origin of man. 1) There is first of all the creation and infusion of the rational soul— 2) Next, we have the raising to the supernatural state. This affected both body and soul. 3) Was there a divine intervention in the formation of the *unsupernaturalized* [sic] body of Adam?. . .We think the formation of the human body may well have required a "special Divine intervention" at least to give it the last disposition necessary for the infusion of the human soul.
>
> There is another line of argument which might be mentioned here. *It is of faith that the whole of the present human race has descended from Adam,* and all theologians would agree that when Adam was formed there was no other human being in existence. If we could be *certain* that there were never any human beings who had existed before Adam's time, we might argue that the fact that the one and only human being was produced, implies that such production was beyond the powers of created nature. . . . But the weakness of this argument lies in the fact that we cannot be *absolutely certain* that there were no human beings before Adam. Theologians agree that the hypothesis of pre-Adamites *who had ceased to exist at the advent of Adam* is not unorthodox, and it does not seem altogether impossible that some such hypothesis may yet be of value in accounting for *the many apparently imperfect types of humanity which recent archaeology has revealed.*

From the above quotation, which was written before the publication of the Encyclical *Humani Generis,* it is clear that Dr. Messenger is in complete agreement with what is stated in that encyclical about the special creation of the human soul and the unity of the human race in being descended from Adam alone.

In his chapter on the formation of Eve in *Evolution and Theology* (pp. 252-256) Dr. Messenger states:

> It is our considered and definite belief that Eve was really formed from Adam. In other words, the *"formatio pimae mulieris ex primo homine"* is literally and historically true, as affirmed by the Biblical Commission. Indeed, this is so certain and so clearly taught both in Scripture and Tradition, that it may well be *de fide.*

Furthermore, he gives the following quotation from *De Deo Creatore* by Van Noort:

> Adam and Eve, both in body and soul, were formed by God, no evolution intervening.
>
> The term "peculiar creation of man" (used in the decree of the Biblical Commission) of itself might admit indeed some latitude, but the term "the formation of the first woman from the first man" manifestly excludes all evolution from the body of Eve. But no prudent person would contend that the body of Adam was formed by evolution, and that of Eve without evolution. (*De Deo Creatore,* p. 115).

The chief reason, therefore, that induced Dr. Messenger to adopt the theory of human evolution as "a working hypothesis, or better still as an inference," was the supposed existence of "the many apparently imperfect types of humanity which recently archaeology has revealed."

When Dr. Messenger was writing, the Piltdown Man (since admitted to be a forgery), the Peking Man (whom we shall show to be also a forgery), the Australopithecinae (the South African ape-men, which Sir S. Zuckermann proved to be merely apes), etc., were put forward by Catholic writers, such as Fr. Teilhard de Chardin and Abbé Breuil, as men in the process of evolution. The responsibility therefore for at least some of the views expressed by Dr. Messenger must rest on those supposed experts who alleged that these fossils represented "imperfect types of humanity." Had Dr. Messenger known the true facts of the case, it is highly probable he would have rejected entirely the theory of evolution as applied to man, seeing the formidable objections which he has given against it.

The Opinion of Present-Day Writers On the Continent

The propaganda of the Count Begouen circle in favor of the evolution of man still continues. The article in *God, Man and the Universe* entitled "The Origin of Man and the Recent Discoveries of the Natural Sciences" by Professor Vanderbroek of Louvain University, is a sample of the gross, out-of-date form of propaganda used in Belgium, and at the same time, of views inflicted on the students of the great University of Louvain, who come to it from all parts of Europe and even from America. We shall discuss the article in the section on "The Origin of Man." Here it is sufficient to say that the arguments in the article in favor of human evolution are based almost entirely on the genuineness of the Java Man, the Peking Man, etc., etc., which, as we shall show, do not represent creatures in the process of evolution.

In France, Fr. Charles Hauret may be said to represent the views of the Count Begouen circle. His views expressed in *Origines de l'Univers et de L'Homme* on the origin of man are very extreme, but they are concealed under protestations of submission to the directions of the Holy See frequently repeated. The following quotation is a fair specimen of the book:

> Chapter III (p. 71).
>
> Let Us Make Man to Our Own Image.
>
> A regional French paper published the following notice on the front page:
>
> ***Man is descended from the ape***
>
> Capetown 27 April 1947. Dr. Broom has discovered a human skull in a cave at Sterkfontain (Transvaal). This skull, according to him, establishes definitely that there is a (genetic) link between man and the anthropoid apes.

Fr. Hauret gives the following commentary on the above:

> At the beginning of the century the slogan "Man is descended from the ape" was often the expression of a materialistic outlook. The objection occupied a prominent place in the anti-religious arsenal. But today more and more Catholics, some of them university professors, declare publically their sympathy for theistic transformism. Their opinion has not remained confined to circles of the initiated, but has won adherents among their students, and among the Catholic elite and is gradually seeping in among the common people...

Fr. Hauret continues:

> We ourselves will not be guilty of the impertinence of discussing on a scientific plane the conclusions of palaeontologists, biologists and anthropologists. We confine ourselves to stating that at present most of the learned, both believers and atheists, hold, at least as a working hypothesis, that the body of man is of animal origin. Exegetes and theologians have no right to ignore this fact or minimize its importance.

In the same Chapter III and the following chapter, Fr. Hauret discusses the origin of man, the origin of Eve, and the question of whether there was one pair or many pairs of ancestors of the human race. He leaves the reader under the impression that modern science has raised objections, to which no answer has been found, against the special creation of man, the formation of the body of Eve from that of Adam, and the teaching of the Church that all men are descended from one pair of ancestors. However, he ends Chapter IV by a quotation from the Encyclical *Humani Generis* which condemns the opinion which says that there were several pairs of ancestors, and in his summary of conclusions on page 237 (French edition), he admits that science is unable to prove that there was more than one pair.

As Fr. Hauret's ambition extends to reforming the method of teaching the Catechism so as to include the theory of the evolution of man as the most probable theory, and the opinion that it is legitimate to hold that Eve's body may have been derived from Adam's, not physically, but as a picture is derived from a model, it is not possible to ignore the book, especially as a translation of it with a few modifications, but substantially the same as the original French edition, has been published in the U.S.A.

Fortunately, Fr. Hauret, unlike Dr. Messenger, gives us a glimpse of the so-called modern scientific proofs on which he bases his belief in the theory that man's body has been evolved from that of a lower animal. They are the fossil remains found at Sterkfontein, now admitted by men like Sir S. Zuckerman to be the fossils of an ape, and the fossils of the so-called Peking Man, which as we shall see, are also fossils of macaques and monkeys. He does not give us any more information on that point, for he says that he would not have the impertinence of even discussing the opinions of paleontologists. Instead of the Mosaic order, he gives his own order which is based on the now defunct theory of Laplace. Contrary to the advice given by Pope Leo XIII in his Encyclical *Providentissimus Deus,* he carves up the first chapters of Genesis according to another defunct theory, the theory of Wellhausen, and endeavors to show that the first chapter was written, not in the order given, but after the second chapter. Fr. Hauret has, however, the merit of letting us see on what he bases his conclusions.

In France another book covering much the same ground as Fr. Hauret's *Origines* (already referred to) and expressing much the same views was published in 1954 by Reverend Fr. Grison, Professor in Saint-Sulpice Seminary under the title *Problèmes d'Origines.* Unlike Fr. Hauret's *Origines* this book claims to be a treatise on the scientific aspect of the problems of Genesis, and in that resembles Fr. Marcozzi's *L'Uomo nello Spazio e nel tempo* which, however, deals only with the origin of man.

His treatment of the problem of the Six Days of Creation is based on the defunct theory of Laplace. On the question of the origin of life on the earth he quotes the experiments of Pasteur, but thinks that the possibility of spontaneous generation must not be ruled out. He adopts the theory of evolution, but makes no attempt to answer the formidable objections against the theory.

Coming to the Origin of Man, which is the principal question dealt with in his book, he gives photographs of the models of the fossil skulls that have been put forward during the past century as skulls of missing links. He does not tell his readers that many of these photographs are photographs of artificial models, not of the actual fossils, and that the claims put forward in the case of all of them to represent "Missing Links" have either been queried or rejected by the best authorities. At the end of his long list of photographs of these models, many of which do not correspond with the original fossils, Fr. Grison says: "Such in brief are the findings of science with regard to the origin of man." (p. 251).

In other words, he claims to give not one "missing link," but a whole series of "missing links," beginning with the *Proconsul* (an ape of the Miocene Period) and continuing his illustrated geneology of man through the Australopithecinae of South Africa, the Pithecanthropus of Java, the Sinanthropus of China, the Neanderthal Man, down to modern man. However, Fr. Grison does not claim to have made any original research, he just gives as evidence in favor of human evolution the list of fossils that he found in French propagandist books.

The most probable explanation of the evident mistakes about the fossils claimed to represent creatures in the process of evolution, which are mentioned in the books by Frs. Hauret and Grison and the other recent French writers, is that these men did not consult the most recent books of reference of the fossils discovered during the past century. The standard book of reference on these fossils is *Les Hommes Fossils* by Boule and Vallois. This book was originally written by Boule alone and published in Paris in 1923. Boule was an evolutionist, but before his death he had rejected the Peking Man and had raised objections against all the other "Missing Links."

After Boule's death, Vallois, also an evolutionist but with more extreme views, published a revised edition of Boule's book in 1946. It is this 1946 edition that Fr. Grison and most of the recent French writers used; it is also the edition used by Frs. Marcozzi and Ezpondaburu, S.J. Now Vallois revised the whole work again in 1952, using the information that had come to light (such as the results of the "carbon 14" tests) between 1946 and 1952. This 1952 edition of *Les Hommes Fossiles* (which is one of the principal books of reference consulted by the present writer) gives sufficient documented evidence (with references) to warrant the rejection of the claims of all the fossils put forward by Fr. Grison and the other French writers as "The findings of science on the origin of man."

Besides Fr. Grison's book, *Problèmes d'Origines,* several other books dealing with the origin of man by Catholic writers have appeared in France in recent years, all of which have this in common, that they put forward as proofs of human evolution the fossils of the Australopithecinae of South Africa, of the Piltdown Man (up to 1954), and of the Java and Peking Men, none of which represent a creature in the process of evolution, and that they even claim that the fossils of the Neanderthal Man afford evidence in favor of evolution, even though these fossils have been written off by practically all non-Catholic evolutionists as of no use to prove their theory.

The following are a few of the recent books by French Catholic authors which have influenced public opinion in favor of the theory of human evolution:

Les Hommes de la Pierre Ancienne, by Abbé Breuil, published at Paris in 1951.

Abbé Breuil gives the same list of fossils as Fr. Grison, except that he has the Piltdown Man fossils, which Fr. Grison does not mention. He gives 550,000 years for the antiquity of man and bases his opinion chiefly on the existence of man in Europe during the hypothetical Interglacial Periods, which authorities on the Glacial Periods such as Howorth say never existed. Abbé Breuil is quoted as an authority on human fossils, but as he accepts as genuine the fossils of the Piltdown Man, the Java and Peking Men, and the Australopithecinae which have been rejected by such authorities as Marcellin Boule, the claim can hardly be maintained. He is an authority on the artifacts of the Old Stone Age, which is quite a different thing.

Les Premiers Hommes, by Frs. Bergounioux and Glory, published at Paris in 1952. This book, which had a great influence on public opinion in favor of human evolution both in France and Spain, gives as evidence the same list of human fossils as Fr. Grison, with the addition of the Piltdown Man fossils.

Les Origines de L'Homme by Nicholas Corte, published at Paris in 1957.

The author, who conceals his identity under the assumed name "Nicholas Corte," also gives the same list of "Missing Links" as Fr. Grison; in addition, he makes the extraordinary claim that the theory which says that there are two different accounts of Creation in the first two chapters of *Genesis* is confirmed by statements (which he does not specify) in the letter of the Biblical Commission to Cardinal Suhard and in the encyclical *Humani Generis*.

For evidence of the real attitude of the Holy See at present toward the above-mentioned theory, see the article in *L'Osservatore Romano* (July 2, 1958) on *L'Introduction à la Bible* (the use of which has been forbidden by the Holy See in all ecclesiastical seminaries in the world).

An English translation of this article is given after the Preface to Part I of this book.

L'Evolution: Hypothèses et Problèmes, by Dr. (Med.) Rémy Collin, published at Paris in 1958. Dr. Collin has been writing books since 1907; this is his twenty-first important book. He is an evolutionist and, like the other French writers referred to, bases his opinion in favor of human evolution on the fossils of the Australopithecinae, Java and Peking Men, etc. He admits that the Piltdown Man was a forgery.

Pierre Teilhard de Chardin by Claude Cuenot, published at Paris in 1958.

This large volume by M. Cuenot, who is an evolutionist, gives a detailed account of the life of Fr. Teilhard de Chardin, S.J., in which he is represented as a great authority on geology, paleontology and biology. The validity of these claims will be examined in Chapter 5 on the Peking Man.

Nouvelle Revue Théologique, Sept.-Oct. 1958.

This number contains an article by Fr. Boné, S.J., of Louvain on the fossils of an ape discovered in a coal mine at Baccinello in Italy on August 2, 1958, which are said to be twelve million years old and to have some resemblance to human fossils. Fr. Boné, who is an advocate of the theory of human evolution, has no precise information about the peculiarities of these newly discovered fossils, but devotes most of his article to what he calls "Hominids," in the list of which he includes the Java Man and the Australopithecinae of South Africa.

The word "Hominid" is used by evolutionists to designate an ape or a monkey in the process of evolution toward man. Many claims have been made for the existence of such creatures, some of which, like *Proconsul* of South Africa, are represented as being still apes, and others like Sinanthropus of China as having crossed the barrier between ape and man, but, as we shall see, the claims of every one of these have been proved to be fraudulent. This new claimant from the Italian coal mine need not be taken seriously.

Two Recent French Commentaries on the Bible Which Deal with the Origin of Man

Two recent commentaries on the Bible by prominent Scripture professors which deal with the origin of man have been published in France during the past few years. The first, entitled *An Introduction to the Study of the Bible,* was published at Paris, Tournai and Rome, and an English translation was published at New York (U.S.A.) in 1955 under the title *Guide to the Bible.* This commentary in two large volumes is the work of a number of French Scripture scholars and is edited by Frs. Robert and Tricot of the Catholic Institute of Paris. The writer who deals with the origin and antiquity of man is an evolutionist. He gives as evidence of human evolution the same list of fossils as Fr. Grison, with the addition of the Piltdown Man, and as evidence of man's great antiquity, he gives Abbé Breuil's unproven claim that man existed during the alleged Interglacial Periods.

Intervention by the Holy See

The second commentary referred to above is entitled *Introduction à la Bible,* and was published in 1958. It was to consist of two large volumes like the last, but the first volume only, which contains the introduction and deals with the problems of the Old Testament, has so far appeared.

The chief editor of this new work is Fr. Robert, who was chief editor of the first commentary; Fr. Tricot is one of the contributors. This first volume, which deals with the problems of the Old Testament, is the work of two editors and nine professors of Scripture from the Catholic Institute of Paris and the Major Seminaries of Lyon, Strassburg, Annecy and Angiers, and has a preface written by the Most Reverend J. J. Weber, Bishop of Strassburg.

Among the subjects dealt with in this book are: inspiration, inerrancy of Scripture, the text of the Bible, literary and historical criticism of the text, the historical background of the Bible, the first five books of the Bible and the problems which they contain.

In the announcement of the book the editors say:

> The book aims at providing a study of the Bible which will be at the same time scientific and religious. While emphasizing the religious aspect it avoids any apologetic attitude which would disguise the real problems or prevent a solution.

The book was evidently intended as a textbook for the Major Seminaries and Catholic universities of the world. It came under the notice of the Holy See, and was examined by the Sacred Congregation for seminaries and universities. The result of the examination was that this commentary was pronounced to be "totally unsuitable," and its use was forbidden in all seminaries and Catholic universities in the world.[1]

These men were, doubtless, the victims of a hundred years of propaganda in France in favor of various dangerous theories underlying the exegesis of the Bible, which they mistook for scientific conclusions. It may be presumed that they accepted as proofs of human evolution the various fossils referred to above, and that they regarded themselves obliged to take them into account in commenting on the first chapters of *Genesis*.

1. See the text of the letter of the Sacred Congregation of seminaries and universities.

Evidence will be given in the present work to prove that not one of them has any claim to represent a creature in the process of evolution.

Italy

Fr. Marcozzi, S.J., of the Gregorian University, Rome, who is also a strong advocate of the theory that man's body was evolved from a brute beast, takes the opposite attitude from that taken by Dr. Messenger and Fr. Hauret, who disclaim all knowledge of the scientific side of the question. He poses as an authority on the scientific aspect of evolution and is the author of several books on the subject, the two latest of which were published in 1953 and 1954, costing £3 4s 6d. and £1 3s. od. respectively. These two books have the external appearances of well-documented scientific treatises, but when carefully considered, they appear to be rather a defense of the position which the author has taken up on the question of human evolution against the criticism of the Spanish Jesuits. In 1952 the Spanish Jesuits of Madrid published a learned treatise on Dogmatic Theology in four large volumes, in the second volume of which they dealt at great length with the teaching of the Catholic Church on the origin of man. (See the last chapter of present book). They defend the traditional view that man's body was directly created by God from inorganic matter, and give reasons to show that the opposite view is devoid of solid probability. On the scientific aspect of the question they say:

> It has been discovered that the alleged scientific solution (that man's body was evolved from living matter) is in no way certain, but is in fact a mere hypothesis, the degree of probability of which cannot be defined by the men of science who hold different opinions on the subject. (Vol. II., p. 639).

Among the adversaries whose opinion they are refuting they mention: Fr. Marcozzi S.J., Fr. Teilhard de Chardin, S.J., Dr. Messenger, and Fr. Sertillanges, O.P.

Whether Fr. Marcozzi's two volumes are meant as a refutation of the above quotation or not, they have certainly failed in establishing that there is sufficient evidence to justify the statement that the evolution of man's body from either an ape or a lemur (as the evolutionists hold) has any real probability.

Fr. Marcozzi, like most evolutionists, bases his argument almost completely on the evidence from the fossil remains of man (or of creatures alleged to be men) discovered during the past hundred years. Though his books are dated 1953 and 1954, his treatment of the question of the fossil remains of man is hopelessly out of date, as will be shown in the present book. He devotes a large part of his 1953 book to the fossil remains of the Neanderthal Man, which constitutes eighty per cent, if not more, of the fossils of the Old Stone Age, and leaves the reader under the impression that the Neanderthal Man represents a race in the process of evolution, whereas it is conceded by such weighty authorities as Marcellin Boule and Henri Vallois, that the Neanderthal Man was an ordinary normal man with more than average brain, who developed prominent brow ridges from life in the open as a hunter, like the aborigines of Australia, and that he became extinct at the time of the *hiatus* or Deluge (see *Les Hommes Fossiles,* 1952 ed.). Of the other candidates for the position of "Missing Links"—the Piltdown Man, the Java Man, the Peking Man and the Australopithecinae—he leaves the reader under the impression in his 1953 book, *L'Uomo Nello Spazio and Nello Tempo,* that all these have a claim to represent creatures in the process of evolution toward man, whereas, as we shall see, the fossil remains in question are all fossils of either apes or monkeys. In his 1954 book, *Le Origini dell' Uomo,* he admits the forgery in the case of the Piltdown fossils, but still keeps the Peking Man, the Java Man and the Australopithicinae, all of which are fossils of apes or monkeys. For dating the fossils of the Old Stone Age, he adopts the theory of Professor Penck, which was propounded back in 1880, and has been rejected by the best authorities of the Ice Age.

If what is stated in Fr. Marcozzi's book were true, there would be a scientific basis not only for the hypothesis of human evolution, but also for the theory of polygenesis, or plurality of human ancestry. The fact is, however, that practically all of Fr. Marcozzi's fossils of men or creatures in the process of evolution have been thrown into the scrap-heap by such writers as Boule and Vallois, and even by Sir S. Zuckerman (See *Les Hommes Fossils* by Boule and Vallois, 1952 ed., and *Evolution as a Process,* pp. 301-349, edited by Sir Julian Huxley).

Spain

In Spain a Jesuit Father named Andérez Alonso had spent several years writing a book on the origin of man, entitled *Hacia El Origen del Hombre,* but died before he was able to finish it. Eight years after his death, another Jesuit Father named Fr. Ezpondaburu undertook the task of finishing it, but called in two laymen to assist him: Sénor Melendaz of Madrid University, an evolutionist, and Dr. V. Von Köenigswald of Utrecht University, notorious for his attempt to revive the case of the discredited Java Man. Fr. Ezpondaburu, who is an evolutionist, tells us in the preface that he found it necessary to alter part of the work of Fr. Andérez Alonso, which had become "out-of-date." The book was published in 1956. Fr. Ezpondaburu gives various quotations from the writings of Fr. Marcozzi and Fr. Teilhard de Chardin. As in the case of Fr. Marcozzi, if what is stated in *Hacia El Origin del Hombre* about the fossil remains of the Neanderthal race and of the various candidates for the position of "Missing Links" were true, there would be scientific basis for the theory of evolution of man and for the theory of polygenesis. The book which is the work of four men, three of whom are evolutionists, is full of contradictions.

Conclusion

The intentions of these men were good. The enemies of the Church had been boasting that modern science had proved that the theory of evolution was no longer a theory but a fact, and that the Mosaic account was therefore wrong, and that Genesis was only a tissue of fables. Men like Dr. Messenger, Fr. Hauret, etc., tried to take the weapon out of the enemies' hands by admitting the very thing they wanted to be believed—the ape origin of man—and even went as far as to say that this was the proper interpretation of the Mosaic account. It was like attempting to put out a fire by throwing kerosene on it, because the enemies of the Church are much more eager to have the man-from-ape theory generally believed than they are to discredit the Bible. Furthermore, most atheistic propagandists for the theory of human evolution are now aware that the arguments from paleontology based on the existence of half-man, half-ape fossils, have collapsed, and men like Sir Julian Huxley have abandoned most of them. These men, therefore, can have nothing but contempt for those Catholic writers who abandon the biblical account of the origin of man for reasons known to them to be worthless.

What St. Augustine said about Christian writers of his time who endeavored to defend the Sacred Scriptures by arguments from natural science, which the learned among pagans knew to be worthless, applies today with greater force to those Catholics who abandon the traditional teaching of the Church for reasons which science of today has proved to be false. St. Augustine said:

> Often, in connection with the earth and the heavens, or other elements of this world, the movement, circuit, or still more, the magnitude of the stars. . .the exact nature of animals, fruits, rocks and many other similar things, it happens that a man, who is not a Christian, professes a knowledge which is so profound that it is guaranteed by certain calculations, or even by experience. Now here is a thing which is too disgraceful, and from which we must above all guard ourselves: a Christian speaks on all these subjects; he thinks that he speaks of them according to our Holy Scriptures, yet the unbeliever may hear him rambling so much that in the presence of such errors, he (the unbeliever) cannot help laughing. (*De Genesi ad litteram.* lib. I, Cap. xix).

The statements of Fr. Hauret quoted above, to the effect that most of the intellectuals of France, both Catholics and non-Catholics, are believers in the theory of evolution, is a gross exaggeration, being merely a common form of propaganda for the theory. The fact is that the bishops, priests and religious of France have been so overworked for the past half-century that they have little time for the study of such questions as paleontology. Propaganda for the theory of human evolution within the Catholic Church in France is the work of a small number of men and, as we shall show, is based on out-of-date information.

The other statement of Fr. Hauret, that he would not have the impertinence to express an opinion on the value of the scientific arguments for evolution, implies that the questions involved are so abstruse and difficult that they are beyond the capacity of men of ordinary learning, and is a common form of propaganda. The only direct arguments for or against evolution are drawn from paleontology. It is within the capacity of any educated man to investigate these arguments and to appraise their worth. Every priest has sufficient knowledge of biology to enable him to judge whether indirect arguments for evolution drawn from that science are valid or not.

In any event, a person may very well ask the question: if Fr. Hauret knows nothing about the merits of arguments in favor of evolution, why does he advocate a change in the teaching of the catechism to include the teaching of human evolution as the most probable theory?

The actual certain conclusions of science of today provide the best refutation of erroneous interpretations of the first chapter of *Genesis*, and the best vindication of the wise rules contained in Papal Encyclicals for their interpretation.

The Popes have always allowed full liberty for scientific investigation, they have allowed full liberty to publish actual findings of science when they are certain, but no amount of propaganda has ever forced any of them to permit the teaching of mere theories on matters touching revealed doctrine. They have given liberty for the investigating of these theories, but as long as they remain theories, they will not allow them to be taught as established facts.

Fr. Hauret devotes the concluding chapter of his book *Origines* to giving advice to catechists about how they were to teach bible history, and actually gives a scheme for teaching it. Most of what is in his scheme is just the sugar-coating for a very bitter pill. On page 237 (French edition) he advises that pupils should be told that the majority of scientists hold as the most probable opinion that the body of man was evolved from a brute beast, and that Eve was derived from Adam, not physically, but as a picture may be derived from a model. On page 235 he puts down as part of the new information to be given to pupils: "Science has established that men were found at the three extremities of the ancient world at the beginning of the Quaternary Period," which is usually put at between half a million and a million years ago.

These questions will all be dealt with in detail in the course of this book. Here it is sufficient to say: 1) the fossils found by Dr. Broom at Sterkfontein were fossils of a large ape: for conclusive proof of this, see the article by Zuckerman in *Evolution as a Process,* edited by Sir Julian Huxley; 2) the opinion which says that man was not evolved but was specially created, even from a scientific viewpoint, is by far the most probable and is the common teaching of the Church; 3) the estimate of 600,000 which Fr. Hauret gives for the age of man in the world has been proved by modern radio-carbon method of dating fossils to be thirty times too high. We shall see in the chapter on "The Antiquity of Man" that 20,000 years is quite sufficient to explain all the human fossils found.

Pope Pius XII, in an audience given to specialists in the science of genetics, concluded his address with the following words:

> If you reflect on what we have said on research and human knowledge, you should understand that neither from the side of reason, nor of thought oriented in the Christian sense, are any barriers placed to scientific research or to the affirmation of truth.
>
> *There are barriers, but they are not for the purpose of imprisoning truth. They have as their end to prevent unproved hypotheses from being taken as established facts;* to prevent people from forgetting the necessity of completing one source of knowledge by another; to prevent people from interpreting erroneously the scale of values and the degree of certainty of a source of knowledge. It is in order to avoid these causes of error that there are barriers; but there are no barriers to truth.

Chapter 1

THE ORIGIN OF MAN

The Mosaic Account

And He (God) said:

> *Let us make man to our image and likeness; and let him have dominion over the fishes of the sea, and the fowls of the air, and the beasts, and the whole earth, and every creeping thing that moveth upon the earth. And God created man to his own image; to the image of God he created him: male and female he created them. And the Lord God formed man of the slime of the earth: and breathed into his face the breath of life, and man became a living soul.* (*Gen.* 1:26-27; 2:7).

The traditional opinion, and still the common opinion, of the above biblical account of the origin of man given in Chapters 1 and 2 of *Genesis*, is that Chapter 1 was written in the order given, and that Chapter 2 supplemented it by adding the details that man's body was formed from the slime of the earth and that his soul was distinct from his body. (See *Introductio in Libros Sacros Vet. Test.* published at Rome, 1958, by Fr. Mariani, O.F.M., for the confirmation of this statement).

However, some modern writers like Fr. Hauret[1] think that they are two different accounts, and that Chapter 1 was written after Chapter 2. (This is denied by Fr. Mariani in *op. cit.* p. 60).

This question has already been discussed in the introductory chapter to Part I. Here it is sufficient to say that both chapters are covered equally by inspiration, for the Council of Trent solemnly decreed that "these books in their entirety and all their parts, as they have been accustomed to be read in the Catholic Church, and as they stand in the ancient Latin Vulgate, must be accepted as sacred and canonical."

---

1. See *Origines* by Fr. Charles Hauret, Chap. 2.

The meaning of the words "The Lord formed man of the slime of the earth" seems to be as plain as words could make it, that God formed man from inanimate matter; this is the traditional teaching of the Church and still remains the official teaching. However, those people who believe in the theory of the evolution of man's body from that of a brute beast contend that in the words quoted, no definite statement is made as to whether God created man directly from inanimate matter, or only indirectly, by using the body of some animal that had been formed from the slime of the earth. While the Teaching Authority of the Church forbids all her children to teach as an established fact that man's body is derived genetically from that of a brute beast, she allows scientific investigation and discussion on the question. Pope Pius XII, however, warns all investigators that they should look for "clearly proved facts" and that they should not imitate the rashness of those "who transgress the liberty of discussion given, when they act as if the origin of the human body from pre-existing and living matter were already completely certain and proved by facts, and as if there were nothing in the sources of revelation which demands the greatest moderation and caution in the matter."

The object of Part II of this book is to investigate whether science of today provides any real scientific basis for the theory 1) that there is a genetic or physical connection between man and the brute beast, that is, for the theory that man's body was evolved from the brute beast; and 2) whether the recent findings of science tend to prove the opposite, that there is no genetic connection between man and the brute beast.

The branches of modern science that deal with the question of the origin of man are paleontology and biology. Paleontology, in this connection, deals with the fossil remains of man from historic times back to the earliest trace of the existence of man in the world. If there is any genetic connection between man and the brute beast there should be some indication of this in the earliest fossils of man. If such an indication can be found, it provides the only direct argument in favor of the theory of evolution: if no such indication can be found, that is, if, as we shall show, the earliest skeletons of man found resemble those of modern man in all essential human characteristics (brain capacity, upright gait combined with evidence of intelligence shown by artifacts), then the conclusion should be that there is no genetic connection between man and the brute beast.

The science of biology can give no direct proof of the evolution of man from the brute beast; it can only discuss the question whether, taking into account the distinctive characteristics of man, the evolution of man from a beast is possible or probable. In practice, as we shall see, nearly all biologists who support the theory of evolution rely, not on biology, but on paleontology for their arguments in its favor.

We shall therefore first deal with the evidence provided by the latest findings of paleontology on the origin of man.

Preliminary Explanations

Paleontology is generally regarded as a very mysterious branch of science, so mysterious in fact that many, if not most, biblical exegetes think themselves excused when they adopt alleged conclusions of people who are regarded as experts on the subject. The ordinary reader when skimming over the pages of the larger books on paleontology, and seeing the illustrations of the dozens of fossils discovered during the last hundred years, and the forbidding names of the various periods to which these fossils are assigned, is inclined to say: this subject is too complicated for me, it is beyond me.

In reality, however, the subject as far as it deals with the origin of man can be made very simple. The history of early man may be divided into three periods: the Paleolithic, or Old Stone Age, the Mesolithic, or Middle Stone Age, and the Neolithic, or Late Stone Age. Now the question of the origin of man belongs to the Paleolithic or Old Stone Age exclusively: all the fossils of early man from the Cro-Magnon, the ancestor of the present European, to the Heidelberg Man, who is supposed to be the earliest inhabitant of Europe, belong to this period.

The Old Stone Age is divided into various periods which

get their names from the places in Europe and Africa where old stone instruments have been found. The names of the periods differ for Europe and Africa. In Europe the names generally used (beginning with the latest period and counting toward the origin of man) are: the Magdalenian, the Solutrian, the Aurignacian, the Mousterian, the Levallosian, the Clactonian, the Acheulian and the Chellean or Abbevillian. The question of the relative lengths of these periods does not concern us here; it will be discussed in the chapter on the Antiquity of Man in the World. In this chapter we are concerned only with the Mousterian period and the periods prior to it. The question can be further simplified by saying that there is an agreed dividing line in the Old Stone Age between the Aurignacian and the Mousterian periods. Between these two periods a catastrophe occurred in Europe and Africa which resulted in the disappearance of the total population of Europe and at least all North Africa, for a period the length of which has not been definitely fixed. The population began to return during the Aurignacian period. The time that elapsed between the disappearance of man from Europe and Africa at the end of the Mousterian period and his re-appearance at the beginning of the Aurignacian is referred to by paleontologists as the *hiatus,* or complete gap. The disaster, as we shall see in a special chapter on the subject, was the Flood of Noe. The race of men who appeared after the *hiatus* (caused by the Flood) is generally called the Cro-Magnon race. It is admitted by all that the Cro-Magnon man, in physical characteristics, size of brain, etc., is the equal, if not the superior to modern man, and that he left after him undoubted signs of a high culture. The problem, therefore, of the origin of man is narrowed down to the study of the period before the *hiatus* or Deluge.

The Search for the Missing Link

It is just over a century since the skull of a man discovered in the year 1856, in the valley of Neander, from which the Neanderthal Man gets his name. A similar skull discovered in 1848 at Gibraltar had passed almost unnoticed. This Neanderthal skull had undoubted peculiarities, but these were grossly exaggerated at the time. The brain capacity was represented to be only 1,270 cc, which is 230 cc below the average for man, whereas it is over 1,500 and thus above the average. It was hailed by the followers of Lamarck and Darwin as a proof of man's simian ancestry, and search began in nearly all parts of the globe for other human fossils. The search has lasted a century. Not only fossil skulls of ancient man, but whole skeletons have been found in various parts of the world.

Naturally the various ages of these fossils did not correspond with the order in which they were found. All these fossils have now been studied and classified by experts. Very definite conclusions have been arrived at on a number of points, while some other points remain to be settled. Just as the search for fossils that might prove to be "missing links" was carried out mostly by evolutionists, so also was the study and classification of them done by believers of the theory of evolution. The conclusions arrived at by these men may be said to be all against the theory of human evolution, and since these men gave their conclusions without any intention of either proving or disproving the theory of evolution, they are not open to suspicion. These conclusions will be studied in detail in the next chapter. Here we shall give merely a brief summary. We shall deal with the question of the *hiatus,* or break in civilization, in Parts III and IV (on *The Deluge and the Antiquity of Man.*).

Chief points on which there is now agreement among experts:

The following points on which there is agreement among experts are the following:

1) There was a *hiatus,* or complete break in civilization, after the Mousterian period and before the Aurignacian.

2) The race that appeared after the *hiatus,* generally called the Cro-Magnon race, were perfectly normal men, whose descendants are found in Europe today. (See Part 3).

3) The race that inhabited Europe, Africa and part of Asia before the *hiatus* was chiefly the Neanderthal race. While this race of men had certainly some peculiarities, they had a normal brain capacity, they walked erect, manufactured tools, and buried their dead with ceremony.

4) Along with the Neanderthal race there existed at least two other races, one of which resembled modern man very closely, while the other appeared to be the result of intermarriage between Neanderthal Man and the other race.

5) So far no fossils belonging to a period prior to the *hiatus* have been yet discovered in either South America or Australia.

6) The only fossils claimed to belong to a period prior to the *hiatus* found in either India, China or Indonesia are those of the Peking Man and the Java Man and, as we shall see in a special chapter, these are certainly not genuine fossils of man.

Chapter 2

EVIDENCE FROM PALEONTOLOGY ON THE ORIGIN OF MAN

In the last chapter we saw that there is now agreement among experts on a number of points concerning the origin of man, the chief of which being that there was a *hiatus* or complete break in the history of man when the total population disappeared from Europe, Africa and part of Asia for a considerable time; and that the families that appeared after that break were composed of normal men like the present inhabitants of Europe. Now the fact that such a *hiatus* or gap occurred, although acknowledged by experts for the past half century, is not generally known, and many biblical commentators appear never to have heard of it. If the existence of this *hiatus* or gap is admitted, it will simplify our study of the origin of man, for it provides a convenient line of demarcation from which to begin our investigation. However, the conclusions from the study of early fossil remains of man which we propose to make in this chapter are completely independent of whether the existence of such a *hiatus* or gap is admitted or not, for in this chapter we shall deal with all the human fossils discovered so far. This does not mean, however, that it will be necessary to deal individually with each fossil, for the fossil remains found during the last century have all been carefully studied by experts and classified, and there is now no controversy whatever about most of them. We shall first deal with the fossils about which there is agreement, and then give the latest scientific information about the fossils that are still the object of controversy.

Fossils Attributed to the Post-Hiatus Period

The first are the Grimaldi skeletons discovered in 1901 in the Grotto of Grimaldi and now in the museum of Monaco.

One is that of an old woman with brain capacity of 1,375 cc, the other of a young man with brain capacity of 1,580. The skulls are dolichocephalic, or long-headed, like those of the Neanderthal race, but are easily distinguished from them. There is no controversy about them and no claim is made for any simian characteristics.

The second are the skeletons of the Cro-Magnon race, so called from the rock shelter in the South of France where five skulls were dug up in 1868 by workmen engaged in the construction of a railway. The Cro-Magnon race are regarded as the ancestors of part of the present European population, and representatives of them are found all over Europe.

POST-FLOOD FOSSILS

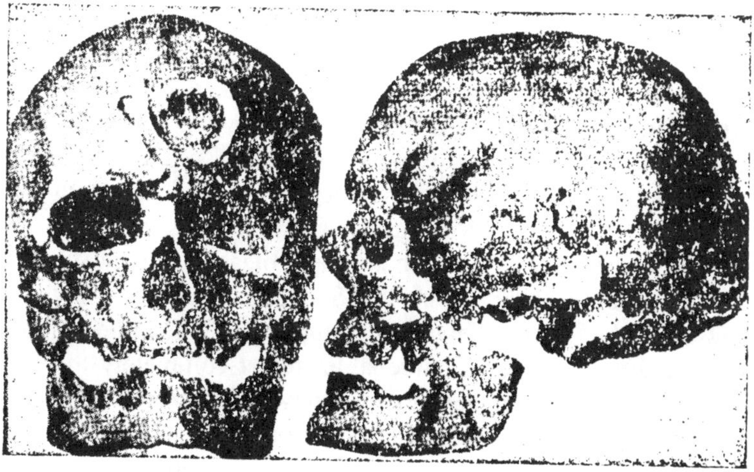

front **profile**

SKULL OF CRO-MAGNON MAN
brain capacity 1,590 cc

This skull resembles the pre-Flood Fontéchevade skulls. No skulls like those of the Neanderthal race have been found anywhere after the Flood, from which it is concluded that the whole Neanderthal race perished in the Flood.

The third is the skeleton found at Chancelade in 1888. The brain capacity is 1,710 cc, and the skeleton presents all the characteristics of the superior races.

These three races or families are believed to have arrived in Europe in the order given, sometime during the Aurignacian, Solutrian and Magdalenian periods, which are generally referred to as the Age of the Reindeer, because the men of these races left behind them in caves and other places numerous drawings of the reindeer. This is taken as an indication that the last Glacial Period had not yet ended when man reappeared in Europe after the Flood. Their culture, as shown in their drawings and paintings and carvings in stone and ivory, was altogether superior to that of the Neanderthal race, but the period is referred to as the Old Stone Age.

Fossils of Earliest Man

We come now to the real question, that is, the consideration of the fossils unearthed in various parts of the world, claimed to be the fossils of man or of beings half-man, half-ape.

Before beginning the examination of the fossils of ancient man or of beings claimed to be in various stages of evolution, let us first see what are the views of the supporters of the theory of human evolution about the manner in which this evolution is supposed to have taken place. As was stated in the last chapter of Part I, men like Professor Leakey (the author of *Adam's Ancestors*) and Sir Julian Huxley, who wish to avoid the inconvenience of attempting to defend an opinion that is now regarded as untenable, reject completely the theory that would represent man as descended from the gorilla or any of the great apes, and propound the view that man and the great apes are descended from a common ancestor back in the beginning of the Tertiary Period. Most of the propagandists, however, still cling to the man-from-ape theory and do not seem to be aware that it is out of date. This latter form of propaganda is usually adopted in primary schoolbooks, museums and sometimes even in universities, and takes the form of a series of pictures or statues representing the supposed stages of evolution from gorilla to Peking or Java Man; from Peking and Java Man to the Neanderthal Man and from the Neanderthal Man to present-day man. It is immaterial which of the two theories the propagandists for human evolution may adopt; for in either theory they have to produce the links between modern man and his supposed animal ancestor. As it is agreed upon by all, that man, whether considered as specially created or as the final result of an evolutionary process, was the last of all the animal kingdom to appear on the earth, it should be possible to find the links with animal ancestors if they exist; the excuses given for the failure to produce the links in the supposed chain of evolution back in the Primary, Secondary and Tertiary epochs are not valid in the case of man, who was the last to appear. Propagandists are aware of this, and hence they have spared no expense or labor in carrying out excavations whenever there was any hope of finding traces of ancient man. We shall now see the fruits of a hundred years of effort.

A List of the Principal Human Fossils Of the Pre-Hiatus Period

The fossils found during the last century and now preserved in museums in various parts of the world consist 1) of remains of the Neanderthal race which constitute the greater part, and which were found all over Europe and Africa in Asia Minor; 2) of a small number of fossils of other races represented by the Fontéchevade skulls of central France, the Swanscombe skull found in Southern England, the skeleton and skulls found in Palestine on the shores of the Lake of Tiberias, at Mount Carmel in the grotto of Es-Soukoul, and at Asselar in the Sahara Desert. Besides these there are the Calaveras skull of California, the Galley Hill and London skulls of England, now regarded as of comparatively recent date, and some fossils discovered in Australia in recent years but for which no great antiquity is claimed; 3) the fossils of the Piltdown man, now minus the ape jawbone, of the Peking man and of the Java man; and 4) the various fossils of the *Australopithecus* class found in South Africa.

It is now admitted by all serious authorities that the men represented by the fossils of class (1) and class (2) had average human brain capacity; that they walked erect, manufactured tools and knew the use of fire. It is admitted by most authorities, including propagandists for the evolutionary theory, that the fossils from South Africa referred to in class (4) have no real claim to be reckoned among other fossils of man, or even of fossils of half-man, half-beast. The whole controversy therefore centers around the Piltdown Man (now rejected), the Peking Man and the Java Man. We shall, however, deal separately with each of the four classes.

The Neanderthal Man

It is now a little over a hundred years since the remarkable skeleton was found by workmen in the valley of the Neander in the year 1856, near Düsseldorf, Germany, which gave its name to the Neanderthal race of men. Lamarck's theory of the evolution of all living things, including man, from primitive forms, had been put forward at the beginning of the century and had been widely accepted by rationalists. There was, however, no tangible evidence for the theory up to the time of the discovery of this skeleton. Its indubitable peculiarities were noted and exaggerated by rationalists like Haekel; the brain capacity was represented as being only 1,270 cc, which is 230 cc below the average for a man, whereas it was found to be over 1,500 cc when measured later on by Marcellin Boule, one of the greatest authorities of his time. On the strength of the skeleton, Haeckel constructed a family tree for man, tracing his origin back to the ape.

Since that time, skeletons or parts of skeletons of the Neanderthal Man have been discovered in all parts of Europe that had not been covered by ice, all over Africa and in those parts of Asia that border on the Mediterranean; but so far none have been found in Asia, east of the Himalaya Mountains or in any other part of the world, except those mentioned above.

The following is a list of the principal Neanderthal fossils discovered to date:

In 1856, the original Neanderthal skeleton was found; in 1864, the skull that had been found in Gibraltar in 1848 was shown to the public; in 1866, a jawbone was found in La Naulette; in the same year, a skull was found at Spy, near Namur in Belgium; in 1899, fragments of 10 or 12 skulls and a large number of teeth and isolated bones were found in Krapina in Croatia; in 1908, a remarkable skull was discovered at Chapelle-aux-Saints in the South of France, with brain capacity of 1,625 cc; in 1909 a skull was discovered at Le Moustier (the place in the Dordogne valley in the south of France that gives its name to the Mousterian age, the age of the Neanderthal Man), and another skull at La Ferrassie in the same valley; in 1911, another skull was discovered at La Quino; in 1924, two Neanderthal skeletons were discovered in the Crimea; in 1925 and 1931, a number of skulls and other human fossils with some Neanderthal characteristics were discovered in Palestine; in 1939 a skull was discovered at Mont Circe, about 100 kilometers from Rome; the latest discoveries of Neanderthal remains were made in 1953 at Saldanha, a hundred miles from Capetown, South Africa, and at Palikao in Algeria; in both these cases stone instruments of the Palaeolithic Age were found along with the fossils; finally, what is regarded as the most ancient Neanderthal fossil yet discovered is the massive jawbone discovered in 1907, at Mauer, near Heidelberg, which gives its name to the Heidelberg Man.

General Conclusions About The Neanderthal Race, Brain Capacity

The estimate given by Boule and Vallois for the average brain capacity of the Neanderthal Man is about 1,540 cc, which is a little above the average brain capacity of present Europeans; and for that of the Neanderthal woman is about 1,290, which is just a little less than that of present-day European women. If, however, we take the average brain capacity of all the different races in the world, we find it to be only about 1,300 cc for men and 1,200 for women. The brain capacity of the Neanderthal race is therefore much higher than the brain capacity of the average men and women in the world at present. From these figures, Weidenreich, who is one of the extremists among the advocates of the human evolution theory, concludes that the development of the human brain had reached its maximum at the time of the Neanderthal race.

THE SHAPE OF THE SKULL

The shape of the brain case of the Neanderthal Man, which is dolichocephalic, or long-headed, used to be given as a proof that he was a man in the process of evolution. It was contended that the form of the brain case of the majority of men in Europe at present, which is brachycephalic, or round-headed, has been gradually evolved, and that the quality of the contents has been greatly improved. This argument had to be abandoned completely for many reasons. In the first place, brachycephalic skulls have been found belonging to the period before the *hiatus,* or Flood, which are regarded as older, or at least as contemporary with the Neanderthal period. In the second place, the skull of the races that came back to Europe after the *hiatus,* or Flood—the Cro-Magnon and the Grimaldi—are dolichocephalic, though differing in other respects. Finally, dolichocephalic skulls are found in present day cemeteries all over the world.

Note: Skulls are classified by the ratio of the length to the width. The length is calculated by measuring the skull from front to back, and the width by measuring from ear to ear. If the ratio of the width of the skull to the length lies between 70 to 75 percent, it is called dolichocephalic, or longer than it is wide; if the ratio is over 80 percent, it is called brachycephalic; if the ratio lies between 75 and 80 percent, it is called mesocephalic. The height of the forehead varies in proportion to the length and width: Long-headed people, like the Neanderthal race, have low foreheads, and wide-headed or round-headed people have high foreheads. There were people of all three kinds in the world before the Flood, and are in the world still, the round-headed being now in the majority.

Both the words "long-headed" and "highbrow" are used to denote more than usual mental capacity or wisdom; however, many people who use this term are not aware that the length of head is accompanied by lowness of brow, and height of brow by shortness of head (measured from front to back), so that it does not appear to matter much whether the same quantity of brain material is housed in a long, low case or in a high, short one.

Peculiarities of the Neanderthal Skeleton

The chief peculiarity of the Neanderthal skeleton is the great strength and solidity of build; this peculiarity escaped notice for a long time while attention was directed to finding similarity between it and the skeleton of the ape, an attempt now almost abandoned. In the hundred years during which the search for fossil remains has gone on, fossils of all the bones of the body of the Neanderthal Man from the head to the toes have been discovered, sufficient to make many complete skeletons. Each of the various bones and joints are of greater size and strength than those of modern man, and each of them has the peculiarities that belong to the human as against the animal skeleton. The Neanderthal man, therefore, though of only medium height, was built for greater strength and endurance than the modern man. The skeletons would indicate also that he was made for a longer life, for all the vital parts are better protected, and he had powerful jaws suitable for thorough mastication of his food, which is conducive to good health. At any rate, the powerfully-built Neanderthal skeletons, which are certainly antediluvian, while they are not sufficient of themselves to prove that man was capable of living for a thousand years, do prove that he was capable of living much longer than the average modern man.

The Neanderthal Man is still represented in illustrations in books and statues in museums as having a short neck with the head bent forward. This idea, however, has long ago been abandoned by the experts. It is clear from the skeletons that the spinal column was perfectly normal, and that the head fitted on it straight and not at an angle, as in the case of the apes.

The only two pecularities that are still criticized as showing some likeness to the ape are the orbital ridges over the eyes and the form of the chin.

The question of the brow ridges of the Neanderthal Man is discussed at length by Vialleton in *L'Origine des Etres Vivants* (pp. 277, 278) and by Leakey in *Adam's Ancestors* (pp. 164, 165). Both authors came to the same conclusion, namely, that the formation of brow ridges in man and ape is different. In the case of the ape, the prominent orbital ridge over the eyes is the result of the thickening of the edge of the bone over the eye; in the case of all men, including the Neanderthal Man, the brow ridges are the result of the uniting of two bones, one of which is joined to the nose and the other to the opposite side. In the case of ordinary men the brow ridge is scarcely noticeable; it is very pronounced in the case of present day Australian aborigines, and of the Neanderthal Man; it is also pronounced in the case of the Cro-Magnon Man.

The Neanderthal jawbone and chin are perfectly human and are easily distinguishable from those of the ape. The jawbone of the ape has what is known as a "simian shelf" on the inside, which served to strengthen it; this is absent in the case of the Neanderthal Man and of all men; instead of it, there is a thickening of the jawbone in front. The Neanderthal chin is receding, a little more so than the Negro chin, but quite different from the chin of the ape.

The Neanderthal Man was a skilled tool-maker and left abundant proofs of his skill everywhere his remains have been found; he knew the use of fire and buried his dead with ceremony.

Chapter 3

PRE-NEANDERTHAL HUMAN FOSSILS

When the fossil skull that gave the name to the prehistoric Neanderthal race was found in the valley or the Neander near Düsseldorf in 1856, it was at first represented as the skull of an ape-man in process of evolution with a brain capacity of only 1,270 cc, which is far below the average for modern man. This was proved to be a mistake; the actual brain capacity is 1,560 cc, which is well above the average. Subsequent discovery of other Neanderthal skulls associated with the instruments of the Old Stone Age showed the Neanderthal Man to be a skillful tool-maker, a clever hunter, and a man who buried his dead with ceremony.

As he had a few physical peculiarities, the chief of which were prominent brow ridges and a receding chin, evolutionists still cling on to the claim that he was a man in the process of evolution. But this position has to be abandoned, for in the present century fossils of men older than the Neanderthal which resemble modern man were discovered in different parts of Europe, and it is now generally admitted that the Neanderthal race has died out completely.

Pre-Neanderthal Fossils of Two Kinds

These pre-Neanderthal fossils are of two kinds: the first kind combines the traits of the Neanderthal Man with those of modern man; the second resembles modern man closely and has none of the characteristics of the Neanderthal Man. To the first kind belong: the Ehringsdorf fossils, the Saccapastore skulls and the Steinheim skull; to the second, the Swanscombe skull and the Fontéchevade skulls. In addition, fossils of the first kind combining the characteristics of the

Neanderthal Man and of modern man, have been discovered in Palestine.

The Ehringsdorf Fossils

In 1914 and 1916 two mandibles, one of an adult, the second of a child of about 10, were discovered at Ehringsdorf near Weimar in Germany. These mandibles had some of the characteristics of the Neanderthal mandible, but other characteristics that at the time were thought by Virchow to be more primitive. Doubts about these mandibles were cleared up by the discovery of the Ehringsdorf skull in 1925. This was found in a broken condition. When the pieces were put together, the skull was found to combine the characteristics of the Neanderthal Man and modern man. As it was found associated with the fossils of extinct animals of the warm climates, it is considered to belong to a race at least contemporary, if not more ancient than the Neanderthal Man.

The Saccopastore Skulls

Two fossil skulls were found at Saccopastore, three and a half kilometers from Rome, one in 1929 by Professor Sergi, the second in 1935 by Abbé Breuil. With them were found the fossil bones of the ancient elephant and the hippopotamus, extinct animals of warm climates. These, like the Ehringsdorf skull, combined the characteristics of the Neanderthal Man and those of modern man, and as they are associated with the fossils of extinct fauna of warm climates they are regarded as belonging to a race at least as old as the Neanderthal.

The Steinheim Skull

In 1933, a skull was found at Steinheim, in Würtemberg, and with it the fossils of fauna of both cold and warm climates. It was found 21 meters underground and is believed to have belonged to a young woman. Neanderthal traits are about equally blended with those of modern man.

The Swanscombe Skull

In 1935, Mr. Marston found a skull at Swanscombe, Kent, in the south of England, in the gravel of the Thames, eight meters below the soil.

Along with it were found the fossil bones of the ancient elephant and the rhinoceros of Merk, extinct fauna of the warm climates, and the stone instruments of the Acheulian (lower Paleolithic) Age.

The skull is believed to have belonged to a woman of about twenty. It is distinctly different from the Neanderthal skull and has practically all the characteristics of the skull of a modern woman. There can be no doubt about its antiquity, for besides the fact that it was found associated with the fauna of warm climates and the artifacts of the lower Paleolithic Age, it was tested by the flourine method, and was found to be of great antiquity. There was just one thing wanting in this remarkable discovery: the skull was not found at a stratified site where its position with regard to the fossils or artifacts of the Neanderthal Man would prove beyond doubt that it belonged to an earlier age. This want was supplied by the subsequent discovery of the stratified cave at Fontéchevade in the center of France, where two fossil skulls were found far below the artifacts of the Mousterian Age, which is the Age of the Neanderthal Man.

The Fontéchevade Fossils

The discovery of the Fontéchevade fossils, which was made by a French lady named Mlle. Henri-Martin in 1947, is of much greater importance for the information which it gives on the physical characteristics of the earliest man than the discovery of the Neanderthal skull, and yet, while everyone has heard of the Neanderthal Man, and pictures supposed to represent him are displayed in museums and inserted in school books, comparatively few have heard of the Fontéchevade Man, and no pictures of him as he appeared in life have been made. The reason is because the Fontéchevade skulls provide a strong, if not unanswerable argument against the theory of human evolution, and most of those who write on the origin of man at the present time are evolutionists who are naturally reluctant to give prominence to a discovery which disposes finally of all claim on behalf of the Neanderthal Man to represent a man in the process of evolution.

The Discovery of the Fontéchevade Fossils

The descriptions of this important discovery which are given in most books on paleontology are both meager and misleading. Some modern books, like Romer's *Man and the Vertebrates,* do not mention the discovery at all. The latest (1952) edition of *Les Hommes Fossiles* by Boule and Vallois gives a good description of these fossil skulls, but does not stress the importance of the find. The best account of this discovery is to be found in *The Testimony of the Spade* by G. Bibby (London, 1957); it is chiefly from this book that the following facts are taken:

The actual cave where the Fontéchevade fossils were found had been known for a long time. In it there was the routine stratified sequence of Magdalenian flints on top, Aurignacian (the Period after the *Hiatus*) next, then the sterile layer of clay without fossils or artifacts that was deposited by the Flood and marked the abandonment of the settlement, and finally, the Mousterian (Neanderthal) flints beneath it. Underneath these four strata was what appeared to be a limestone floor.

In 1937 Mlle. Henri-Martin discovered that this was not a floor at all, but a layer of limestone that had fallen from the roof of the cave before the Neanderthal Man occupied it. When this layer was removed, no less than twenty feet of debris were found beneath it, which contained the fossil remains of animals of warm climates, the stone instruments of the Lower Paleolithic Age and two human skulls. These latter were not found until 1947.

In *Les Hommes Fossiles,* Vallois says:

> The fact that the stalagmite floor which covered these deposits was found to be intact, guarantees the absolute authenticity of what was found beneath them. The fluorine test (which was

applied in 1951) confirms the antiquity of the fossils. . . .The skulls resemble those of men of our own time in form and dimensions. . .and have a brain capacity of about 1,450 cc . . .Viewed from above they have a pentagonal contour without any trace of the post-orbital contraction which is characteristic of the Neanderthal skull. (p. 197).

This latter statement of Vallois disposes effectively of the argument for the evolution of the human skull found in most books, from the so-called primitive form of the Neanderthal Man, which is long, low and narrow, to the pentagonal form of modern man, which is short (measured from front to back), high and broad. The form of the Fontéchevade skulls corresponds with the commonest form of the skull of modern man.

The Fontéchevade cave is the best example of a stratified cave that we have in Europe. It shows the fossils of artifacts of the various families or races in the order in which they came to Europe. The earliest (i.e. those of the Fontéchevade Man) resembled modern man very closely; next came the Neanderthal Man with his marked peculiarities; above him was the flood deposit of earth, probably laid down by the Deluge, containing neither fossils nor artifacts; above that was the post-*hiatus* Aurignacian stratum, and finally the stratum of the Magdalenian hunter who brought the Old Stone Age to a close.

Palestine

France and Germany were the first countries to receive the attention of the paleontologists. The periods into which the Old Stone Age was divided and subdivided were named almost exclusively after the places in France where the various types of stone instruments were found. The Chellean (also called the Abbevillian) and Acheulian were named after places in the Somme valley in the north of France; the Tayacian, the Mousterian, the Aurignacian, the Solutrian and Magdalenian, after places in the center and south of France; the Clactonian after Clacton-on-Sea in the south of England. It was not suspected at the time that these names were adopted, that stone instruments of similar kinds would be found all over the Middle East, where they were first manufactured, and, strange to say, no one at the time dreamt that Palestine would be found to be one of the very oldest centers of pre-Flood civilization in the world.

The instruments of the very earliest Old Stone Age—the Chellean and Acheulian—were found in the open and in many places in Palestine, but as the actual flint shops in which those were made are to be seen in Egypt along the upper reaches of the Nile and as far down as Tanganyika, it is probable that these ancient stone instruments had their origin in Northern Africa and were brought from there by the hunters on their way to Palestine on the East and to Europe on the West. These stone instruments were suited for the nomadic hunters that roamed over both Europe and Palestine for thousands of years. The earliest human fixed settlements, where houses were built and agriculture practiced, are to be found in the rich alluvial valleys of Mesopotamia, Syria and Palestine, and these have the stone instruments suited for agriculture and domestic uses.

The Human Fossils of the Caves In Galilee

BEFORE THE DELUGE

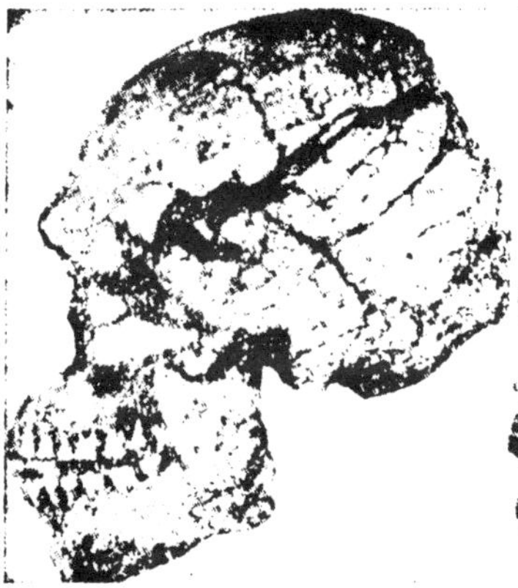

Skull of a mixed race found in Palestine. It is not as long as the Neanderthal skull, and the brow ridges are not so prominent.

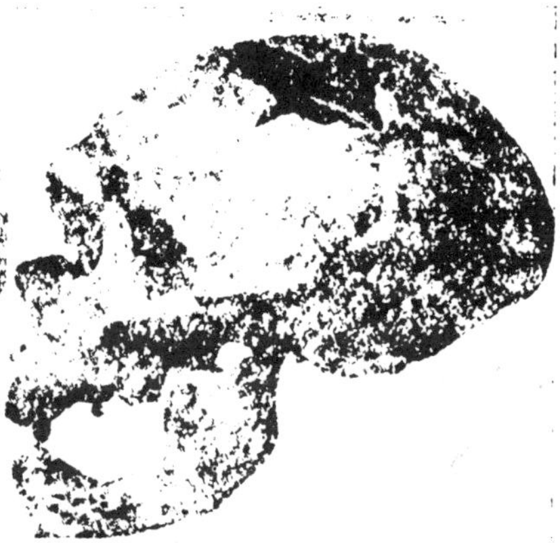

Skull of a Neanderthal Man found at Chapelle aux Saints in France. Brain capacity 1,625 cc. It is long-headed, has large brain capacity and prominent brow ridges.

The first stratified cave discovered in Palestine is situated at Mugharet-el-Zuttiyeh to the northeast of the Sea of Tiberias. The discovery was made in 1925 by an Anglo-American party who explored the caves of Galilee and of Mount Carmel, while M. Neuville of France carried out his investigations of the caves around Bethlehem and Nazareth.

In the cave of Mugharet-el-Zuttiyeh were found the broken pieces of a skull which, when put together, showed all the peculiarities of the Neanderthal skull. There were two strata in this cave; the upper one contained the stone instruments of the Mousterian (Neanderthal) period, while the lower one contained those of the earlier Acheulian period.

The Mount Carmel Fossils

Still more important discoveries were made in 1931 and 1932 by Miss Garrod and Mr. T. D. McGowan of the Anglo-American party, and in 1934 and 1935 by MM. Neuville and Stekelis of the French party.

At Mount Carmel two caves were discovered which contained human skulls that combined the characteristics of the Neanderthal and modern man, and with them were found the stone instruments of the Mousterian, Acheulian and Tayacian (pre-*hiatus*) Ages. In the first of these caves, called El Taboun, were found the complete skeleton of a woman, the mandible and thigh-bone of a man and no less than 10 strata which contained the stone instruments of the Lower Palaeolithic Age, i.e., the stone instruments of the period before the *hiatus* or Deluge. On the very top were found the artifacts of the Bronze Age, showing that the cave had not been inhabited again for a thousand years or more after the Mousterian Period when the Neanderthal Man disappeared. This is a most valuable confirmation of the fact of the existence and the extent of the *hiatus*.

In the second cave at Mount Carmel, called Mugharet-es-Soukhoul, were found the fossil remains of 10 individuals, men, women and children, associated with the stone instruments of the pre-*hiatus* (Levalloisian and Mousterian) Periods.

As in the case of the first Carmel cave, this one was also abandoned for a long time after the *hiatus*.

The skulls of these 10 individuals, while having some of the characteristics of the Neanderthal Man, resemble modern man much more closely.

The Cave at Nazareth

In a cave near Nazareth, called Djebel Kafzeh, skeletons whole or partial of five individuals were found. The most of these fossils were fragmentary, but among them was one skull well-preserved with a brain capacity of 1,560 cc, which is well above the average of modern man. Like the Mount Carmel skulls, it combines the characteristics of the Neanderthal Man and modern man.

Various explanations have been given for the mingling of the characteristics of two different races in these Carmel and Nazareth fossils, but the most likely explanation appears to be that they are the result of intermarriage between the Neanderthal race and the race represented by the Fontéchevade skulls. We have definite information in the Bible of the intermarriage between the descendants of Cain and those of Seth during the period before the Flood. As these Carmel and Nazareth fossils of a mixed race are found in the stratum just before the end of the Mousterian Age when the *hiatus* or Deluge occurs, they can be regarded as a confirmation of the statement in the Bible, and a proof that Palestine was covered by the waters of the Deluge. (See *Les Hommes Fossiles,* 1952 ed., pp. 392-396).

Further Discoveries in Palestine—the Natufians

The fossils and artifacts of a race to which the name Natufian has been given were discovered in the vicinity of both Carmel and Bethlehem. Between 1928 and 1931, Miss Garrod of the American party unearthed the fossil remains of 45 individuals in the cave of Shukbah, and 87 in the cave of Mugharet-el-Wad in the vicinity of Carmel, and in 1931

M. Neuville of the French party found the fossils of six or seven individuals at Erq el Ahmar to the south of Bethlehem.

Instead of the stone instruments used by the nomadic hunters of the Carmel and Nazareth caves, which were of the Egyptian type, these had the stone instruments suited to agricultural and domestic purposes. These stone instruments were not polished like the Neolithic instruments, and the fact that they were small in size may be due to the smallness of the blocks of flint found in Palestine. The Natufians were of rather small stature; they cannot be identified with any living race, but in general they resembled the Fontéchevade Man. They practiced agriculture and kept domestic animals. Their stone instruments closely resembled those dug up in the excavations of the lower strata of the city of Jericho.

It is at least possible that these Natufians were contemporary with the later dwellers in the Carmel caves, who were hunters from Egypt with the African stone instruments, while the Natufians belonged to the settled population of Palestine and used the stone instruments suited for agriculture which were manufactured in Palestine. When those writers who are evolutionists hear of agricultural instruments being found at any ancient site they conclude immediately that they belong to the Neolithic Age. For instance, W. F. Albright in *From the Stone Age to Christianity* states: "The true Neolithic was first discovered by L. Garstang in his excavation of the lowest occupied levels of Jericho in 1935-36." Now the Neolithic stone instruments are made by friction and are therefore polished. The stone instruments found in the lower strata at Jericho were made in the same manner as those of the Old Stone Age, i.e., by flaking, and were not polished. Garstang, who was not an authority on the instruments of the Old Stone Age, refers to them as Neolithic, but in the photographs which he gives of them in *The Story of Jericho* (facing p. 51) they look like the instruments of the Old Stone Age. (See *The Story of Jericho* by Garstang and *The Archaeology of Palestine* by W. F. Albright).

Conclusions To Be Drawn From the Existence of Pre-Neanderthal Human Fossils which Resemble Modern Man

Readers who still believe that paleontology furnishes any solid argument for the organic evolution of men would do well to read pages 199 and 200 of *Les Hommes Fossiles* by Boule and Vallois (1952 edition). The conclusion arrived at by these two authorities is: 1) that as the discovery of pre-Neanderthal skulls is of comparatively recent dates (1925 to 1947), and as they are certainly as old as the Neanderthal fossils, conclusions previously arrived at about the Neanderthal fossils must be revised; 2) that as these pre-Neanderthal skulls have none of the peculiarities of the Neanderthal skulls, such as the very pronounced brow ridges, but resemble closely the skulls of modern man, the peculiarities of the Neanderthal skulls must be regarded as representing a development in a particular race or family. The large eye-sockets and prominent brow ridges of the Neanderthal Man, which are found in a lesser degree in the present Australian aborigines, are explained by some authorities as due to the life of a hunter in the open air.

A final conclusion is that as it is now generally admitted that the Neanderthal race became extinct at or before the time of the *hiatus* or Flood, and as men with skulls of modern form existed before them and along with them, the argument from the peculiarities of the Neanderthal skull that was formerly used as evidence of the evolution of the human skull collapses completely.

We have dealt with all human fossils so far discovered except the fossils of the Piltdown, Peking and Java Men, and the fossils of the *Australopithecus Africanus* class, and have seen that there is now no controversy whatever about the fossils so far mentioned, and that it is now admitted that they represented men and women of good average brain capacity who left behind them undoubted proofs of high intelligence and of a civilization in keeping with the times in which they lived.

We shall now consider the two remaining classes, and we shall see that there is strong evidence of fraud and deception in the cases of the Piltdown Man, the Peking Man and the Java Man; and that the fossil remains of the *Australopithecus Africanus* class are considered by the best authorities to be merely fossils of great apes, and that the claim for a brain capacity greater than that of the great apes—a maximum of 640 cc—is unfounded.

Chapter 4

THE PILTDOWN MAN

That the Piltdown Man was a forgery is now universally accepted both by those who support and those who reject the theory of evolution. In fact, the incontrovertible evidence that all the proofs given for the primitive character of the human fossils alleged to have been found at Piltdown were a series of forgeries were furnished by well-known propagandists for the evolutionary theory. It had long been an open secret among prominent evolutionists that there was no Piltdown Man in the sense claimed, for there were several people in the Piltdown district, among whom was Captain Guy St. Barbe, who had evidence that the whole case was a forgery.

The news of the discovery of the Piltdown Man fossils was announced in the *Manchester Guardian,* and on December 18, 1912, Arthur Smith Woodward, the keeper of the British Museum and Charles Dawson of Piltdown gave a detailed account of the alleged fossils to a crowded house at a lecture room of the Geographical Society of Burlington.

The fossils consisted of a human skull, the face of which was missing, a mandible in all respects like that of an ape, except that the teeth were worn in the same manner as the human teeth. The condyle or joint was broken off and a canine tooth was missing, but this was found a year later by Teilhard de Chardin, a French Jesuit student who was studying at Hastings. Primitive flint tools, a piece of carved ivory and eighteen fossil bones of various animals were also produced. On account of the mandible, which had all the characteristics of the ape mandible, including the "simian shelf," the age of the skull was estimated at 500,000 years. The Piltdown Man was accepted generally in England as a "Missing Link," but some prominent foreign authorities on

Paleontology such as Marcellin Boule of France and Fairfield Osborn of America refused to accept it on the grounds that a purely human skull and a purely ape jawbone were an impossible combination.

In 1915, fossils of another alleged ape-man, including part of the brain-case and the molar teeth of an ape, were discovered at Sheffield Park, two miles from Piltdown, and were accepted by Arthur Smith Woodward for the British Museum. This silenced all opposition. Catholic apologists such as the late Archbishop Sheehan, who rejected the theory of human evolution, tried to explain away the peculiarities of the mandible as well as they could, but they did not attempt to deny the alleged facts. Dawson died in 1916, but the Piltdown skull continued for 40 years to do propaganda work and to influence opinion all over the world in favor of the theory of human evolution. The Piltdown skull was also used as an argument for polygenesis, or the existence of more than one ancestor for the human race.

When the doubts about the genuineness of the Piltdown fossils began to be voiced, an attempt was made to settle them by applying the fluorine test to the fossils. The fluorine method of testing fossils was discovered by a French scientist in 1892. It is based on the fact that bones of living organisms contain no fluorine, but when they are buried in the ground they absorb fluorine from the damp soil at a regular rate, and the amount of fluorine that they absorb continues to increase indefinitely. Hence, the more fluorine fossils contain, the greater their geological age. When the test was applied to the Piltdown skull and the ape-like mandible by Messrs. Oakely and Hoskins, they claimed that it showed that both skull and mandible contained the same proportion of fluorine and that they were therefore of the same age, but that the age, instead of being 500,000 years, as had been stated, was only 50,000 years. This test by a modern method should have settled all doubts, but it did not, because the evidence for the forgery was too strong and too widely known, and there was serious danger that it would be published.

It was decided therefore to submit the fossils to a second

test, the result of which was known in advance, and then to discard them.

The second test was carried out by J. S. Weiner, K. P. Oakley and W. E. Le Gros Clark, all three of whom were supporters of the human evolution theory. The results of their tests were published in *The Bulletin of the British Museum* (Vol. II No. 3, 1953).

Besides the fluorine test, the radio-carbon test also was applied to the various fossils. The radio-carbon method of testing was invented by Dr. Libby of the United States, and is based on the fact that all living organisms constantly absorb radio-carbon and radiate it at the same rate, so that the amount in the system remains constant as long as the organisms are living, but when they die, absorption of radio-carbon ceases, and the radiation continues at a constantly decreasing rate. A given quantity of radio-carbon diminishes by half in a period of about 5,570 years. It is possible to judge with approximate accuracy the date of organic remains by measuring the rate at which the radio-carbon disintegrates. When the fluorine and the radio-carbon tests were applied to the Piltdown skull and mandible, the result of both tests was the same: that the mandible contained about the same percentage of fluorine and radio-carbon respectively as a fresh specimen, while the skull contained a high percentage of fluorine and low percentage of radio-carbon, both of which facts proved that it was a genuine fossil of considerable age.

These findings caused great surprise abroad and were questioned by Weinert, a German expert, and by some others. Representatives of various scientific bodies from London, Oxford and other places were called in, and the skull and mandible and all the other fossils found at Piltdown were again examined. The results of this third examination not only confirmed the findings of the second tests, but demonstrated that the fraud had been much more extensive than had been thought at first. The experts from the universities and other scientific centers agreed unanimously that the mandible belonged to an ape that had been dead for only a few years, while the skull was a fossil belonging to the Neolithic age, that is, only a few thousand years old. It was agreed also by them that the teeth of the mandible had been filed by a modern instrument to make them look like human teeth; that the condyle or joint of the mandible had recently been broken so that it would not appear that it did not belong to the skull; that the canine tooth had been filed in order to make it fit; that the fresh mandible and teeth of the ape had been stained to make them look like ancient specimens; that the various other fossils and ancient flints were a heterogeneous collection that had come from various places in England and on the Continent, but which could have been purchased in London, or even at Hastings. Readers who wish to have further details about the Piltdown case will find them in *The Bulletin of the British Museum,* 1953, or *The Piltdown Forgery* by J. S. Weiner (London 1955) or in *The Piltdown Fantasy* by Francis Vere of Piltdown (London, 1955), or in *Lessons of Piltdown,* also by Francis Vere (London, 1959), in which he gives evidence to show that Charles Dawson was not implicated in the forgery.

Chapter 5

THE PEKING MAN—PART I

The case of the Peking Man fossils is discussed in greater detail here than that of the other fossils, firstly, because no complete account of the case has yet been published, for the reason that full information on the facts of the case was not available until recently, and secondly, because now that the Piltdown Man fossils and the fossils of the Australopithecinae (of South Africa) have been rejected by the experts, the Peking Man fossils remain as the chief argument from Paleontology for the evolution of man.

Readers who are not interested in the details given in the second part of this chapter may pass on to the conclusions given at the end of it.

In the domain of Paleontology, various candidates for the Missing Link have been put forward during the past century, but they had to be discarded one after the other for various reasons. The Neanderthal Men were found to have a larger average brain capacity than the modern man; they were skilled hunters, they manufactured tools, buried their dead with ceremony and finally disappeared altogether at the time of the *hiatus* (or Deluge). (See *Les Hommes Fossiles,* Boule & Vallois, Paris 1952, p. 268). The Piltdown Man went down in disgrace; the Australopithecinae or African Ape-Men put forward by Drs. Dart, Broom and Robinson were shown to be just great apes. (See *Evolution as a Process,* chapter by Sir S. Zuckerman, pp. 300-349); the original Java Man has been rejected by such authorities as Marcellin Boule; and Dr. Dubois, who found the fossil of the skull, admitted before his death that it was part of the skull of a gibbon. (See *Les Hommes Fossiles* by Boule and Vallois, pp. 111-132). Dr. Von

Königswald made an attempt to re-open the case. In that attempt he used the same tactics as those employed in the first attempt: he produced fossil skulls so mutilated that the brain capacity could not be estimated, and claimed that they were similar to the portion of fossil skull produced by Dr. Dubois, forgetting that the fossil produced by Dr. Dubois was pronounced by experts such as Boule to be that of a gibbon.

The fossils of the Peking Man are the only ones that have the support of great names. Hence they are used by advocates of the theory of evolution to support their contention. Dr. Frederick Zeuner, in his standard work, *Dating the Past* (Methuen, 1952), uses them as evidence of the antiquity of man and says that they date back 500,000 years. (See p. 274). They are given in schoolbooks of several countries as proofs of the evolution of man; statues or pictures of the supposed ape-man of Peking are found in museums, such as the Natural History Museum of London, which is much visited by foreign visitors to London. Accounts of the Peking Man, representing him as an ape-man or as a man in the process of evolution, are found in books by prominent Catholic writers who support the theory of evolution, such as Fr. Marcozzi S.J. of the Gregorian University, Rome (in *L'Uomo Nello Spazio E Nel Tempo,* 1953), Fr. Espondaburu S.J. of Comillas University, Spain (in *Hacia el Origen del Hombre,* 1956) and Dr. Vanderbroeck of Louvain University (in *God, Man and the Universe* pp. 123-124).

When so-called Catholic experts boldly claim that the Peking Man represents man in the process of evolution, other Catholic writers who protest that they are ignorant of the merits of the case (such as Fr. Hauret in *Origines de l'Univers et de l'Homme,* p. 72 and Fr. Bruce Vawter in *A Path Through Genesis,* p. 51) think themselves justified in informing their readers that the animal origin of man has been established by scientists, "at least as a working hypothesis."

Fortunately there is available on the case of the Peking Man a mass of evidence that makes possible a solution quite as definite as that found for the Piltdown Man, and which proves that the Sinanthropus or Peking Man, in the sense of being a man in the process of evolution, is just another forgery.

The present writer was in China all the time that the excavation at Choukoutien was being carried out, all during the Japanese occupation, and long after the departure of the Japanese. Though he has not gone to Peking to make personal investigation, he has had the advantage of seeing the accounts published in the Chinese papers, native and foreign, which convinced him that the whole facts of the case had not been given to the public and that no "missing link" had been found. Much the same views were expressed in a manual of Christian Doctrine published by the Jesuit Fathers at Hong Kong. This manual had a chapter on the origin of man and expressed the view that no "missing link" had been found at Choukoutien.

Before giving in chronological order the history of the case, we shall first call attention to certain important facts which have either been concealed from the public or grossly misrepresented. 1) Skulls whole or partial to the number of about 30, 11 mandibles and 147 teeth of the so-called Sinanthropus were found in the course of the excavations at Choukoutien. *All these have disappeared completely;* instead of them there are a few casts or models alleged to have been made from them. In an article entitled "New Light on the Peking Man" published in 1954 by Dr. Pei (who has been in charge of the men at Choukoutien since 1926) in the Peking periodical, *China Reconstructs,* he tells us that (under communist rule), three rooms in which the objects found at Choukoutien are on display have been opened to the public. In the first room are the *casts or models* of a few of the skulls of Sinanthropus (made by Dr. Black and Dr. Weidenreich) and a selection of the stone instruments found. In the second room are the *fossil remains* of the various animals. In the third room is a collection of stone instruments, etc., found in other parts of China. *According to Dr. Pei, therefore, everything found at Choukoutien has been preserved, including the casts of the skulls, except the fossil remains of Sinanthropus.*

He says nothing about why these fossils disappeared. H. Vallois, in the 1952 edition of *Les Hommes Fossiles* (by Boule and Vallois), tells us that the Japanese seized the boxes containing the fossils of Sinanthropus (footnote p. 136); Dr. Vanderbroeck in his chapter in *God, Man, and the Universe* (p. 124) says: "All the invaluable material gathered at Choukoutien disappeared when that part of China was occupied by the Japanese." Neither of these accounts is true. The facts are that the work of excavation was carried on without hindrance during the Japanese occupation. Dr. Weidenreich, who was the representative of the Rockefeller Foundation, carried on the work of excavation during the Japanese occupation from 1937 (when the Japanese occupied Peking) until 1940, when he went to America. He made no complaints about Japanese interference. On the contrary, in 1943 after his return to America, he wrote an article on the skulls found at Choukoutien in 1934 and it was published in *Palaeontologia Sinica,* which means that the article passed through the hands of Japanese and that the fossil skulls were still preserved in 1943. He made reference to these skulls again in 1945 in a series of lectures which he gave at the University of California and which were published under the title, *Apes, Giants and Men.* Weidenreich therefore believed that the skulls were still preserved in 1945 at the time of the surrender of the Japanese.

The story circulated in China and outside it that the Japanese seized the fossils after their surrender is evidently false, because after their surrender the Japanese were simply prisoners of war. They could not have brought them to Japan, because all Japanese, both soldiers and civilians, were evacuated from China and were not allowed to take anything with them.

Dr. Pei, who had carried on the work under the Japanese after the departure of Dr. Weidenreich, had very good reason to destroy the fossils, for the models supposed to have been made from them did not correspond with the description of the skulls published by three independent eye-witnesses: Dr. Marcellin Boule, Fr. Teilhard de Chardin and Abbé Breuil.

The skulls were therefore destroyed before the Chinese Government returned to Peking in order to remove the evidence of fraud on a large scale. It is to be noted that it was under the Communist Government that Dr. Pei resumed the work of excavation which he describes in his article published in 1954 in *China Reconstructs.* It is also to be noted that while, during the later excavations, he found fossils of animals, roughly hewn stones, etc., he found no more tell-tale skulls of Sinanthropus. 2) The second fact that was concealed from the public is the magnitude of the industry carried on at Choukoutien. It was admitted that a large number of roughly-hewn stones, some instruments of bone, and some heaps of ashes were found, but from the accounts published (with the exception of the account in *La Pensée Catholique,* of 1948), no reader could guess what went on at Choukoutien in former times.

The following are the facts: In ancient times (but not very ancient) a large-scale industry of quarrying limestone and burning lime was carred on at Choukoutien about 50 kilometers from Peking. This quarrying was carried on at two levels on a front of about 200 meters, and to a depth of about 50 meters into the hill. The limestone hill was undermined, with the result that there was a landslide. The top of the hill slid down and buried everything beneath at both levels under thousands of tons of stone.

With the aid of large grants from the Rockefeller Foundation, the whole of the fallen stone of the upper level and part of the lower level was cleared away. On the upper level was found an enormous heap of ashes and debris 100 meters long, 30 meters wide and seven meters high, tightly compressed under the great weight of stone. On the lower level the heap of ashes was 12 meters high, and the full extent is not known, because the excavation at the lower level was not finished. It was probably larger than the heap at the higher level.

At the bottom of the debris at both levels were found thousands of quartz stones that had been brought from a distance to construct the lime-kilns. Two thousand of such stones were found in a section of the lower level; the number found in the upper level was so large that it went beyond counting. These stones had a layer of soot on one side.

It was in these heaps of ashes and débris that the skulls of the so-called Sinanthropus were found. Now, stones brought from a distance and dressed for building found beside a limestone quarry, and enormous heaps of ashes can mean only one thing, namely, that lime-burning was carried on. Lime-burning on the scale carried on at Choukoutien means the building of houses on a considerable scale. It may be presumed then that the lime-burning was for the ancient city of Cambaluc on the site of the present city of Peking.

It may be regarded as certain that the 30 broken skulls found among the ashes and débris were the skulls of baboons and macaques (large monkeys), fossil remains of which were found in great numbers in the vicinity of Choukoutien. (See *Apes, Giants and Men,* p. 19). Three human skulls of modern type and skeletal remains of six human beings (afterwards increased to 10), were reported to have been found by Dr. Pei in 1934. This information was published in France in an article in *Revue des Questions Sc.* of the same year by Fr. Teilhard de Chardin. It was not released officially for publication for five years (until 1939) by Drs. Pei and Weidenreich, who were in charge of the excavations after the death of Dr. Black. It was denied by Fr. T. de Chardin in an article in *Études* in 1937, but was confirmed by Dr. Weidenreich in an article in *Palaeontologia Sinica* in 1939, who says that skeletal remains of 10 human beings (including the three skulls of adults) had been found. He repeated this information in his lectures to the students of the University of California in 1945. However, the fact remains that both he and Dr. Pei concealed the information for five years.

Very few of the public who have heard of Sinanthropus are aware that fossil remains of 10 human individuals of modern type have been found at the exact same site as the skulls of Sinanthropus. Some books that deal with Sinanthropus make no reference at all to these human fossils; that is true of Romer's book entitled *Man and the Vertebrates*. Other books on human fossils or on the origin of man put the account of these fossils in a different part of the book from that dealing with Sinanthropus and represent them as belonging to a later date. This is true of *Les Hommes Fossiles,* 1952 edition by Vallois, which devotes 17 pages (133-150) to Sinanthropus, but only gives a passing reference to these fossils of real men near the end of the book (p. 405). The same is true of the recent Spanish book by Fr. Andérez S.J., which was altered and finished by Fr. Espondaburu S.J., and published under the title *Hacia el Origen del Hombre.* A passing reference is made on page 78 to these human fossils found at Choukoutien—and this is probably the work of Fr. Andérez, but in the detailed 18-page account of Sinanthropus (pp. 124-142), no reference whatever is made to them, so that a reader would conclude that they had no bearing on the case.

There is no justification for representing these human fossils as belonging to a later date than the skulls of Sinanthropus, for both were found buried under the same landslide that killed the human beings and covered the ashes and debris in which the skulls of Sinanthropus (i.e., the skulls of baboons and macaques) were found. Weidenreich, who was in charge of the excavations after the death of Dr. Black, denied that these human fossils were found in a cave, as is alleged by some.

History of the Case of the Peking Man

The popular account of the discovery of Sinanthropus, or the Peking Man, is that some Chinese workmen who were engaged in quarrying limestone at Choukoutien discovered what they believed to be the opening of a natural cave, inside which they found a skull and some bones of animals. This account representing the Sinanthropus as a cave-dweller who hunted animals for his food is still current and is still, with some additions such as that the primitive creature left traces of fire, the popular account.

The credit, or responsibility, for directing the attention of explorers to Choukoutien appears to belong to Fr. Lincent, S.J., director of the Geological Survey of China. The article in *La Pensée Catholique* (Paris, 1948) already referred to tells us that as early as 1912 Fr. Lincent S.J. obtained several grants of 20,000 francs from France for the purpose of exploring the site at Choukoutien. However, the official version of the story of the Peking Man begins the account at 1921 when Dr. Anderson, an official of the Geological Survey which was being made for the Chinese Government, dug up a lump of quartz which had evidently been brought from a distance because no quartz was found in the district. Dr. Anderson asked Dr. Zdansky, an Austrian Professor of the University of Upsala, who happened to be at Peking, to continue the excavation at Choukoutien, and he, in 1922, found two isolated molar teeth, but no account of them was published until 1926. In 1926, Dr. Anderson left China and in the same year the Geological Survey Service, then under Dr. Wang, and the Union Medical College of Peking, which was financed by the Rockefeller Foundation, joined hands to carry out the excavation. Dr. Davidson Black, Professor of Anatomy in the Medical College at Peking, represented the Rockefeller Foundation and obtained from the United States a yearly grant of $20,000.

The field operations were put in charge, first of Drs. Li and Bochlin, but in 1927 Drs. Young and Pei took their place. After a couple of years Dr. Pei alone superintended the excavations and is still carrying on work under the communist government. Fr. Teilhard de Chardin, S.J. was an unofficial observer at Peking.

A yearly grant of $20,000 in China of 1926 was a big sum of money, for then one United States dollar would be sufficient to pay the daily wages of at least four workmen. Besides, the limestone extracted was in great demand, and if sold, as it probably was, the proceeds alone should have been sufficient to pay the workmen. The work went on from 1926 until 1941 (even during the Japanese occupation). In 1941 the United States entered the war, and the representative of the Rockefeller Institution at the time, Dr. Weidenreich, left. A yearly grant of $20,000 from 1926 to 1941 amounted to the sum of $300,000, the present equivalent of £100,000. (See *Hacia el Origen del Hombre,* p. 127, and *Les Hommes Fossiles,* 1952 ed., p. 133).

In 1927 Dr. Bohlin, who with Dr. Li was in charge of the field operations, found another isolated molar tooth and handed it over to Dr. Black at Peking, whose function it was to give the official description of the fossils found.

In the same year, 1927, Dr. Black published an account of

the tooth in *Palaeontologia Sinica* at Peking in an article entitled, "On a Lower Hominid Tooth from the Choukoutien Deposit." (Let the reader note here that the word "hominid" corresponds to nothing that actually exists; it is merely a part of the jargon used by those who hold that man was evolved from an animal). In this article the word *Sinanthropus* was used for the first time. Dr. Black claimed that in this tooth he had proof that a primitive creature, in some respects resembling a man, existed in former times in the locality. The claim was not so mad as it might appear, for in the first place the reception given to the Java Man represented by only the top of the ape-like skull, and to the Piltdown Man with its human skull and ape jawbone, showed that there was a large section of the public that would welcome any excuse for the belief that man was not created by God; and in the second place, fossils of two species of large monkeys were found in abundance in the district. Dr. Weidenreich, who succeeded Dr. Black as representative of the Rockefeller Foundation, in *Apes, Giants and Man,* gives us the following information on that subject:

> In Choukoutien, skeletons of macaques (large monkeys) and baboons had been found in the same district that yielded the Peking Man; these monkeys do not differ from the living forms except for their greater size. (p. 19).

The chief interest in this publication about a single tooth lies in the fact that Dr. Black made it plain that he was going to produce a new species of ape-man and that he was quite confident that the public that he had in view would not be too exacting in demanding proofs.

Dr. Black was right in his forecast, for accounts of the Peking Man under his new name *Sinanthropus* began to appear in the daily press all over the world. We find an example of this in *The Daily Telegraph* (July 20, 1929) in which it was stated that 10 fossil skeletons had been found in the cave at Choukoutien which dated back a million years, and that Elliot Smith had said that it was a most important discovery because it would help to interpret the Piltdown Man!

New Version of Sinanthropus

The first version, then, represented Sinanthropus as the most primitive "hominid" yet discovered, who was just able to make rough instruments of stone, but did not know the use of fire. (See *L'Apparition de l'Homme* by Fr. T. de Chardin, p. 90). This version was amended so as to make Sinanthropus leave faint traces of fire.

However, as the work of excavation proceeded, large heaps of ashes were found, and a number of quartz stones that had to be brought from a distance, which showed that an industry on a considerable scale had been carried on. A new edition of Sinanthropus had to be produced to suit the altered circumstances. Broken pieces of skull were alleged to have been found in the summer of 1928, and a preliminary report of the fact was published by Dr. Black in *The Bulletin of the Geological Society*, Peking, of 1929. Finally a skullcap,[1] a little more complete than the one produced by Dr. Dubois to represent the Java Man, but still only a skullcap, was found at the bottom of a great heap of ashes on the lower level at Choukoutien. This skullcap was selected to represent the official Sinanthropus. Dr. Black promised a detailed description giving measurements, brain capacity, etc., but this official description making the Sinanthropus creature more like man than ape, with a brain capacity more than twice that of a monkey, did not appear until 1931, two years later.

Fr. Teilhard de Chardin, however, was eager to give the people of France an account of the new Sinanthropus as soon as possible, and wrote an article about him dated April, 1930 which was published in the July issue of *Revue des Questions Scientifiques*, Paris, 1930. This article was republished in the collection of Fr. T. de Chardin's articles published in 1956 by an international committee of evolutionists. It contains a minute description of the skullcap found at the bottom of ashes and debris in 1929 and selected to represent Sinanthropus No. 2.

---

1. The fossil when found appears to have been a complete skull and to have contained the braincase.

At the time of writing the earth or ashes had not yet been cleared out of the interior of the skull.

PEKING MAN
Artificial model by Dr. Black

JAVA MAN
Skull-cap found by Dr. Dubois

These are pictures of the skull-caps of the Peking Man and the Java Man. In each case the lower part of the skull has been removed so that the brain capacity claimed cannot be checked. The evidence given on this page shows that the skull of the Peking creature (which was probably a monkey) contained the braincase when it was found, and that the brain capacity was small, probably not more than 400 cc. The above picture of the Peking skull-cap does not correspond with the descriptions given by Fr. Teilhard de Chardin.

The Java skull-cap is probably the skull-cap of a gibbon.

Fr. Teilhard de Chardin begins his description by referring to the fossil in question as a skull *(crane),* not as a skull-cap *(callotte),* as it was afterwards represented. On page 92 of *L'Apparition de l'Homme* he says:

> The skull (crane) of Sinanthropus is of great scientific value. The front portion of this magnificent fossil (the jawbone and the face below the eye-sockets), is missing *but the whole cerebral part is admirably preserved* and in no way deformed, except the region round the occiput, which is damaged.

> At the time of writing, the earth filling the cerebral cavity has not been cleared out so that neither the cerebral capacity, *which is probably small because of the relatively small dimensions of the skull* and the considerable thickness of the bone walls, nor the details of the inner form of the skull are yet known. The exterior of the skull has been cleared of foreign matter so that a first impression of the morphological peculiarities of the skull can be given.

Fr. Teilhard de Chardin then asks the question whether the skull of Sinanthropus resembles the skull of the Neanderthal Man or that of the Java Man, and decides that it resembles the Java Man. He then says:

> This, however, is only a rough guess. According as a closer study of the anatomical details became possible, Dr. Black perceived that Sinanthropus presented a series of cranial peculiarities which assign him a place apart among all the known "hominids" (ape-men). We may cite as an example the curious development of the tympanal bone which forms under the external orifice of the ear a large double apophysis, the equivalent of which exists only in the large apes. We might mention also the important disposition of the cranial architecture, in virtue of which the maximum width of the cerebral case, instead of being situated at the level of the parietal bone, about halfway up the head (as in man), is found much lower down (as in apes). Looked at from behind the top of the skull of Sinanthropus is of grossly triangular shape like that of monkeys, rather than oval-shaped, as in man.

That is Fr. T. de Chardin's account of Dr. Black's first impressions of the skull. He gives his own impressions in *Anthropologie,* 1931. They are as follows:

> Sinanthropus manifestly resembles the great apes closely: by the length of the face and the bony projections over the eye-sockets; by the strength of the post-orbital construction; by the receding disposition of the forehead; by the triangular aspect of the contour of the skull, which in man is of elliptical shape; finally by the tympanal bone which, instead of being reduced and contracted at the level of the external cavity, opens out and forms two large singular growths above the orifice of the ear.

This skull of Sinanthropus as here described had no resemblance to the skull of the Neanderthal Man or of any other man. It was the skull of a baboon or monkey, for no fossils of apes have been found in China.

The Views of Abbé Breuil

In 1930, the year before he wrote this 1931 article (which was written in France), Fr. Teilhard de Chardin went to France bearing an invitation to Abbé Breuil (a well-known authority on the industry of the Old Stone Age, and an advocate of the theory of evolution) to come out to China. Abbé Breuil accepted the invitation and visited both Peking, where the fossils were kept, and Choukoutien, where the work of excavation was going on. In all he remained 19 days.

On his return to France he wrote a seventeen-page article which was published in the March issue of *Anthropologie,* 1932. It gives the first glimpse of the magnitude of the industry carried on at Choukoutien; in a section on the lower level of 132 square meters, 12 meters deep, no less than 2,000 roughly shaped stones were found at the botom of a heap of ashes and debris which contained the skulls of Sinanthropus and the bones of about 100 different animals.

He next gives us a brief description of the skulls in which he says that they bore no resemblance to any human skulls so far found, and then he raises the question whether the beings that were represented by these animal-like skulls could have been responsible for the large-scale industry, as Fr. Teilhard de Chardin and Dr. Black contended. In answering that question he avoided directly contradicting Fr. Teilhard de Chardin and Dr. Black, who had invited him to come out to China, but limited himself to saying that the objections that could be raised against such a theory were very strong, if not unanswerable.

As to the age of the industry, Abbé Breuil merely stated that the industry bore no resemblance to that of the Old Stone Age and therefore could not be used as an argument for the great antiquity of Sinanthropus.

The Evidence of Marcellin Boule

Marcellin Boule, who is regarded as one of the greatest, if not the greatest authority in the world on fossil skulls, was brought up a believer in the theory of evolution, and though he never formally renounced the theory, he demolished bit by bit the evidence from Paleontology put forward by propagandists in its favor. It was he who first measured the original Neanderthal skull accurately and showed that instead of it being only 1,270 cc (230 cc below the average for man) that it was over 1,500 cc and quite up to average. His visit to Peking and Choukoutien was after that of the Abbé Breuil, and he was aware of the claims made by Dr. Davidson Black, Fr. Teilhard de Chardin and Abbé Breuil. He published his verdict on the fossil remains of the Peking Man in *L'Anthropologie* (1937, p. 21).

In *L'Anthropologie* he writes:

> To this fantastic hypothesis (of Abbé Breuil and Fr. Teilhard de Chardin), that the owners of the monkey-like skulls were the authors of the large-scale industry, I take the liberty of preferring an opinion more in conformity with the conclusions from my studies, which is that the hunter (who battered the skulls) was a real man and that the cut stones, etc., were his handiwork.

In the same article in *L'Anthropologie* he writes:

> It seems to me rash to deem Sinanthropus the monarch of Choukoutien since he appears in the deposits in which he is found in the aspect of common game, like the animals associated with him.

Boule's description of the skulls is substantially the same as that of Fr. Teilhard de Chardin. He adds the additional information that in the case of all the skulls of Sinanthropus there was a hole in the top of the skull at the occiput, supposed to have been made for the purpose of extracting the brain, which is considered a delicacy for eating. In connection with this fact, the question was raised as to whether Sinanthropus was a cannibal. If Boule's verdict is accepted that the Sinanthropus was a macaque or monkey killed by the workmen at the limestone quarry, there would, of course, be no question of cannibalism.

Boule's verdict is confirmed by the further circumstance that all the skulls found (except those of the real men) were found battered by a blunt instrument, the blow which caused the death being struck from outside. (See *La Pensée Catholique,* 1948, no. 7, p. 95).

Dr. Black's Second Version of Sinanthropus

The first version, as we have seen, based on the evidence furnished by a single tooth, was that Sinanthropus was the most primitive "hominid" yet found. The second version was that he was the most advanced of the "hominids," bigger and better than the Pithecanthropus, or Java Man, but inferior to the Neanderthal Man.

It took Dr. Black two years to make the model of the skull of Sinanthropus and to write a description of it, giving the measurements and a comparison with the model of the skull of Pithecanthropus and the skull of the Neanderthal Man as represented by propagandists for the theory of human evolution. This was a document of 110 pages with appendix giving photographs of the model. It was published in *Palaeontologia Sinica* (Series D, vii, fasc. 2, 1931) under the title "On an Adolescent Skull of *Sinanthropus Pekinensis*."

The first thing to be noted about this model is that it is an artificial model of the skull of the mythical Sinanthropus, not a cast of the skull described by Fr. Teilhard de Chardin, Abbé Breuil and Dr. Boule. In the first place, there was a hole in the top of all the skulls found among the debris, supposed to have been made in order to extract the brain matter (see *Les Hommes Fossiles,* 1952 ed., p. 138), and Fr. Teilhard de Chardin says that this was true in the case of this particular skull (See *L'Apparition de l'Homme,* p. 92). In the case of the model made by Dr. Black, there is no hole, there are only indications of cracks in the skull. In the second case, Dr. Black made the brain capacity of the model 960 cc by his calculation, which turned out to be wrong, for Dr.

Weidenreich measured the model and found the capacity to be 915 cc. (See *Les Hommes Fossiles,* p. 139). Now Fr. Teilhard de Chardin in his description of the skull as it was before the clay inside it was cleared out, says that the skull was small, that it resembled that of an ape, broad below and narrow at the top (where the brain is), and that the brain capacity was small *(faible)*.

There was no room, therefore, in the skull described by Fr. Teilhard de Chardin for a brain of 960, or 915 cc. Being the brain of a baboon or macaque (as already noted), not of a great ape, it was most probably not more than 400 cc. in size.

The model, then, was not a cast of the actual skull, but an artificial representation of a creature of the imagination; the 110-page document which purports to be a description of this model is equally artificial, and is not even an accurate description of it. The avowed aim of the document was to represent the skull of Sinanthropus as intermediate between the skull of the Neanderthal Man and that of the Java Man. Now it is acknowledged at the present time by all leading authorities on human fossils (such as Boule, Vallois and Weidenreich), that the brain of the Neanderthal Man was on an average larger than that of the modern man and that the shape of the skull, which was dolichocephalic (long-headed), was no indication of inferior intelligence (See *Apes, Giants and Men,* Chap. V). There was no point then in instituting a comparison between the skull of the mythical Sinanthropus and that of the Neanderthal Man; there was even less point in comparing it to the skull of the Java Man, for the skull of the Java Man of Dr. Dubois has been pronounced by Marcellin Boule to be that of a large gibbon, and was acknowledged to be such by Dr. Dubois himself more than once before his death.

The 110-page document is a tedious, artificial production. It gives the measurements of some of the smaller Neanderthal skulls from all possible angles, those of the model of the skull of the Java Man, and endeavors to fit in those of the Peking Man between them, making them sometimes nearer to the

Java Man and sometimes nearer to Neanderthal Man (of small brain capacity). This tedious document has not even the merit of being an accurate description of the artificial model, for, in the first place, Dr. Black gave the brain capacity of the model as being 960 cc, while Dr. Weidenreich found it to be only 915 cc. If Dr. Weidenreich or any expert had examined the other measurements given by Dr. Black, he would in all probability have found them all to be inaccurate, for Dr. Black had set himself a most difficult task in endeavoring to construct a model of a skull just halfway between that of a given Neanderthal skull and of the Java Man.

This 110-page document of Dr. Black (which is an inaccurate description of an artificial model) has been taken very seriously by some prominent Catholic writers. For instance, Fr. Marcozzi, S.J. of the Gregorian University, Rome, goes to the trouble of analyzing it and finds that of the 121 characteristics of Sinanthropus, 50% are intermediate between ape and man, 36% are human, 10% belong to the ape and 4% are peculiar to Sinanthropus. (See *La Vita e l'Uomo* by Fr. Marcozzi, p. 342). Fr. Marcozzi's analysis is copied into *Hacia El Origen del Hombre* by Fr. Ezpondaburu, S.J. of the Pontifical University of Comillas, Spain.

Now, the first thing that both Fr. Marcozzi and Fr. Expondaburu should have done before quoting Dr. Black's document as an argument for human evolution was to ascertain with reasonable certainty whether the document in question gave an accurate and faithful description of the skull selected to represent Sinanthropus. Neither the model nor the description given by Dr. Black corresponds with the description given by three independent eye-witnesses; the description does not even correspond with the artificial model described, and the actual skull and all the other skulls, which if they had remained would be evidence of the fraud, have been destroyed.

Dr. Black, having finished the model of the skull of Sinanthropus, made models of two mandibles, one of a young specimen, the second of an adult. He claimed that these bore a striking resemblance to human mandibles. However, in the 1952 edition of *Les Hommes Fossiles,* the author, Dr. Vallois, tells us that the mandible supposed to belong to the adult was composed of two parts, one of an adult, the other of a child, and he adds that Dr. Black had gone much too far in claiming that there was a resemblance between the mandible of Sinanthropus and that of man. (*Les Hommes Fossiles*, p. 141).

The document of 110 pages describing the artificial model, which was in technical language and was confined to the description of the model, was followed by a popular account of what had been found in the excavations up to date and was signed by Dr. Davidson Black, Fr. Teilhard de Chardin, C. C. Young and Dr. Pei. This contained nothing beyond what had been already published; it was merely a summary for propaganda purposes.

Discovery of Skeletons of Real Men and Women

In 1934, Fr. Teilhard de Chardin published an article in *Revue des Questions Scientifiques* consisting of two parts.

In the first part of the article, which was written in 1933 and left unpublished for five months, Fr. de Chardin describes the progress made in the work of excavation up to the date of writing. He tells us that the work of quarrying (in ancient times) had extended on a front of nearly 200 meters; that the workmen employed for the excavation (after digging down to the rock on the lower level) had gone up to the top of the hill and were clearing away the stones that had fallen down in the landslide; that already the outside portion had been cleared and that it was hoped that most of the upper level would be cleared by 1934. He tells us further that pieces of broken skulls of Sinanthropus were found at the upper level similar to those found below; that there were now abundant traces of fire and of industry in stone and bone, and—a more important detail—that Dr. Black, having finished the model of the head of Sinanthropus, was now working on a model of the jawbone.

Later on, as we have seen, Dr. Weidenreich examined this model of the jawbone of Sinanthropus and found that it was made from *two* portions of jawbones, one of a grown specimen, the other of a young one. This was done, he said, in order to make the jawbone resemble a human one. (See *Les Hommes Fossiles,* 1952 ed., pp. 141-142).

Finally, in this 1933 part of the article, Fr. de Chardin discusses Marcellin Boule's objection that the owners of the monkey-like skulls could not possibly have produced the large-scale industry, and answered it by saying that although externally the skulls appeared to be those of animals yet they had a brain capacity of nearly twice that of the great ape, and that hence there was no need for Boule's hypothetical man who, he said, killed those creatures.

This 1933 part of the article remained unpublished for five months until Dr. Pei (who was in charge of the excavation) one evening brought in three complete human skulls of adults (not battered like those of Sinanthropus), some smaller ones, a number of thigh bones and other parts of human skeletons. There was no doubt whatever that these were the skulls and bones of real men. As soon as these fossil remains of real men were brought in, Fr. de Chardin finished his 1933 article in great haste, apparently without consulting the others and even without their knowledge, and sent it to France to be published.

In the 1934 part of the article he states that five months had elapsed since he had written the first part. With regard to the three skulls, the thigh bones and other parts of the skeleton, he states most emphatically that these did not belong to Sinanthropus, but to a real *homo sapiens.* (See *L'Apparition de l'Homme,* p. 107, in which the article is included). As Fr. de Chardin had not gone out to Choukoutien to examine the site, the remaining three pages of the article in which he tries to show that these skulls and bones must be of a later date than the skulls of Sinanthropus is of no particular interest. The important point that he makes plain in the article in question is that these skulls were found at the same site as those of Sinanthropus, and that they were not found in the rubbish and ashes as the skulls of Sinanthropus were found, but apart and undamaged, and that they were the fossil remains, not of Sinanthropus, but of real men.

Chapter 5 (Cont'd.)

THE PEKING MAN, PART II

Death of Dr. Davidson Black

On the 15th of March, 1934, Dr. Black, in white overalls, went to his laboratory at Peking to examine the human skulls and bones that Dr. Pei had brought in from Choukoutien, and *was later found dead among the human fossils.* His long article in *Palaeontologia Sinica,* 1931, had been very well received by prominent advocates of the man-from-animal theory all over the world, and as a reward for his work he had just been made a Fellow of the Royal Society of London when his death occurred.

Dr. Franz Weidenreich Succeeds Him

Work at Choukoutien was suspended for a time after Dr. Black's death until a suitable successor could be found. The choice fell on Dr. Weidenreich, an American citizen of German origin, and an advocate of the theory of human evolution with some reputation as a scientist.

The Chinese Dr. Pei continued to be in charge of the field operations at Choukoutien. It was his responsibility to find the fossils and bring them into the laboratory at Peking.

One would have expected that Dr. Weidenreich's first task would be to examine the human fossils found in 1934 and publish an account of them. But no, he kept silent about them for five years; eventually he published a full account of them in the 1939 issue of *Palaeontologia Sinica,* which he repeated in his lecture to the students of the University of California in 1945. (See *Apes, Giants and Man,* p. 86). In that account he says:

> From the *so-called Upper Cave of Choukoutien* which yielded the remains of Sinanthropus, three well-preserved skulls, several fragments of some more and skeletal bones of about ten individuals have been recovered. [The individuals appeared to be of the one family.] The three skulls represent an old male, a middle-aged woman and a younger woman.

Though of the one family, they had different traits: the old man's skull was of Mongolian type, with some Neanderthal traits; the middle-aged woman's skull resembled an Eskimo's, while the young woman's resembled a Melanasian's.

How are we to explain the silence of Dr. Weidenreich about these skulls for five years? It is highly probable that Dr. Pei knew nothing about the article of Fr. Teilhard de Chardin in *Revue des Questions Scientifiques* to which we have referred; it is also probable that Dr. Pei did not show these skulls to Dr. Weidenreich. As it was, he accepted Dr. Black's version of Sinanthropus with some modifications. He corrected Dr. Black's figures for the capacity of the skull of the *model* from 960 cc to 915 cc, and in the article on it published in *Palaeontologia Sinica* in 1935, he referred to it, not as the *skull* of Sinanthropus, but as the *cast* of the skull. He rejected outright the cast of the mandible of Sinanthropus made by Dr. Black, pointing out that it was made from parts of two different mandibles, one of an adult, the other of a young specimen, in order, as he said, to make it look like human. (See *Les Hommes Fossiles* by Boule and Vallois, 1952 ed., p. 141).

Third Version of Sinanthropus

Dr. Weidenreich then proceeded to make his own model of the skull of Sinanthropus, bigger and better than Dr. Black's.

In an article to *Études* (a French Jesuit periodical) dated July 5, 1937, Fr. Teilhard de Chardin tells us that in December, 1936 Dr. Pei "found" three complete skulls of Sinanthropus and portions of others; that one of these skulls was that of a great male, the other two of females. These may be presumed to be the skulls of real men found in 1934 which Fr. de Chardin mentioned in his article in *Revue des Questions*

Scientifiques already referred to. The brain capacity of the "great male" was 1,200 cc; the others were between 900 cc and 1,200 cc. It was from the largest of these skulls (the one of 1,200 cc) that Weidenreich made his cast, but he made it the model of a skull of a *woman,* and later on got a lady sculptor named Swan to produce the head of this woman as she had appeared in life. This head sculptured by Miss Swan looks exactly like the usual caricature of the Neanderthal Man published in propagandist books. Weidenreich christened this model of Mrs. Sinanthropus "Nelly." (See *L'Apparition de L'Homme,* pp. 120-121).

The reader is asked to note that while photographs of the skulls of the real human beings were published by Dr. Weidenreich in his 1939 article in *Palaeontologia Sinica* and again in *Apes, Giants and Men* (1940), no photographs of the three skulls of Sinanthropus alleged to have been found in 1936 have ever been published, and there is now no trace of these skulls. It is also to be noted that Fr. T. de Chardin gives no description of these skulls as he had done for the skull found in 1929. The evidence points to the conclusion that the finding of the three skulls of large brain capacity in December, 1936 is a pure invention.

As in the case of Dr. Black's Sinanthropus No. 2, we have nothing except the model of this imaginary skull made by Dr. Weidenreich and the head sculptured by Miss Swan to represent it.

The finding of the three skulls of real human beings and of the other fossils mentioned by Fr. T. de Chardin in his 1934 article has been confirmed by both Dr. Weidenreich and Dr. Pei (See *L'Apparition de l'Homme,* p. 146).

The work of excavation at Choukoutien was continued with Dr. Pei in charge, thanks to the yearly grant of $20,000 from the Rockefeller Foundation. He brought the fossils found to the laboratory at Peking, where Dr. Weidenreich examined them and issued bulletins periodically about them. The principal of these bulletins were: *The Sinanthropus Population of Choukoutien* (Peking, 1935); *Observations on the Form and Proportions of the Endocranial Casts of Sinanthropus* (Palaeontologia Sinica, 1936); *The Mandibles of Sinanthropus* (Palae. Sin. 1936); *The Dentation of Sinanthropus* (Palae. Sin. 1937); and *The Extremity Bones of Sinanthropus* (Palae. Sin. 1941).

We shall deal first with Dr. Weidenreich's description of the mandibles and teeth of Sinanthropus, and then with his account of the skulls.

He begins his account of the mandibles by pointing out that Dr. Black's model of the mandible of Sinanthropus was made from portions of two mandibles, one, that of a grown specimen, the other, of a young one, and he adds that this was done in order to make it resemble a human mandible. He then rejects Dr. Black's claim that the mandibles of Sinanthropus were very like those of modern man, saying that this was going much too far.

In the article in question (Palae. Sin. 1936), Dr. Weidenreich dealt with eleven broken pieces of mandibles. He remarks that certain characteristics of them, such as polymorphism, were never found in man, but were found in apes. In man the mandibles of male and female differ very little; in those of Sinanthropus, the difference was very marked, and besides, they differed one from another, and the difference was so pronounced that Weidenreich concluded that there must have been more than one species.

There were other characteristics, such as the inside of the mandible and the form of the dental arch not found in the great apes. The conclusion therefore is that the mandibles of Sinanthropus belonged neither to man nor to the great apes. Weidenreich refrained from drawing the further conclusion, namely, that they belonged to two different species of monkeys, baboons and macaques, fossils of which existed in great quantity in the neighborhood of Choukoutien, as he admitted later on. (See *Apes, Giants and Men,* 1945, p. 19).

In his article on *The Dentation of Sinanthropus* (Palae. Sin. 1937), Dr. Weidenreich made a careful study of 147 teeth, 83 of which were still in the jawbones and 64 isolated. He again comments on the polymorphism. The difference between the teeth of male and female was very pronounced, as in apes and monkeys; this does not occur in man. The teeth differed from one another and were far larger than human teeth. The canine teeth protruded like those of animals. However, they differed in some respects, principally in size, from the teeth of the great apes. The conclusion from the study of the teeth is the same as that from the mandibles: that they belonged neither to man nor to the great apes, and that in all probability, they belonged to baboons and macaques.

In his article on the *Extremity Bones of Sinanthropus,* Weidenreich admits that these told us nothing about the form of the skeleton. They consisted of a portion of a collarbone, two broken pieces of the humerus, a small portion of the spinal column and seven broken parts of thighbones without their joints. The next important point to be noted in the article is that *Dr. Weidenreich made no claim to have found evidence that the creature walked erect.*

In Fr. T. de Chardin's 1934 article already referred to, in which he announced the finding of fossils of real men, he says that, besides the five skulls, a pelvis with the two thigh bones was found. The broken bits of thighbones without their joints referred to by Weidenreich are therefore different from these, and may have belonged to Sinanthropus (i.e., either to baboons or macaques).

There is no evidence therefore for the claim made by Fr. Ezpondaburu S.J. in *Hacia el Origen Del Hombre* (p. 135) that the thighbones of Sinanthropus found proved that he walked erect. He gives no reference and is probably confusing the complete thighbones of the real man mentioned by Fr. T. de Chardin, with the broken bits without the joints referred to by Dr. Weidenreich.

We now come to Weidenreich's description of the skulls of Sinanthropus. He published two articles on the question in *Palaeontologia Sinica,* one in 1936, the other in 1943. The first dealt with Dr. Black's model of 1931. Dr. Weidenreich is careful about the title of this article, which is: "Observations on the Form and Proportions of the Endocranial Casts of Sinanthropus." His article is on the *casts* (he should have said artificial models) of Sinanthropus, not on the actual skulls. The only notable feature of the article is that he corrects the figure 960 cc given by Dr. Black for the brain capacity of the model and makes it 915.

In the 1943 article he deals with his own *model,* but calls his article "The Skull of Sinanthropus. . ." Dr. Weidenreich constructed a model of a skull of a *female* Sinanthropus and made the brain capacity 1,200 cc, which is not far below the average for a woman. This model was supposed to be based on the skulls alleged to have been found in 1936, but of which fact there is no proof. In making the brain capacity of the *female specimen* 1,200 cc, Weidenreich differed from Fr. T. de Chardin, who in his article in *Études,* 1937, already referred to, says that the skull with the 1,200 cc capacity, alleged to have been found in 1936, was that of *a great male.*

There is no evidence that the original from which this new model is supposed to have been made ever existed. No photographs[1] of the three skulls supposed to have been found in 1936 have been published, only photographs of the model, while actual photographs of the skulls of real men found in 1934 have been published and have been reproduced in the books by Weidenreich, Boule and Vallois, etc. This model, as far as one can judge from the photograph, resembles an ordinary dolichocephalic (long-headed) skull with prominent brow ridges like the Australian aborigines. It is possible that Dr. Pei, who was in charge during the period between the death of Dr. Black and the appointment of Dr. Weidenreich, concealed the skulls found in 1934 and produced others.

One thing, however, is certain: the model produced by Dr. Weidenreich has no resemblance whatever to the skulls of Sinanthropus as described by Fr. T. de Chardin, Abbé Breuil and Boule. Weidenreich was a most credulous man: he based his theory of the existence of a race of giants on the casts of three isolated teeth which his friend Von Königswald picked up in a chemist's shop in Hong Kong (See *Apes, Giants and Men,* p. 57). He was an advocate of the theory of polygenesis, or plurality of human ancestors and based his theory on the reality of the Peking Man, the Java Man and the Australopithe-

1. In 1937, Dr. Weidenreich published an article in *Nature* in which he gave photographs of three *incomplete* skulls, i.e., photographs of the artificial models.

cinae of South Africa, all of which are rejected by the best authorities.

After the Departure of Dr. Weidenreich

As we have already seen, Dr. Weidenreich left China in 1940 when America entered the war. He had been allowed to continue his work all the time during the Japanese occupation from 1937 till their departure in 1940, and even after his departure the Japanese allowed his articles which he sent from America in 1941 and 1943 to be published in *Palaeontologia Sinica,* a Peking periodical.

Dr. Pei was free to carry on the work if he wished, but he had no longer the annual grant of $20,000 from America. Fr. Teilhard de Chardin was not interned, as is proved by his 1942 lecture in the Catholic University of Peking, which he published in pamphlet form in 1943.

Fr. Teilhard De Chardin's Lecture In the Catholic University of Peking

The lecture was delivered in English to the Chinese students under the title "Fossil Men: Recent Discoveries and Present Problems." Fr. de Chardin dealt with the Peking Man, the Java Man, the Australopithecinae of South Africa and the Neanderthal Man. He represented the Australopithecinae as great apes on the verge of becoming human, and the rest as "hominids," in the process of evolution.

The lecture was an all-out attempt to convince the Chinese students that they had been evolved from animals. He ended the lecture by stating that now that he had proved that man had been evolved, it should follow that all animals had been evolved from primitive cosmic material and that man himself should go on indefinitely evolving toward great perfection. (See *L'Apparition de l'Homme,* pp. 172-173).

How the Peking Man Fraud Was Discovered

The two things that contributed chiefly to the discovery of the Peking fraud were the publication of a French translation of Fr. Teilhard de Chardin's 1942 lecture in the French periodical *Psyche* in 1948, and the collection of his various articles on the subject of evolution after his death by an international committee of advocates of the theory of human evolution (which included Sir Julian Huxley, Le Gros Clark, Von Königswald, Romer, etc.) and their publication in book form in 1956 under the title *L'Apparition de l'Homme.*

Among the small number of Frenchmen who had read Abbé Breuil's articles in *Anthropologie* (1932 and 1935) on the evidence of a large-scale industry at Choukoutien were Dr. A. Dubois and O. Fribault. When the French translation of Fr. Teilhard de Chardin's article was published in *Psyche,* these two men noticed that in the account of Fr. Teilhard de Chardin, no mention was made of the enormous heap of ashes discovered, that no reference was made to Abbé Breuil's article, and that the difference between the two accounts was evident. They then published in *La Pensée Catholique* of 1948 all the information about what was actually found at Choukoutien that was available up to the date of writing. This information was taken from the articles of Abbé Breuil already referred to, and the writings of Marcellin Boule in *Les Hommes Fossiles* and various periodicals. But it was not until the writings of Fr. Teilhard de Chardin were collected together and published in book form that it was possible to give the whole story of the Peking Man.

The Publication of the Writings of Fr. Teilhard de Chardin

After the death of Fr. Teilhard, an international committee composed of the most prominent advocates of the theory of evolution from France, Italy, England, Holland, America and South Africa collected the various articles that Fr. Teilhard had written on the subject of evolution during his lifetime and published them in book form in 1956 under the title *L'Apparition de l'Homme.* It is a monument erected to the memory of Fr. Teilhard de Chardin by men, many of whom were atheists, for his life's work as propagandist of the theory of evolution, and should open the eyes of those Catholic writers who accepted and published his views on the origin of man, which were based chiefly on the discoveries claimed to have been made at Piltdown and Choukoutien, but which were not genuine. It provides evidence, if further evidence is necessary, to convince unbiased readers that the whole Peking Man case is a huge fraud.

Information Contained in These Articles

The chief points of information contained in these articles have been already mentioned. For the convenience of the reader we will give them together here.

In the 1930 article in *Revue des Questions Sc.* Fr. Teilhard says that so far no trace of fire nor any sign of industry had been found (*L'Apparition, de l'Homme* p. 90). This is an extraordinary statement in view of the fact that both Abbé Breuil and Marcellin Boule, who visited Choukoutien about that time, found abundant traces of fire and proofs of the existence of a large-scale industry.

In this article he describes the skull of Sinanthropus as being just like that of a monkey, and says that the brain capacity must be small. The 1934 article in *Revue des Questions Sc.*, as already stated, consisted of two parts. In the first part he admits that there were traces of fire and signs of industry, but so far no fossils of the hypothetical *Homo Sapiens* that Boule spoke of. In the second part of the article, written five months later, he tells of the finding of three skulls of adults which, he said, were the skulls of real man *(Homo Sapiens)*, of a human pelvis with the two thigh bones and other parts of human skeletons. In the end of the same article, he admits the finding of a skeleton of a large baboon not far from Choukoutien.

His 1937 article was in *Études* (a Jesuit publication). For the benefit of his new readers he goes over the whole story again, giving the popular, but inaccurate, version that the fossils were found in a cave. The existence of any natural cave at either the lower or the upper level is denied categorically by Weidenreich, who was in charge from 1934 until 1940.

He then tells of the finding of three skulls belonging to Sinanthropus, one of them being of a large male and having a capacity of 1,200 cc. On the very same page (*L'Apparition de l'Homme,* p. 129), he says that no trace of the hypothetical *Homo Sapiens* demanded by Boule to explain the industry had been found. He thus flatly contradicts what he had written in his 1934 article in *Revue des Questions Scientifiques* and which both Weidenreich and Pei confirmed. His 1942 lecture in English to the students of Peking Catholic University, published in 1943 in pamphlet form and translated into French and published in *Psyche* in 1948 (a copy of the English original of which was received by the present writer while in China) has already been described. The chief points of his account of the Peking Man in the lecture to be noted are that he still insists that the fossils were found in a natural cave (which Weidenreich denies) and that he makes no mention whatever of the finding of the fossils of real men.

Fr. Teilhard de Chardin Has Been Very Much Misrepresented

Both during his lifetime and after his death Fr. T. de Chardin has been represented as a great authority on Paleontology, human fossils, etc., both by Catholic and non-Catholic evolutionists. With regard to the effect produced by his writings in Catholic circles, Dr. Dubois and O. Fribault in their article in *La Pensée Catholique* already referred to, wrote as follows:

> While among laymen Fr. Teilhard de Chardin's affirmations are accepted with reserve, in the religious world his conclusions are accepted without discussion both by members of the Religious Orders and of the Secular Clergy. People go as far as to say that his articles have influenced the teachers in French Catholic Schools and even in the Ecclesiastical Seminaries.

He is quoted by Count Begouen of Toulouse (the head of the movement in France to introduce the teaching of evolution into Catholic institutions) as a great authority on human fossils; he supplied the information on the Peking Man to Fr. Bergounioux for his book, *The First Men*, published a few years ago, in which the doctrine of human evolution is propounded, and in turn Fr. Bergounioux's views on the Peking Man are quoted by Fr. Ezpondaburu in *Hacia El Origin del Hombre*.

What then is the value of Fr. T. de Chardin's opinion on the origin of man? An answer to that question can be found by reading either *The Piltdown Forgery* by J. S. Weiner, or *Lessons of Piltdown* by Francis Vere, or the collection of his own articles published by the international committee of evolutionists under the title *L'Apparition de L'Homme,* to which we have referred.

J. S. Weiner was one of the three men who tested the Piltdown fossils and proved that the jawbone was that of an ape that had recently died, that it had been stained to make it look like a fossil, that the teeth had been filed, etc.; he is a strong propagandist of the theory of evolution and shows that in his book. He tells us that Fr. T. de Chardin, who at the time of the discovery of the Piltdown skull was finishing his studies at the Jesuit house at Hastings, became a close friend of Dawson, who found the skull, and that Dawson introduced him to Arthur Smith Woodward in a letter in which he said: "Teilhard is perfectly safe" (*op. cit.*, p. 88) and afterwards introduced him to Sir Arthur Keith. He tells us that it was Fr. Teilhard who was allowed to find a number of the fossils (which had been planted) and that in particular he had "found" the canine tooth which had been missing from the ape jawbone and which Sir Arthur Keith had called for. This canine tooth had been filed to make it fit into the jawbone and stained to make it look like a fossil. Fr. Teilhard could see nothing wrong with it.

He returned to France in October, 1913, before the fossils of the second Piltdown Man had been found two miles away from Piltdown. Like other French priests, he was conscripted for the First World War. After the war he got a position as Professor of Geology in the Catholic University of Paris in 1923 and became involved in the case of the Peking Man, with the results that we have seen.

His claim to be considered an authority on ancient human fossils has rested almost completely on his connection with the cases of the Piltdown Man and the Peking Man. In neither case did he give any indication whatever of critical ability or independent judgment. He was just a child that never grew up. He had a marvelous knowledge of all the technical terms used by geologists and paleontologists, but that was all. However, he was able to describe the outside of the skull of Dr. Black's Sinanthropus, and to tell us that three skulls of adult human beings had been found in 1934; and apparently after being warned, he reported the same skulls as those of Sinanthropus and found them again in 1936.

It is tragic, however, that the opinions of such a man, which are utterly worthless, should have influenced the teaching of prominent Catholic scholars such as Fr. Mancozzi, S.J. of Rome, Fr. Expondaburu, S.J. of Spain and Dr. Vanderbroeck of Louvain University (see *God, Man and the Universe,* pp. 123-124).

Conclusions on the Case of the Peking Man

1) The skulls and portions of skulls (about 30 in number found in the ashes and debris) were certainly not human. Externally they looked just like the skulls of the large monkeys (baboons and macaques, fossils of which were found in the district).

The mandibles and teeth in some respects resembled those of the great apes, and in others differed; these were certainly not human and may therefore be presumed to be those of baboons and macaques.

2) There is no doubt whatever about the fact that the three skulls of adults reported by Fr. Teilhard de Chardin to have been found by Dr. Pei in 1934 were real human skulls. This was acknowledged by both Dr. Weidenreich and Dr. Pei.

3) (*a*) Sinanthropus No. 1 based on the evidence of a single tooth, which was certainly not human, is a mere figment of Dr. Black's imagination.

(*b*) Sinanthropus No. 2, based on an artificial model, which does not correspond with the descriptions of the skull from which it was supposed to be made, given by three independent witnesses (Dr. Boule, Abbé Breuil and Fr. T. de Chardin), is also a product of Dr. Black's imagination, as is also his 110-page document describing it.

(*c*) Sinanthropus No. 3, of Dr. Weidenreich, has nothing in common with Dr. Black's except the name. The skull (of the *woman*) on which it was said to have been modelled has been destroyed; there is not even a description of it to be found, nothing but the model and photographs of the model, in which it looks like a human skull.

There is no evidence whatever to prove that the three skulls of Sinanthropus alleged by Fr. T. de Chardin to have been found in 1936 ever existed. They may be presumed to be the skulls of the real men and women found in 1934.

4) There were no natural caves at Choukoutien, either at the lower or the upper level. The pocket found at the lower level and referred to as the "Kotsetang cave" is called the "artificial cave" by Drs. Pei and Weidenreich and Abbé Breuil. That it was an artificial cave formed by the landslide is proved by the fact that a section of 132 square meters was dug down in the floor of it to a depth of 12 meters through debris and ashes. It was at the bottom of that section that the skull of Sinanthropus, referred to in Dr. Black's 1931 document, was found.

The place at the upper level where the fossils of real men and women were found, which Fr. T. de Chardin calls "the upper cave," is referred to by Dr. Weidenreich as the "so-called cave." Weidenreich tells us that skeletal bones of about 10 human individuals were found, that they evidently belonged to the same family, and that they died a violent death. They were evidently buried in the same landslide that covered up the skulls of the monkeys (Sinanthropus) and the ashes.

The very great quantity of ashes is explained by the fact that as there was no coal available, the lime was burned in ancient times, as it still is in China, by grass, straw, reeds, etc.

As Choukoutien was 50 kilometers from Peking, Fr. de Chardin had little opportunity of observing what was done there; besides, since he did not speak Chinese (as is shown by the fact that he gave his lecture to the Chinese students in English), he could not obtain information from the Chinese workmen. This explains, in part at least, the contradictions in his evidence.

5) The Sinanthropus described by Fr. Marcozzi, S.J. in *La*

Vita e l'Uomo (p. 342) as having 121 different characteristics or traits, 50% of which were of the Missing Link, 36% human, 10% animal and 4% peculiar to Sinanthropus, is an imaginary creature part of which is of baboon, part of macaque, parts of Sinanthropus Nos. 1, 2 and 3, and part of the *Homo Sapiens* found in 1934, and is much more wonderful than the chimera, which has only three parts: (head of a lion, body of a goat and tail of a serpent).

The same may be said of the Sinanthropus of Fr. Ezpondaburu, S.J. in *Hacia El Origen del Hombre*.

Two More Important Conclusions

Besides the above conclusions, which eliminate Sinanthropus as a candidate for the Missing Link and a proof of human evolution, there are two other very important conclusions.

The first of these conclusions is in favor of monogenesis, or the unity of the human race. Sinanthropus has been used by such writers as Dr. Weidenreich as an argument to prove the plurality of human ancestors (polygenesis). That argument disappears.

The second conclusion is in favor of the traditional moderate estimate of the antiquity of the human race.

Sinanthropus has been used to prove that man existed in Asia, according to some, for 500,000 years (see *Dating the Past,* p. 274); according to others, for 100,000 years. With the disappearance of Sinanthropus, the argument for his great antiquity disappears also.

Drs. Weidenreich and Pei and Fr. T. de Chardin are agreed that the skulls of *Homo Sapiens* found in 1934 do not date back as far as those of the Cro-Magnon Man, which means that they are long after the *Hiatus* or *Deluge*. No claim for great antiquity has been made in favor of any human fossils, except in the cases of the alleged Peking and Java men, found in India, China, or anywhere east of the Himalayas, that would make them earlier than 7000 B.C., which, as we shall show in Book II, is the approximate date of the Deluge. Neither have any fossils of the Neanderthal race, which was the predominant race before the Deluge, been found east of the Himalayas.

The Chinese brought with them to China a fairly well developed form of writing similar to that used in ancient Mesopotamia and Egypt; the presumption, therefore, is that their ancestors did not leave Mesopotamia until long after the Deluge. It is true that stone instruments have been discovered at Ordos in China and in parts of India which are assigned to the Paleolithic Age by Fr. Teilhard de Chardin, but in the first place, it is impossible to base a conclusion on the finding of stone instruments alone, because the Stone Age varies in different countries, and in the second place, Fr. Teilhard's opinion is based on his experience at Choukoutien, the value of which has already been discussed.

As stated at the beginning of this chapter, the Sinanthropus or Peking Man is still being used by prominent writers, both non-Catholic and Catholic, as an argument for the evolution of man. The models made by Dr. Black and Dr. Weidenreich (without the fossils that they are supposed to represent) are to be seen in the display rooms opened at Peking by Dr. Pei, who informs the Chinese people that they are the descendants of the Peking ape-man.

Thus the fraud which was connived at by foreigners, and subsidized by foreign contributions, is being used to confirm the Red Propaganda that Christianity is based on myths such as the existence of a human soul and a divine origin of the body.

Statues or pictures of the Peking ape-man are on display, not only in the museums of Warsaw, Moscow, Peking, etc., but in the British Kensington Museum and in museums in America. The people of America who contributed the large sum of $300,000 have not even been told what the costly excavations have revealed; instead, they have had the compliment conveyed to them through these artificial models, that they are the blood relations, if not the descendants of monkeys and apes.

It is time that Catholic writers should cease using these artificial models of an imaginary creature as evidence to prove that man's body was not *specially created* by God (in the traditional sense of these words), but *evolved* from a brute beast.

Two Recent Attempts to Find a "Missing Link"—the Oreopithecus Fossil

These fossils were found in abundance near a coal mine in Baccinello in Northern Italy in 1870. A French paleontologist named Gervais examined them in 1872, and gave his opinion that they belonged to an extinct species that resembled apes. A German paleontologist named Schlosser thought that they resembled fossils of baboons or long-tailed monkeys. In 1958 Dr. Hurzeler of Switzerland claimed that he had found fossils of the same creatures in the coal mine, but of this fact there is not sufficient evidence, and, as Hurzeler himself admitted, the fossils that he produced had no real resemblance to man.

The Zinjanthropus

In two articles in *The National Geographic Magazine* in 1960 and 1961, Dr. Leakey, the author of *Adam's Ancestors,* informs his readers that the *National Geographic Society* had awarded him a "generous grant" (the amount of which he does not specify) for the purpose of exploring the Olduvai Gorge, in Tanganyika, with a view of writing some articles for their magazine. He had already explored the gorge to get material for *Adam's Ancestors*, with results unfavorable to the theory of evolution, of which he was an ardent supporter.

On this occasion, he found 400 fragments of what he claimed to be a prehistoric skull. He tells us that he attempted to reconstruct the skull and find the brain capacity, but he hinted that he did not expect his readers to take him seriously. In his *Adam's Ancestors,* he tells us that the workshops in which real men manufactured the instruments of the Old Stone Age, found all over Europe and Africa, had been discovered in this gorge. It may be presumed, therefore, that the 400 splinters belonged to the skull of a real man, and that Dr. Leakey's claim to have reconstructed the skull need not be taken seriously.

Chapter 6

THE JAVA MAN, OR *PITHECANTHROPUS ERECTUS*

Java is a most unlikely place to find fossils of the earliest man. Geologists say that it did not emerge from the ocean till the Pliocene Period. Its flora and fauna came from the Continent of Asia during that period. It was selected as a place to look for the "Missing Link" by the Dutch surgeon, Dr. Dubois, because it was a Dutch possession, and also because, being remote from Europe, claims made could not be checked.

Four attempts were made to find a "missing link" in Java. The first attempt began in 1889, when the first alleged fossils were discovered at Trinil. These were exhibited at the International Congress of Zoologists at Leyden in 1895. Dr. Dubois, a Dutch army doctor, was entrusted by the Dutch government with the task of carrying out excavations in Java. He brought home a great quantity of bones of various animals, two simian teeth, the thigh bone of a man, and the cap of a skull which some say is that of a man, others, that of an ape, and others still, that of a "missing link." As the brain case is missing, it is not possible to decide to which category it belongs.

He brought home at the same time two human skulls, known as the Wadjak skulls, of a large brain capacity; one of them was that of a man with brain capacity of 1,650 cc; the other was that of a woman with brain capacity of 1,550, both well above the average for human skulls. Dr. Dubois concealed these on his return and did not produce them at the International Congress. He produced them, however, in 1925, 30 years later, when the results of the second expedition, carried out by Madam Selenka, became known, and when his claim to have found a "missing link" was generally rejected.

At the International Congress, he made the bold claim that he had found the fossil remains of a real "missing link." He gave the age of the fossil as belonging to the Pliocene, that is to a time before any of the normal human species appeared on the earth. As the claim was evidently absurd for a place that emerged from the ocean in the Pliocene, later propagandists placed these fossils in the Pleistocene Period.

He claimed that the brain capacity of the skull was 850 cc, that is halfway between man and ape; that the thigh bone, which was certainly that of a man, and the skullcap, belonged to the same individual, and that therefore the creature to which both belonged walked erect. This was also an absurd claim; there is the same objection to it as was made against the jawbone found at Piltdown, which was evidently that of an ape belonging to the skull found at the same place, which was certainly that of a man.

The scientists at the International Congress gave their verdicts according to nationalities: the British members said that the skullcap belonged to a man, the German that it belonged to an ape, and the French, that it belonged to a "missing link."

The production of the Wadjak skulls (found at the same time as this skullcap) by Dr. Dubois himself in 1925 when the results of the Madam Selenka expedition were announced was a practical confession that he had been guilty of fraud, and that is the general belief of serious scientists. Dr. W. R. Thompson refers to the Java Man in his preface to *The Origin of Species* as an evident case of fraud.

The second attempt was made by Madam Selenka, the widow of a German scientist, who organized an expedition in 1906 to search the original site at Trinil for human fossils. The men engaged in it dug the site to a depth of 36 feet. The only fossil found was a human tooth, but a hearth where fire had been kindled and some charcoal were found also. The members of the expedition disagreed with Dr. Dubois about the date of the stratum where Dr. Dubois' fossils were said to have been found. Dr. Dubois had said that it dated from the Pliocene, but the Madam Selenka expedition proved that it belonged to the Pleistocene.

The third attempt to find fossils began in 1931 and was conducted by the Geological Service of Java. During this attempt 11 skulls or parts of skulls were found, five of which were in a fairly good state of preservation. Different estimates for the brain capacity are given in different books: Romer gives the figures as 1,316 cc for the man's skull and 1,175 cc for the woman's. These skulls were found at Ngandong on the Solo river about 30 kilometers from Trinil. They are undoubtedly human. With regard to their date, Fr. Teilhard de Chardin, S.J., who in this case is probably right, places it about the middle of the Pleistocene. They would therefore date to about the same time as the human fossils found in the upper part of the Choukoutien limestone hill near Peking, which would place them after the *hiatus*.

The final attempt was made by Dr. Von Königswald between 1936 and 1939 at Sangiran, 60 kilometers from the original site at Trinil. The result of this attempt was much the same as that of the first attempt by Dr. Dubois. Dr. Von Königswald produced parts of four skulls so broken that the brain capacity could not be determined. Romer, in *Man and the Vertebrates,* describes these as "three more skullcaps, a lower jaw and an upper jaw"; Vallois, in *Les Hommes Fossiles* numbers them ape-man Nos. 1, 2, 3 and 4. As there were only skullcaps, it is impossible to tell what was the brain capacity, but Romer, Vallois and other propagandists for the man-from-ape theory, give the capacity as much the same as that given by Dr. Dubois' first specimen—between 800 and 900 cc.

Dr. Weidenreich gives us the interesting piece of information in his *Apes, Giants and Men* (p. 48) that Von Königswald came to him to Peking in January, 1939, bringing with him a fragment of the upper jaw that he had found at Sangiran in Java, and *that it had been recently* broken. Weidenreich tells us further that he returned to the United States bringing with him *molds* of the skullcaps found by Königswald, and that he made a reconstruction of the largest skull (generally referred to as the skull of the Robust Ape-Man).

Conclusions About the Various Fossils of The So-Called Java Man

1) There is now no controversy about the two skulls found at Wadjak by Dr. Dubois in 1891, which he concealed for 30 years, or about the skulls found along the Solo River during the third attempt. All these skulls belonged to normal men of comparatively recent date.

2) With regard to the original Java Man found at Trinil, the human thigh bone produced by Dr. Dubois and the hearth with traces of fire and charcoal discovered during the Selenka expedition prove the presence of a real man in the place. It is not, however, possible to say definitely whether the human femur and the skullcap belonged to the same individual, or whether the skullcap was that of a man or of an ape.

Fr. Marcozzi, S.J. in his article in *Gregorianum,* 1956 (pp. 290-297) tells us that Bergman and Kasten of Amsterdam applied the fluorine test to the human femur and the skullcap, and that both contained an equal amount of fluorine. With regard to this conclusion we must remember that the same test was applied to the fossil skull of Piltdown and the jawbone of the ape that had died only a short time previously, and that both were pronounced to be of the same age in the first test made in 1948. In the second place, even if the test had been properly made, all it proves is that the thigh bone and the skullcap dated from about the same time; it does not tell us whether they belonged to the same individual or what was the brain capacity of the skull. Of one thing we may be quite certain, that as there is no way of estimating the real brain capacity of the skull, and as there is evidence of fraud, we may reject as without foundation the estimate of 850 cc for the brain capacity of the skull.

A similar line of reasoning can be applied to the three skullcaps found by Von Königswald between 1936 and 1939. The brain capacity cannot be estimated from the skullcap alone. It is extraordinary that complete fossil skulls were found at several places on the island of Java, and that no complete skull of the supposed ape-man could be found anywhere. Furthermore, the finding of the skullcaps by Von Königswald, a noted propagandist for the man-from-ape theory, was an attempt to answer the difficulties raised against the claims made for Trinil fossils by the results of the Madam Selenka expedition in 1906 and by the excavations of 1931-1932; and it resembled the attempt made at Piltdown to prove that the first Piltdown Man was genuine by finding the second.

It is a remarkable fact that Weidenreich, who reconstructed the largest of the three skullcaps from a mold supplied to him by Von Königswald, gives no estimate of the brain capacity of the skull, but in the illustration in his book represents it as a skull of large brain capacity and closely resembling a Neanderthal skull. He uses this portion of a skull to prove the thesis of his book, that the first men who appeared on the earth were giants, for the skull was large and of great strength. He seemed to have no doubt that the skull was human. We have therefore an additional reason for rejecting the estimate of from 800 to 900 cc for the skulls represented by the three skullcaps found by Dr. Von Königswald. Furthermore, we are justified in concluding at this stage of our investigation that all claims made to have found skulls of a brain capacity halfway between man and ape are fraudulent.

Chapter 7

OTHER FOSSILS SUPPOSED TO REPRESENT CREATURES IN THE PROCESS OF EVOLUTION TOWARD MAN

The Dryopithecus and the Australopithecus

In 1856, a Frenchman named Edward Lartet claimed to have found the mandible of a missing link at St. Gaudens, and gave the name *Dryopithecus* to the supposed owner. Another more complete specimen was found in the same place in 1890 by Gaudry, which was proved to be that of an ape. No further attempt was made to press the claim. Nevertheless, the name *Dryopithecus* and the claim that it represents a "missing link" still find a place in books by propagandists for the theory of human evolution. (See *Les Hommes Fossiles*, pp. 81-84).

The Australopithecinae

This is the name given to the creatures supposed to be half ape and half man, represented by half a dozen fossil skulls, found by Drs. Dart, Broom and Robinson in various parts of South Africa, principally in the Transvaal. The brain capacity of the skulls varied from 400 to 600 cc, which is the average for the great apes. There were no artifacts of any kind found in connection with them; and the claim that man was descended from the great apes was regarded as unorthodox by the European evolutionists and was rejected by such men as Sir Julian Huxley. Drs. Dart and Broom chose fancy names for the supposed owners of the skulls; it is possible that they meant the whole proceeding as a jibe at the theory of human evolution.

The following is a list of these fossils, with the dates at which they were found:

1) In 1925, Dr. Dart found a fossil skull at Taungs, about 80 miles from Kimberly, and called the owner *Australopithecus Africanus*. The brain capacity of the skull was only 500 cc, that is, 100 cc below the average for the gorilla. There were no artifacts.

2) In 1936, Dr. Broom found a similar fossil skull near Johannesburg and called the owner of it *Plesianthropus*.

Soon after he found another skull at Sterkfontein and called the owner *Paranthropus robustus*.

The search was discontinued during the war, but was resumed by Dr. Broom in 1947, when he found another fossil skull at Swartkrans, the owner of which he called *Paranthropus crassidens*. It was probably this skull that was referred to in the telegram alleged by Fr. Hauret in Chapter III of *Les Origines* to have been sent from Capetown in 1947, and not the one found at Sterkfontein before the war, as he says.

3) About the same time Dr. Broom and Dr. Robinson found at Swartkrans, near the place where Dr. Broom had found *Paranthropus crassidens,* parts of two mandibles claimed to be human, one having five molar teeth and the other two. The name *Telanthropus capensis* was chosen for the owners of the mandibles.

With regard to this last case, there is no reason to believe that these mandibles belonged to the ape skull found some distance away by Dr. Broom in 1947; neither Dr. Broom nor Dr. Robinson makes any such claim; instead, they claim that they belong to a type of real man in the process of evolution whom they call *Telanthropus* and think he belonged to the Neanderthal race.

Fr. Marcozzi, S.J. discusses the case of the Australopithecinae in his article in the 1956 issue of *Gregorianum,* entitled "Recent Findings of Palaeontology." He says that attempts have been made during the last few years to show that these creatures made use of rough stone instruments, but the only proof so far brought forward to establish the claim was a single stone found in a grotto at Makapangsgat, and some bones of animals that appeared to have been killed. Fr. Marcozzi is given by the Jesuit author of the chapter on "The Origin of the Human Body" in *Sacrae Theologiae Summa,* published by the Spanish Jesuits, p. 641, as a defender of the theory of mitigated human evolution. His article in *Gregorianum* by no means gives the latest findings of Paleontology on the origin of man available in 1956; he makes no mention of the definite conclusions arrived at about the Neanderthal Man already referred to, which were published in the 1952 edition of *Les Hommes Fossiles* by Boule and Vallois, and leaves the reader under the impression that the Java Man and the Peking Man are genuine.

If the roughly hewn stone referred to and the heap of mangled bones are the work of someone endowed with intelligence, there is no difficulty in explaining that fact without attributing it to the *Australopithecinae*, for the Broken Hill skull found in Rhodesia in 1921, and the Saldanha skull, found near Capetown in 1953, have both normal human brain capacity, and being of the Neanderthal type prove the presence of members of the Neanderthal race in various parts of South Africa before the *hiatus* or deluge.

With regard to the various skulls and bones of the Australopithecinae class, with the exception of the parts of the two mandibles just referred to, in the first place, the claim that they be regarded as "missing links" is rejected even by evolutionists on the general grounds that the great apes to which these fossils belong are already too highly specialized to be regarded as the ancestors of man. This has been made clear in the previous chapter by quotations from such authors as Sir Julian Huxley and Dr. Leakey (author of *Adam's Ancestors*). In the next place, no artifacts or indications that these creatures possessed intelligence beyond the ordinary ape were found in connection with them.

A belated claim, that one of them that was named *Australopithecus prometheus* knew the use of fire, is rejected by all; another belated claim that some of these skulls had a brain capacity of 750 cc is also rejected. Boule and Vallois in *Les Hommes Fossiles* (p. 89) give the brain capacity for them as between 400 and 600 cc; Romer in *Man and the Vertebrates* gives it as between 450 and 650 cc; the latter figure, which is a little above that of the brain capacity of the gorilla, may be regarded as a slight exaggeration. The only author that I can find who agrees with the claim of 750 cc for the brain capacity of some of the *Australopithecinae* is Professor Vanderbroek of Louvain University. He gives the figure 750 cc in his article on "The Origin of Man" already referred to. Professor Vanderbroek is not an authority on Paleontology. He is Professor of Comparative Anatomy, but appears to think that his subject provides no cogent argument for human evolution, for he states in the second page (p. 94) of a 50-page article that "the most spectacular argument is provided by Palaeontology." He devotes practically the whole of his long article to arguments from a department on which he is not an authority, and embodies in it claims made on behalf of the Australopithecinae, the Peking Man, the Java Man, and even on behalf of the Piltdown skull, but has to admit that the mandible that was supposed to belong to it was that of an ape.

Chapter By Sir S. Zuckerman In "Evolution as a Process"

We are not depending on general considerations alone to form definite opinions about these *Australopithecinae* fossils. We have available a detailed study of them, bone by bone, made by Sir S. Zuckerman and published in *Evolution as a Process,* which was edited by Sir J. Huxley, A. C. Hardy and E. B. Ford.

On page 303 of his 50-page article Sir S. Zuckerman lays down the following principles, according to which the claim of these *Australopithecus* fossils should be judged:

> If material signs of these essential evolutionary changes were to be sought in fossil remains, attention would have to be directed to: 1) the development of a brain of human shape and proportions; 2) a decrease in the size of the teeth and of the face, with the associated changes in the curvature of the dental arcade; 3) evidence of an upright posture, with the appropriate dimensional relations of limbs and trunk.
>
> This three-fold pattern of physical change is necessarily pre-

supposed by the belief that man is descended from a non-human Primate—however many other specifically hominid features of a less obvious kind may also have been evolved in the process.

In this article I propose to examine some of the evidence put forward to support the proposition that the tripartite pattern of major change, or a significant piece of it, is manifested by the fossil Primates now assigned to the *Australopithecinae*.

Then a detailed examination of each of the fossils mentioned above is presented, and on pages 346 and 347 he gives the following conclusions:

The conclusions to which the present analysis points are clear. In the first place, our safest inference from the available facts is that the brains of the fossil *Australopithecinae* did not differ in size or conformation from those of such modern apes as the gorilla. In the second, we may conclude that the fossils provide no significant evidence of the major decrease in size of jaws and teeth which is presupposed by the thesis that the *Hominidae* evolved from non-human primate forms. And thirdly, the evidence is also clear that the skull of the *Australopithecinae* was balanced on the vertebral column as in apes, rather than in man, whereas it is far from certain that the innominate bones that are associated with these fossils betoken an upright gait of the kind characteristic of the *Hominidae*.

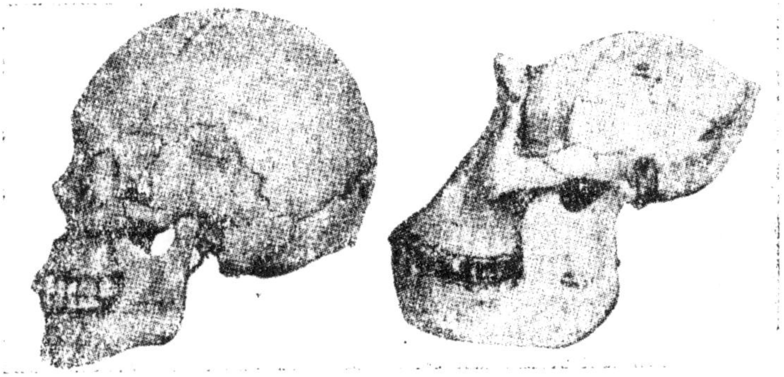

HUMAN SKULL SKULL OF GORILLA

Note the great difference between these skulls. The human skull is small below and large and voluminous above; the skull of the gorilla, which among the apes has the largest brain capacity, is large below and small and narrow above.

The skulls of the Australopithecinae resembled gorilla skulls at the top, but had pointed muzzles.

The view about the poise of the head is based (*a*) on the position of the occipital condyles in *Plesianthropus* 5; and (*b*) on the fact that the two specimens assigned to the species *Paranthropus crassidens* possess sagittal crests. The correlation that exists between the relevant cranial features makes it plain that the presence of these crests presupposes prominent nuchal crests and a nuchal shelf, and correspondingly, the presence of neck muscles as powerful as those which we find in modern apes. . . .

If we combine these various conclusions, the safest overall inference that can be drawn from the facts which have been discussed here is that the *Australopithecinae* were predominantly ape-like, and not man-like creatures. While the specimens assigned to this sub-family add considerably to our information about the Primate fossil history, they provide no clean indication of the major anatomical changes one would expect in the transformation of a non-human Primate into a big-brained bipedal animal possessing articulate speech and the capacity to use his hands to work with artificially fashioned tools. The answer to the question put on page 303, whether the characteristics of the *Australopithecinae* conform with the whole or a large part of the pattern of change that must have occurred during the transformation to manhood of a non-human Primate is, then in general in the negative.[1]

The Rabat Man of Morocco

In 1933, parts of a skull which appears to have been destroyed by the explosion of a mine were found at Rabat in Morocco. The only parts that could be identified were a broken mandible with a few teeth and part of the roof of the mouth. Propagandists for the theory of evolution refer to these bits of a skull as "The Rabat Man."

There is no indication whatever about the brain capacity of the skull and the evidence available about the alleged peculiarities of the fragments found is not reliable. The claims, therefore, that these fragments represent a "hominid" or "missing link" may be safely dismissed. (See *Les Hommes Fossiles,* 1952 ed., pp. 443-444).

---

1. From a chapter by Sir S. Zuckerman in *Evolution as a Process,* published by Allen and Unwin, London, and by the Macmillan Company, New York.

General Conclusions About the Origin of Man From the Results of a Hundred Years' Search For a Link Between Man and Beast

Our first conclusion is that the hundred years' search has provided us with a reasonably certain account of man on earth and his activities back to the time of Adam and Eve.

Our second conclusion is that the study and classification of the fossils found show that the predominant race in Europe during the Old Stone Age (which provides us with specimens of man's first tools) was the Neanderthal race. It is now agreed that the men of this race were of powerful physique; that they had all the characteristics of the *homo sapiens,* or normal man; that they had prominent brow ridges and receding chins; and that the race became extinct, and therefore cannot be regarded as a link in the development of man. As the Neanderthal man is found all over those parts of Europe not affected by the Ice Age, all over Africa and Asia Minor, and as only a small number of fossils of other races of families belonging to the Old Stone Age have been found, it is most probable, if not certain, that the Neanderthal race was the race of Cain, and that, of the other fossils of the same period which have been found, some belonged to the race of Seth, and others to the race that resulted from the intermarriage between the race of Cain and the race of Seth.

Our third conclusion is that the remaining fossils put forward as fossils of missing links—the *Australopithecinae,* the Peking Man and the Java Man fossils—have no claim to be called fossils of "missing links," they are just fossils of apes or monkeys.

Our fourth conclusion is that as no fossils of man belonging to the part of the Old Stone Age which was prior to the *hiatus* or Deluge, have been found in South America, Australia, India, China, anywhere east of the Himalaya Mountains, or anywhere affected by the Ice Age, it is very probable, if not certain, that man before the Deluge was confined to Europe, Africa and the part of Asia west of the Himalaya Mountains and possibly to North America.

Our fifth conclusion is that the Fontéchevade fossil skulls (which were discovered by Mlle. Henri-Martin in 1947) represent a race that was certainly as old, and most probably older, than the Neanderthal race. As these skulls are perfectly formed, and resemble in all important details well-formed skulls of modern man, they afford a strong scientific confirmation of the common belief of all Christians that the first man, Adam, was a perfectly formed human being and not the result of evolution from a brute beast.

Our sixth conclusion is that the early accounts of the Neanderthal Man were wrong, not only because they represented him as a creature in the process of evolution—a position now abandoned by experts—but also because they represented his primitive mode of life as a hunter who neither tilled the ground nor kept domestic animals, as the mode of life of earliest man. Abundant evidence will be given in the section on the Deluge, which follows this, to show that agriculture and stock-raising were practiced by the descendants of Seth in Palestine, and in Iran by the descendants of Tubalcain who, in addition, manufactured instruments by hammering copper, while the Neanderthal Men roamed over Europe and Asia, hunting wild animals and living in caves.

Our seventh conclusion is that the Neanderthal race was a branch, but not the main branch, of the race of Cain. This conclusion is based, not on the repulsive physical characteristics of the race, which could have been acquired by their life in the open as hunters, but on two other considerations. The first is, because during the age before the Flood, the Neanderthal race had practically the exclusive use of the hunting grounds all over Europe and Africa, and only the predominant race, which before the Flood was the race of Cain, could have held that position. While fossils of the Neanderthal race and of a race with some of their peculiarities were found all over Europe and Africa, only in two places were fossils of any other race found; at Swanscombe in England, where the fossil skull of a woman was found, and at Fontéchevade in France, where two skulls resembling skulls of modern man were found, but in this case there are indications that the owners of the skulls were murdered. (See *Testimony of the Spade* by Bibby).

The second consideration is that fossils of a mixed race with pronounced Neanderthal traits were found in Palestine, which must have originated from intermarriage between the Neanderthal race and the race that inhabited Palestine. Palestine, as we shall see, was the home of the descendants of Seth, and we are told in the Bible that the descendants of Seth intermarried with the descendants of Cain, with the result that the morals of a race that had lived previously in isolation became corrupted. (*Gen.* 6:2).

Our overall conclusion is that Paleontology furnishes us with an unanswerable argument for the traditional teaching that there is no genetic link between man and beast, but that man was specially created by God.

There is a further conclusion which will be discussed in the chapter on the teaching of the Church about the origin of man, which is, that as the argument for polygenesis, or plurality of the ancestors of man, was based entirely on the genuineness of such fossils as those of the Java Man, the Peking Man, the Australopithecinae, and on the unfounded assumption that man was found in America, India, China and Indonesia, as early, if not earlier, than in Europe and Africa, this argument collapses, and thus there is a practical, scientific solution of the question of man's ancestry which is in harmony with the teaching of the Catholic Church.

Finally, as it was on the genuineness of the fossils claimed to be those of "missing links," such as the Australopithecinae, Peking Man and Java Man fossils, that demands were based by those Catholics who advocated a relaxation of the restrictions of the Holy See on the teaching of human evolution, and a reform of the Catechism so as to include the theory of evolution as the most probable explanation of the origin of man, the conclusive proofs that we have given that these fossils are not genuine, but are only a mumbo-jumbo to frighten people, abundantly justifies the wisdom of the Holy See in remaining firm.

Note: Before the Deluge the great bulk of the human race lived in the Fertile Crescent—Egypt, Palestine, Mesopotamia and Iran—where the inhabitants built towns and cities, while the Neanderthal Man lived in caves.

Chapter 8

BIOLOGISTS AND THE ORIGIN OF MAN

Conclusions arrived at during the past few years on the various questions that have reference to the origin of man, and admissions made by prominent scientists such as Sir Julian Huxley which have been given in the last Chapter of Part I and Chapter 2 of Part II of this book, make the writing of the present chapter largely a matter of summarizing what has been already said and drawing conclusions from it.

The statement made in Chapter 7 of Part I, that biologists cannot settle the question of whether species arose by evolution or not and that the theory of evolution must stand or fall by the evidence of the fossils which furnish the only direct evidence, applies with much greater force to the origin of man. In *Evolution in Action,* Sir J. Huxley writes:

> For the biologist who wants to study the time relations of evolution, fossils are the basic documents; the facts of comparative anatomy and ontogeny, of adaptation and geographical distribution and ecology, all shed essential light on the process; but fossil remains provide direct "evidence."

This is admitted in practice by those biologists who hold the theory that man's body was evolved from an animal, for in practically all books on the origin of man by them, they give 1) a list of fossils of beings alleged to represent "missing links" and 2) they apply their knowledge of biology to interpret these fossils. This is true both of textbooks on biology for schools and universities such as *Biology and Man* by F. G. W. Knowles for primary schools, and *Biology and the Vertebrates* by Walter and Sayles, for universities, and of the more ambitious books of reference on the origin of man by Catholic authors such as Frs. Marcozzi, Ezpondaburu and Grison referred to above. As already stated, these three authors from Italy, Spain and France respectively, give as beings in the process of evolution toward man the Piltdown Man (in the editions before 1954), the Australopithecinae (the Southern Ape-Man of Drs. Dart, Broom and Robinson) and the Peking Man, and they apply their expert knowledge of biology to show that some of the traits of these beings belong to the ape species, and some to man. Now it is admitted by all that the Piltdown Man was a forgery; Sir S. Zuckerman proved conclusively in his chapter in *Evolution as a Process* edited by Sir J. Huxley, that the Australopithecinae of South Africa had no claim whatever to be regarded as beings in the process of evolution toward man; in Chapter 5 of Part II evidence has been given to show that the Peking Man is even a worse case of fraud than the Piltdown Man, and in addition evidence was given to show that of all the candidates put forward by evolutionists during the past hundred years not a single one is genuine in the sense that it represents a being in any stage of evolution toward man, all the candidates being either men in the full sense of *homo sapiens,* or simply apes or monkeys. So therefore the slate of "missing links" is wiped clean, and not even one remains for the biologist to quote as a proof of human evolution or to exercise his biological skill in explaining it.

From the time when the evolution of man from one of the great apes was first propounded by Darwin, all advocates of his theory, including biologists, relied chiefly on the evidence of fossils to prove the theory. A fossil skull of the Neanderthal Man was discovered at Gibraltar in 1848, but its peculiarities escaped unnoticed for the very good reason that it differed very little from the ordinary human skull, as is now admitted. A second Neanderthal skull was found in the valley of the Neander in Germany in 1856, three years before Darwin's *Origin of Species* was published and 15 years before the publication of his *Descent of Man.* When this fossil skull was found in the Neander Valley, fraud was resorted to immediately: the brain capacity was minimized and the peculiarities were exaggerated. The Neanderthal Man has been used for a hundred years by evolutionists, including biologists, as proof of the evolution of man, and is still being used by propagandists in spite of the evidence to the contrary given by experts, most of whom are evolutionists. As pointed out already, the Neanderthal Man had on an average a larger brain capacity than the present day man; though of average height, he had the bones and joints of a giant; he was a skillful tool-maker; he buried his dead with ceremony in carefully prepared graves; his chief peculiarity was a prominent ridge over the eyes much like the aborigines of Australia of the present day, which is most probably due to his open air life.

Retreat of the Propagandists for the Theory of Human Evolution

The history of the propaganda for the evolution of man since the time of Darwin is the history of a disorderly retreat from one position to another, with the scientists who had a reputation to maintain leading the way, and the mere propagandists following far behind. In the case of genuine scientists, who inherited the theory of evolution, like Sir Julian Huxley, the scientist usually prevailed over the propagandist, and they abandoned arguments in favor of evolution that had been in common use, when science demanded it. The following are the principal admissions made:

Man is not evolved from any of the great apes, or from any of the monkey tribe. Both apes and monkeys are too highly specialized, hence it would have been biologically impossible for man to be evolved from either an ape or a monkey. So say Sir Julian Huxley and all prominent scientists. In *Evolution as a Process,* Huxley writes: "High specialization of one mode of life restricts the possibilities of switching over to another," and in the last chapter we gave the quotation from Leakey's *Adam's Ancestors* which says that man could not have been evolved from either a monkey or an ape, because they were too highly specialized.

However, in *The Descent of Man* (1871), Darwin wrote as follows:

> As soon as some ancient member in the great series of the primates (monkeys and apes) came to be less arboreal, owing to a change in its manner of procuring subsistence, or to some change in the surrounding conditions, its habitual manner of progression would have been modified.
>
> We can, I think, partly see how he has come to assume his erect gait. . . It would have been an advantage to man to become a biped; but for many actions it is indispensable that the arms and the whole upper part of the body should be free: and he must for this end stand firmly on his feet. To gain this great advantage the feet must have been rendered flat. . . . (*The Descent of Man,* p. 76).

This explanation of how an ape was gradually transformed into a man has been dropped by Darwin's present-day followers as a biological absurdity. They retreat back a few million years and fix on the lemur as the common ancestor of monkeys, apes and men, forgetting that they only increase the difficulties, for they have to seek for "missing links" not only between man and the lemur, which, as we have seen, cannot be found, but between the lemur and the monkey and ape, which are still missing. In other words, evolutionists have retreated from one biological absurdity to another.

Note: The lemur is a small animal with a thick coat of hair, a bushy tail and a pointed muzzle. It resembles the squirrel in its arboreal habits, and is still found in Madagascar.

Abandonment of the Principal "Missing Links"

The two principal "links," the Piltdown Man and the Australopithecinae, have been abandoned. The Piltdown Man can never again be mentioned, but we still find the Australopithecinae or South African ape-men mentioned in recent books by evolutionists like Sir Arthur Keith. In *A New Theory of Evolution* (1948), Sir Arthur Keith refers to them in a chapter headed "Crossing the Rubicon 'twixt Ape and Man."

Dr. Dubois, who brought the fossil skull home from Java that gave its name to the Java Man *(Pithecanthropus erectus),* admitted before his death that, instead of its representing the skull of a creature with a brain capacity halfway between ape and man (850 cc), it was the skull of a common gibbon. Three attempts made subsequently, including the most recent attempt by Dr. Königswald, have failed to establish the Java Man as a "missing link."

The Neanderthal Man has been finally abandoned as an argument for human evolution. He is now acknowledged to have been a *homo sapiens* in the full sense who developed a few peculiarities, and became extinct at the time of the *hiatus*.

The Peking Man has been shown to be an even worse case of fraud than the Piltdown Man.

The above-mentioned fossils have been used during the past century in books both by non-Catholics and Catholics as the principal argument for the theory of human evolution. Their abandonment by the leading authorities on human fossils means that the argument for human evolution based on the fossil remains of man has collapsed completely.

In 1950, when Pope Pius XII issued the Encyclical *Humani Generis,* to which Catholic evolutionists are so fond of referring, doubts about the claims made in favor of these fossils had not been resolved, and they were represented in books by Catholic authors like Fr. Marcozzi S.J. of the Gregorian University, Rome, as fossils of beings in the process of evolution toward man. Nevertheless, His Holiness refused to give anything more than a mere permission to discuss the possibility of the origin of man from pre-existing living matter, on the conditions that the theory was not to be taught as an established fact, and that the Biblical account of man's creation by God was not to be ignored.

Now that the claims in favor of all these fossils to represent creatures in the process of evolution have been disposed of, and that the principal arguments from biology have been abandoned, it is vain for Catholic evolutionists to hope that the Holy See will relax its restrictions on the teaching of the theory of human evolution.

Abandonment of the Principal Biological Arguments

Among the biological arguments most commonly used, even by Catholic writers, is Haeckel's argument from embryology. This argument is found in most present-day books on the origin of man by evolutionists, non-Catholic and Catholic alike. The theory which was first propounded by Haeckel is that every embryo recapitulates the history of the race; that the embryo appears first as a shapeless mass, then assumes during its development the forms of the various creatures from which this embryo, whether of man or animal, has been evolved. Haeckel faked a series of photographs of embryos in the various stages of its development to illustrate his theory. Present-day evolutionists give illustrations in their books which they claim are not faked. A refutation of the theory was given in Fr. Wasmann's *Modern Biology and the Theory of Evolution;* it was again refuted by Douglas Dewar in *Is Evolution Proved?*, but it is only during the past few years that it was abandoned by prominent evolutionists. Professor Hardy contributed a chapter to *Evolution as a Process* (pp. 122-142) under the title *Escape from Specialization,* in which he showed that Haeckel's theory that the embryo in its different stages of development resembles the ancestors from which it was evolved, is absurd, and he proved by experiment that just the opposite is the truth. (See *Evolution as a Process,* edited by Sir J. Huxley, A. C. Hardy and E. B. Ford).

Sir J. Huxley summarizes Professor Hardy's chapter on page 20 of the introductory chapter as follows:

> Following de Beer and Garstang, A. C. Hardy shows that Haeckel's "Law of Recapitulation" is false, and that consequently many so-called evolutionary sequences that have been deduced from comparative anatomy and embryology should really be read in the opposite direction.

Presence of Vestigial Organs in Man

The argument for evolution based on the presence of alleged vestigial organs in man has been refuted in *L'Origine des Etres Vivants* (pp. 161-167) by Louis Vialleton of France, who was acknowledged to be one of the greatest authorities of his time on the subject.

The general argument for evolution based on the presence of vestigial organs in animals is refuted in the introduction to the Everyman's Edition of Darwin's *Origin of Species,* by Dr. W. R. Thompson, Director of the Commonwealth Institute of Biological Control, Ottawa, who ranks among the leading authorities on biology of our time, and who is a strong opponent of the theory of human evolution (*op. cit.* pp. xiv, xv).

The whole question of vestigial organs in animals and men is treated at considerable length in *Is Evolution Proved?* by Douglas Dewar, and the argument is refuted in detail (pp. 222-248). On page 224, he says:

> Some transformists realise how rare vestigial organs are. Thus E. S. Goodrich, late Regius Professor of Zoology at Oxford, writes (*Ency. Brit.* Vol. 8, p. 926): "It is doubtful whether any really useless parts are ever preserved for long unless they are significant, and many of the so-called useless organs are now known to fulfil important functions."

Darwin's Machinery to Effect the Evolution of Species

According to Darwin's theory, the chief agency that effects the transmutation of one species into another is natural selection acting on small fortuitous mutations. We have already given a quotation from Dr. W. R. Thompson's introduction to *The Origin of Species,* which reads:

> Darwin's conviction that evolution is the result of natural selection acting on small fortuitous variations, says Guenot, was to delay the progress of investigations on evolution for half a century.

Sir Julian Huxley, in his introductory chapter to *Evolution as a Process,* says:

> Muller has calculated that the most conservative odds against a higher organism, such as a man, a mammal, or even a fruit fly, coming into existence fortuitously without the operation

of selection by the union of one stock of all the necessary mutations are given by a number with so many noughts after it that it would take an average book of 300 pages to write it out.

Sir Julian defines the mysterious agencies "natural selection" and "struggle for existence" as "highly metaphorical terms" (*Evolution in Action,* p. 39). He makes large demands on the credulity of his followers when he claims that natural selection which he calls "a highly metaphorical term" working on the extremely rare favorable mutations is capable of producing from the first living organism spontaneously generated all the myriad species of plants and animals, including man himself. On p. 40 of *Evolution in Action,* he rules out all other agencies except natural selection and struggle for existence as mere superstitions in the following words:

> With the knowledge which has been amassed since Darwin's time, it is no longer possible to believe that evolution is brought about through the so-called inheritance of acquired characters—the direct effects of the use and misuse of organs, or of the changes in the environment; or by the conscious or unconscious will of organisms; or through the mysterious operation of some vital force; or by any other inherent tendency. What this means in the technical terms of biology, is that all the theories lumped together under the heads of orthogenesis and Lamarkism are invalidated, including Lysenko's Michurinism, which is now the officially approved theory of genetics and evolution in the U.S.S.R. They are "out"; they are no longer consistent with the facts. Indeed, in the light of modern discoveries, they no longer deserve to be called scientific theories, but can be seen as speculations without due basis of reality, or old superstitions disguised in modern dress.

So, then, most of the old arguments used in proof of the theory of evolution, including arguments at present in use in the U.S.S.R., fall under Huxley's guillotine.

The Great Difficulty: Could Human Language, Intelligence, Sense of Right and Wrong, Religion, Have Been Acquired by Evolution?

Sir J. Huxley states the difficulty, on page 12 of *Evolution as a Process,* as follows:

> Anatomically the human type constitutes one Family of one Order, of one Sub-class, of the Class Mammilia; biologically, he represents a new Phylum and indeed a new Kingdom. It is quite possible that even if man were to be miraculously removed from the scene, the remaining animal types would all prove to be so specialized that not one of them would be capable of the only new step which would constitute further biological progress—the step towards concept formation, language, and a tool-making, psycho-social mode of existence.

In his own book, *Evolution in Action* (published by Chatto and Windus, London, 1953), Sir Julian deals at greater length with the uniqueness of man among the animals, because of his possession of human language, intelligence and the power of distinguishing between right and wrong. He points out that man is the only animal that possesses speech and a common pool of organized experience for a group; that he is the only animal subject to mental or emotional conflict, and capable of practicing repression and of making a choice; that he alone has a sense of the sacred or is capable of practicing religion.

He points out that while parrots can learn elaborate phrases, they cannot be taught to associate words with purposes, for instance to say "food" when hungry, and that while apes can learn a number of tricks, they cannot be taught to speak. (See *op. cit.* pp. 104, 107).

Then we have the famous passage by Shakespeare in *Hamlet* on the uniqueness of man, which reads:

> What a piece of work is man! How noble in reason! How infinite in faculties! In form and musing how express and admirable! In action how like an angel! In apprehension how like a god! The beauty of the world! The paragon of animals! (Act II, Sc. II).

Much more might be added about man's uniqueness: about his gifts of music, poetry, painting; about his capabilities for unselfishness, heroism, patriotism, and the sublime heights to which he can rise by sacrificing himself in the service of God and his fellow men.

It is not in the power of any biologist, Catholic or non-Catholic, to show from biology how these various powers of man could have been acquired from a lower animal by a process of evolution. Since the fossils of the Piltdown Man, etc., have been thrown into the scrap heap, biologists have been deprived of their "missing links" and "hominids," and have now to show how an ape or a monkey could suddenly be transformed into a rational creature. If a Catholic evolutionist falls back on the assumption that Almighty God, when infusing the human soul, at the same time changed the body of the monkey or ape to suit it, let him explain why it would not be in keeping with God's Almighty power and wisdom to create man's body directly from the slime of the earth, as we are told in *Genesis,* than to take the body of an animal and unmake it, changing its instincts and the purpose for which it was created. Why should a Catholic scientist attempt to change God into what Cardinal Newman calls the "constitutional deity" of the heretics, on whom they impose a constitution according to which He must act? When the Second Person of the Blessed Trinity was on earth, He refused to be bound by any such constitutional laws. When occasion arose, He ordered the winds and waves to be made calm, He called Lazarus from the grave where he had been for four days, He multiplied the loaves and fishes, etc., why then could not "He through Whom all things were made" have made our first parents from the slime of the earth?

Cardinal Ruffini, who is a member of the Biblical Commission, in commenting on the words, "special creation of man" which occur in the decree issued in 1909, writes as follows:

> The Commission, with its very high authority, requires, therefore, that a special intervention of God in the creation of man must be admitted; but it does not determine in what constitutes this special intervention.
>
> The attempt to maintain that, in the act of infusing the spiritual soul, the Creator transformed the body of an animal in such a way as to render it fit to receive the human soul, is quite sufficient to exclude that evolution which the transformists defend. In fact, to affirm that a particular intervention of God was necessary in order to render the body of a brute beast fit to become the body of the first man is the same as saying

> that such a privileged body did not and could not reach the stage of development (required for the rational soul) by a law of nature, and this strikes precisely at the basis of all evolutionism.
>
> Now, we ask, if there must be a special divine action, why is an animal assigned as the matter rather than the dust of the earth of which the Bible speaks? It is certainly no more difficult for the Almighty to form Adam's body directly from the clay of the earth than it would be to produce it from the body of an animal.[1]

Enough has been said in this chapter to show that Catholics have now nothing to fear from the arguments of biologists in favor of the Man-from-Ape or Man-from-Lemur theory. If readers want further details about biological arguments that have been used (including those which have fallen under Sir J. Huxley's guillotine) and their refutation, they will find both in the famous book by Louis Vialleton *L'Origine des Etres, L'Illusion Transformiste* (Paris, 1930), referred to above, or in *Modern Biology and the Theory of Evolution* by Fr. Wasmann, S.J. (published by Paul Keegan in 1910) or in *Is Evolution Proved? An Argument between H. S. Shelton and Douglas Dewar* (published by Holles and Carter in 1947). For an account of modern theories of evolution, readers are referred to *Recent Theories of the Origin of Man* (The Victoria Institute, Surrey, 1953) by Douglas Dewar in which he analyzes 10 modern (contradictory) theories about the origin of man, which includes a good account of the now unorthodox theory of Drs. Dart, Broom and Robinson, that man was evolved from a South African ape (the Australopithecinae), and Sir Arthur Keith's latest theory, which he calls *The Group Theory of Human Evolution* (London, Watts & Co., 1949). For a recent biological study of species and the modern arguments against the theory of evolution, see *Species Revalued* by Rev. Desmond Murray, O.P., F.R.E.S. (London, Blackfriars, 1955); see also *The Theory of Evolution Judged by Reason and Faith,* by Cardinal Ernesto Ruffini (New York, J. F. Wagner; London, Herder, 1959).

1. See *The Theory of Evolution Judged by Reason and Faith* by Cardinal Ruffini, New York, 1959.

Chapter 9

THE TEACHING OF THE CATHOLIC CHURCH ON THE ORIGIN OF MAN

As stated in the preface, serious doubt still exists in the minds of some Catholics as to what exactly the Church binds them to believe, what is a matter for discussion, and what may be taught (in spite of the very definite teaching on this subject found in the Encyclical *Humani Generis,* one of the objects of which was to settle these doubts). We pointed out that the origin of these doubts was the acceptance as established facts of what are mere theories, and a consequent straining both of the words of Holy Scripture, and of the directions given by the Teaching Authority of the Church through Papal Encyclicals and other channels, to make these fit in with imaginary scientific conclusions.

We have given the conclusions which an impartial examination of the latest evidence seems to justify. We now give a summary of the teaching of the Church as expressed in the definitions of Councils of the Church, in Papal Encyclicals, in the tradition of the Church and in the teaching of the Fathers. In order to give greater authority to this summary of the teaching of the Church on this question (which is one of the most important of our time) we take it from *Sacrae Theologiae Summa,* to which we have referred in the introductory chapter. In this important four-volume textbook on dogmatic theology which was published at Madrid in 1952 by the Spanish Jesuits, a chapter of Volume II is devoted to the teaching of the Church on the origin of man. The following is a translation of this chapter:

"The Origin of the Human Body"

Article I The creation of our first parents as regards their bodies.
Thesis: Our first parents were formed as regards their bodies immediately by God.

506. The question concerning the origin of the bodies, whether of our first parents or of the rest of mankind, is of special moment to theologians. We shall here speak of this.

The body of each man proceeds from his parents: what about the bodies of Adam and Eve, who had no parents? Did they come from some inorganic or organic element, or were they created immediately by God Himself? This question concerns theology in a very special way, because in *Gen.* (1:26; 2, 7:21) God is represented as creating with special care and solemnity the being who was to be set over visible things as king and priest, to be divinely adopted, to be called the progenitor of Christ, and because in general the origin of the human body is treated of in the theological sources.

507. "Natural science" (biology, paleontology) also has a contribution to make to the solution of this question. If it were once established by scientific proofs that the body of man is certainly the result of evolution, then theologians would admit the fact without further discussion. But the evolution of man's body is far from being an established fact: it is in fact a mere hypothesis, on the probability of which even the scientists hold different opinions. There are some among them who even deny it, others merely claim for it a certain degree of probability, or think that it is very obscure, or at least not more probable than the contrary hypothesis.

Indeed, since this is not a theory which can be established experimentally, the scientists, besides answering all the serious difficulties which confront transformism, would need to prove that the first man could not have been produced by any other means.

508. *Explanation of our thesis: Our first parents, or Adam and Eve,* with whose origin we are principally concerned, since it is certain that all other men proceed from them by generation, *were formed,* i.e., by an act of molding or forming,

since, as is clear enough, it is supposed that our first parents, in regard to their bodies, were not made immediately from nothing, but from some pre-existing matter, organic or inorganic.

In regard to their bodies (quoad corpora). The origin of the body alone of our first parents is under consideration, since the origin of their souls is both clearly expressed in Scripture and is proved elsewhere later on. The body is taken to be a *human* body, i.e., one aptly and proximately disposed for the reception of a rational soul and hence demanding it *(exigens)*.

Immediately by God. These words in our thesis mean that God did not employ, even as instrumental cause, a brute from which to form the human body, by means of some kind of evolutionary process of the said brute, but made the body of Adam directly from inorganic matter, and the body of Eve directly from the body of Adam (from a rib or in some other way). This immediate action on inorganic matter excludes even special transformism. God therefore would be the *one and only efficient* cause of the human body.

The body of Adam could have proceeded from a brute by an act of special intervention of God, but in our thesis we propose to prove that *de facto* it did not, so that not only natural transformism but transformism of any kind is excluded.

Our thesis does not state that the formation of the human body by its evolution from the brute is altogether *impossible,* since it would be difficult to prove this, but that *de facto* it was not formed in that way.

Likewise our thesis neither affirms nor denies the instrumental cooperation of the Angels toward the formation of Adam's body, into which God infused a soul. (1 q. 91 a. 2 ad 1). However, there is no solid reason for saying that the angels cooperated, since in the sources of God alone is said to be the maker of the human body.

The creation of man must not be conceived as if God infused a soul into a body *already* completely organized; but rather as an instantaneous action, by which God *at the same time* organized the body, created the soul and infused it into the body, although the formation of the body may be conceived as prior in the order of nature to the infusion of the soul. (1 q. 90 a. 4; 2 q. 91 a. 4 ad 3).

510. *Adversaries, Transformists,* or rather many naturalists (biologists, paleontologists) who, to omit their other views and their disagreements, hold that all living created things, including man, resulted from one or from a few organisms by a process of evolution.

They attribute the origin of man to evolution: 1) some entirely, or as regards both body and soul (rigid transformism). So Darwin, Huxley, Haeckel, many other non-Catholic scientists. 2) Some partially, or only as regards the body (mitigated transformism). There are not a few Catholics who defend this view as more or less probable; among them are: Mivart, Leroy, Zahm, and to mention a few of the more recent: Bergounioux, Colombo, Elliott, Kaelin, Marcozzi, Melendez, Messenger, Leonardi, Teilhard de Chardin, Sertillanges, De Saint-seine, Denis, Carles, Muller, etc.

Those of them who state simply the fact of transformism without mention of a special action of God, need not necessarily be thought to exclude that action.

511. *The Doctrine of the Church* (*a*) The Provincial Council of Cologne (1860).

> Our first parents were formed immediately by God. Therefore we declare that the opinion of those who do not fear to assert that this human being, man as regards his body, emerged finally from the spontaneous continuous change of imperfect nature to the more perfect, is clearly opposed to Sacred Scripture and to the Faith.

By these words *natural* mitigated transformism is condemned, but not necessarily *special* transformism.

(*b*) Reply of the Biblical Commission (D. 2123) to the question:

> Whether in particular the literal historical sense can be called in doubt, where there is question of facts narrated in these same chapters (the first three chapters in *Genesis*) which touch on the foundations of the Christian religion, as are, among

> other things. . .the special creation of man, the formation of the first woman from the first man, the unity of the human race?

Reply: Negative.

In these words it is stated that Eve was formed by God immediately, and that Adam was created by special action, not only as regards his soul, which is evident, but as regards his body. In this declaration the word "special" is not used to describe the creation of the soul of the man or of the woman (there is no distinction made between them in that matter), because Catholics have no doubt about the special creation of the soul; and because otherwise the words "special creation of the soul" would have been used. Our conclusion, therefore, is that *natural* transformism is ruled out by the above decision, but not necessarily *special* transformism.

512. *Pius XII:*

> God made man and crowned him with His own image and likeness. . . .only from man can another man proceed, who could call him father and progenitor. The helper given by God to the first man came from him also and she is flesh of his flesh. . . .taking her name from man, because she was formed from him. At the summit of the scale of living things, man endowed with a rational soul, has been placed by God as prince and sovereign of the animal kingdom. The many sided investigation, whether palaeontological, biological or morphological, about the origin of man has so far yielded no clear and certain results of a positive kind. The question looks to the future, then, for a solution, when science, illuminated by faith and under the guidance of revelation, may be able to arrive at secure and definitive conclusions concerning a matter of such great moment. (Pius XII to the members of the Pontifical Academy of Science, 1941).

513. Therefore Eve has been formed from a man. The man, having been made by God to His own Image, standing out as king among the animals by reason of his rational soul, cannot call any brute beast his father and progenitor.

From this we deduce that man, even as regards his body, has not proceeded from a brute beast at least by purely natural generation (or without special intervention by God) nor, *a fortiori,* as it seems, through any other form of natural process. But whether (allowance being made for a special divine intervention) man's body has in some way come from a brute is an open question to which investigations of natural science with the help of the truths of the faith and under the guidance of revelation may perhaps at some future date provide an answer.

514. *Pius XII.* (Encyclical *Humani Generis,* 1950):

It remains for us to say something about these questions which, although in part belonging to these sciences usually called "positive" are, however, more or less connected with the truth of faith. Not a few [Catholics] persist in demanding that the Catholic religion attach the greatest possible importance to (the conclusions of) natural science. This indeed may be commended when there is question of conclusively proved facts, but caution must be used when dealing with mere hypotheses, even though these may have some foundation in human science, whenever doctrine contained in Scripture or in tradition is touched on. But whenever such conjectural opinions are directly or indirectly opposed to doctrine revealed by God, then a claim of this kind can in no circumstances be admitted.

Wherefore in view of the present state of opinion in the domains of natural science and of theology, the teaching authority of the Church *(Ecclesiae Magisterium)* does not forbid free inquiry through research and discussion by experts in both fields into the question as to whether evolution from pre-existing living matter may have taken place in the case of the human body—for the Catholic Faith binds us to believe that human souls are directly created by God. This investigation and discussion should be so conducted that the reasons for both opinions, namely of those who favour [the theory of evolution] and those who are opposed to it, should be weighed and adjudged with gravity, moderation and restraint. [This permission to investigate and discuss is given by Catholics] on the condition that all are prepared to bow to the decision of the Church to which the duty of interpreting the Sacred Scriptures authentically and of safeguarding the dogmas of Faith has been entrusted by Christ. (cf. *Allocut. Pont. ad membr. Academiae Scientiarum. 30 novembris 1941*). Not a few [Catholic writers] are rashly and defiantly transgressing the bounds of this liberty

> of discussion and are so conducting themselves [in the discussions] as if the origin of the human body from existing living matter were a fact that had been demonstrated with certainty by discoveries actually made, and by deductions from these discoveries, and as if there was nothing contained in the sources of divine revelation, which calls for the greatest moderation and caution when dealing with this question.

515. In this Encyclical it is presumed and positively asserted that evolution of the human body is not a fact that has been actually proved but only a hypothesis, and one, too, that touches upon doctrine contained in Scripture or tradition; that this hypothesis is not certainly directly or indirectly opposed to revelation since otherwise it would have to be entirely rejected; that in view of the present state of opinion among theologians and natural scientists it may be freely discussed since the Church does not forbid it (and this does not mean that this doctrine may be propounded at will); that the discussion is permitted to experts in both fields, and provided that the reasons for and against the theory of transformism be stated with due gravity and moderation, and that those who take part in the discussions are prepared to submit to the judgment of the Church; and that anyone who states that the theory of human evolution has been demonstrated with certainty or that no information about the question at issue is found in the sources of revelation is guilty of "rashness" (in the ecclesiastical sense).

The hypothesis, therefore, of the evolution of the human body is a question that belongs to both theology and natural science; it is one for which no solution has yet been found and which can therefore at present be freely discussed among experts with the Catholic Church as judge.

It is to be noted that as regards the method in which evolution may be supposed to have taken place the words used in the Encyclical are "from already existing living material." Undoubtedly the words "from a brute beast" were avoided lest it might be supposed that man, if evolved, could have been derived from a brute beast by natural generation, an obvious supposition, but impossible, since there would be no proportion between cause and effect. But the formula "from existing living material" makes it clear that if evolution did take place, it was through some power given from outside to the material and therefore by the special action of God.

The admission of liberty of discussion about the fact of transformism must not be taken to mean that special action or influx on the part of God may be excluded from the hypothesis.

516. They speak according to Scripture and therefore they should be interpreted in the same way as Scripture: *Pope Pelagius I* (D. 228a) says: "They (our First Parents) were not born from other parents but one of them was created from clay, the other from a rib of the man." *The definition prepared by the Vatican Council reads:*

> This, our Holy Mother the Church believes and teaches: When God was about to make man, He breathed the breath of life into his body which He had formed from the slime of the earth. And blessing the First Man and Eve his wife who was formed by divine power from his side, He said: *Increase and multiply.*

The fact that Leroy was compelled to retract his opinion and that Zahm was ordered by the Holy Office to withdraw his book from circulation does not necessarily indicate that transformism, properly understood and taking due account of the sources of revelation, is either directly or indirectly opposed to revealed truth, since the explanation can be given that this action was taken either for the purpose of avoiding confusion among Christians, especially since the theory of transformism was not proved by facts, or that those authors were censured because they seemed to advocate a purely natural evolution of the human body.

517. Theological note of the Thesis: If the several quotations from the sources are taken in their obvious meaning, the thesis must be said to be of faith, but since these quotations do not necessarily exclude transformism of every kind, it appears that the thesis, taking into account revelation on the one hand and the sciences on the other, must be given

a milder theological note.

(*a*) The thesis is of *Catholic faith* insofar as it excludes any kind of transformism in the formation of Eve's body. (*b*) With regard to the body of Adam, it is theologically certain insofar as it demands action on the part of God, and rules out purely natural transformism; it is *most probable* insofar as every form of transformism is excluded.

There is no positive theological reason for the theory of transformism. Indeed the theological sources taken in themselves as they read would appear to exclude the hypothesis completely. But that cannot be absolutely proved as long as there is at least some probability for the theory of transformism so that the greater the probability, the more the probability of the above interpretation of the sources of revelation is lessened. But the degree of scientific probability for the theory of transformism is so uncertain that not even those scientists who hold the theory agree in defining it; therefore we maintain that it is most probable that every form of transformism is ruled out.

Besides, this view is held at least more commonly by theologians; for example in our own days it is held by Cardinal Ruffini, Ternus, Boyer, Basi, not however in the sense that every form of transformism is absolutely and certainly opposed to the theological sources.

518. *Proof from Sacred Scripture:* Sacred Scripture makes several references to the formation of the body of Adam. Either these references are couched in such figurative language as merely to indicate the production of man and the special creation of the soul, or they are to be taken in their obvious meaning, as indicating that the formation of Adam's body was the direct action of God, an action moreover that appears to have been exercised directly on inorganic matter. That the references are to be taken figuratively cannot be proved either from Scripture or tradition, therefore we are to accept them in their obvious meaning.

An examination of the following passages shows that this opinion is the more probable:

> And he said: Let us make man to our image and likeness; and let him have dominion over the fishes of the sea. . . .and the beasts and the whole earth. . . .and God created man to his own image; to the image of God he created him. Male and female he created them. (*Gen.* 1:26-27).

These words which refer to the creation of the body also, since mention is made of the whole man and to sexual distinction, when taken in their obvious sense, imply: (*a*) that there was *special* action on the part of God. This is clear from the solemn description in the first person of God with the plural of Majesty and from the fact that there is no mention of any second cause, while the creation of plants and animals is attributed to God in the third person with an indication that there were secondary causes: "And he said: Let the earth bring forth the green herb and such as may seed. . . ." "And he said: let the waters bring forth the creeping creature having life. . . ." (*Gen.* 1:11-12); (*b*) that man was not produced by evolution since in the references to his creation in *Genesis* there is no mention of any material *(ex qua)* from which he was produced except earth.

519. "The Lord God made the heaven and the earth and every plant in the fields;. . .and there was not a man to till the earth. And the Lord God formed man of the slime of the earth and breathed into his face the breath of life; and man became a living soul." (*Gen.* 2:4, 7).

By these words which also concern the formation of the body, since there is clear reference to a twofold action, and since the soul is said to be infused into the face or nostrils of the body, it is stated that man as regards his body was made by God, (*a*) by special action, for God alone is represented as Himself forming man's body by an action parallel to the act of creating man's soul, which was certainly a direct action on the part of God; (*b*) not by evolution, since the starting point *(terminus a quo)* is said to be inorganic matter and the *terminus ad quem* is said to be "a living individual," which implies that he did not come from something with life.

520. If our thesis is accepted, other passages of Sacred

Scripture are easily explained, e.g.:

> In the sweat of thy face thou shalt eat bread until thou returnest to the earth out of which thou wast taken; for dust thou art, and unto dust thou shalt return. (*Gen.* 3:19). Thou madest Adam of the slime of the earth and gavest him Eve as a helper. (*Tob.* 3:8). God created man of earth, and made him after his own image. (*Ecclus.* 17:1). And all men are from the ground, and out of the earth, from whence Adam was created. (*Ibid* 33:10). I myself am a mortal man, like all others, and am of the race of him, that was first made out of the earth. (*Wis.* 7:1). The first man, Adam, was made into a living soul. . . .The first man was of the earth, earthly. (*1 Cor.* 15:45, 47).

521. As we shall see presently, Eve was formed immediately by God. Therefore, *a pari,* the same should be true of Adam, especially since man surpasses woman in dignity. "For the man is not of the woman but the woman of the man. For the man was not created for the woman." (*1 Cor.* 12:8-9).

522. B. *The formation of the body of Eve.*

> Then the Lord cast a deep sleep upon Adam; and when he was fast asleep, he took one of his ribs and filled up flesh for it. And the Lord built the rib *[sela]* which he took from Adam into a woman. (*Gen.* 2:21-22).

From this it follows clearly that the body of Eve was formed by God, (*a*) by a special act (of whatever kind it might have been), and (*b*) not by evolution, as is plain from the obvious meaning of the words, and because otherwise Adam could not have said: "This now is bone of my bone and flesh of my flesh." (*Gen.* 2:23). St. Paul's words are in agreement with this: "Man. . .is the image and glory of God, but the woman is the glory of the man. For the man is not of the woman, but the woman of the man." (*1 Cor.* 11:7-8). "Adam was first formed and then Eve." (*1 Tim.* 2:13) cf. (*Eph.* 22-23).

N.B. The Hebrew word *"Sela"* need not necessarily be taken in the strict sense of "a rib" since 1) the word is variously translated by scholars and 2) even though it is translated by "rib" (in *Gen.* 2:23 and *1 Cor.* 11:8) it might be taken to indicate not a rib in the strict sense, but some part of the body of Adam. Hence in the reply given by the Biblical Commission it is stated that we are bound to hold from *Genesis* that "the formation of the first woman was from the first man" (D. 2123), as if some liberty is permitted in further determining the meaning of the passage.

The Probative Force of the Texts From Genesis 1:2 and 2:4

523. These texts (at least the second one) are certainly sufficient to prove that there was special intervention on the part of God for the formation of the human body, whether the material be said to be inorganic or organic. They do not necessarily exclude the possibility of evolution, since these words might be taken absolutely as stating the *fact* of the formation of the body from inorganic matter, but not as determining the *mode* of the formation—whether it was immediate or through evolution—so that even the words "and he became a living soul" might with regard to the word "living" in the context be a continuation of the anthropomorphism preceding it (the fashioning of the body and the breathing into it of the spirit), indicating simply that the body became a human individual by the infusion of the soul without intending primarily to declare that it was "living." And indeed, are not we ourselves said to be produced from the earth, even though we do not proceed immediately from it, but only immediately? (*Ps.* 104, 14; *Is.* 64:7; *Eccles.* 12:7; *Job* 10:9; 33:6).

A fortiori the same is true of the proving force of the other passages of Scripture cited above. Hence some modern exegetes think that the fact of transformism can be reconciled with Scripture.

But even granting that hypothesis, difficulties which appear to be insoluble arise against it. For example (besides other difficulties such as the obvious and natural sense of Scripture): (*a*) Adam is represented in *Genesis* only as an adult capable of generating (1:27), of tilling and taking care of the garden (2:15), of precept (2:17), of matrimony (2:23), of sinning (3:6-19). Now these texts cannot be so interpreted (to buttress up transformism) that their historical substance would not be jeopardized. (D. 2123).

Hence the fathers and exegetes always represent Adam as an adult.[1]

But the supposition of a man proceeding from a brute beast as an adult is so preposterous that even the transformists suppose that the transition of brute to man took place in the embryonic state. (*b*) If Eve was formed from Adam by the special intervention of God, without evolution, why could not Adam also have been formed from the earth without evolution?

Nevertheless, in spite of these and other difficulties it does not seem that transformism is absolutely excluded by teaching of Scripture although it is exceedingly difficult to reconcile it with it.

524. *Proof from Tradition.* The Fathers, although not directly refuting the theory of transformism since they did not know about it, have, however, so spoken that it cannot be reconciled with their statements taken in their obvious meaning. This is easily admitted by all.

Here the author gives a number of quotations from the fathers in proof of the above statement.[2]

528. *Proof from theological reason.* Against natural transformism: All men are descended from Adam and Eve. But if many men were evolved from brutes, as would have happened if the theory of natural transformism were true, why have all of them except Adam and Eve perished?

The first woman was formed from man by God. But according to transformism she should, like the man, have proceeded from the brutes by evolution. If, however she was not evolved from the brute beasts, by the same right we should suppose that the man was not the result of evolution but was

1. *Ceuppens.* p. 171. "With the exception of St. Augustine whose testimony is very much disputed, the Fathers admit the immediate formation of the first man by God; God directly and by Himself formed the body of Adam from the slime of the earth. The modern theory of evolution or transformism was unknown to them; they did not doubt about the stability and immutability of species; it is no wonder, then, that there is no trace of the theory of evolution to be found in the writings of the Fathers."
2. See Introductory Chapter to Part II for quotations from the Fathers.

formed immediately by God.

The man whom *Genesis,* Chapters 2 and 3 represent as being from the beginning corporally, physically and intellectually perfect, does not easily fit in with the man who was in the beginning weak and imperfect such as natural transformism supposes.

Against Special Transformism

According to Tradition, the first man was an adult from the beginning of his existence. But this would be denied by transformism if the body of the brute was changed into a man in the embryonic stage, nor does transformism explain, without postulating gratuitously several great miracles, how that infant arrived at adult age. If it asserts that the body of the brute already in adult stage was changed into a human body, it gives no solid reason for such a miracle. Therefore the theory of special transformism cannot be admitted, unless some further proofs can be given.

529. Philosophy cannot either rule out or confirm special transformism; at best it can establish its possibility. But it can refute the theory of natural transformism for this reason among others, that it gratuitously supposes, contrary to the principle of causality, that any nature (with God's ordinary *concursus*) can tend to produce an effect more perfect than itself, i.e., that the body of a brute had evolved naturally to such a state of perfection that it called for the infusion of a human soul or that a brute can give birth to a man.

530. *Transformism considered scientifically.* The theory, especially as applied to man, labors under the following difficulties which make it extremely doubtful.

In General. The theory cannot be proved directly, but only indirectly or by indications. Some living things have continued to be the same as they were many thousands of years ago. Some organisms differing among themselves seem to have appeared simultaneously and suddenly. There are reversions (to former type) not corresponding in order to the principles of evolution. Those forms are lacking which could really be proved to be intermediate or transitionary from one class or type to another. It cannot be proved that acquired characteristics or qualities are transmitted by heredity; sudden changes (in the embryonic period) in which characteristics in some respects new are acquired do not reach considerable proportion and may explain the origin of new breeds or varieties but not of new types. Nor is there any proof for the transformation of instincts which differ in different series of living things.

531. *In particular with reference to man.* No animal (or fossil) has yet been found from which it might be said with sufficient probability that man was derived. Man is the only animal that lacks that aptitude for defending himself and living an independent life with which other animals are endowed almost as soon as they are born; therefore it would be necessary to make the supposition that he was evolved from some animal less fitted to defend itself than he is; unless contrary to the principles of transformism it be gratuitously stated (presuming special intervention by God is not invoked) that man in the embryonic stage, interrupting the normal evolutionary process, came forth suddenly endowed with an altogether new kind of life.

The family tree constructed by the transformists: Anthropoids, Sinanthropus, Pithecanthropus and Neanderthalensis is open to such serious objections that it may be said to be just a figment of the imagination.

534. *Corollary.* Prudence is necessary when dealing with the question of the origin of man. It is not the business of a priest as much to defend or propagate the theory of transformism, or to speak about this theory to the laity without some cogent reason. If the necessity for doing so should arise, let him explain the theory with great moderation and let him point out the great difficulties against the theory which have led many scientists to reject it. He should be aware that the common people are not able to take in subtle theological distinctions about this matter and that they might easily be led to believe to the detriment of their faith that a doctrine that had been taught them as contained in the Scripture, namely that man was formed from the slime of the earth, had been found to be false. Indeed, they might easily be drawn into

error, assuming that the theory of transformism was certain because it is proposed by a priest, when in fact it is only a mere hypothesis bound up with such difficulties that perhaps in the near future it may be pronounced to be false. *(End of the translation).*

The Question of Polygenesis

The part of the Encyclical *Humani Generis* which deals with the theory of polygenesis reads as follows:

> When however there is question of another conjectural opinion, namely polygenesis, the children of the Church by no means enjoy such liberty. For the faithful cannot embrace that opinion which maintains either that after Adam there existed on earth true men who did not take their origin from him as from the parent of all, or that Adam represents a certain number of first parents.
>
> Now it is in no way apparent how such an opinion can be reconciled with that which the sources of revealed truth and the documents of the Teaching Authority of the Church propose with regard to original sin actually committed by an individual Adam, and which through generation is passed on to all and is in everyone as his own.

Letter of Msgr. Montini On Behalf of Pope Pius XII

Since the above translation was made of the Chapter on the Origin of Man in Vol. II, Part III, Chapter 1 of the 1952 edition of *Sacrae Theologiae Summa,* a new edition of this volume was published in 1958.

From this new edition we learn that the original 1952 edition (from which our translation was made) was submitted to the Holy Sce for examination and then presented to His Holiness; that His Holiness was very pleased with it for many reasons, but especially because it contained extracts from Pontifical documents, particularly the latest ones, relating to the points of doctrine expounded, and accurate explanations of these documents.

His Holiness instructed Monsignor Montini[1] to write the following letter on his behalf to the authors of this volume expressing his satisfaction with it and imparting to them his Apostolic blessing:

The Vatican
April, 24 1954

Reverend Father,

The copy of *Sacrae Theologiae Summa* which you presented to His Holiness. . . .has been received by Him with great pleasure for more than one reason.

In the first place He is deeply impressed by the zeal and energy displayed by the authors in composing this elaborate treatise destined for the instruction and formation of candidates for the priesthood. His Holiness noted with special pleasure that the book excelled not merely in scholarship but in clarity of exposition.

What pleased His Holiness most, however, was the fact that Pontifical documents, especially the most recent ones (relating to the questions discussed) were quoted in their proper context, and by their application to the theological problems that have arisen from the conditions of the age in which we live, fair and accurate solutions have been found.

His Holiness therefore confidently trusts that clerics nourished on the healthy fare provided by this manual will be ever mindful of the injunction contained in Canon 129 "that they follow the solid doctrine handed down by the Fathers and commonly received by the Church, and avoid profane novelties and false scientific theories. . . ."

J. B. MONTINI

As all the Pontifical documents concerning the Origin of Man have been quoted in the Chapter of this volume, which we have translated and which have been interpreted in the sense that man's body is not the result of evolution, but has been specially formed by God, it is legitimate to conclude that this interpretation has the approval of His Holiness.

The same opinion that man's body was specially created

---

1. Pope Paul VI.

from inanimate matter is expressed and defended in this 1958 edition.

To the list of adversaries whose opinions (that man's body was evolved from a lower animal) were refuted in the 1952 edition three notable additions were made in the 1958 edition. They are: Fr. Grison and Abbé Breuil of France; and Professor Vanderbroek of Louvain University. A brief account of the books and articles written by these three men has already been given in the introductory chapter of Part II of this book.

Cardinal Ruffini Rejects the Theory of Evolution

In his book entitled *The Theory of Evolution Judged by Reason and Faith,* to which we have already referred, Cardinal Ruffini devotes two chapters to an exposition of the teaching of the Catholic Church on the question of the origin of man. Like Fr. Sagues, S.J., whose chapter on the subject we have just quoted, His Eminence gives evidence from the Old and New Testaments, from the writings of the Fathers, the schoolmen and the theologians of the Church and from the various Papal Encyclicals on the subject to show that the theory that man's body was evolved from a lower animal is incompatible with the teaching of the Catholic Church properly understood. There had always been permission for Catholic scientists to carry out investigations about the origin of man before the Encyclical *Humani Generis* was issued. In that Encyclical the permission was renewed, but it is expressly stated in it that no Catholic is allowed to teach as an established fact that man's body was evolved from pre-existing living matter, or to ignore what the Bible says about the origin of man.

Part III

The Biblical Account of The Deluge

PREFACE—PARTS III AND IV

The traditional opinions on the Deluge and the antiquity of man which are still held by the vast majority of both clergy and laity—that the whole human race except those in the Ark perished in the Deluge, and that man's existence on the earth is of comparatively short duration—have been questioned by several writers of our time under the mistaken impression that they are either incompatible with the findings of modern science, or that modern discoveries have pushed back both the Deluge and the origin of man so far into the dim and distant past that nothing certain will ever be known about them.

The truth is to the contrary: the traditional opinions on these subjects have always been supported by contemporary science; today that support is so definite as to give moral certainty that the traditional opinions on them are right opinions.

The object of Parts III and IV is to make available the most recent findings of paleontology, archaeology and ancient history regarding the Deluge and the antiquity of man.

A conviction of the historical reality of the exemplary punishment recorded in *Genesis,* inflicted by God on the wicked descendants of Cain and on those of Seth who became partners in their crime, was never more necessary than now, when the great majority of the descendants of Noe act as if God did not exist, or that He dare not punish sin, at the very time when the threat of another chastisement more dreadul even than that of the Deluge hangs over the human race.

Rationalistic writers, and indeed some Catholic writers as well, are endeavoring—in ignorance of the most recent findings of both paleontology and archaeology—to reduce the Deluge of Noe to a mere overflowing of the rivers Tigris and Euphrates or an inundation of the low-lying country around the Caspian Sea, apparently under the impression that it was beyond the power of the Almighty to destroy the whole human race except one family that had remained faithful to Him.

Even at the beginning of the present century there was sufficient scientific evidence in books by geologists, such as Sir Henry Howorth, to show that the Deluge was of vast extent and that the human race had disappeared mysteriously from Europe, Africa and Western Asia for a long time. The two World Wars prevented further investigation of the Deluge or the Ice Ages in Europe, and in the meantime the books written by geologists of the beginning of the century got hidden away in libraries and escaped the notice of modern Scripture commentators, who imagined that the first real scientific evidence on the Deluge was provided by the excavations at Ur of the Chaldees, and that it indicated the Deluge was confined to Mesopotamia. More recent excavations carried out in Palestine and Iran, however, have shown that the flood that blotted out the cities of the low-lying plain of Mesopotamia extended not only to Palestine and Egypt, but even to the high plateau of Iran 5,000 feet above the plain of Mesopotamia.

For the composition of the present work, both the books by the geologists of the beginning of the century and the most recent books and articles on the excavations carried out in the Middle East have been consulted. It will be shown that the conclusions arrived at by the geologists at the beginning of the century have been confirmed by recent excavations.

We tender our thanks to Messrs. Ernest Benn Ltd., Fleet St., London, for permission to quote from *Excavations at Ur* and *Ur of the Chaldees* by Sir Leonard Woolley, and to reproduce illustrations from these books; to Messrs. A. D. Peters, Buckingham St., London, for permission to quote from *The Track of Man* by Henry Field; for Messrs. Collins, St. James's Place, London, for permission to quote from *Testimony of the Spade* by Geoffrey Bibby; and to The Victoria Institute, London, for permission to quote from the lecture on the Deluge delivered before the members of the Institute by Col. Merson Davies, D.Sc., PhD., F. G. S., F.R.S.E.

February 2, 1959 Patrick O'Connell

INTRODUCTORY

Some modern Scripture scholars such as Fr. Louis Pirot and Canon Albert Clamer (*La Sainte Bible,* Paris, 1955), when writing their commentaries on the Deluge, were under the erroneous impression that modern scientific research has been unable to throw any light on the question of the Deluge, and under that impression, they have thought it safe to support the theory that the Deluge was only an unusually great river flood, or in other words that there was no Deluge at all. These views have been copied into some recent books by authors who disclaim any expert knowledge on the question. This impression is completely erroneous, for the fact is, that paleontologists in their hundred years' search for the fossils of earliest man, and the archaeologists in their explorations of ancient centers of civilization, have furnished us with a mass of scientific evidence which leaves us in a position to answer with reasonable certainty all the principal questions that can be put about the Deluge.

The principle questions concerning the Deluge that call for solution are the following:

1) What is the approximate date of the Deluge?

2) Had the descendants of Adam reached all the principal countries in the world before the Deluge, and if not, what countries had they reached?

3) Did the whole human race, except Noe and the seven others with him in the Ark, perish in the Deluge?

4) Did the waters of the Deluge cover the whole earth and destroy not only all the men, but all the animals in the world except those in the Ark?

We shall first give briefly the answers which modern scientific research has provided for these questions, and then proceed to discuss each question in detail and give the evidence for the answers.

1) The approximate date of the Deluge is somewhere between the end of the Mousterian period, when the Neanderthal race disappeared, and the beginning of the Aurignacian, when the Cro-Magnon, Grimaldi and Chancelade men made their appearance. Modern methods of dating enable us to fix the date at somewhere around 7,000 B.C.

2) At the time of the Deluge, it is doubtful whether members of the human race had reached North America; it is certain that they had not reached those parts of the earth still under the ice of the last Glacial Period; and it is almost certain that they had not reached India, China, Indonesia or Australia; there is positive evidence to show that they had reached all parts of the Continent of Europe that was free from ice, all parts of Africa, and those parts of Asia west of the Himalaya system of mountains.

3) There is evidence to show that those countries above mentioned to which the human race had reached were submerged beneath the waters of the ocean less than 10,000 years ago; that the predominant races that existed in those countries before the Deluge which were populated disappeared completely; and that after an interval a new race similar to the antediluvian minority race, whose fossils have been found, began to appear.

For the information that the actual number of those who survived the catastrophe was eight persons only, we have to fall back on the account given by Moses in the Bible. If the main fact that the whole human race, with the exception of a very small minority, perished before the dispersal of the descendants of Noe to the remote parts of the world, can be established by evidence from scientific investigation, there should be no difficulty about accepting the statement in the Bible that the actual number of survivors was eight.

4) It has long been regarded as certain that the waters of the Deluge did not cover the whole world, and that all the animals did not perish. The principal reasons for this view are: *a*) There is positive evidence to show that all of Europe that was free from ice, at least all North Africa, Asia west of the Himalaya Mountains, and the plains of India, China

and North America were covered with water at the end of the last Glacial Period; there is no such evidence for the rest of the world; *b*) it would have been absolutely impossible to accommodate pairs of all the species of animals in the world (well over half-a-million) in a vessel of the dimensions of Noe's Ark, no matter how the cubic measure is computed.

PREFACE AND INTRODUCTION TO THE SECOND EDITION OF PARTS III AND IV

The Deluge and the Antiquity of Man

Like Parts I and II, Parts III and IV were written at a time when the evidence for definite solutions for the two important problems discussed in it had just become available. What were believed to be certain traces of the Deluge of Noe were discovered soon after the First Great War in the lower reaches of the Tigris and Euphrates, at Ur of the Chaldees and Kish, which gave rise to a controversy about the date and extent of the Deluge; nearly 30 years later two discoveries were made which settled this controversy. Sir Leonard Woolley, who superintended the excavations of Ur of the Chaldees, gave as his opinion that the Deluge was confined to the plains of Mesopotamia and that the date was about 4,000 B.C., and his opinion was accepted by many Scripture exegetes. In 1951, 25 years later, Dr. R. Ghirshman, a French archeologist, published a book entitled *Iran* in which he gave the results of elaborate excavations that he had superintended on the high Plateau of Iran, which proved conclusively that the same great Flood that destroyed both Ur and Kish reached up to the Plateau of Iran, destroyed the towns and cities there and left behind a deposit of salt which turned a fertile valley into an arid desert. The Flood, therefore, which destroyed Ur and Kish was not a local flood in Mesopotamia, as Woolley thought, but one of vast extent. In 1956, a lecture delivered at Oxford on May 5, 1956 which was published in the December issue of *Antiquity* gave the final results of the long-drawn-out excavations of the ancient city of Jericho. In this lecture Dr. Kathleen Kenyon described the ancient pre-Flood city of Jericho in the ruins of which clear evidence was found: 1) that the ancient inhabitants of Jericho practiced agriculture and kept the common domestic animals; 2) that the city was destroyed by a flood and 3) that the date of the flood was approximately 7,000 B.C. The flood that destroyed ancient Jericho was the same flood that destroyed Ur and Kish of Mesopotamia and the cities of Iran, and the date was not 4,000 B.C., as Woolley had guessed, but 7,000 B.C. The date 7,000 B.C. was arrived at by several carbon 14 tests carried out on charred wood found both above and below the Flood deposit. These tests confirmed the date arrived at by Baron de Geer of Sweden for the zero year of the Ice Age when a great flood also occurred in Europe and, as both great floods occurred at the same time, they must have been one and the same flood.

For a summary of the conclusions arrived at by the great geologists of the beginning of the century about the Ice Age and the great Flood that followed it, the reader is referred to Chapter 12, pp. 317-319. The account given there of the origin of the Ice Age and of the Deluge—that the Ice Age was caused by an elevation of the northern hemisphere above the snow-line and that the Deluge was caused by the sinking of the earth under the weight of ice—is confirmed in the article on the Glacial Period in the 1962 edition of *The Encyclopedia Britannica,* which says that there is evidence that the Northern Hemisphere was actually elevated by thousands of feet at the time of the Ice Age as the result of pressure from other parts of the globe.

A number of books by geologists and biblical scholars dealing with the problems of the Deluge and the early history of man have appeared since this book was written. The two most recent books by geologists were *The Genesis Flood* by John C. Whitcomb and Henry M. Morris, published in 1961, and *The Biblical Flood and the Ice Epoch* by Donald W. Patten, published in 1966. Neither of these books give the very important results obtained at the excavations of Jericho, and neither of them gives either the date arrived at by Baron de Geer for the zero year of the Ice Age or the date of the flood which destroyed Jericho.

There are several books by biblical exegetes which deal with the Flood and the early history of man, the best known of which are: *The Word of God in the Words of Man* by Fr.

Jean Levie, S.J. of Louvain, *God's Story of Creation* by Bruce Vawter, and *The Two-Edged Sword* by Fr. John McKenzie, S.J. Fr. Levie, S.J. gives Sir Leonard Woolley's mistaken opinion that the Deluge did not extend beyond the plain of Mesopotamia; Fr. Bruce Vawter says that the Mosaic account of the Deluge was only a story borrowed by Moses from the Babylonians to dramatize the punishment of sin; and Fr. McKenzie says that the chapters of *Genesis* that deal with the Flood and the early history of man have no roots either in time or in space. Though these three books are the books best known in England and America, they do not represent the views of the best biblical exegetes. On p. 94 of this work, reference is made to *Introductio in Libros Sacros Vet. Test.* by Fr. Mariani, O.F.M., which was published in Rome in 1958. This book, which became available only when the composition of the present work was completed, contains all the latest scientific information, and the conclusions arrived at by the author are the same as those expressed in this book.

There is no need, therefore, to make any change in the views expressed in the first edition of this book for they were based on definite scientific evidence, which has since had additional confirmation.

Parts III and IV Provide Additional Evidence for the Special Creation of Man and the Unity of the Human Race

By means of the scientific information assembled in Parts III and IV we can trace the history of man back to the Great Flood at the end of the Ice Age in which the whole human race, except a small remnant, perished about 7,000 B.C.; we can ascertain with certainty that the great bulk of the human race was confined to the Fertile Crescent with a relatively small nomadic population that lived on hunting wild game in Europe, Africa and possibly North America; we have evidence that it was in Mesopotamia that the first towns and cities were built after the Flood and that the art of writing was invented and developed in Mesopotamia before the dispersal of the human race. The first beginnings and the gradual development of the hieroglyphic system of writing can be traced to ancient Babylon (now called Kish); this form of writing was brought by Egyptians to Egypt in a developed form, by the Chinese to China and by the American Indians to America, and neither in Egypt, nor in China, nor among the Indians in America has it been possible to trace the system of writing to a primate form. The conclusion to be drawn from the possession of a common form of writing by the ancient Egyptians, the Chinese and the Americans, which was invented in Mesopotamia, is that the ancestors of the Egyptians, the Chinese and the Indians originally lived together in Mesopotamia while this system of writing was being developed. This fact affords important evidence that the present world population is descended from a common post-Flood pair of ancestors.

Before the Flood

As will be seen in the course of Part III, the excavations carried out during the present century have not only traced the history of man back to the Great Flood, but have also traced his history back from the Flood to earliest man. It is a most remarkable fact that the great organized expeditions composed of experts from both Europe and America never claimed to have discovered the fossils of any creature half-man, half-beast. The so-called discoveries of the mythical "hominids" or "missing links" were all made by one or a few individuals who were advocates of the theory of evolution and, as we have seen in Parts I and II, every case of these "missing links" put forward during the century has been found to be a case of fraud or error. Abundant evidence is given in Parts III and IV to show that not only is the present human race descended from the few survivors of the Deluge (Noe and his family), but also that these were the descendants of men of great intelligence whose earliest ancestors kept domestic animals, tilled the ground, invented mechanical aids—at first made from flint but as time went on, made from copper—and developed the art of making pottery and of painting to a high degree of perfection.

As the title of this Part indicates, its principal object is to deal with the period of the Deluge and the period from the Deluge to earliest man, hence only the information derived from the results of the excavations that concern these periods has been given and only those ancient sites whose history goes back to the time of the Deluge (about 7,000 B.C.) have been chosen for detailed examination. It has not been possible to add accounts of the excavations carried out at sites such as Ras Shamra (Ugarit), from which valuable information has been derived that throws light on the manners and customs of the Mosaic period.

However, some general information has been given on the period (which lasted about 5,000 years) between the Flood and the time of Abraham and a solution of the difficulties about the chronology of that period (to which the early Pharaohs of Egypt belong) has been offered. This general information and the solution of chronological difficulty will be found in Chapters 3, 4 and 5 of Part II of this book, dealing with the *Antiquity of Man.* The most recent edition of one of the world's greatest works of reference, *The Encyclopedia Britannica,* which was published in 1962, supports the accounts given in this book about the results of the excavations in the Middle East and confirms the solution of the chronological difficulty given in the first edition of this book. The following is some additional information on the chronological difficulties.

The Chronological Difficulties

There are two important dates in ancient history about the fixing of which there has been and still is much controversy; the date of the Deluge and the date of the beginning of the reign of Menes, the first of the Egyptian Pharaohs.

The Date of the Deluge

Two dates are given for the Deluge which differ by 3,000 years: the date 7,000 B.C., which is given in the first edition of this work (see p. 345, Part IV) and the date 4,000 B.C., which is given in some books by Scripture commentators.

Half of the difference between the estimates is due to the adoption of different systems of chronology and the other half, to the difficulty of getting information about the results of the excavation in the Middle East. The question has been dealt with in considerable detail in Chapter 5 of Part III (pp. 249-268) and Chapter 3 of Part IV (pp. 340-345). Further confirmation of the date 7,000 B.C. given for the Deluge in this book will be found in *Digging up Jericho* by Dr. Kathleen Kenyon and in the most recent edition of *The Encyclopedia Britannica* published in 1962. The estimate 7,000 B.C. for the date of the destruction of Jericho by water given on p. 284 of Part III was based on carbon 14 tests made on charred wood found *above* the flood deposit of Jericho; since the publication of the first edition of this book further tests on charred wood found both *above* and *beneath* the flood deposit have confirmed the date 7,000 B.C. as the approximate date of the destruction of the ancient city of Jericho by water.

The discovery at Jericho of a city that goes back to earliest times which was destroyed by water in approximately 7,000 B.C. is of very special significance, because Jericho is situated in close proximity to the Dead Sea and, according to geologists such as Sir Henry Howorth F.R.S., the saltwater in the Dead Sea and in other salt lakes with no openings to the sea was brought from the ocean in the great flood which occurred at the end of the Ice Age in 7,000 B.C. (see Chapter 12, Part III, pp. 310-319). Thus we have the results obtained by geologists at the beginning of the century confirmed by carbon 14 tests carried out in our own time.

The Second Difficulty: The Fixing of the Dates of the Reigns of Menes and the Other Egyptian Pharaohs

Though the ancient records of Egypt which were written in hieroglyphic characters have perished and a history of Egypt by Manetho, an Egyptian priest of the third century B.C., has also perished, there is still available abundant material for a history of Egypt if the date of the first of the Pharaohs could be fixed. Epitomes of Manetho's History of Egypt are included in the works of Josephus, the Jewish historian, of Eusebius and other writers; there are in addition elaborate inscriptions on the tombs of the Pharaohs and much information derived from excavations.

Two sets of figures are given for the beginning of the reign of Menes, the first of the Pharaohs, which differ by 1,460 years, the length of a Sothic cycle, and which differ also among themselves: Sir Flinders Petrie, who spent 40 years in research work in Egypt and who lived until 1942, fixed the date of the beginning of the reign of Menes at 4,777 B.C.; other authorities such as Boekh, Unger and Mariette, who, like Petrie, follow the older system of chronology, are in substantial agreement with Petrie but fix the date somewhat above 5,000 B.C.

German authorities, who accepted the Penck and Brückner theory of the four Glacial Periods without any extensive Deluge, have reduced Petrie's estimate by the length of a Sothic Cycle, which is 1,460 years; their system of chronology is referred to as the "short chronology." This system was adopted by Professor Breasted in his book *Ancient Records of Egypt* and was copied from there into the first edition of *The Catholic Encyclopaedia*. The same system with some modifications was adopted by Dr. Allbright of America in his book *From Stone Age to Christianity.* But first, before giving the objections against the "Short Chronology," for the convenience of some of our readers, let us explain what is meant by a Sothic Cycle.

A Sothic Cycle

The Egyptians had a solar calendar in which the year was divided into 12 months of 30 days each with five days added; they did not, however, add an extra day every four years for the leap year. Their year was supposed to begin on the day that Sirious, the Dog Star, which they called Sothis, appears on the horizon at the same time as the sun, which is July 19, but as there was an error in their calendar of one day every four years the simultaneous rising of the Sirius (of Sothis) and the sun occurred only once in 4 x 365 or 2,460 years, and when it did occur, the years was called a "Sothic year" and the period of 1,460 years was called a "Sothic Cycle." If a record had been kept of the occurrences of the Sothic years there would be no difficulty about Egyptian chronology, but there are records of only two Sothic years, one of which occurred between 139 and 141 A.D. and the other in the seventh year of the reign of Senusret III of the 12th Dynasty. Now the question arises, how many Sothic Cycles were there between 141 A.D. and the seventh year of Senusret III? Petrie and those who follow the older system say that there were three cycles and that consequently the seventh year of Senusret III was 4,241 B.C. Petrie fixed the date of the beginning of Menes, the first of the Pharaohs, at 4,777 B.C., but some of those who follow the old system fix it a little before 5,000 B.C. Those who have adopted the "short chronology" allow only two Sothic Cycles between 141 A.D. and the seventh year of Senusret III and fix the date of the seventh year of Senusret at about 2,781 B.C. and the beginning of the reign of Menes between 3,500 B.C. and 2,850 B.C.

The Difficulties Against the Short Chronology

1) Those who adopt the "short chronology" either deny or ignore the fact that a great flood occurred at the end of the Ice Age and ignore the *hiatus* (which was a complete break in the civilization due to the disappearance of the population) which it caused. Now there is abundant evidence to show that such a flood occurred and covered Egypt and Europe and a large part of Asia; there is also evidence to show that the date of that flood was about 7,000 B.C. The dates given by the "short chronology" for Menes—between 3,500 and 2,850—would leave an interval of from 3,500 and 4,150 years between the Great Flood and the beginning of the reign of Menes, which is altogether too long. Evidence of the first crude attempt at the developing of a hieroglyphic system of writing has been found at the excavation of Jamdet Nasr in Mesopotomia. The stratum in which it was found is dated

at about 500 years after the Flood. Clear evidence of the further development of the same system was found in the excavation of other post-flood strata in various other places in Mesopotamia. This same system in a *developed form* has been found in Egypt, China and in America without any indication in any of these three countries of the existence of a crude undeveloped form. This affords valuable evidence that the ancestors of the Egyptians, the Chinese and the American Indians had been together in Mesopotamia after the Flood and that at the dispersal, they brought the same system of writing to their respective countries; it also helps to date the time of the arrival of the Egyptians, Chinese and Indians in Egypt, China and America. Two thousand years should be ample to account for the development of the hieroglyphic system from the crude form of Jemdet Nasr period and for the establishment of the first central government in Egypt under Menes; this is approximately the date arrived at by Sir Flinders Petrie, the greatest of the Egyptologists, who lived until 1942 and who rejected the "short chronology" which he had every opportunity to examine.

The Second Difficulty Against the Short Chronology

With the additional evidence provided by the 1962 edition of *The Encyclopedia Britannica* the "short chronology" may be said to have been put out of court. The "short chronology" allows only about 200 years for the six dynasties between the twelfth, to which Senusret III belonged, and the eighteenth. There is still preserved at Turin, the Turin Papyrus, which goes back to the 13th century B.C., which contains a list of the Pharaohs for this period. Of these six Dynasties the 15th Dynasty alone consisted of six Pharaohs whose reigns, according to Manetho, the Egyptian historian, lasted 260 years (and even according to the "short chronologists" they lasted over 100 years). If one Dynasty lasted 100 years, as the "short chronologists" contend, six Dynasties could not possibly be fitted into a period of 200 years.

One of the chief arguments used in favor of the "short chronology" is that the pottery of the eighteenth Dynasty is not much better than the pottery of the twelfth, and that 200 years should be ample to account for the slight improvement.

Petrie, who was an authority on pottery, took this into account. There are two kinds of painted pottery from Egypt and Mesopotamia to be found in museums: one kind is handmade, beautifully painted, but not quite symmetrical; the other kind is made on the potter's wheel and therefore symmetrical, but is not quite so well painted. Those who, like Petrie, accept the evidence for the submergence of Egypt in the Deluge and the *hiatus* which followed it, attribute the beautifully painted, handmade pottery to the period before the Deluge, and the painted pottery made on the potter's wheel to a period two or three thousand years after the Deluge; those who, like Dr. Albright, deny that there was any break in civilization as the result of the Deluge, put these two different kinds of pottery in close succession, and do not see the need for a long period between them. It is absurd to allow half-a-million years, or even a hundred thousand years (the figure given by Dr. Albright) for the duration of the Old Stone Age, and only 200 years for six Egyptian dynasties. (See *From Stone Age to Christianity* by Dr. Albright).

The Chronology of Asia

As in the case of Egypt there are two different sets of dates for the events of the early history of Asia and two accounts that differ very widely. As a rule, those who follow the "short chronology" accept the theory of human evolution and the version of the Deluge which says that it was only a local river flood in Mesopotamia which did not cause a break in civilization. For the "short chronologists," therefore, it is impossible to write an approximately accurate history of early man in Asia or elsewhere: for them the serious history of Asia begins with the Babylonian Empire, before which there was a Sumerian kingdom, the beginning of which, according to them, goes back to the distant past without any reliable record.

The date of Sargon I, who partially conquered the Sumerian

kingdom, is brought down from 3,800 B.C., of the older system of chronology, to 2,360 B.C. and the dates of early events in other Asiatic countries, including Palestine, are altered to suit the "short chronology."

The objections against the system for Asia are even stronger than the objections against it for Egypt. It ignores the results obtained from the elaborate excavations of all the principal ancient towns and cities of the Middle East which were carried out by organized expeditions from Europe and America, and which have continued, with short interruptions, from the last half of the last century up to our own time. These expeditions have furnished abundant evidence which shows: 1) that the human race began in Mesopotamia; 2) that there was a great flood at about 7,000 B.C. which caused a break in the civilization of Asia, Europe and Africa; 3) that it was in Mesopotamia that the first kingdom, which is known as Sumeria, was established after the flood; 4) that the kingdom of Sumeria continued for 5,000 years with one major break caused by the partial conquest of Sargon I, which occurred in 3,800 B.C., as is proved by the excavations, and that the Sumerian kingdom came to an end with the conquest of Hammurabi, who lived before the time of Abraham, and 5) that during these 5,000 years the descendants of Noe increased and multiplied, that they established settlements which developed into kingdoms in various parts of Asia, such as China and India and in Egypt and America.

Here it may be noted that the earliest accounts of the Deluge which have come down to us, such as the Babylonian account, were written 5,000 years after the event and, as they were written by the descendants of Noe, they can give testimony that a great Flood occurred in which all men, except one family, perished, but they cannot give accurate details such as we find in the Mosaic account, which was written with divine assistance.

The Chronology of Europe

There are two systems of chronology for the early history

of Europe: the system of the evolutionists, among whom are many who claim to be scientists, and the system of those who reckon the dates by acknowledged scientific findings.

According to the evolutionists, man existed in Europe in a semi-evolved state for at least half-a-million years, during which he lived on hunting wild game with the aid of stone instruments, but did not till the ground or keep domestic animals. Toward the end of the period, the Cro-Magnon race appeared and was represented as the first of the real *homo sapiens* race that was fully evolved. The date that used to be given for the appearance of the Cro-Magnon race (and the Grimaldi and Chancelade races that appeared about the same time) was about 100,000 years ago; this date has been brought down to about 5,000 B.C. by Dr. Albright in *From Stone Age to Christianity.* There is a big difference between 100,000 years ago and 5,000 B.C., which is less than 7,000 years ago, but no two evolutionists agree about the dates of early events, because there is no basis from science for the dates.

The System Based on Acknowledged Scientific Findings

In their book *Les Hommes Fossiles* by Boule and Vallois, who were atheists and evolutionists, but who were recognized authorities on the early history of Europe, we get the following account in the 1952 French edition: 1) The fossil skulls of the earliest known men in Europe were discovered in a stratified cave at Fontéchevade in France by *Mlle* Martin in 1947. These skulls resembled the skulls of present-day Europeans and were found just beneath the Mousterian stratum, in which the remains of the Neanderthal man is always found. 2) There are evident signs all over Europe, chiefly in the form of deep deposits of mud in caves, that all Europe was submerged at the end of the Ice Age, which is about 7,000 B.C. and that the Neanderthal race (which according to Vallois was composed of men like ourselves) perished in the flood, and that there was an interval called *hiatus* during which there were no inhabitants in Europe; that after the *hiatus,* representatives of three new families or races called the Cro-Magnon, the Chancelade and Grimaldi appeared at about 6,000 B.C., which is a little earlier than the date given by Dr. Albright. These three races had still the tools of the Old Stone Age, which was soon succeeded by the Middle Stone Age, to be followed after a short interval by the New Stone Age, during which the common domestic animals first appeared.

It is an interesting fact that in the period before the Flood the practice of cultivating the land and of keeping domestic animals was confined to the Fertile Crescent (Egypt, Palestine, Mesopotamia and Iran) as was also the art of building towns and cities and of manufacturing painted pottery and agricultural instruments. This is in accord with the biblical account of the early history of man, and is at least an indication that the common domestic animals were provided by Almighty God for our First Parents.

It is another very interesting fact that the excavations in the Middle East have shown that the same domestic animals that had been in the Middle East and nowhere else before the flood appeared again in the Middle East immediately after the flood. All the animals in the Middle East must have perished in the flood, unless they had been in the Ark with Noe and his family. The domestic animals did not appear in Europe until the Neolithic Age in Europe, the date of which is generally given as between 4,000 and 3,000 B.C.

The Chronology of the Mosaic Period

Before the "short chronology" was adopted generally by biblical exegetes, the chronology of the Mosaic period was based on *Exodus* 2:40 and *3 Kings* 6:1. In verse 1 of *3 Kings* 6, we read:

> And it came to pass in the four hundred and eightieth year after the children of Israel came out of the land of Egypt, in the fourth year of the reign of Solomon over Israel. . .he began to build a house to the Lord.

The fourth year of the reign of Solomon was 967 B.C. The 480 years mentioned in *3 Kings* 6:1, includes the 40 years in the desert; 480 plus 967 B.C. gives us 1,447 B.C. as the approximate date of the Exodus. There is no difficulty in fitting in this date with the older system of chronology followed by Petrie, but it cannot be fitted in with the "short chronology." Those biblical exegetes who have adopted the "short chronology" change the date based on *3 Kings* 6:1 to various dates that center around 2,500 B.C. and even allege that the date given in *3 Kings* 6:1 is wrong and give this as an excuse for rejecting the decrees of Trent and Vatican I and the teaching contained in two Papal Encyclicals, *Providentissimus Deus* of Leo XIII and *Divino Afflante Spiritu* of Pius XII, which state that the Bible contains no error of any kind and that statements in the Bible about historical facts and the physical universe are covered by inspiration equally with statements about faith and morals. In the case with which we are dealing, the dates given in *4 Kings* 6:1 are in agreement with the findings of present-day science, whereas the dates based on the "short chronology" which have been adopted by many biblical exegetes cannot be fitted in with these findings.

Conclusions

From the evidence given above, which is confirmed by additional evidence given in the 1962 edition of the *Encyclopedia Britannica,* we can safely conclude: 1) that the chronological system of Dr. Petrie which allows three Sothic Cycles between 141 A.D. and the seventh year of Senusret III, instead of the two cycles of the "short chronologists," is the right system; 2) that the dates of the Egyptian Pharaohs, of the Babylonian Emperors and of the events of the Mosaic Period as given in the Old Testament which are based on this chronology are in perfect accord with the most recent findings of science; and 3) that Biblical exegetes who have adopted the "short chronology" (which conflicts with the teaching of the Church on the inerrancy of Sacred Scripture) without sufficient research and consideration, are now encumbered with an erroneous system which must ultimately be changed back to the older system based on science.

It is high time for professors in universities and major ecclesiastical seminaries to abandon their ostrich-like attitude of ignoring the evidence of geologists, paleontologists and archaelogists accumulated since the end of the last century, and giving their students instead old superstitions about mythical "hominids" and a discredited system of chronology which is in conflict with both the Bible and the findings of modern science.

Chapter 1

THE BIBLICAL ACCOUNT OF THE DELUGE: THE FATHERS OF THE CHURCH AND THE DELUGE

Who Were Destroyed in the Deluge?

The Mosaic account reads:

> *And all flesh was destroyed that moved upon the earth, both of fowl and cattle. . .and all men. And Noe only remained, and they that were with him in the ark.* (*Gen.* 7:21, 23).

The part of the account which says that all men except Noe and those in the ark perished in the Flood is repeated in *Ecclesiasticus* 44:18-19; *Wisdom* 10:4 and 14:6; *1 Peter* 3:20; *2 Peter* 11-56; but no reference is made to the destruction of animals except in the passage from *Genesis* quoted above.

The Mosaic account of the destruction of all men, except those in the ark, is confirmed by Our Lord Himself in *Matthew* 24:38-39 and *Luke* 17:26, 28. The reference of Our Lord to the destruction of mankind at the time of the Flood, which He compares to the destruction that will take place at the end of the world *("and the Flood came and took them all away"),* is omitted by those commentators who hold that all the people who were not in the ark did not perish. The emphasis in Our Lord's account, and in the other biblical accounts referred to above, is on the destruction of all men not in the ark; in fact, with the exception of the Mosaic account in *Genesis,* no reference is made in other parts of Scripture to the destruction of animals.

How Far Did the Deluge Extend?

For the extent of the Deluge the Mosaic account reads:

> In the six hundredth year of the life of Noe, in the second month, in the seventeenth day of the month, all the fountains of the great deep were broken up, and the flood gates of heaven were opened. And the rain fell upon the earth forty days and forty nights. (*Gen.* 7:11-12).
>
> And the waters. . .began to be abated after a hundred and fifty days. And the ark rested in the seventh month, the seven and twentieth day of the month, upon the mountains of Armenia. . . .In the tenth month, the first day of the month, the tops of the mountains appeared.
>
> And after that forty days were passed, Noe. . .sent forth a raven. . .He sent forth also a dove after him. . . .but she returned. And having waited seven other days, he again sent forth the dove out of the ark. And she came to him in the evening, carrying a bough of an olive tree, with green leaves in her mouth. . .And he stayed yet another seven days: and he sent forth the dove, which returned not any more unto him. Therefore, in the six hundredth and first year, the first month, the first day of the month, the waters were lessened upon the earth. (*Gen.* 8:3, 5, 6, 8-13).

From the above quotation, it appears that the Deluge began on the seventh of the second month and lasted till the first of the New Year, which is a period of about 10-1/2 months, or about 300 days. Within that period a few of the details are given, such as the date on which the tops of the mountains appeared and the sending forth of the raven and the dove, but there are many details which are not given.

There are a number of points in the Mosaic account given above which are the subject of controversy. The chief of these are:

1) Whether the account of the Deluge found in *Genesis* is a simple account written by Moses, or whether it is a composite account compiled at a later date.

2) Did Moses use documents for the composition of his account?

3) Whether the Deluge was universal.

   (*a*) with regard to all men not in the ark;

   (*b*) with regard to the animals not in the ark;

   (*c*) with regard to the extent of the world which it covered.

Was the Account of the Deluge Given in Genesis Written by Moses, Or Was It Compiled at a Later Date?

On this question, the ruling of the Church is contained in the answer given by the Biblical Commission on June 27, 1906, to the following question:

> Whether the arguments amassed by critics to impugn the moral authenticity of the sacred books of the Pentateuch are of sufficient weight to justify the statement that these books have not Moses for their author, but have been composed from sources for the most part posterior to the time of Moses?
>
> Answer: In the negative.

The German rationalist Wellhausen claimed to be able to trace back the whole of the Pentateuch to four sources, which he called the Yawhist, the Elohist, the Deuteronomist, and the Priestly Code, and said that all four sources dated to periods long after Moses, and that the Pentateuch did not receive its present form until about 400 B.C.

Pope Leo XIII makes the following statement about the above theory in his Encyclical *Providentissimus Deus*:

> There has arisen, to the great detriment of religion, an inept method dignified by the name of the "higher criticism," which pretends to judge the origin, integrity and authority of each book, from internal indications alone. It is clear, however, that in historical questions, such as the origin and handing down of writings, the witness of history is of primary importance and that historical investigation should be made with the utmost care; and that in this manner internal evidence is seldom of great value except as confirmation. To look upon it in any other light will be to open the door to many evil consequences. It will make the enemies of religion bold and confident in attacking and mangling the sacred books and the vaunted "higher criticism" will resolve itself into the reflection of the bias and the prejudice of the critics.[1]

---

1. See *Introductio in Libros Sacros Veteris Testamenti* by Fr. Mariani, O.F.M. (Rome, 1958), which gives the latest information on this subject and defends the view that there are not two accounts of Creation and of the Deluge in *Genesis*, but only one. See also the quotation from *Osservatore Romano* given after the preface to Part I.

In spite of the above warning, some modern Catholic commentators think themselves justified in carving up the Mosaic account according to Wellhausen's method and in using his terminology. Frs. Pirot and Clamer and several other modern authors in their commentary on *Genesis* (p. 179) adopt Wellhausen's division of the Mosaic account, alleging as justification that there are evident divergences in the account which show that it is of composite origin. The divergences which they allege are: 1) in the number of birds and animals taken into the ark. Chapter 6:20 says that the number was one pair of every sort of bird and animal; Chapter 7:2-3 says that seven pairs of clean animals and birds were taken in; 2) in the length of time that the Deluge lasted. According to Wellhausen, the biblical account is made up from two independent accounts, one of which gives 308 days as the duration, the other only 101 days; 3) in the use of the names of God: in some places Yahweh is used, in others, Elohim.

These difficulties are more apparent than real, and do not justify the introduction of Wellhausen's theory to explain them. With regard to the first, in Chapter 6:20, Moses says that one male and one female of all the kinds of beasts and birds were taken into the ark; in Chapter 7:2-3, he gives the additional information that seven pairs of clean beasts and birds were taken in. There is no need to interpret the second statement as contradicting the first; there might be an excuse for seeing a contradiction, if the order had been the reverse.

With regard to the alleged divergence in the Mosaic account concerning the length of time that the Deluge lasted, the validity of this objection depends on whether Wellhausen's artificial division of the biblical account into two independent, contradictory accounts can be justified or not.

Wellhausen arrives at his two accounts by separating verses 11 and 12 of Chapter 7, and verses 4 and 5 of Chapter 8.

He takes verse 12 of Chapter 7, which says that the rain fell for 40 days, along with verse 5 of Chapter 8, which says 40 days after the ark had rested on a mountain, Noe sent forth a raven; these two periods make 80 days; to this he adds 21 days for the three periods of seven days, during which the raven and the doves were sent out, which gives a total of 101 days.

In order to get the second account, which contradicts this, he combines verse 2 of Chapter 7, which says that the Deluge began on the 17th of the second month and was caused by an invasion of the sea, with verse 13 of Chapter 8, which says that the Deluge ended on the first day of the New Year. Reckoning by the Lunar month, there are about 308 days from the 17th of the second month till the New Year.

Now even if the account in *Genesis* were an ordinary human account compiled from two different sources, as rationalists contend, no editor would be so stupid as to combine two contradictory accounts that differ so widely, one giving 308 days for the duration of the Deluge, the other only 101 days. But the Mosaic account is not a mere human account; it is an inspired account which has the Holy Ghost for its Author.

The object of Wellhausen is evidently to discredit the Mosaic account so as to leave room for his theory. It is hard to see, however, how any Catholic commentator can justify himself in adopting this carving up of the Mosaic account of the Deluge, especially in face of the warning given by Pope Leo XIII in his Encyclical *Providentissimus Deus*.[1]

With regard to the question whether the use of the names Yahweh or Elohim for God indicates that the passages in which these different names occur are the work of different writers, the best modern commentators, both Catholic and non-Catholic, now hold that it does not. The name Elohim occurs in several Jawhist passages, and neither the Jawhist, Eloist nor Priestly Code passages by themselves make up a connected narrative. (See article on "Higher Criticism" in *A Catholic Commentary on Holy Scripture;* and *Modern Discovery and the Bible* by A. Rendle Short; see also *Introductio in Libros Sacros Vet. Test,* pp. 46, 47).

1. See *Introductio in Libros Sacros Vet. Test.*, pp. 62 and 63.

Did Moses Use Documents for The Composition of His Account?

The Holy See has so far made no pronouncement on this question beyond that contained in the reply of the Biblical Commission with regard to the Mosaic authorship of the Pentateuch, already quoted, which condemns the opinion that the Pentateuch was composed from sources posterior to the time of Moses. Catholics are free to hold that Moses used documents to aid him in the writing of the Pentateuch.

Whatever be the sources from which Moses composed it, the definition of the Council of Trent binds all Catholics to believe that the whole text as found in the Vulgate, including the account of the Deluge, is the inspired word of God. In addition, the opinion which would limit inspiration to matters of faith and morals, to the exclusion of what belongs to the physical or historical order, was condemned by both Pope Leo XIII, Pope Benedict XV and Pope Pius XII. In his Encyclical *Divino Afflante Spiritu,* Pope Pius XII says:

> Later on, this solemn definition (by the Council of Trent) which claims for these books, in their entirety with all their parts, a divine authority such as must enjoy immunity from any error whatsoever, was contradicted by certain Catholic writers who dared to restrict the truth of the Sacred Scripture to matters of faith and morals alone, and to consider the remainder, touching matters of the physical or historical order as *obiter dicta,* and having no connection with the faith. These errors found their merited condemnation in the Encyclical *Providentissimus Deus,* published on the 18th November 1893, by Our Predecessor of immortal memory, Leo XIII.[1]

Did Moses Receive Revelation About the Deluge?

The Holy See binds all Catholics to believe that Moses was guided by inspiration in writing his accounts of the Deluge, but leaves it an open question as to how he got his information. His account is immeasurably superior to any of the other

1. This is confirmed in the Decree on Divine Revelations of Vatican Council II.

accounts that have come down to us, and indeed to all of them combined. It is very detailed and quite dogmatic; the author spoke as one who was sure of his facts. The account may have been handed down from Noe, through the Patriarchs to Abraham, and from him through his descendants to Moses. This is a possible explanation, but it involves many difficulties. If 7,000 B.C. is accepted as the most probable date of the Deluge, over 5,000 years would have elapsed between it and the time of Moses; it would have been very difficult to preserve an accurate detailed account so long. Moses certainly received revelation from God on Mount Sinai, and he was present as witness to Our Lord on Mount Thabor, hence there should be no difficulty about believing that he received revelation concerning the Deluge. (See *Introducio in Libros Sacros Vet. Test.* by Fr. Mariani, O.F.M., p. 109).

Was the Deluge Universal in Every Respect?

The answer to the third question, namely, whether the Deluge was universal, both with regard to the extent of territory covered and destruction of the whole human race except those in the ark, is contained in what has been already said. It is now generally admitted that the Deluge did not extend to the whole earth, for reasons already given.

Opinion was unanimous that the whole human race except Noe and his family perished in the Flood, down to about the middle of the 16th century. Since that time, the opinion that only a portion of the human race perished has continued to gain ground, but this opinion is based on three false assumptions: (*a*) that members of the human race had reached all the principal countries of the world, including the two Americas, before the Deluge; (*b*) that the total submergence of even one continent was a practical impossibility; and (*c*) that it was safe to propound this theory (which contradicted the plain meaning of the Mosaic account) because scientific investigation provided no information on the subject.

(*a*) It is now reasonably certain that the human race had not reached all the principal countries of the world before the Deluge. Reasons for this opinion will be given later on.

(*b*) Scientific investigation has shown that not only is the submergence of a continent possible, but that it actually occurred about the time to which the Deluge is attributed.

(*c*) Recent writers who adopted and defended the theory of Abbé Montais, that the race of Cain survived the Deluge, showed that they were not aware of the recent discoveries by archaeologists in Syria, Iran and Mesopotamia, who were satisfied that they found evidence that at least the use of copper, if not the use of iron, was known before the Flood, and that the disaster that occurred in Mesopotamia and Syria, in which the cities of Iran, Mesopotamia and Syria were destroyed, could not have been caused by a mere river flood. They showed also that they were not aware of the discoveries made by paleontologists in Europe and Africa who are unanimous in stating that the total population of Europe and Africa disappeared at the end of the Mousterian period, and that a different race appeared at the beginning of the Aurignacian period, or of the very strong evidence brought forward by eminent geologists which proves that the whole country from the Caspian Sea to the Arctic Ocean was invaded by the water of the ocean about the end of the Last Glacial Period. (See the last chapter of Part I of this book).

The Fathers of the Church and the Deluge

There is agreement among all Catholic writers on the Deluge, irrespective of their own views about its universality with regard to mankind, that the Fathers taught that all men in the world except Noe and those with him in the ark perished.

The Schoolmen are all of the same opinion. Very few of the Fathers discussed the question whether the waters of the Deluge covered the whole world, and those of them who did discuss it were of the opinion that the waters did not cover the whole surface of the world and that all the animals did not perish.

Fr. Pirot and Canon Clamer, in their commentary on *Genesis* already referred to, get over the difficulty about the unanimous opinion of the Fathers on the universality of the Deluge by saying that the question of the Deluge is not a question of faith and morals, but one of science and history, and that the comparison so frequently used by the Fathers between the ark, outside of which no one was saved, and the Church of Christ, holds good equally in the case of a restricted flood in which the ark was the only means of salvation in the area under water. (*Genese,* pp. 200-201).

This solution of the difficulty is given also by Fr. Sutcliffe, S.J., in his C.T.S. pamphlet entitled, "Who Perished in the Flood?"

The solution cannot be said to be satisfactory, for the Fathers were unanimous in their opinion that the *whole* human race, with the exception of those in the ark, perished in the flood. The appeal to the findings of science by Frs. Pirot and Clamer is equally unhappy, for they display complete ignorance of the very definite results of the hundred years' investigation by paleontologists of the early history of the human race, and a very limited acquaintance with the work of modern archaeologists.

Chapter 2

ACCOUNTS OF THE DELUGE IN PROFANE LITERATURE

Accounts of the Deluge are found in the books or records of all countries that have an ancient literature. They are found in the ancient records of Sumeria, Babylonia, Assyria, Egypt, Persia, Greece, India and China. These accounts, while differing in details, all agree on the essential point: that there was a real Deluge in which the whole human race perished, except a few in a boat or ship, who were saved through the intervention of some god or goddess.

When the Spaniards settled in North and South America, no matter where they went, they found the tradition of a deluge in which all men perished except a few who were saved in a ship or boat. Strange to say, the details of the account preserved by the Indians of America resemble those of the Mosaic account more closely than does any of the other accounts. This may be due to one or other of two facts: either to the fact that the ancestors of the Indians left Asia soon after the Deluge and brought a true account of it which was preserved in tradition, or that Christian missionaries had reached America long before the time of Columbus. Dr. J. Walsh, in his book *The World's Debt to the Irish,* gives evidence to show that Irish missionaries reached North America about 1,000 A.D.

The Babylonian Account of the Deluge

The earliest recorded account of the Deluge which has come down to us is known as the Babylonian account. This account dates back to about 1,900 B.C., which is 500 years earlier than the Mosaic account.

Though it is generally known as the Babylonian account,

it is really a Sumerian account. Before the first Babylonian Empire was founded by Sargon I (in 3,800 B.C., according to the older and better system of chronology), another empire called the Sumerian had existed for at least 2,000 years and probably more. The First Dynasty of the Empire lived at Kish (near Babylon) for a very long period until the hegemony of Mesopotamia was wrested from Kish by another town called Uruk (the Arach of the Bible, *Gen.* 10:10), situated in the south of Mesopotamia, opposite to Ur of the Chaldees. This city, in the height of its glory, had an area of over a thousand acres (as shown by the excavations) and an estimated population of half-a-million. It used to be referred to as a post-Flood town like Jemdet Nasr in the North, but recent excavations carried out by a German expedition have brought to light the Flood stratum and a pre-Flood town like that of Ur on the opposite bank of the river.

The first king or emperor of Uruk was called Gilgamesh, a great historic personage, whose name went down in history. Long after his death, a book was written by an unknown author, recording the exploits and adventures of this Gilgamesh, something on the lines of the Labors of Hercules. This epic was divided into 12 parts, each giving an account of a different adventure. In the eleventh book the adventure recorded is a voyage in search of the elixer of immortality. In the course of this voyage he met Uta Napisthim (the Sumerian equivalent of Noe). This Uta Napisthim told Gilgamesh the story of the Deluge and the part he himself had played in it, for which he was rewarded by being made a god.

Several versions of the description of the Flood by Gilgamesh have come down to us. The first of these to be published was deciphered by George Smith from baked clay tablets found at Niniveh in the library of King Assurbanipal (688-626 B.C.) and published by him at London in 1876. Another incomplete account which dates back to about 1,900 B.C. was discovered at Nippur by an American expedition, and published in 1914. This account agrees substantially with the former one.

According to the latest calculations, a period as long as 5,000 years may have elapsed between the Flood and the earliest account that has come down to us, which dates about 1,900 B.C. There was therefore, plenty of time for this account handed down by tradition alone, without the help of either inspiration or revelation, to have become corrupted.

It is to be noted that all the traditional accounts of the Sumerians, Babylonians etc., attribute the Flood to the action of rain alone, and that for *seven days only;* while the Mosaic account tells us that the Flood was caused by the waters that came from the ocean and by the rains which continued *for forty days.* It is to be noted also that the cause, which alone is capable of explaining the magnitude of the Flood that covered the mountains, namely, the inrush of the waters of the ocean, is put first in the Mosaic account. This alone should be sufficient to show that the Mosaic account was not derived from either the Sumerian or the Babylonian account, as a few writers like André Parrot (to whom we have referred in the introductory chapter) contend.

The following is a brief summary of the account published by George Smith in 1876:

The gods decided to exterminate the human race. One of them named Ea revealed the secret to a man named Uta Napisthim and told him to construct a great ship, the dimensions of which were indicated. Uta Napisthim constructed the vessel, which was larger than Noe's ark, and took into it his family, his gold and silver and pairs of animals both tame and wild. When the waters began to rise, the gods got alarmed and quarrelled among themselves. According to this version the storm of rain lasted only six days and ceased on the seventh. The vessel rested on Mount Nisir and remained motionless for seven days. Uta Napisthim sent forth a dove and a swallow which returned, and finally a crow which did not return. He then left the vessel and offered sacrifice to the gods. He and his wife and daughter were subsequently admitted among the gods, and he afterwards appeared to this man named Gilgamesh and told him the story of the flood.

There are points of similarity in this account with the biblical account, but the differences about the details, even apart from the introduction of the pagan gods, are so many that the biblical account could not have been derived from it. The chief thing to note about this account attributed to Gilgamesh is that it represents the whole human race, except those in the great vessel, as perishing in the Deluge. The idea of universality with regard to human beings could hardly have arisen from any flood in the Tigris or Euphrates; in fact, no river-flood of which there is record could give rise to a story in which even half-a-million people could be represented as perishing.

From the history of Sumeria which has come down to us, written in about 2,000 B.C., it appears that the people of the first city at Kish worshipped one god with great ceremony, and regarded him as their protector. When the population increased and new cities were built, some of the cities adopted new gods with new names. When war was waged between rival cities, the people of the victorious city believed that they had conquered the god of that city and had taken him captive. In that way, then, the religion that had been purified by the chastisement of the Flood became again corrupted and adopted a plurality of gods. As 5,000 years had probably elapsed between the Flood and the recording of this Sumerian account by Babylonians, there was plenty of time for this corruption of the true religion to take place.

In *The Track of Man* (p. 176), Henry Field quotes Professor Langdon (who assisted in superintending the excavations at Kish and Jemdet Nasr) as saying that the evidence from the excavations shows that "the history of the oldest religion of man is a rapid decline from monotheism to extreme polytheism." This opinion is confirmed by Sir Leonard Woolley in his book entitled *Sumeria*.

Chapter 3

THE ORIGIN OF THE RIVER-FLOOD THEORY OF THE DELUGE

The universality of the Deluge with regard to the human race was first challenged about the middle of the 16th century by Fr. Oleaster, O.P. of Portugal, who held that the race of Cain did not all perish. He based his opinion on an incorrect version of *Numbers* 24:21, in which he read "Cainite" for "Cinite." The Cinites were a tribe in the Sinai peninsula, but there is no evidence whatever that they were the descendants of Cain. This reading was adopted by the German rationalist Wellhausen (1844-1918), but it is generally rejected.

A century later, Voltaire (1694-1778) endeavored to prove that there was no deluge at all. He delivered an address on the subject to the Academy of Bologna and wrote an article in the Philosophical Dictionary. Like all rationalists, he rejected the testimony of the Bible and poured ridicule on the arguments current at the time in support of a universal deluge. In particular he rejected the evidence from the presence of marine shells all round Paris and at Touraine, brought forward to prove that France was inundated in comparatively recent times. He was answered by the German poet, Goethe, whose evidence will be quoted later on.

Another century later, D'Omalius d'Halloi (whom Canon Dorlodot quotes in favor of the theory of evolution) supported the theory that all men outside the ark did not perish in the Deluge, in an address to the Belgium Academy delivered in 1866.

Toward the end of the same century, Abbé Montais of the Oratory of Rennes wrote a book entitled *Le Deluge biblique devant la Foi, l'Ecriture et la Science* (Paris, 1885), in which he propounded the theory that only a small minority of the human race perished in the Deluge, and that this small minority was of the race of Seth, not of Cain. He said that the whole race of Cain escaped; if this were true, most of the people in the world would be of the race of Cain.

Fr. Sutcliffe S.J. adopts and attempts to defend this theory of Abbé Montais, that the whole race of Cain survived the Deluge, in his pamphlet entitled, *Who Perished in the Flood?* and again in his article in *A Catholic Commentary on Holy Scripture* (p. 190). The theory of Abbé Montais that the whole race of Cain survived the Deluge is absurd and has no solid reason to support it. There is against it the testimony of *Genesis* that all except those in the ark perished; that testimony is repeated several times in both the Old and New Testaments; the Fathers are unanimous in saying that all the human race except those in the Ark were drowned; and, as we shall see, both archaeologists and paleontologists have found traces of the Deluge in Europe, Asia and Africa. Fr. Sutcliffe quotes *Genesis* 4:22, which says that Tubalcain was "a hammerer of brass and iron" in favor of his view. He argues that as the use of metals was not known till thousands of years after the Deluge, the mention of the use of brass and iron proves that Moses is referring to what had been done by the descendants of Tubalcain long after the Deluge, and therefore they must not have perished in it. This argument is invalid for several reasons. In the first place, the words "brass and iron" can mean no more than the metals or metal that was known before the Deluge. As we shall see, the use of hammered copper ore was known before the Deluge, and it is not impossible that the use of iron ore was known also. Iron, like most metals with the exception of copper and gold, dissolves and leaves no trace after it, except in very special circumstances. Pieces of hammered iron were found between two of the inner blocks down one of the air-shafts in the Great Pyramid (built during the 4th Dynasty); another piece was found in a building at Abydos in conjunction with bronze tools of the 6th Dynasty. Iron was found also in Syria in buildings belonging to the Third Millenium B.C. After this, the use of iron in Egypt appears to have become a lost art and was not rediscovered till the beginning of the Iron Age between 1,000 and 800 B.C. (See *Egypt and Western Asia in the Light of Recent Discoveries,* pp. 112-116, London, 1907). There is just the possibility that these few pieces of iron found in buildings of the 4th and 6th Dynasties of Egypt may have been hammered out from iron ore before the Deluge by descendants of Tubalcain who had migrated into Egypt. However, the question whether the whole human race except Noe and his family perished in the Deluge will not be settled by an argument over the meaning of the words "a hammerer of brass and iron."

Chapter 4

EVIDENCE FROM PALEONTOLOGY OF A GREAT FLOOD THAT EXTENDED OVER EUROPE AND AFRICA

In the early stages of the controversy about the universality of the Deluge, initiated by the publication of Fr. Oleaster's book, there was much confusion about the arguments used. Those who held for the absolute universality appealed to the testimony of fossils of fish found embedded in rocks on the tops of high mountains, as well as to the presence of countless sea-shells found in the Paris basin, all over plains of Italy and in the Rhine Valley. Voltaire rejected not only the argument based on the fossils of fish found on the mountaintops, but also the argument from the presence of sea-shells scattered over the surface of the plains.

Geology has long ago disposed of the argument from the fossils on the tops of mountains, but the argument from the presence of sea-shells in the Paris basin, the Rhine Valley and the plains of Italy still holds good. Voltaire tried to get over it by saying that these shells, which were of Syrian type, were brought back by "the numberless bands of pilgrims who carried their money to the Holy Land and brought back shells." He was answered by the German poet, Goethe, who wrote:

> When I learned that to weaken the tradition of the Deluge, he (Voltaire) had denied all petrified shells, and only admitted them as *lusus naturae,* he entirely lost my confidence; for my own eyes had, as I stood on the Bashberg mountain, plainly enough shown me that I was looking down on an old dried-up sea. . . .These mountains had certainly been once covered by waves, whether before or during the Deluge did not concern me. It was enough that the valley of the Rhine had been a monstrous lake, extending beyond the reach of eye-sight.

Paleontologists have followed the example of Goethe by refusing to enter into any controversy over the Deluge; in fact they have gone further than Goethe, for they never even mention the Deluge at all. They give the evidence which proves that there is a clear line of demarcation between the men of the modern world, beginning with the Cro-Magnon race, and those who preceded them, and that this line is between the periods known as the Mousterian and the Aurignacian. They tell us about the races that lived before that time and what countries they occupied. They tell us that there is palpable evidence that the surface of the earth was churned up over large areas of Europe, Africa and Western Asia sometime between the Mousterian and the Aurignacian periods; that the whole population disappeared for a time after the Mousterian, and that a different race appeared about the beginning of the Aurignacian period. They refer to the interval between these two periods as the *hiatus,* that is, the complete break in civilization caused by the disappearance of one race and the appearance of another. The men who gave this evidence were for the most part advocates of the theory of human evolution and were searching for "missing links"; their evidence is therefore all the stronger, because it can be used against their own theories.

There is no indication in their writings that they even thought on the Deluge of Noe, or that they were giving valuable information about it. Evidence of experts for the existence of the *hiatus* caused by a flood of great dimensions has been available for the past 50 years, and yet some modern Scripture commentators make no mention of it, but give us instead fantastic theories which contradict the unanimous opinion of the fathers and the universal belief of the faithful.

The Extent of the Hiatus

We can only speak of a *hiatus,* or break in the civilization, to have existed in a country where inhabitants lived prior to it. As we have just mentioned, no fossils prior to the Mousterian period have been found in South America, Australia or anywhere east of the Himalaya Mountains, except the disputed fossils of the Peking Man and the Java Man. There are undoubted signs of the *hiatus* all over Europe and all over North Africa. It may be regarded as certain that the *hiatus* extended to Mesopotamia, the only doubt being whether there were two major disasters in Mesopotamia: the *hiatus* and the great flood in the valley of the Tigris and the Euphrates, or whether these two—the *hiatus* and the local flood—were parts of the same disaster.

With regard to South Africa, it is quite certain that members of the Neanderthal race made their way as far as the Cape of Good Hope, and that they all died out, as they did in Europe and everywhere they had existed; it is quite certain also that there are abundant paleolithic instruments in South Africa, and the other signs of the *hiatus,* such as the deep deposits of sand, have been found in the Kalahari Desert South of the Equator.

Proofs for the Existence of the Hiatus

The *hiatus,* or complete break in the civilization that occurred between the disappearance of the Neanderthal and the appearance of the Cro-Magnon, Grimaldi and Chancelade races, has been recognized by scientists for over 40 years and is now regarded as certain. Sir Bertram Windle writes in *The Church and Science* (1918 ed., p. 253):

> What at present seems to be undeniable is that in the northern parts of Europe, Palaeolithic man did disappear off the face of the earth, which was left without human inhabitants for a lengthy period during which the physical conditions as well as the character of the fauna were profoundly altered.

He quotes the well-known authority Dr. G. F. Wright as saying:

> Even the south of England affords evidence of this general exodus, for there is a complete break both in strategraphical relations and the style of implements of the two periods. Between Palaeolithic and Neolithic culture of Great Britain there is a great gulf fixed, and no amount of research has succeeded in finding any trace of transition between the two.

Marcellin Boule, the greatest modern European authority on Paleontology, agrees with this view; and Henri Valois, another well-known authority, who edited the last (1952) edition of Boule's *Les Hommes Fossiles,* writes:

> The Neanderthal Man, whose origin certainly goes back to ancient times, has become extinct without leaving posterity. He is doubly fossil, because he goes back to the geological epoch prior to the present one, and because we know of no descendants of his from the time of the upper Pleistocene. (pp. 267-268).

Boule and Vallois give the Mousterian period as the time of his disappearance, and the Aurignacian period as the time when the Cro-Magnon, Grimaldi and Chancelade races appeared.

Boule and Vallois agree also with both Windle and Wright about the profound change that took place in the surface of the earth between the time of the disappearance and reappearance of man in Europe. Boule remarks that the deposits in caves and other places subsequent to the time known as the *hiatus,* or break with the past, are insignificant compared to the deep deposits made between the disappearance of the Neanderthal and the appearance of the Cro-Magnon, Grimaldi and Chancelade races.

To explain this we must postulate either a very long period, or some disaster or upheaval.

Some people, and among them many who are highly educated, find it difficult to conceive a whole continent submerged for a time beneath the sea—even by the power of God. Hence, we have modern writers representing the Deluge of Noe as merely an unusually large river-flood. Fr. Sutcliffe, S.J. in his C.T.S. pamphlet on the Deluge is willing to concede that the low-lying country around the Caspian Sea (where he gathers together the descendants of Seth to have them drowned) might have been the scene of the Deluge. The fact is, however, as has been established with certainty by geologists, that during the geological period before the mountains arose, the whole earth was covered with water, and that even after the dry land emerged it was again submerged, and again submerged time after time until the Tertiary Period. Even during the Quaternary Period, parts of the Continent of Europe were invaded by the sea at various times.

Major Submergence of Europe About the End of the Old Stone Age

Two modern standard reference books that deal with prehistoric man, *Les Hommes Fossiles* by Boule and Vallois, and *Dating the Past* by Zeuner, agree in placing a major submergence of the countries of Europe about the end of the Old Stone Age, the age of the Neanderthal Man and the age of the Deluge of Noe. (See Goodwin's chart in *Dating the Past,* p. 108, and the chronological table in *Les Hommes Fossiles,* pp. 46, 37). In the chronological table in *Les Hommes Fossiles* the authors tell us that it was after this transgression of the sea that the caves of Europe were filled up and that a layer of loess was deposited in many parts of Europe. All this happened toward the end of the last glacial period, when the level of the sea had returned to normal as a result of the melting of the ice.

There is no difficulty therefore in imagining the Continent of Europe submerged beneath the sea at the time to which the Deluge is attributed; in fact, there is solid evidence to show that it was actually submerged. This does not mean, however, that the Deluge was a purely natural occurrence; God uses natural causes (which are His work) as far as they help to bring about the effect He desires, but supplements them when they are insufficient.

Boule and Vallois place the return of the human race to Europe (the Cro-Magnon, Grimaldi and Chancelade races) after the regression of this invasion of the sea, and say that there was a minor transgression of the sea after the return of these races, which would account for the upper deposits in the caves. As these caves, where prehistoric remains of man were found, were all in the valleys along the rivers, this second marine transgression need not have done more than cause river floods.

This is confirmed by evidence given by Zeuner which shows that there were several minor transgressions of the sea about the end of the last glacial period. There is also evidence to show that there were several transgressions of the sea in Asia Minor about the same time. It may be presumed that the continent of Africa was affected also in like manner.

The Sahara Desert

It is a well-known fact that what is now the Sahara Desert was once fertile territory, well-watered and with a teeming population.[1] There are the traces of rivers and lakes that became silted up, and all over the desert, particularly near what once were rivers or lakes, tools and pottery manufactured by man have been found in great quantity. (See *Reader's Digest,* Oct., 1958, p. 129).

According to both paleontologists and archaeologists, the transformation of this fertile region into a desert took place in comparatively recent times; a date as late as from 8,000 to 10,000 years B.C. is mentioned. (See *Les Hommes Fossiles,* pp. 436-452).

The fossil remains of a man, in many respects resembling the Neanderthal Man, were found at Asselar in the middle of the desert.

Before the Sahara became a desert, tools of the early period of the Old Stone Age, associated with hand-made pottery, were plentiful all over; after the event that turned it into a desert, neither the tools of the later part of the Old Stone Age, nor of the Middle Stone Age were found: instead, the tools of the New Stone Age, associated with pottery fashioned on the potters' wheel and instruments cast from smelted copper, made their appearance. The *hiatus* was even more pronounced in the Sahara region than in Europe.

Egypt

Archaeologists have been working in Egypt for nearly a century. By the end of the first quarter of the present century

---

1. The same is true of the Kalahari Desert south of the Equator.

their work there was as far advanced as it is now in Mesopotamia or Iran. The conclusions now being arrived at from the latest excavations made in Mesopotamia and the adjoining countries agree perfectly with conclusions reached by those who worked in Egypt at the beginning of the century and with conclusions recorded in books long out of print.

Among the means used by archaeologists for comparing the civilizations of ancient countries and arriving at comparative dates, one of the principal is a comparison of the potteries of the countries. Early pre-*hiatus* pottery has been found over a stretch of country reaching from Egypt to Iran. It is of distinctive type, very easy to recognize, for it is hand-made and painted. The perfection of the painting and the beauty of designs reached its acme just before the *hiatus* in Egypt and the flood in Mesopotamia. This beautiful handmade pottery was found along the Nile in Egypt, at the pre-Flood city of Jericho, in a dozen pre-Flood cities of Syria and Mesopotamia and, just a few years ago, in several places in Iran. In all these places this distinctive pottery disappeared suddenly and never appeared again. After the *hiatus* in Egypt and the flood of Mesopotamia, rough unpainted pottery made on the potter's wheel appeared for the first time, and soon after, tools made from smelted copper; painted pottery did not appear again for several centuries.

The upper Nile flows down through an arid desert, with only a thin border of alluvial land on either side. Artifacts buried in the desert in the remote antiquity are still preserved intact. Great numbers of human skeletons[1] lie crouched in shallow graves, with the flint instruments of the Old Stone Age and painted pottery within reach of their hands. The actual flint-shops, where the flint was chipped and the instruments made, can still be seen. Both the flint instruments and the pottery increased in perfection, until finally a kind of buff pottery with elaborate painted designs was found. With this last kind of pottery there were found very simple hammered

1. As there was no apparent difference between these skeletons and those of modern man, as in the case of Neanderthal man, they were not removed to museums.

copper weapons, and then the painted pottery ceased. When it appeared again in the First Dynasty, it was of a rough, unpainted kind; the painted pottery did not again appear until the time of the Fourth Dynasty. Egypt is therefore a country where the flood of Mesopotamia and the *hiatus* meet on common ground, showing that these were parts of the same disaster. (See *Egypt and Western Asia in the Light of Recent Discoveries,* London, 1907).

All over the rest of the continent of Africa, right down to the Cape, fossils of the Neanderthal Man have been found with tools and pottery belonging to the Old Stone Age. The fossil record shows that the Neanderthal Man disappeared at the same time as in Europe, but no attempt appears to have been made to ascertain whether the *hiatus,* or complete break in the civilization, extended over all Africa. As the Neanderthal race became extinct, the presumption is that it did.

Chapter 5

EVIDENCE OF A GREAT FLOOD FROM THE EXCAVATIONS IN THE SOUTH OF MESOPOTAMIA

Excavations on a large scale have been carried out in many different places in Mesopotamia, Syria and Palestine over a stretch of more than a thousand miles: at Ur of the Chaldees, the city from which Abraham came, at Kish near ancient Babylon, at Tepe-Gawra, near the ancient city of Nineveh, and at several other places.

It is reasonably certain that the flood, or transgression of the sea that filled the caves of Europe, scattered sea shells from the coasts of the Mediterranean all over Italy, France and Germany, and turned the fertile, well-watered Sahara into a desert, extended to the low-lying country around the Caspian Sea and into Mesopotamia. The question that arises, whether the flood or transgression of the sea was the same as the great flood in Mesopotamia, evident traces of which were discovered in the course of the excavations carried out during this century in Mesopotamia, Syria and Palestine, can now be answered in the affirmative, as will appear in the course of our study of these excavations. Here it is sufficient to say that a few modern writers, like Millar Burrows, have been deceived in thinking that experts have dated this flood in Mesopotamia at about 4,000 B.C. Experts have not been able to give even an approximate date for this flood, for there were two periods, about the length of which nothing is yet known for certain. These two periods are: the length of time that elapsed between the earliest certain date in the history of ancient Babylon and this flood, and the length of time that elapsed between the disappearance of the people who perished in that flood and the arrival of the new race.

The carbon 14 (or radio-carbon) method has given us figures as low as 8,000 + or − 900 for the age of a charred bone found in Iran, that belonged to the early Mesolithic Age, which was the age after the *hiatus* or Deluge. This would be only 6,500 B.C. The usual date given (according to the old method of guessing) for the early Mesolithic Age used to be around 60,000 years.

This great Mesopotamian flood, which we are now about to consider, can be fitted in with a date even earlier than 6,500 B.C., for the two unknown periods referred to above may have lasted many thousand years. As we shall see, the most recent evidence available indicates that the date was about 7,000 B.C.

The Excavations at Ur of the Chaldees

Ur of the Chaldees had been known only as an uninhabited mound called "the Mound of Pitch" for more than a thousand years, until Mr. J. E. Taylor unearthed inscriptions in 1854 which revealed the fact that the mound of Pitch was none other than Ur, the home of Abraham. No organized attempt, however, was made to excavate it until 1918, when Dr. Hall carried out preliminary excavations at Ur itself, and at 'Al Ubaid, four miles from it.

In 1922 the University Museum of Pennsylvania and the British Museum organized a joint expedition which was put under the direction of Sir Leonard Woolley. Besides issuing bulletins as the work proceeded, Sir Leonard published a general account of the excavations both at Ur and Ubaid, under the title *Ur of the Chaldees,* in 1928. A revised Pelican edition of this book was published in 1950 and reprinted in 1954. Sir Leonard found no change necessary for the new edition so far as the facts were concerned. The only change made was to adopt the shorter system of chronology proposed by Dr. Albright, although he (Sir Leonard) admits that this system (which fixes the date of Sargon at 2,360 B.C. instead of 3,800 B.C.) is not accepted by all writers on the subject.

As we shall see from quotations from this book, Sir Leonard

makes it perfectly plain that it was the same flood that destroyed both Ur and the village of 'Al Ubaid, four miles away, and that this flood caused a break in the civilization in Mesopotamia. He tells us that in the case of Ur, the excavations revealed that it had been covered by eight feet of earth deposited by the flood that destroyed it, that after an unknown period, a new city was built on top of this deposit of earth, and that it was destroyed and rebuilt several times during a period of three or four thousand years, with the result that the city that existed before the flood was buried down 40 feet beneath the ruins accumulated during several milleniums.

In the case of the village of 'Al Ubaid four miles away, it appeared to have been inhabited for only a short time before the flood, and after the flood nothing was built upon the deposit of mud over it, except a temple which covered only a corner of it.

'Al Ubaid, therefore, was easy to excavate, unlike the ancient cities buried in the flood at Ur, Babylon and Nineveh, over which cities were built and destroyed and rebuilt during thousands of years. Hence Sir Leonard Woolley began work at 'Al Ubaid and finished it in a short time. It took him several years, however, to excavate a small part of the remains of the cities built, one over the other, at Ur before he came to the ancient city beneath, the excavation of which was never finished. Sir Leonard gives as his opinion that the flood that left the eight feet of deposit over Ur was the Deluge of Noe. However, for the present, we shall leave aside the question whether this undoubtedly historic flood in Mesopotamia, the like of which has never occurred since in any part of the world, was the Deluge of Noe or not, and confine our attention to exploring the extent of this historic flood and to the evidence that shows that a different race with a different civilization replaced the race that perished in it.

Before giving the evidence, we shall first deal with objections put by Professor Millar Burrows in *What Mean These Stones?* (U.S.A., 1941 and London, 1957), which, he says, is based on a report of excavations carried out at Kish (near the site of ancient Babylon) about the same time as those at

Ur, by another joint American-British expedition under the direction of Mr. Watelin for the U.S.A. and Professor Langdon for England. (Mr. Watelin was the director of the expedition, and it was he who wrote the report; Professor Langdon had left Kish long before the excavations were finished).

The objections are as follows: Evidence of several floods was found in the excavations carried out at Kish. Two of these floods were of very great dimensions, and left deposits differing in depth by 19 feet. The flood represented by the upper level was dated by Langdon at about 3,500 B.C.; the lower one at about 4,000 B.C. It is this lower one which he equates with the inundation at Ur. "None of these inundations," says Mr. Burrows, "is contemporary with Ur, and none at either place marks a division between two civilizations.

> In Woolley's own excavations at 'Al Ubaid, only four miles from Ur, there was no silt at the levels corresponding to those at which it was found at Kish. As a matter of fact, representations at Gilgamesh were found at a lower level than the Deluge at Kish, showing that the Babylonian story was more ancient than this. (Pg. 70 of *What Mean These Stones?*).

These objections of Mr. Burrows are quoted by Fr. Sutcliffe in his article in *A Catholic Commentary on Holy Scripture* (148,d), who accepts the statement of Burrows as far as the part referring to "representations of Gilgamesh being found at a lower level than the deluge deposit," which he thinks can be explained. Fr. Sutcliffe's conclusion is that this historic flood in Mesopotamia, which blotted out several cities, could not have been the Deluge of Noe, because the date given by experts in chronology (4,000 B.C.) was too early to account for the known development of the human race, and because he does not think the evidence for a complete break in the civilization of Mesopotamia given by Woolley, sufficient.

Fathers Pirot and Clamer in *La Sainte Bible* (Genèse pp. 199, 200) also give the above objections. They quote Sir Leonard Woolley as saying that there was "an enormous *hiatus*" between the civilization represented by the pottery, written tablets and other artifacts found above the flood deposit, and the civilization represented by the artifacts below it. They also quote Langdon as being even more convinced than Woolley that the historic flood was of gigantic proportions and that it wiped out the pre-flood city of Kish. Nevertheless, Fathers Pirot and Clamer reject the evidence of the two experts who conducted the excavations and give their own conclusions.

A Reply to the Objections of Millar Burrows, Fr. Sutcliffe and Others

The whole question of this historic flood of enormous dimensions has been cleared up by further excavations and further publications since Mr. Burrows wrote *What Mean These Stones?* in 1941, so that it is now very easy to give definite replies to all these objections.

In the first place, it may be pointed out that Mr. Burrows has completely misrepresented the report of the excavations given by Mr. Watelin. Mr. Watelin and his party carried out excavations at two places 18 miles apart: at Kish itself and at Jemdet Nasr, 18 miles from Kish. The report of the excavations at these two places is given together under the title "Excavations at Kish." Now at Kish there was a pre-flood city rebuilt several times until the buried debris reached a height of 20 feet. The great flood blotted out this city and left a deposit of mud on top of it. A post-flood city was built on this deposit, and rebuilt several times, leaving a further 35 feet of buried debris before it was finally abandoned.

Jemdet Nasr was a post-flood town, 18 miles from Kish, built in the plain on *top* of the flood deposit. There was therefore a difference of about 20 feet (or 19 feet, according to Burrows) between the level of the deposit left *on top* of pre-flood Kish (which was about 20 feet above thc plain), and the deposit *under* post-flood Jemdet Nasr (which was built on the plain) but it was the *same flood* that left the deposits in two different places. There was, therefore, only one great flood, and not two, as Mr. Burrows says. It was easy to make the mistake, for Mr. Watelon gave only one diagram, on which he represented the levels of two places 18 miles apart, so that a person might easily be misled into thinking that Jemdet Nasr was at Kish.

At present the words "Jemdet Nasr" are commonly used in books dealing with the chronology of Mesopotamia, to denote an ancient settlement built a considerable time *after* the great flood in Mesopotamia, while 'Al Ubaid is used to denote a settlement or town built *before* the flood.

The statement of Mr. Burrows (quoted by Fr. Sutcliffe, S.J. in the article already referred to) that the flood that destroyed Ur of the Chaldees, leaving a deposit of eight feet of mud over it, did not extend to 'Al Ubaid, only four miles from this city, is absurd, for no one denies that this flood extended at least as far as Nineveh, 400 miles north of it, and at least a hundred miles on each side. What Sir Leonard Woolley actually states is that 'Al Ubaid is a pre-flood settlement over which no town was built after the flood.

With regard to the part of Burrow's objection which says that representations of Gilgamesh (who was certainly post-flood, because he wrote the story of the flood) being found at levels below the flood, the answer should be apparent from what has just been stated. No such representations were found *beneath* the flood deposit at Kish or anywhere else; they were found in the post-flood town of Jemdet Nasr, which was built on *top* of the flood deposit.

The Difficulty About the Date 4,000 B.C. As the Date of the Deluge

Fr. Sutcliffe says 1) that the date of the historic flood in Mesopotamia is, according to the experts on chronology, 4,000 B.C. and 2) that this date would not leave time for the known development of the human race from one family (assuming that the whole human race, except one family, perished in the Deluge) to the number of people in the world at the time of Christ.

Now it is not at all certain that 4,000 years would not suffice for the multiplication of the human race from one family to the number of people in the world at the time of Christ if there had been no wars or other disasters, but it may be readily admitted that in the actual circumstances that obtained, 4,000 years would not have sufficed.

It is not true, however, to say that experts on chronology are agreed that 4,000 B.C. is the actual date of this historic flood. Evidence from several sources will be given in this and the next Part of this book (on the Antiquity of Man) to show that the actual date of this flood was somewhere around 7,000 B.C., and that this same flood extended to Palestine, covered the high plateau of Iran (5,000 feet above sea level) and reached the Arctic Ocean.

The Length of Time Required for The Multiplication of the Human Race and The Development of the Various Languages

Dr. G. F. Wright in his book *The Origin and Antiquity of Man* (London, 1912) gives evidence to show that it would be possible for the descendants of one human pair to increase to a million in 500 years, and to 500,000 million (more than 200 times the present population of the world) in 1,000 years, if there were no wars, famines, etc., to check the increase.

With regard to the development of the languages of the world, present-day authorities do not demand a very long time for the development of new languages. Isolation of families or tribes, especially among illiterate peoples, will produce new dialects which will become distinct languages in a comparatively short time.

As for the development of the arts of peace and war, it is not the time factor that is important, but continuous contact with the existing civilization. The civilization that existed at the time of Noe (of the character of which there is now plenty of evidence) was developed by Sumerians after the flood; humane laws were enacted which were copied by Hammurabi later on; the art of writing was invented; copper was smelted, etc.; this developed civilization was brought to Egypt, from Egypt to Crete, from Crete to Greece and Rome, and from them it has come down to us, transformed and enriched by Christianity.

The races that lost contact with this civilization, especially those that remained pagan, either stagnated or gradually deteriorated.

Objections Raised by André Parrott Concluded from Small-Scale Excavations Carried Out in Mesopotamia

The objections raised by Millar Burrows are found also in a book by André Parrott entitled *Deluge et Arche de Noe,* published at Paris in 1953 and translated into English and published at London in 1955 under the title *The Flood and Noah's Ark.* On page 50 of the English translation, readers will find a diagram which is supposed to represent the findings from the excavations carried out at Kish. In this diagram Jemdet Nasr (which is also written Jamdat Nasr) is represented as being at Kish and as being *beneath* the flood deposit, whereas, as we have seen, Jemdet Nasr is 18 miles from Kish, and is *above* the level of the flood deposit.

On page 49 of the same book M. Parrott speaks of images of Gilgamesh impressed on cylinder seals being found *beneath* the flood deposit (at Jemdet Nasr). Cylinder seals are regarded as the first step in the development of the art of writing and have never been found anywhere beneath the flood deposit in Mesopotamia. This is quite certain.

They have been found in the excavations at the *post-Flood town* of Jemdet Nasr carried out by the joint British-American expedition. (See *The Track of Man* by Henry Field, in the chapter on Jemdet Nasr).

There are many other errors in this book about dates etc., which are probably due to the fact that M. Parrott, like most French writers, drew his conclusions from small-scale excavations carried out in Mesopotamia by Frenchmen during the first quarter of the present century. The evidence provided by the more recent large-scale excavations carried out by German, British and American expeditions not only in Mesopotamia but also in Iran, Palestine and Syria (an account of which will be given in this and the following chapters) shows that the conclusions based by French writers, such as André Parrott, on the partial results of earlier excavations were erroneous.

Sir Leonard Woolley's Account Of Excavations at 'Al Ubaid

Having dealt with the objection raised by Millar Burrows and other writers against regarding the great historic Flood of Mesopotamia as part of the Deluge, we now give Sir Leonard Woolley's account of what he found in the excavations of the pre-Flood village of 'Al Ubaid.

The following is his account of the excavations at 'Al Ubaid:

> At 'Al Ubaid, four miles from Ur, we have dug out part of a primitive settlement. Here a little knoll, fortunately never covered afterwards with buildings, preserved the remains of huts constructed with mud and wattle or slight timber framing filled in with reed mats, with floors of beaten mud and fire-places of crude brick and wooden doors whose hinge-poles turned on stone sockets.
>
> In the ruins we found quantities of the fine painted hand-made pottery such as occurs in the lowest levels touched at Ur (Plate Ia), rougher household wares used for cooking, and storage, hoes and adzes of chipped and polished stone, saw-toothed flints and flakes of imported volcanic glass, sickles made of hard-baked clay (Plate Ib), all the evidence of a very simple culture. It was clear that these people cultivated the soil and reaped their harvest of grain; they kept domesticated cattle, sheep and goats; they fished in the marshes (for we found fish-hooks and model boats), and, judging from fragments of painted terra-cotta figures of men and women, they seem to have painted or tattooed their bodies; stone weights showed that the loom was known.
>
> There was nothing to show to what race these first inhabitants of Mesopotamia belonged. . . .
>
> At 'Al Ubaid the settlement seems to have been comparatively short-lived; at Ur a similar settlement, but on a much larger scale, must have endured for a very long time. (*Ur of the Chaldees,* pp. 15, 16).

The following is his account of the excavations at Ur of the Chaldees:

> The shafts (through the upper, post-Flood city of Ur) went deeper, and suddenly the character of the soil changed. Instead of the stratified pottery and rubbish, we were in perfectly clean clay, uniform throughout, the texture of which showed that it had been laid down in water. The workmen declared that we had come to the bottom of everything, to the river silt of which the original delta was formed, and at first looking at the sides of the shaft I was disposed to agree with them, but then I saw that we were too high up. It was difficult to believe that the island on which the first settlement was built stood up so much above what must have been the level of the marsh, and after working out the measurements I sent the men back to work to deepen the hole. The clean clay continued without change—the sole object found in it was a fragment of fossilized bone which must have been brought down with the clay from the upper reaches of the river—until it had attained a thickness of a little over eight feet. Then, as suddenly as it had begun, it stopped, and we were once more in layers of rubbish full of stone implements, *flint cores from which the implements had been flaked off* (which was the method employed in the Old Stone Age), and pottery.
>
> But here there was a remarkable change. The pottery was of the hand-made painted ware which distinguishes the village settlement of 'Al Ubaid, while the numerous flint implements, which evidently were being manufactured on the spot, were similar to those from 'Al Ubaid and further differentiated this from the higher strata, where flints were very rarely to be found. The great bed of clay marked, if it did not cause, a break in the continuity of history: above it we had Sumerian civilization slowly developing on its own lines; below it there was a culture of that 'Al Ubaid type which seems not to be really Sumerian, but to belong to the race which inhabited the river-valley before the mixed race of the Sumerians had come into being.

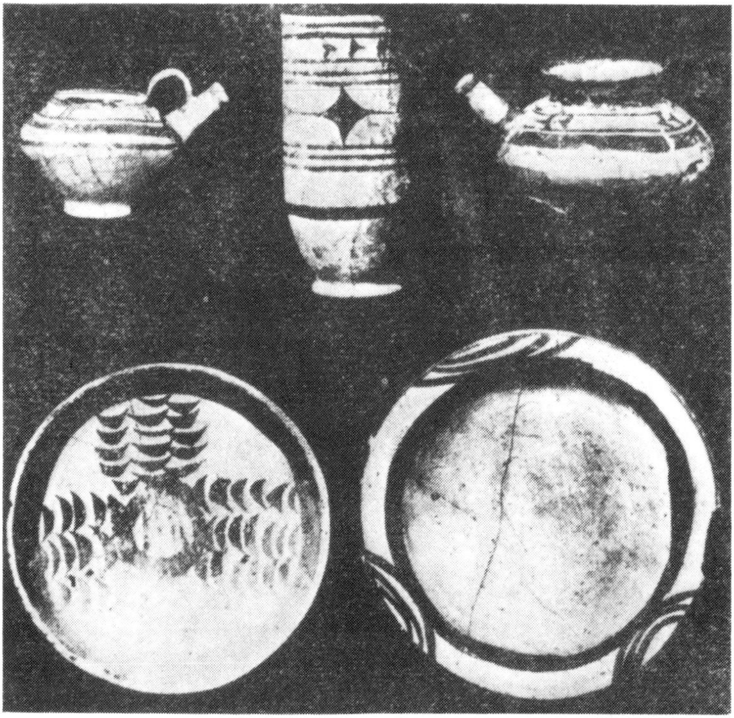

Hand-made painted pottery of the pre-Flood 'Al Ubaid period.

Post-Flood pottery made on the potter's wheel of the Jemdet Nasr period, probably about 1,000 years after the Deluge.

> We had long before this seen the meaning of our discovery. The bed of water-laid clay deposited against the sloping face of the mound, which extended from the town to the stream or canal at the north-east end, could only have been the result of a flood; no other agency could possibly account for it. Inundations are of normal occurrence in Lower Mesopotamia, but no ordinary rising of the rivers would leave behind it anything approaching the bulk of this clay bank: eight feet of sediment imply a very great depth of water, and the flood which deposited it must have been of a magnitude unparallelled in local history. *That it was so is further proved by the fact that the clay bank marks a definite break in the continuity of the local culture; a whole civilization which existed before it is lacking above it and seems to have been submerged by the waters.*
>
> *Taking into consideration all the facts, there could be no doubt that the Flood of which we had thus found the only possible evidence was the Flood of Sumerian history and legend, the Flood on which is based the story of Noah.* A pit sunk 300 yards away to the north-west gave us the same bed of water-laid clay, with beneath it the same flints and coloured pottery of the "non-Sumerian" folk.

Ur of the Chaldees, from which we have quoted, gives the results of the excavations carried out at Ur up to 1929, when the book was written. These excavations were continued for five more years, still under the direction of Sir Leonard Woolley. Sir Leonard rewrote the original book, and in the new book, entitled *Excavations at Ur,* he gives the results of 12 years of work. As most of the work consisted in excavating the various strata of the post-Flood city, which continued to exist for at least 3,000 years, and probably more, before the Babylonian empire was founded and reached a very high standard of civilization, most of this book is devoted to the description of the various objects found in this post-Flood strata. Our present work, however, is concerned with the pre-Flood period, and hence we quote only from the part of the book dealing with the pre-Flood strata. Readers interested in the history of the thousands of years that elapsed between the Flood and the foundation of the Babylonian empire will find most valuable and interesting information on that subject in *Excavations at Ur* by Sir Leonard Woolley, published by Messrs. Ernest Benn, Ltd., London, in 1954.

The results of the excavations described in this new book show that the contrast between the pre-Flood and post-Flood civilizations at Ur is not so marked as was first thought. The objects found in the smaller shaft, such as a potter's wheel and metal instruments, told of a people who arrived long after the Flood with a much more highly developed civilization than that reached before the Flood, while the new excavations carried out over a much wider area revealed the presence of another people with a civilization definitely much inferior to pre-Flood civilization. How is the presence at Ur of this people with the primitive civilization to be explained? Are they the degenerate survivors of the pre-Flood city of Ur, or the descendants of Noe who moved in sometime after the Flood? This question cannot be settled by the results of the excavations at Ur alone. Evidence will be given from recent excavations carried on at Jericho, on the high Plateau of Iran and at other places, which shows that the Flood which blotted out the great cities of Mesopotamia not only extended to Palestine but reached the high Plateau of Iran, and that it was not merely a river flood 25 feet deep caused by the rising of the Tigris and Euphrates, but that it was an incursion of the sea that submerged the high Plateau of Iran and turned its once fertile plains into a salty desert, and drowned whole herds of mammoth as far north as the Arctic Ocean.

These new excavations, a description of which we quote here, confirmed Sir Leonard in the opinion which he expressed in his earlier book that he actually discovered traces of the Deluge of Noe. That claim has been disputed by a few biblical commentators who maintain that what he discovered was merely a local flood, but we shall provide evidence from many sources to substantiate his claim to have discovered traces of the Flood described in *Genesis*.

The following is Sir Leonard's description of the new excavations:

Excavations at Ur

In the year 1929 the work of excavating the Royal Cemetery at Ur was drawing towards its end. On the evidence then to hand I was convinced that the cemetery came before, but only just before, the First Dynasty of Ur; the treasures recovered from its graves illustrated a civilization of an astonishingly high order and it was therefore all the more important to trace the steps by which man had reached that level of art and culture. That meant, presumably, that we had to dig deeper; but it was just as well to begin by a small scale test of the lower levels which could be carried out with a minimum of time and cost. Starting then below the level at which the graves had been found we sank a little shaft, not more than five feet square at the outset, into the underlying soil and went down through the mixed rubbish that is characteristic of old inhabited sites—a mixture of decomposed mud bricks, ashes and broken pottery, very much like that in which the graves had been dug. This went on for about three feet and then suddenly it all stopped: there were no more potsherds, no ashes, only clean water-laid mud, and the Arab workman at the bottom of the shaft told me that he had reached virgin soil; there was nothing more to be found, and he had better go elsewhere.

I got down and looked at the evidence and agreed with him; but then I took my levels and discovered that "virgin soil" was not nearly so deep down as I had expected, for I had assumed that the original Ur was built not on a hill, but on a low mound rising only just above the surrounding swampy land; and because I do not like having my theories upset by anything less than proof I told the man to get back and go on digging. Most unwillingly he did so, again turning up nothing but clean soil that yielded no sign of human activity; he dug through eight feet of it in all, and then, suddenly, there appeared flint implements and fragments of painted 'Al Ubaid pottery vessels. I got into the pit once more, examined the sides, and by the time I had written up my notes was quite convinced of what it all meant; but I wanted to see whether others would come to the same conclusion. So I brought up two of my staff and, after pointing out the facts, asked for their explanation. They did not know what to say. My wife came along and looked and was asked the same question, and she turned away remarking casually, "Well, of course, it's the

> Flood." That was the right answer. But one could scarcely argue for the Deluge on the strength of a pityard square; so in the next season I marked out on the low ground where the graves of the Royal Cemetery had been a rectangle some seventy-five feet by sixty, and there dug a huge pit which went down, in the end, for sixty-four feet.

Here Sir Leonard describes the objects found in the various strata above the Flood level. Immediately above it were found the remains of houses constructed with reeds and mud, and primitive unpainted pottery, much inferior to the pre-Flood pottery; then came pottery made on the potter's wheel; later on smelted copper and samples of the first attempts at writing; then the gold and silver objects of the royal tombs, and finally samples of the Babylonian culture of the time of Abraham, showing the development of the arts and crafts during a period of probably 5,000 years.

He then gives the following account of the objects found beneath the Flood deposit which throw light on the manner of life of pre-Flood man:

> At this point the clean silt measured about eleven feet in thickness and except for one scarcely noticeable stratum of darker mud, was absolutely uniform throughout; microscopic analysis proved that it was water-laid, subject to the action of gentle currents, and it was composed of material brought down from the middle reaches of the Euphrates. Below it came the level of human occupation—decayed mud brick, ashes and potsherds, in which we could distinguish three successive floor levels; here was the richly-decorated 'Al Ubaid pottery in abundance, flints, clay figurines and flat rectangular bricks (preserved because they had been accidentally burnt) and fragments of clay plaster, also hardened by fire, which on one side were smooth, flat or convex, and on the other side bore the imprint of reed stems, the daub from the walls of the reed huts which, as we saw at 'Al Ubaid, were the normal houses of the pre-Flood people, as they are of the Marsh Arab today.
>
> The first huts had been set up on the surface of a belt of mud which was clearly formed, for the most part, of decayed vegetable matter; in it were potsherds (thicker at the bottom of the belt) all lying horizontally as if they had been thrown

there and had sunk of their own weight through water into soft mud; below this again, three feet below modern sea level, there was stiff green clay pierced by sinuous brown stain which had been the roots of reeds; here all traces of human activity ceased and we were at the bottom of Mesopotamia.

Both at Ur and on other Mesopotamian sites there has been found evidence of local and temporary water action occurring at various times in history; sometimes this was no more than the effect of rain in an enclosed area, and never is there anything approaching what we found in our "Flood-pit." There, it can safely be said, we have proof of an inundation unparalleled in any later period of Mesopotamian history. We were lucky to find it at all because a flood does not, of course, pile up silt everywhere—on the contrary, where the current is strongest it may have a scouring effect; the silt is deposited where the current is held up by some obstacle. To settle this point we dug a whole series of small shafts, covering a large area, in which the depth of the mud differed considerably, and when these were duly plotted it was clear that the mud was heaped up against the north slope of the town mound which, rising above the plain, broke the force of the floodwaters; on the plain east or west of the mound we should probably have found nothing. Eleven feet of silt—the maximum—would probably mean a flood not less than twenty-five feet deep; in the flat low-lying land of Mesopotamia a flood of that depth would cover an area about three hundred miles long and a hundred miles across; the whole of the fertile land between the Elamite mountains and the high Syrian desert would disappear, every village would be destroyed, and only a few of the old cities, set high on their built-up mounds, would survive the disaster. We know that Ur did survive; we have seen that villages such as 'Al Ubaid and Rajeibeh were suddenly deserted and remained desolate for long or forever. The compilers of the King-lists regarded the Flood as something that made a breach in the continuity of their country's history; we find that it put an end to the 'Al Ubaid culture as such; they dated the Flood as coming two "dynasties" before the First Dynasty of Ur.

The Sumarian version describes antediluvian man living in huts made of reeds, which at 'Al Ubaid and at Ur we found to be the case; Noah built his ark of light wood waterproofed with bitumen, and just on top of the Flood deposit we found a big lump of bitumen bearing the imprint of the basket in which it had been packed, as I have myself seen the crude bitumen from the pits at Hit on the middle Euphrates being packed in baskets for export downstream.

As we shall see in the following chapters, excavations carried out in Palestine, Syria and Iran subsequent to those at Ur have revealed the fact that the flood that left a deposit of 11 feet of mud at Ur extended not only to Palestine, but even reached the Plateau of Iran, 5,000 feet above the plain. The opinion therefore of Sir Leonard that the flood at Ur may have been only 25 feet deep and that some of the pre-Flood cities of the plain may have survived is no longer tenable.

Sir Leonard Woolley has been unfairly quoted as saying definitely that the flood which left the deposit over Ur of the Chaldees occurred about 4,000 B.C., and that its extent was only 400 miles in length by 100 in width.

Among those who quote Sir Leonard for this opinion is Werner-Keller in *The Bible as History* (English translation, London, 1957). It is true that these statements are found in the 1950 edition of *Ur of the Chaldees,* but this edition was printed from the standing type of the 1928 edition with a few verbal changes. One of these changes was a change in the system of chronology adopted. In the 1928 edition Woolley adopted the older and better system which dates the beginning of the reign of Sargon I at 3,800 B.C.; in the 1950 edition, in order to avoid controversy, he adopted Dr. Albright's system of "short chronology" which dates the beginning of the reign of Sargon I at 2,360 B.C., 1,460 years later. He accepted the short chronology with two reservations: 1) that the figure, whether 4,000 B.C. of the 1950 edition or 5460 B.C. of the 1928 edition, was not a date, but a mere guess; 2) that the "short chronology," which is not accepted by all, is not his own.

The Excavations at Uruk

Evidence of the same flood that destroyed Ur of the Chaldees was found at Uruk (the Arach mentioned in *Gen.* 10:10) in Southern Mesopotamia, a little higher up on the opposite bank of the Euphrates. This Uruk, or Arach, which in post-

Flood times became a great city with half-a-million inhabitants, used to be regarded as a post-Flood town built on top of the Flood deposit. Excavations begun as early as 1912 showed much the same results as those obtained by Woolley in the post-Flood city of Ur. These excavations were not completed until recently, when a German expedition under Noldeke and Heinreich found the same flood stratum as Woolley had found at Ur, and beneath it a pre-Flood town which differed in this from the great pre-Flood town of Kish and Tepe Gawra, which had many strata, that it had only one stratum which had been rebuilt twice. However, the results obtained from the excavation of this pre-Flood stratum confirmed the view expressed by Woolley that the great flood of Mesopotamia marked a break in the continuity of the civilization there; that an ancient race with a peculiar type of culture disappeared forever, and was replaced long after by a different race with a different culture.

Could an Inundation of the Tigris and Euphrates Have Caused the Destruction Wrought at Ur, Kish And Tepe Gawra, and the Other Places?

The few modern writers who say so cannot deny the evidence that all the dwellers in the valley of the Tigris and Euphrates perished in this flood.

Now, in the first place, if this flood had extended for only a hundred miles on each side of the rivers, the dwellers in the regions to which the flood had not extended would immediately have rushed in and seized the fertile lands. These neighboring peoples must have had a civilization somewhat similar to that of the people who perished; but the evidence just quoted proves that the newcomers had a very different type of civilization from that of the people who perished, and that they did not arrive till after the lapse of a long period. In the next place, there is no flood of which there is a record in the whole history of the world which wiped out the entire population of even one river valley, except this flood in Mesopotamia, the flood that caused the hiatus in Europe and

Africa, and the Flood of Noe, and it may be regarded as certain that all these three floods were one and the same.

The present writer was in China when several river floods occurred, including one of the greatest in the history of China, which left several sub-prefectures or counties under water from summer until Christmas, and he often travelled by boat on missionary work in the inundated area. The loss of life in the greatest of these floods was negligible, and when the waters of the flood had receded the people of the district all returned to their houses. The next spring, a stranger travelling through the district could see nothing to make him suspect that a flood had occurred. The same is true of floods that have occurred in various other countries such as France, Italy, Canada and the U.S.A.

In the case of the flood of Mesopotamia, however, all are agreed that at least the population of the valley of the Tigris and Euphrates perished, and that several great cities were not only destroyed but that a deposit of eight feet of mud was left on top of them.

Chapter 6

EVIDENCE OF A GREAT FLOOD FROM THE EXCAVATIONS IN THE NORTH OF MESOPOTAMIA

Since Sir Leonard Woolley wrote his account of the excavations carried out at Ur in 1928, other experts have carried out excavations not only in Mesopotamia but in Syria, Palestine and Iran. We shall give brief accounts of the principal of these excavations and compare the results obtained with the results quoted above.

It is well to bear in mind that we are not depending on the results obtained by archaeologists from excavations in Mesopotamia and the surrounding countries for confirmation of the biblical account of the Deluge; we have also the evidence of the paleontologists which has been given, and the evidence from geologists which will be given later on.

The evidence, however, from the recent excavations carried out all over the Middle East confirms the Mosaic account of the Deluge and of the manner of life of early man, and is very important.

We shall therefore give here an account of the most important of these excavations, adding the testimony of geologists, and then give the very strong evidence of geologists which shows that Europe and Siberia were submerged under the waters of the ocean about the same time—7000 B.C.

The Excavations at Kish

Contradictory opinions have been expressed about the excavations carried out around Kish near the ancient city of Babylon, not by the experts who superintended the excavations, but by book reviewers and commentators. A book, published as late as 1955 which deals with the last phase of the excavations by Henry Field, one of the men in charge of the "Chicago Field Museum-Oxford University Joint Expedition," gives first-hand information which settles these difficulties. In this book entitled *The Track of Man,* which describes the author's travels abroad exploring ancient sites, he devotes two chapters to the last phase of the excavations around Kish. Among the illustrations inserted after page 224 is the following diagram:

Surface of Mound . . . . .feet	0
Non-Babylonian Building levels	5
Later Dynastic	20
Plain level	30
FLOOD STRATUM	35
Early Dynastic Building Levels and Chariot Tombs . .	45
Jemdet Nasr Period	50
Virgin Soil	55

The above diagram is evidently the work of a draftsman who did not understand the situation at Kish clearly, for he represents Jemdet Nasr, which is 18 miles from Kish and five feet above the level of the plain as being at Kish, and 20 feet below the flood deposit on the top of the artificial mound there. This diagram was probably responsible for the mistake made by Millar Burrows and others referred to above. The words "Jemdet Nasr Period" mentioned on the diagram are also misleading, for being written on the space beneath the words "Flood Stratum," they seem to indicate that the Jemdet Nasr Period was prior to the flood, whereas it was at least 500 years after it. Henry Field, who succeeded Professor Langdon in superintending the excavations at Jemdet Nasr, states in his book *The Track of Man* (p. 176): "All antiquities found at Jemdet Nasr belong to the period 3,500 B.C.," that is, 500 years after the date 4,000 B.C. given by Millar Burrows for the flood.

Among the antiquities found there Henry Field mentions tablets written in the Sumerian language. Now, no evidence of writing, even the most primitive, has been found anywhere beneath the deposit left by the Mesopotamian flood.

The following is an account by Henry Field of some sensational discoveries made in the strata below the flood deposit at Kish:

> The great day finally came when Watelin (the U.S.A. Director of the excavations) decided to cut through the red earth stratum in Y trench to the levels below (before Christmas 1927). I wrote a personal note to Professor Langdon at Oxford. I told him that we were now at Flood level expecting to find the Flood of Noe. A report came from a Paris laboratory that the red-earth stratum was a water-borne deposit. Watelin was thus able to establish that this was the deposit laid down by the Flood of Noe. On the floor of one of the small rooms just beneath the red-earth stratum, we discovered bones of small fishes drowned (i.e., entombed) in the Flood.

This quotation shows that Frs. Pirot and Chalmer in their book, which is generally regarded as a scholarly modern commentary on *Genesis,* did not take sufficient pains to get the truth about the results of the excavations at Kish.

The discovery of the fish was made before Christmas, 1927. During the following year, a much more sensational discovery was made. Henry Field (who was present) describes it as follows:

> The most sensational discovery of the 1927-28 season was excavated a few feet above water level (about 10 feet below the Flood level). At a depth of 43 feet below the summit of the mound, Ali Daud, one of our best pickmen, who was working at the lowest levels of the Y trench, shouted that he had found something. Watelin (the Director), Eric and I descended into the trench. Ali proudly held up a copper nail with a large head. Ali had found the nail below the artificial staircase cut into the earth so that the basket-boys could carry the earth from the lower levels to the dump above. Soon he found a handful of copper nails. . . . After about an hour we suddenly saw five copper nails arranged in a semi-circle. Watelin looked up and said quietly, "This is a chariot wheel." Our faces whitened with excitement as we realised the significance of the find—a wheeled vehicle used before the Flood of Noe. Slowly the wheel was uncovered with the *copper nails* still in place around the rim. (*The Track of Man,* pp. 166, 167).

Henry Field immediately sent a telegram to London announcing the find in which the words "Chicago Papers please copy" were added. That evening the London papers published an account of the find, and the Chicago papers published it on the following day.

A week later, while excavating the large tombs below the Flood level, a four-wheeled chariot was unearthed and beside it a human skeleton, a copper saw and a copper dagger. Several other human skeletons were found in the tomb, as well as numerous pottery vessels. (*ibid,* p. 170).

Both Henry Field and Mr. Watelin, the director of the excavations, were satisfied that the remains of the primitive four-wheeled vehicle with the copper nails in the rims of the wheels belonged to the period before the Flood, for there appeared to be no sign that the belt of red earth had been dug through for a post-Flood burial. There is nothing very extraordinary in the finding of a primitive four-wheeled cart or of copper nails and a copper saw belonging to a period prior to the Flood, for, as we shall see, primitive tools made from hammered copper ore were found in the pre-Flood strata in Iran and other places in the Middle East. Nor is there anything extraordinary about the tomb found, which was not very elaborate, for carefully dug graves of Neanderthal men belonging to the pre-Flood period have been found all over Europe and even in South Africa.

The Excavations at Tepe Gawra Near the Site of Ancient Nineveh

The most remarkable, but least-known of the excavations in Mesopotamia, were those carried out at Tepe Gawra, which is situated about 15 miles northeast of the ancient city of Nineveh. At present there is no book in English, at least no book in circulation, which tells the story of these excavations. The account given below is taken partly from *The National Geographic Magazine* (January, 1951), partly from an American magazine (probably *The Scientific American*) which the present writer received in China between the years 1937 and 1940, and partly from *Foundations in the Dust* by Seton Lloyd (1955 ed.).

E. A. Speicer, the author of the article in *The National Geographic Magazine,* who directed the excavations for four years, gives the following account of Tepe Gawra.

> Tepe Gawra (the Great Mound), which rises 75 feet above the surrounding plain, is situated 15 miles northeast of Mosul and ancient Nineveh. . . .Systematic excavations were begun in 1927 and carried on through eight separate campaigns, five of which I had the opportunity to direct in person. The final results exceeded our greatest expectations. Tepe Gawra proved to contain 26 occupation levels, *yet only the upper six of these fell within the historic age.* The long period prior to the introduction of writing, reaching back to the fourth millenium B.C. and beyond, was no longer obscure. . .The continuous account of early man could be pushed back by perhaps 20 centuries.

Further Descriptions of the Excavations at Tepe Gawra

The account given in the American periodical (probably *The Scientific American*) which the present writer received between 1937 and 1940 when he was in China, refers to the same excavation. This account says that when the excavators had been down through 16 occupation levels, each containing records of the past, they found a belt of solid earth similar to that described by Woolley at Ur of the Chaldees; and that having dug through this belt they found 10 more occupational levels beneath it. The 16 levels above the belt of clay showed the development of the civilization of Nineveh from primitive beginnings after the Flood, to its zenith and the gradual decline until Nineveh was finally abandoned. The first buildings just above the clay belt appeared to have been constructed of mud and wattle; the buildings went on improving as the civilization developed.

Immediately below the belt of earth they found solidly constructed buildings built of burnt brick, just as they had found evidence of brick buildings at Ur of the Chaldees below the clay deposit. They found also beautiful hand-made painted pottery similar to that found at 'Al Ubaid near Ur of the Chaldees. In addition they found the kilns in which this pottery was baked. These antediluvian kilns were so constructed that the temperature was kept constant. This was done by having the fire, not in the chamber in which the pottery was baked, but in an adjoining one. An arrangement like this for keeping the temperature constant is necessary for the production of high-class pottery. This art was lost at the time of this flood and was not rediscovered until hundreds of years after it. The pottery that appeared after this flood was of a completely different kind; instead of being hand-made it was made by the potter's wheel, but it lacked the finish and beauty of the pre-Flood pottery. Among the excavations carried out in the three placed under Flood level the only one that was completed was the one at 'Al Ubaid, four miles from Ur. The artifacts found in that excavation belonged to the Old Stone Age and included hand-made painted pottery similar to that found at Tepe Gawra.

About this painted pottery Sir Leonard Woolley writes:

> One of the great puzzles of South Mesopotamian archaeology is the *sudden and complete disappearance of the painted pottery* which at one time seem to have been universally distributed over the southern sites. . .Certainly they (those who came after the Flood) did bring new inventions, for whereas the 'Al Ubaid pottery was handmade, the vases that came immediately above the Flood deposit are made on the potter's wheel and metal tools replace the flints of an older day. (*Ur of the Chaldees,* pp. 24-26).

The above affords valuable evidence of the fact that not only was there a break in the civilization, but that a long time, perhaps a thousand years or more, must have elapsed between the sudden disappearance of those who made the hand-made painted pottery, and the people who came after them who knew the use of the potter's wheel and of metal tools.

Further Evidence of the Flood From The Latest (1932-1957) Excavations in Mesopotamia

Between 1932 and 1957, the British School of Archaeology have carried out excavations at a number of sites in Mesopotamia and Syria. As their main object was to investigate the earliest works of man, they selected for the most part sites containing pottery of the 'Al Ubaid (pre-Flood) type, which had not been built upon after the Flood. Attempts had been made to excavate the pre-Flood cities of Ur, Kish and Nineveh, but such colossal heaps of rubbish had accumulated over them, because successive cities had been built on the same sites, that it was impossible to do more than dig a few shafts through the rubbish down to the belt of earth left by the Flood, and through the pre-Flood cities below it down to virgin soil. Of these attempts, Mr. M. E. L. Mallowan, Director of the British School of Archaeology in Iraq writes:

> Two cities on the Southern Euphrates had been dug down to virgin soil. Sir Leonard Woolley had found evidence of what he believed to be the Biblical Flood at Ur. A German expedition had dug deep in the sand at Uruk, where the beginnings of town life in Sumer, which later was called Babylonia, were thus revealed, and were given character by rich collections of painted pottery, graves and the remains of houses which were assigned to the pre-Flood "Ubaid period." Eight hundred miles to the north some slight evidence of the "Ubaid period" had also come to light in a deep shaft which had been sunk from the top of the great mound at Nineveh (Quyunjik) through 92 feet of debris down to virgin soil. At a depth of more than 60 feet we found many shreds of a finely finished and brilliantly painted pottery (regarded as earlier than Ubaid pottery) of a type known as "Halaf" ware. (*Twenty-five Years of Mesopotamian Discovery,* p. 1).

Of this latter shaft dug at Nineveh, Mr. Seton Lloyd writes in *Foundations in the Dust:*

> From this shaft, as the excavators descended stage by stage, came pottery, cylinder-seals, beads, and even sculpture, representing all the successive phases of Iraq's history. Passing through Assyrian, Babylonian, Akkadian and Sumerian periods he reached the (post-Flood) three and two phases, and the (pre-Flood) phase one pottery of the south, and beneath it the brilliantly decorated jars of the (earlier) Tell Halaf period. . . . From the two or three metres remaining above virgin soil all that was found was a handful of potsherds decorated with peculiar scratched designs never before seen.

The excavations at the two southern cities, Ur and Babylon, revealed the same 'Al Ubaid pottery at the levels below the Flood deposit, while the northern city of Nineveh, while showing the 'Al Ubaid pottery at the levels below the Flood belt of earth, showed also another earlier type of hand-made pottery, called the Halaf pottery, from a pre-Flood settlement west of Nineveh, called Tell Halaf.

Excavations at Arpachiyah

The British School of Archaeology in Iraq, having seen for themselves the type of pottery and other artifacts at the lowest levels of ancient Nineveh, 92 feet beneath the surface, selected for excavation the mound of Arpachiyah which had the same relation to ancient Nineveh as 'Al Ubaid had to Ur; for it was just four miles from Nineveh, no town had been built on it after the Flood, and the pre-Flood occupation had been of short duration.

The following is the account given by Mr. Mallowan, the director of the excavation, of what was found:

> The mound of Arpachiyah contained at the top four superimposed settlements which consisted of small houses with meanly built rooms. . .The walls were of crude clay. . .The contents consisted of only a few potsherds, beads and clay articles of the Ubaid period, but fortunately a cemetery containing forty-five graves yielded an extensive collection of pottery decorated with geometric designs in a dark paint on a light ground. Some of these pots closely matched types which had been discovered in the earliest levels at Ur, while some terra-cotta beads with incised designs provided indisputable proof of the similarity of the north Ubaid fabrics to those discovered in the south. This pottery is hand-made without any mechanical aid. *A very simple flint industry is an obvious carry-over from the earlier Halaf period, and a flat open-cast (i.e., hammered) copper axe provides proof positive that metal tools were available, though it is clear that copper was still very rare at the time.*
>
> Subsequent work by an American expedition at Gawra (near Nineveh) proves that the Arpachiyah 'Al Ubaid pot styles persisted through five main periods of occupation. (*Twenty-five Years of Mesopotamian Discovery,* p. 2).

This early settlement at Arpachiyah resembled that at 'Ubaid in containing primitive flint tools similar to those of the Old Stone Age, and thus were associated with hammered copper tools. This corroborates the evidence of Henry Field already quoted, that copper nails were found at Kish below the Flood level (which may be presumed to be "hammered," not smelted).

Excavations at Chagar Bazar

Chagar is a mound in the north of Mesopotamia 63 feet above the level of the surrounding plain. From its summit, 200 other ancient mounds could be seen, which shows that the district had been thickly populated in ancient times. The excavations which had been made down to virgin soil revealed that there had been 15 occupational levels, some of which had been built upon several times. There was a dividing line between the fifth level (from the top) and the sixth beneath it. Mallowan fixes the date of this fifth (post-Flood) level at about 3,000 B.C., but as we shall see, it was very much earlier. Between the fifth level and the sixth there was a *belt of clean clay that had become bleached,* which is a sign that a long period had elapsed before it was built upon again. At the lowest level (level 15) there was evidence that the place had been used as a camping ground, as there were broken pieces of pottery of a primitive kind. The remaining levels up to the dividing line between level 6 and level 5 showed the gradual development in the making of pottery. All the pottery found up to level 5 was of the hand-made, painted kind found at the lowest levels at Ur, Kish and Nineveh. There were, however, several varieties which showed that they had been the work of many potters.

When the site was occupied again after a long interval, the new inhabitants used part of the site as a cemetery. They had pottery which was completely different from any on the lower levels, and on the very first levels *above* the dividing line metal tools were found. Tools made of iron which dated back to 2,300 B.C. were found in the upper levels. This find confirms the one made at Abydos in Egypt which dated back to about the same time. Seventy written tablets dating back to 1,800 B.C., as well as ornaments of gold and silver, were found on the first level.

Excavations have been carried out by the British School of Archaeology at several other sites in the northern reaches of the Euphrates and in the Balikh Valley. In all cases handmade painted pottery of the Ubaid and Halaf types have been found at the lowest levels. As has been already stated, fossil remains of the Neanderthal Man and of a mixed race, that certainly belonged to the pre-Flood period, were found in Palestine.

The evidence from these excavations in Mesopotamia, Syria and Palestine points to the conclusion that these countries had been thickly populated before the Flood, that inhabitants were proficient in the arts of pottery-making and painting, in the manufacture of stone implements; and that they had begun to develop the art of metallurgy.

On the other hand, excavations carried out at the ancient sites in Europe, the principal of which were in the south of France, in the Dordogne Valley, and in the north in the valley of the Seine, would point to the conclusion that the inhabitants were people who had wandered far from the ancient centers of civilization, and who were slow in developing the art of metallurgy, because no metals were to be found on the surface of the earth, as they were to be found in abundance in the mountains of Mesopotamia and Syria. (See past numbers of *Iraq* from 1932 to 1937, and *Twenty-five Years of Mesopotamian Discovery* by M. E. L. Mallowan, London, 1956).

Chapter 7

EVIDENCE OF A GREAT FLOOD FROM EXCAVATIONS IN PALESTINE

The Excavations at Jericho

The discoveries made in the stratified caves of Galilee and Carmel show that Palestine was inhabited from the earliest period of the Old Stone Age both by the Neanderthal Man and by a mixed race combining the characteristics of the Neanderthal Man and those of modern man.

Palestine can lay claim also to the possession of early fixed settlements which rival those of Mesopotamia in antiquity. Several of those ancient sites have been excavated, such as Megiddo and Ghassoul, but the most important results were obtained at Jericho.

Excavations there were begun by a German expedition before the First World War and suspended during it. They were resumed in 1929 by an English expedition under John and J. B. E. Garstang. These two give the results of the expedition in *The Story of Jericho* which was published in London in 1940, and revised and published again in 1948.

The history of this ancient city may be divided into three clearly defined periods: the prehistoric period, lasting from the earliest times down to the occurrence of some great disaster, when the city was destroyed and abandoned for a long time; the period beginning with the building of the first city wall by a new race, at the end of which it was taken by Josue and burned; and the period lasting from the time when the site was reoccupied about 500 years later and lasting till the present day.

It is with the first period only that we are concerned here. No dates can be given for the beginning or end of this period; the figures 5,000 B.C. for the beginning and 3,000 B.C. for the end of this period given by Garstang and others are merely guesses and do not correspond with the more modern figures given for ancient towns in Mesopotamia and Iran.

When Garstang resumed the excavations in 1929, his first care was to establish the dividing lines between the different periods. This he did by digging a trench which cut through the different city walls down to virgin soil. He found that this virgin soil, on which the earliest settlement was built, was 64 feet below the first city wall of the second period.

The first general conclusion to be drawn from the excavation of the lower city is that it lived in splendid isolation almost to the end of this period, without contact either with Mesopotamia or Egypt. During this whole period no trace either of the polished stone instruments of the Neolithic Age or of hammered copper was found. Because of the fact that the stone instruments found consisted chiefly of agricultural instruments such as sickles, writers who hold the theory of evolution, such as W. F. Albright, insist on placing this first period in the Neolithic Age: Garstang, who superintended the excavations, places it in the Mesolithic Age, but it appears to be quite certain that the lowest strata belong to the Paleolithic Age. The stone instruments found in the lower city were all made by flaking, like those of the Old Stone Age, and not by grinding, like the polished instruments of the Neolithic. They were small in size, of the kind usually referred to as microlithic, and were made locally, while the weapons of the hunters who lived in the caves in Galilee and Carmel were of the type manufactured in Egypt and were probably imported from there.

The various strata of the first period appear to correspond closely with the strata of Tepe Gawra, Kish, etc., before the flood of Mesopotamia, but the instruments, the pottery and the houses were of a more primitive kind. A house excavated in one of the lowest strata had been rebuilt no less than six times, and had the floor level raised each time. It is of large dimensions, its largest room being 15 by 18 feet. It was probably built long after the settlement was first made, possibly a thousand years or more. Garstang dates the house as he found it at 5,000 B.C., but it is almost certainly much earlier.

Near the top of the prehistoric mound (before the first walled town was built) a very large building was found. It was probably a temple and had figurines representing cows, goats, sheep, pigs and dogs, showing that not only agriculture, but also stock-raising was carried on there during the early period.

Among the stone tools belonging to the early period were 800 sickle blades, as well as a great variety of other tools for agricultural and domestic purposes. Pottery was found in the lowest strata. It appears to have been invented and developed locally, not borrowed from outside. Its earliest appearance took the form of a basin scooped out of the floor and made water-tight, evidently for holding water. The art of making pottery was gradually developed from that primitive form. Simple utensils of clay mixed with chopped straw or fiber that could be moved about appeared soon after the invention; then baked pottery was developed, and finally painted pottery.

Even in the latest stages of this prehistoric period, the hammered copper instruments used in contemporary Iran and Egypt never found their way to Jericho; the isolation continued almost to the end of the period. On the top of the last stratum of this period, two objects of Egyptian origin, a stone palette and a mace-head of alabaster, were found. These belonged to the pre-Dynastic period of Egypt which, as we have seen, was also the pre-*Hiatus* period.

In forming an idea of the antiquity of the prehistoric settlement at Jericho, the first thing to bear in mind is that the figures given as dates: 3,000 B.C. for the end of the period, and 5,000-6,000 for the beginning, are not dates at all, and can hardly even be called estimates. The various objects found in the topmost stratum of the first period, stone instruments and pottery in different stages of development, all appear to have been invented and developed locally, and did not reach the perfection of similar objects found in the last stratum before the flood of Mesopotamia. It is highly probable, then, that the date of this last stratum of the first period of Jericho corresponds with the date of the great flood of Mesopotamia, and that it was this flood that caused the city to be abandoned for what was evidently a long period of time, for the new inhabitants belonged to a different race and brought with them a completely different culture.

A further argument that helps to strengthen the conclusion that the whole first period of Jericho belongs to the pre-Flood period of Mesopotamia is that no trace of writing or of any primitive attempt at writing was found in any of these early strata.

Garstang introduces his account of Jericho of the second period when the first city wall was built, as follows:

> The new world now enfolded Jericho where a complete change of civilisation coupled with signs of the destruction of the previous settlement, argues a change of race...The new population brought with it the radical features of Babylonian (or Sumerian) civilisation; there can be little doubt but that the new city was founded and fortified by a people migrating either from further north in response to pressure from beyond, or from Mesopotamia itself. (*The Story of Jericho,* p. 69).

The walled city was built and destroyed four times, the fourth destruction being caused by the Israelites under Josue, when the city was burned and not rebuilt again for more than 500 years. The only part of the history of this second period that concerns us here is the time immediately after the building of the first city walls. This period is referred to as the Early Bronze Age in most books, but in Jericho, copper only, without any alloy, was used for a long time, and the stone instruments of the new settlers were much inferior to those of the last part of the first period. The making of wine and apparently of a kind of beer also were introduced. This corresponds with what is related in the Bible of the making of wine by Noe. When pottery made its appearance again it was better shaped because it was made on the potter's wheel, but it was of rougher finish. In a word, the new city went through the same stages of development as the post-Flood towns of Mesopotamia.

The following is a description of the walls of the Fourth City of Jericho which was destroyed by Josue (both before and after the destruction), given in the field report dated March 2, 1930:

> The main defences of Jericho in the Late Bronze Age followed the upper brink of the city mound, and comprised two parallel walls, the outer six feet and the inner twelve feet thick. Investigation along the west side show continuous signs of destruction and conflagration. The outer wall suffered most, its remains falling down the slope. The inner wall is preserved only where it abuts upon the citadel, or town, to a height of eighteen feet; elsewhere it is found largely to have fallen, together with the remains of buildings upon it, into the space between the walls which was filled with ruins and debris. Traces of intense fire are plain to see, including reddened masses of brick, cracked stones, charred timbers and ashes. Houses alongside the walls were found burnt to the ground, their roofs having fallen in upon the domestic pottery within. (*The Story of Jericho,* p. 133).

The story of Jericho as revealed by the excavations is an admirable confirmation of the biblical account of early man, of the Deluge and of the destruction of the city by Josue. The Bible tells us that the sons of Adam and Eve practiced agriculture and stock-raising and that their descendants attained a high degree of material civilization before the Deluge; that the Deluge occurred in comparatively recent times, that the art of making wine was invented after it, and that the walls of Jericho fell suddenly and that the city was burned and abandoned about 1,400 B.C. (See *3 Kings* 16).

The Most Recent Excavations at Jericho

The work of excavating the lowest strata of the ancient mound of Jericho which had been carried on by Dr. Garstang between 1930 and 1936 has been resumed in recent years, and what are regarded as sensational results have been obtained. These results have been summarized by Dr. Kathleen Kenyon (who helped to superintend the excavations), in a lecture delivered at Oxford on May 5, 1956, which was published in the December issue of *Antiquity* of that year.

Dr. Kenyon begins her lecture by admitting that the credit of discovering the lower strata, to which we have referred above, belongs to Dr. Garstang, and then goes on to say that the new excavations were carried out at a different part of the tell, or mound, which is about eight acres in extent. In the course of the excavations a clearly marked dividing line was found between the upper and lower strata which was also the dividing line between two completely different civilizations.

Though Dr. Kenyon does not say so, it may be presumed to be the same dividing line as that discovered by Dr. Garstang's expedition to which we have referred. Whether it is the same or not, the new evidence provided by the recent excavations proves conclusively that an ancient civilization of a unique type, different from any discovered elsewhere, suddenly ceased, and that after a long interval a new civilization totally different replaced it.

An examination by the carbon 14 method of the objects found in the upper strata of the mound showed that the event which caused the mound to be abandoned at the time referred to occurred about 7,000 B.C., which is the date given by geologists for the great inundation which covered a large portion of our earth at the end of the Ice Age. The date of the dividing-line between the two civilizations was given tentatively by Garstang as 3,000 B.C.; the carbon 14 examination shows that the date is about 7,000 B.C. It is reasonable to conclude that the 4,000 B.C. date given by Millar Burrows, which we have endeavored to show was altogether too late, should have been 7,000 B.C., and that the great flood of Mesopotamia was really the Flood of Noe.

The description of the houses and artifacts of the upper strata given by Dr. Kenyon is much the same as that given by Dr. Garstang; the houses were well-built and had all the conveniences of a civilized people. Both the walls and floors of the houses were covered with a layer of gypsum plaster which was finished off with a fine coat of highly burnished plaster, pinkish or creamy in color. As this was characteristic of nearly all the houses, Dr. Kenyon refers to the people who inhabited them as "the Plastered Floor People."

In the strata beneath "the Plastered Floor" houses, evidences of a completely different civilization were found. This civilization was, however, of a high order. The remains of a town wall were found beneath the town wall referred to by Garstang, and within the wall the remains of a tower built with great stones transported from a distance. But there was another surprise: a still earlier massive town wall was found at a still lower level enclosing a smaller space. Both of these town walls were pre-Flood and were earlier than those described by Garstang. Now comes the greatest surprise of all, of which we will allow Dr. Kenyon to tell:

> This brings me (Dr. Kenyon) to what I regard as the major discovery of the season. Over the face of what has now become the second earliest town-wall known, was a great tipped fill, with a layer of soft dark earth tailing up and over the tower. Above this is a long series of the usual "Plastered Floor" houses. Many people have wondered why this excellent town wall was allowed to go out of use. *The answer is that there was a major interruption in the life of the site.*

Dr. Kenyon had described the "Plastered Floor" houses as rectangular in shape, with large rooms and a lavish supply of household utensils. In contrast with this, the houses beneath the earth deposits were bee-hive shaped and were built with bricks of a different kind from those of the strata above the deposit. The equipment of these houses was however lavish and consisted of flint instruments, bowls made from limestone, querns for grinding corn and a remarkable bone industry.

Dr. Kenyon then continues:

> It is clear therefore that we have the remains of the occupations of two separate groups of people. Fortunately the strategraphical evidence of the separation is very clear. At the northern end of the tell (mound) there was evidence of a streambed, probably of stormwater which cut through the remains of buildings of the earlier type. The streambed was cut down and silted up again on three occasions, indicating an appreciable lapse of time, though one, of course, which it is impossible to estimate accurately. Immediately above the filled-in streambed appears the first of the Plastered Floors.
>
> But one thing of major importance for Near Eastern archaeology is already clear. The latter group, the Plastered Floor people, arrived at Jericho with a fully blown civilization; with house

> plans and building methods already stereotyped, and with an equipment so adequate to their needs that it seems to show very little development in the many successive levels (above it) excavated. Of where they came—there is at present not a scrap of evidence. (See *Antiquity,* December, 1956, pp. 187-191).

At the time the lecture was being printed, the results of the examination of objects found by the carbon 14 method had not yet come to hand, but the author had ventured to express the opinion that the earliest strata might date back to the sixth millennium B.C., that is, to somewhere between 5,000 and 6,000 B.C.

The results came in when the printing was finished and a footnote was added to page 190 which reads:

> Since the date at which the lecture [by Dr. Kenyon] was delivered, the preliminary results of the Carbon 14 examination made under the direction of Professor Zeuner have become available. These give dates in the seventh millennium B.C. [between 6,000 and 7,000 B.C.] for material from layers considerably later than the beginning of the Plastered Floor stage.

The date of the destruction of the early settlement must therefore be about 7,000 B.C., which is the date of the end of the Ice Age, and the date given for the Deluge by authorities on geology such as Howorth. The strata beneath the dividing line made by the earth deposit must belong to dates long prior to 7,000 B.C. It is quite possible that the earliest of them may go back to near the time of Adam.

The evidence from the excavations carried out under the direction of Dr. Kenyon supports the conclusion of Dr. Garstang that the early settlers of Jericho lived in splendid isolation and developed a civilization of their own up almost to the time of the destruction of the settlement. It appears from the evidence of Dr. Kenyon just given that the destruction of the settlement was by water. Therefore, as the date of the destruction is the date given by the best authorities for the Deluge, as the destruction was by water, and as there is clear evidence that the destruction caused a break in the civilization, it is legitimate to conclude that the Deluge of Noe extended to Palestine.

The pre-Flood civilization of Mesopotamia and Iran was much more advanced and very different: the peoples of these countries manufactured beautiful painted pottery and they knew the use of hammered copper. This is in accordance with what we read in the Bible about the descendants of Cain, among whom was Tubalcain, who was the father of "the hammerers of brass and iron."

There is a tradition, which is supported by private revelations (See *The Dolorous Passion of Our Lord Jesus Christ,* London, 1951, p. 305), that Adam and Eve went to Palestine when they were expelled from the Garden of Eden; that Seth was born at Bethlehem, that Adam and Eve were buried at Calvary, and that their bones, covered deep by the Deluge, were under the spot where Our Lord's Cross was erected. If we cannot claim that the excavations carried out in various places in Palestine confirm these traditions, we can at least say that they do not render them improbable.

Note: The Dead Sea with its salt water is less than two miles from Jericho. Geologists tell us that the salt water of the Dead Sea was brought from the ocean by the Great Flood at the end of the Ice Age and remained there because the Dead Sea is under the level of the ocean. It must have been this Great Flood that destroyed the earliest city of Jericho. The results of the Carbon 14 tests referred to above give us not only the date of the destruction of the earliest city of Jericho, but also confirm the date of the zero year of the Ice Age arrived at by Baron de Geer of Sweden, which was also the year of the Great Flood.

Chapter 8

EVIDENCE OF A GREAT FLOOD FROM EXCAVATIONS IN IRAN

Iran was one of the last places to receive the attention of the archaeologists, and yet it is the home of what appears to be one of the oldest civilizations of the world. Excavations carried out there in recent times show that the flood in Mesopotamia was not a mere local river flood, as some modern Scripture commentators allege, but that it reached the high plateau of Iran; these excavations also afford evidence that the Mosaic account which says that Tubalcain was "a hammerer of brass and iron" was correct, for they show that copper ore had been hammered (not smelted) and that tools were made from it before the time of the great flood in Mesopotamia.

Iran is a high plateau lying between the Persian Gulf and the Caspian Sea; it is bounded by the Zagros Mountains (5,500 feet high) on the north and east, and by the Elburz Mountains on the south (19,000 feet high). In the center of the plateau thère is an extensive salt desert, the most arid in the world, where nothing grows or lives. What is today a great salt desert was once a fertile plain with an extensive lake in the center into which the rivers from the mountains discharged their waters. Around the fringe of this great salt desert, prehistoric villages have been discovered where stone instruments and pottery in various stages of development have been found. Instruments of various kinds made by hammering copper ore were found in considerable quantity all over the plateau. This shows the marvelous accuracy of the Mosaic account of the pre-Flood civilization, which describes Tubalcain as a "hammerer," not as a "smelter" of brass and iron. Hebrew scholars tell us that the proper translation of the Hebrew passage is "A hammerer of *copper* [not brass] and iron." There is no doubt whatever about the fact that hammered copper ore was found both in Iran and Mesopotamia before the flood. It is probable that iron ore was also "hammered" at the same period, for iron ore exists in Iran. Iron, unlike copper, rusts and dissolves, and hence instruments made from hammered iron ore, if such existed, would have dissolved during the thousands of years that have elapsed since then. As already stated, a "hammerer in brass and iron" can hardly mean more than a hammerer of some kind of metal.

Excavations at Siyalk

Excavations have been carried out at many places in Iran: down in the plain at Susa, in the sides of the mountains that surround the Plateau, and around the edge of the salt desert high up on the Plateau.

Mr. Ghirshman, who superintended these excavations, gives us an account of some of them in his book entitled *Iran*.

He tells us that he found remains of primitive habitations dug into the sides of the mountains, and sometimes caves that had been used as habitations. In these he found hand axes and other stone instruments fashioned by flaking, which was the method employed in the Old Stone Age. He found also coarse pottery, which is a proof that pottery and the instruments of the Old Stone Age were contemporaneous in places where there were fixed habitations. As well as these, he found agricultural instruments, which shows that agriculture goes back to the earliest times.

On the high plateau itself, the oldest human settlement discovered was that at Siyalk, near Kashan, south of Teheran.

The excavations carried out there show that the settlement lasted for a very long time, and that its history might be divided into three periods, the first two of which were prior to the flood of Mesopotamia and the third after it. In the strata of the first period the tools were all of stone, among which were sickle-blades and other agricultural instruments. Toward the end of the period, hammered copper instruments appeared. During this period the pottery, which originally had consisted of wicker baskets daubed with clay, was gradually improved. The pottery was baked and painted, the paint being made from iron oxide, which is very common on the Plateau, mixed with fruit juice. Evidence of the breeding of the common domestic animals was also found in the strata of this same period.

The strata of the second period show a great improvement in the manufacture of pottery. The ovens in which it was baked were better made, the various utensils were beautifully painted and decorated with rows of birds and animals. The use of copper tools became more common, but they were still made by hammering, as smelting and casting had not yet been invented.

During this second period the plough appeared for the first time and samples of barley and wheat were found. The same type of kiln or oven in which the heat was generated outside the chamber where the pottery was baked, and the same type of well-baked buff pottery as was found beneath the flood deposit at Tepe Gawra, were found at the dividing line between the strata of the second and third periods and may be presumed therefore to belong to the second period, though Ghirshman attributed them to the third.

In the strata of the third period, evidence was found that the potter's wheel was used, that copper was smelted and cast and that a primitive mode of writing was developed.

The Flood deposit left on the top of the mound of Siyalk appears to have been small, and when the new settlers came after the Flood they probably dug through it and used some of the utensils of the upper strata. At Susa, 5,000 feet lower down on the plain, the dividing line between the pre-Flood and post-Flood strata was just as marked as at Ur or Kish.

The great proof that the Flood reached the high plateau of Iran is the presence of the arid salt desert where there had been a fertile plain with a freshwater lake in the center sometime about 7,000 B.C.

Sir Arthur Keith devotes a chapter in his book entitled *A New Theory of Evolution* (London, 1949) to the "Antiquity of Village Settlements," in which he gives an excellent summary of the results of recent excavations in the Middle East.

In this chapter he states:

> Much (of the plateau of Iran) is now desert or arid steppe, but in the closing phases of the Ice Age (i.e., about 7,000 B.C.) most of it was rolling grassland, well watered and providing, in the words of Professor Hadden (in *The Races of Man,* 1924, p. 143) "a very desirable land and well-fitted for human habitation."

We have, then, in the salt desert of the Plateau of Iran, a proof that the waters of the Deluge rolled over it, and an indication of the date at which the disaster happened.

In the same chapter Sir Arthur admits that the excavations carried out in the Middle East between the two World Wars have shown clearly that the civilization of Asia (Iran and Mesopotamia) as shown by the practice of agriculture, and the manufacture of pottery etc., is older than the civilization of Egypt. Skulls were found at Abydos on the Nile in one of the earliest agricultural settlements, which were of Asian type and had a larger brain capacity than the later pre-Dynastic skulls.

He admits also in the same chapter that both the upper sandy wastes of the Nile as well as Arabia were habitable up to the latter part of the Pleistocene, i.e., up to the end of the Ice Age.

The Cause and Date of the Disaster in Iran

The arid salt desert in the plateau is not an isolated case. There are several other salt deserts and salt lakes on plateaus cut off from the sea in various parts of Asia and Africa. Besides the salt desert of Iran there is the Sahara Desert in Africa, which contains large deposits of salt, and the Gobi Desert in Asia; then there are the salt lakes of the Caspian, the Dead Sea and Lake Baikal in Asia, and Lake Chad in Africa, to mention only the principal ones. Geologists give the same explanation for all these inland salt lakes and salt deserts, which is, that these places were inundated by ocean water at some time in the geologically recent past, and that when the ocean water receded from places connected with the ocean, it was trapped in those places mentioned above. The water remained on all the parts of these plateaus cut off from the ocean and, as there was great evaporation, at first there was heavy rainfall. This, however, was not sufficient to counterbalance the evaporation and to keep these lakes from shrinking. It is by estimating the rate of shrinkage, or what is called "desiccation" of these inland salt lakes, that geologists come to the conclusion that the inundation of ocean water must have occurred within the last 10,000 years. In the quotation given above by Arthur Keith from *The Races of Man,* the date of this inundation of the Plateau of Iran is given as somewhere about the end of the last Ice Age (about 7,000 B.C.).

This inundation of ocean water that left the salt deposits on the Plateau of Iran may be reasonably presumed to have been the same inundation that caused the *hiatus* in Europe and Egypt and is sufficient to account for the sudden cessation of the beautiful painted pottery in Mesopotamia, Egypt and Iran. It helps us then to fix the date of the *hiatus,* as well as of the flood in Mesopotamia.

It also shows the accuracy of the Mosaic account of the Deluge, which says: "The waters increased and lifted up the ark high from the earth. . .and the waters prevailed beyond measure upon the earth; and all the high mountains under the whole heavens were covered." (*Gen.* 7:17, 19).

How the Inundation Was Caused

We say that the disaster in Iran was caused by a flood that came from the sea, but if we ask how the flood was caused, was it by a rising of the sea or a depression of the dry land, the explanation usually given by geologists is that it was caused by a depression of the land, but this may have been accompanied by an elevation of the bottom of the sea. There have been several cases of such depressions of the land even in historic times. For instance, in 1819 a wide expanse of the delta of the Indus of an area of about 2,000 square miles was converted into an inland sea by a sudden depression of the land caused by an earthquake. In fact, depressions of the land on a larger or smaller scale have accompanied most earthquakes of which we have records.

The illustrious Baron Cuvier (1769-1832) in his *Theory of the Earth* states:

> I agree with MM. Deluc and Dolomieu in thinking that if anything in geology be established, it is, that the surface of our globe has undergone a great and sudden revolution, the date of which cannot be referred to a much earlier period than five or six thousand years ago.
>
> This sudden catastrophe was occasioned by an elevation of the sea-bottom and a submergence of the land.

This depression of the surface of the earth of which Cuvier speaks was not universal, for there are large tracts of the earth, especially at the Equator, where there are no traces of such depression.

Chapter 9

EVIDENCES OF A GREAT FLOOD THAT EXTENDED FROM THE CASPIAN SEA TO SIBERIA

Did the Flood of Mesopotamia And Iran Extend to Siberia?

A glance at a relief map of Asia indicating the heights of the various places above sea level will show that in the plain that runs east of the Ural Mountains from the Caspian Sea to the Arctic Ocean there is no place more than a thousand feet above sea level, and that the whole coastline from the Ural Mountains to the Bering Strait is not more than a few hundred feet above sea level. A flood, therefore, such as left the big deposit in Mesopotamia and reached the Plateau of Iran would certainly reach the shores of the Arctic Ocean. On this question we are not depending on mere conjecture; we have definite proof that such was the case.

It is an established fact that carcasses of mammoths in great numbers have been found preserved in ice all along the Arctic Ocean from the Bering Strait to the Urals. There is difference of opinion as to whether these belong to a variety that was indigenous to the northern regions, or to the tropical variety, the general opinion now being that they belonged to an extinct species with long, woolly hair, indigenous to the cold north.

For information about the mammoths found in great numbers along the coastline of the Arctic Ocean, it is necessary to go back to writers of the end of the last and beginning of the present century. The great authority on the subject is Sir H. Howorth, F.G.S., who wrote *The Mammoth and the Flood* in 1887 and continued writing on the same subject until his death in 1918.

In modern books by non-geologists, readers will find reference to one or two mammoths found frozen in Siberia with the remains of the last meal they had eaten in their stomachs, and will get the impression that only a few specimens have been found. The facts as related by Howorth, who was an eminent geologist and speaks from evidence, are very different. He tells us that whole herds of these huge beasts, of all ages, from full-grown specimens to baby mammoths, have been found together in various places in Siberia, chiefly along the coastline of the Arctic Ocean and in the islands near the coast. Many of these have been found intact with the skin and hair, and with the flesh so perfectly preserved that it can still be eaten. Along with them the remains of other animals have been found, such as the woolly rhinoceros, the bison, the horse and many other animals, both living and extinct. These have been found frozen, being buried beneath the surface along with great masses of trees, branches and other vegetation, much of which has been transported from the south. Of the animals from the south only the skeletons remain, while the whole carcasses of many of the mammoths are still intact and in a perfect state of preservation. Obviously the trees and other vegetation belonging to the tropics must have been transported from the south as well as the animals of which only the skeletons remain, but the mammoths found intact and fresh must have belonged to the north; they must have perished suddenly and have become frozen soon after their death, for otherwise they would have rotted.

The Deluge Alone Can Explain the Presence of the Mammoths from the North Found Frozen Along With the Skeletons of Animals from the South, in Debris Consisting Mostly of Tropical Vegetation Transported from the South to the Arctic Ocean

The presence in the Arctic Ocean of the well-preserved mammoths with the skeletons of other animals, all buried among the debris of trees and plants from the south, raises the following questions: 1) Why did some animals remain intact and fresh for nearly 10,000 years, while others rotted and became skeletons before they were buried? 2) How did the trees and plants from the south get transported to the Arctic Ocean? 3) How did it happen that the mammoths and other animals got buried deep in a place which has remained frozen to a depth of 600 feet ever since they were buried? 4) How was it that the ground got thawed at the particular time that the mammoths and debris from the south arrived, so that the animals and debris were found, not on the top of the ground, but buried among the debris carried from the south, and why did the ground freeze so soon that the mammoth had not time to decay?

The complete answer to all these questions is very simple and easily understood, but strange as it may appear, though several attempts have been made to answer these questions, the first complete answer to them all is given here for the first time.

Most geologists who have written about the Deluge are agreed that it took place about the end of the Ice Age, and yet none of them so far as I have been able to find out, has thought of referring to the effect of the inrush of the warm water from the tropics on the ice that still remained to be melted.

The Waters of the Deluge Accelerated the Melting of the Ice of the Last Glacial Period

The amount of heat, reckoning from freezing point to the temperature at the tropics, contained in a body of water thousands of miles in extent and deep enough to cover the Plateau of Iran, is so great that it is almost beyond reckoning.

Now if the Deluge occurred during the Last Glacial Period, as many geologists believe, it must have passed over the ice both in the Scandinavian countries and in Siberia, and if so, it must have accelerated the melting. We all know the effect that the warm water of the Gulf Stream has on the temperature of the air in the countries whose shores it washes; the direct contact of the water of the Deluge with the ice of the Glacial Period would have been much more pronounced, and if this actually happened, there must be some proofs of the facts. Are such proofs available? There are at least two clear proofs. The first is, as already indicated, the sudden softening of the ground along the Arctic Ocean that allowed the mammoth and other animals to sink down and get buried before they were frozen; the second proof is furnished by Baron de Geer of Sweden, who calculated almost to a year the time it took for the ice of the Last Glacial Period which covered the Scandinavian countries to melt.

The Country Around the Caspian Sea

The country all around the Caspian Sea resembles the salt desert on the Plateau of Iran very closely. Hugh Millar in *The Testimony of the Rocks* (Edinburgh, 1890) speaks of it as follows: "Vast plains, white with salt and charged with sea-shells, show that the Caspian Sea was at no distant period greatly more extensive than it is now." He believes that the presence of the salt and the sea-shells can be explained only by an inrush of the water of the ocean which was trapped in the depressed area but gradually evaporated, leaving the salt and the sea-shells behind. So far he has the support of other geologists, for no other satisfactory explanation of the presence of the salt and sea-shells can be given. But he goes on to propound a theory of how the Deluge of Noe occurred, which need not be taken seriously. He says that "the whole human race, greatly reduced by exterminating wars and exhausting vices" were confined to that area and were all destroyed except Noe and his family. Millar's theory of the Deluge is untenable, because the fossils of men who lived long before the Deluge have been found all over Europe and Africa and in Asia west of the Himalaya Mountains.

Fr. Sutcliffe, S.J. in his C.T.S. pamphlet, *Who Perished in the Deluge?* combines the theories of Millar and Fr. Montais. He congregates the descendants of Seth into the area around the Caspian Sea, where they are all destroyed except Noe and his family, and puts the descendants of Cain at a safe distance from the scene of the disaster. The theory in this amended form is also untenable because, as we have seen, traces of the Deluge have been found in Europe and Africa, in Asia west of the Himalaya Mountains and in the low-lying plains of India and China.

Millar is quite right in saying that "the Caspian Sea was greatly more extensive than it is now."

Col. L. M. Davies, D.Sc., F.G.S. in a lecture entitled "Scientific Discoveries of the Deluge" delivered in 1930 before the Victoria Institute, London, gives many proofs of this. He quotes Mr. B. Carpenter as saying:

> Great deposits of salt are to be found in different parts of the great area of the steppes of Southern Russia . . . Everywhere the sand of these steppes contains an admixture of salt; and there are various local accumulations of salt often associated with marl, having shells and fish-bones embedded in them, and thus clearly marking the sites of lakes which survived for a time the reduction of level and recession of the northern border of the Caspian, but which are now entirely dried up.

Though the level of the country immediately around the Caspian Sea is lower than the sea, the steppes of Russia to which this Sea formerly extended are far above sea level. The explanation given by geologists of the presence of salt and marine fauna in the country round the Caspian is the same as that given for the presence of salt and marine fauna on the Plateau of Iran, which we have already dealt with. There was an incursion of the water of the ocean in comparatively recent times, and, as there was no outlet to the ocean from the plateau, the water was trapped but gradually evaporated leaving the salt and the fishes behind.

The Salt Mines

Salt mines are found in various parts of the world, in some of which the layers are more than 3,000 feet in depth. There is a salt mountain at Cardana in Spain, towering above the surface of the earth, and there are salt mines in Poland and New Mexico deep down in the bowels of the earth. Geologists believe that the origin of these goes back to before the Tertiary

Period, a hundred million years ago, but so far no completely satisfactory explanation of their formation has been given. Dr. Heribert Nilsson in *Synthetische Artbildung* propounds the theory that they are the result of enormous tidal waves raised by the moon at a time when it approached the earth. These tides, according to Nilsson's theory, drew the air toward the Equator, causing intense cold; as they were ebbing, ice was formed and the salt was deposited.

Whether this theory be true or not, the salt mines date back millions of years and are in no way connected with the Deluge of Noe.

Excavations in the Caspian Sea Area

Remarkable results were obtained at the beginning of the present century from excavations carried out by Mr. Raphael Pumpelly at Anau, near Askabad, 300 miles east of the Caspian Sea. These results correspond closely with those obtained by Sir Leonard Woolley and other excavators in Mesopotamia and Iran during the past 50 years, but they have not got the same publicity.

These excavations revealed the fact that a pre-Flood civilization similar to that of Mesopotamia existed in the Caspian Sea area from a very early date, that it lasted for thousands of years and then suddenly came to an end. According to Pumpelly's calculation the earliest settlement, which was very primitive, was founded about 9,000 B.C. and continued developing till about 6,000, when it suddenly ended.

Two mounds, locally called "Kurgans," which contained the remains of pre-Flood settlements, were excavated at Anau. The northern one was abandoned after the Flood and was never built on again. The southern one was abandoned for a period calculated by Pumpelly to have lasted 800 years, after which a new settlement was built. It was 38 feet from the top of the mound down to virgin soil, 18 feet of which are under the present level of the country, which means that there was a flood deposit of 18 feet. In the strata below the Flood level, there were found the flint instruments of the Old Stone

Age; hand-made pottery; a small number of hammered copper instruments in the higher strata; the bones of domestic animals—the ox, the pig, the horse and the sheep; some wheat and barley. The presence of wheat and barley and domestic animals along with the flint instruments of the Old Stone Age in the early pre-Flood strata is another proof that the normal life of earliest man was life in a fixed settlement where both agriculture and stock-raising were practiced, as is stated in *Genesis,* and not the life of a nomadic hunter, like the Neanderthal Man.

In the strata of the southern settlement, which was reoccupied 800 years after the Flood (according to Pumpelly's calculation), there were found weapons and instruments of copper, and pottery that was made on the potter's wheel, all of which are indications that a long interval had elapsed between the abandonment of the site and its reoccupation. As there is convincing evidence (which has been given above) of a great flood in the Caspian Sea area about 7,000 B.C., it may be regarded as certain that the destruction of these early settlements was caused by that flood, and that the date of the destruction was 7,000 B.C., not 6,000 B.C. It is, however, remarkable that Pumpelly's calculations came so near those arrived at by the carbon 14 tests carried out at Jericho. This is a further proof that the date of the great flood in Mesopotamia was 7,000 B.C., not 4,000 B.C. (See *Excavations in Turkestan* by Raphael Pumpelly, 2 vols., 1904).

Chapter 10

THE ACTUAL DATE OF THE DELUGE

Baron De Geer Gives a Proof of the Deluge And Fixes the Actual Date[1]

The famous Baron de Geer of Sweden, who calculated the time that it took to melt the ice of the Last Glacial Period, without either knowing it or intending it, furnished us with a proof that the water of the Deluge not only accelerated the melting of the ice, but practically finished it, and at the same time, by calculating the date of the year on which the altogether abnormal melting of the ice occurred, he gives us the date of the Deluge. The proof furnished by the Baron, that the Deluge accelerated the melting of the ice, is supported by the evidence from Siberia.

The Baron has discovered that the melt water of the glaciers of the Last Glacial Period left each year a deposit that could easily be distinguished from the deposit of the preceding and succeeding years, because the melting of the ice took place during the summer and ceased in winter, thus allowing the heavier material (coarse sand) of the deposit to sink to the bottom. These deposits are called "varves" in Swedish, a name now generally used to designate them. The Baron with a party of 20 collaborators patiently counted these varves, beginning with the outermost one at the Dani-Gotiglacial moraine in Denmark, and tracing them along the path of the receding

---

1. See article on the Ice Age in *The Readers Digest* of December, 1958.

The evidence given in this article indicates that the Last Glacial Period was coming to an end about 9,000 B.C., but does not fix the date when all the ice had melted in America and Europe, and therefore does not contradict the findings of Baron de Geer and M. Suaramo, who fix the date for Scandinavia at about 7,000 B.C. This new evidence supports the conclusion of these men that the Last Glacial Period ended in comparatively recent times.

glaciers up to Ragunda, in the northern half of the Scandinavian peninsula. These varves, which were easily distinguishable from one another, varied in thickness from a few millimeters to a couple of centimeters. At Ragunda, however, Baron de Geer found one enormous varve of about 40 times the average thickness. He found also that at Ragunda the melt water had begun to flow in two directions the year the varve was deposited, which indicated that the ice had melted far above Ragunda. It has been calculated from the counting of the varves that this year was 6,839 B.C. Baron de Geer called it the Zero year of the Last Glacial Period, which marked the beginning of the post-Glacial Period.

A Finnish geologist named Suaramo counted the varves on the other side of the Baltic in Finland, and arrived at substantially the same result as Baron de Geer; there was a difference of only 39 years between them. He also found one enormous varve 40 centimeters in thickness, the date on which it was deposited being also at the end of the Last Glacial Period.

An American geologist named Antevs attempted to do the same for America, but as whole series of varves were missing he had to fall back on estimates (which are the same as guesses) to replace counting of the varves. However, his conclusions agree with those of Baron de Geer and Suaramo. (See *Dating the Past* by Zeuner, 1952 ed., p. 33).

The most satisfactory explanation (given here for the first time) for the depositing of the enormous varves found in Sweden by Baron de Geer, and in Finland by Suaramo, about the year 6,839 B.C.—which represented an abnormal amount of melt water for that particular year—is that this was the year of the Deluge, and that it was the warm water from the ocean that caused the abnormal melting of the ice. The fact that both Baron de Geer and Suaramo were concerned only with scientific investigations and not with proving theories, makes their evidence all the stronger. This evidence is supported by the evidence from Siberia, which geologists like Howorth regard as conclusive, that there was a great and sudden thawing of the ground in the Arctic regions at the end of the Last Glacial Period.

As the two events occurred about the same time, we are justified in using the figures arrived at by Baron de Geer and Suaramo—about 6,839 B.C.—for the date of the burying of the mammoths in Siberia.

The explanation for the freezing of the mammoths found intact and fresh, given in some books—that it was due to a sudden and permanent change of temperature in the Arctic regions—is put forward by men who regard it as certain that these animals were drowned in the Deluge, but who have not adverted to the effect which the ocean water must have had in melting the ice and softening the ground. Hence, in order to explain how these animals sank down and got buried, they said that the ground was soft, due to mild climate, when they arrived, and in order to explain how they got frozen soon after they had died, they had recourse to the unnecessary and fantastic explanation that the temperature dropped suddenly and has remained so ever since.

The answer to the five questions raised above should now be plain: the Deluge of Noe explains them all. The trees and tropical plants found in the Arctic Ocean were transported there from the south by the ocean water; the skeletons found were skeletons of animals from the south, which had plenty of time to decay, as the Deluge lasted several months; the carcasses of the mammoths found fresh and intact belonged to the north, where the temperature was then—and has been ever since—far below the freezing point, so that they were chilled as soon as they died, and frozen along with the debris from the south when the waters receded.

Besides furnishing us with a probable date for the Deluge, the labors of Baron de Geer and Matti Suaramo have given us with certainty the earliest date at which it was possible for men to enter the Scandinavian peninsula and the remaining part of Europe that had been covered with ice. Antevs, the American authority on the Ice Age, has not been able to furnish us with a corresponding date for North America; however, the estimate which he gives is substantially the same as that of Baron de Geer and Suaramo.

We can therefore safely fix the date of the Deluge at

somewhere around 7,000 B.C. The date arrived at by Baron de Geer's investigations is not guaranteed by him to be absolutely accurate, but as it has been checked by Suaramo of Finland, and by the method known as the pollen-analysis method, the error, if any, cannot amount to more than 50 years.

Chapter 11

EVIDENCE OF A GREAT FLOOD IN INDIA, CHINA AND NORTH AMERICA

Were India and China Affected By the Deluge?

Under this heading there are two questions which must not be confounded: 1) Did man reach India and China before the Deluge? and 2) did the waters of the Deluge reach India and China?

With regard to the first question, there is no sound evidence either from human fossils or artifacts to show that man existed in either India or China before 7,000 B.C., or even much later than that date.

No claim at all for human fossils of an earlier date than 3,000 B.C. has been made for India, and for China the only claim made is for the Peking Man, alleged to be half-ape, half-man. The case of the Peking Man has been dealt with in detail in *The Origin of Man,* Chapter 5, where readers will find conclusive evidence that the Peking Man was another forgery, like the Piltdown Man.

The oldest of the Chinese classical books of China, which is the Chou-King, claims to give the history of China from 2,357 B.C. Modern scholars say that no actual written document can be claimed with certainty to date before 728 B.C., or 1,200 at the earliest. Excavations at An-Yang in Honan revealed the existence of pottery of the post-flood Chalcolithic Age, similar to that of Mesopotamia of the same period. The system of writing which was developed after the Flood and which still obtains in China was also borrowed from Mesopotamia.

India

With regard to the antiquity of the human race in India, the opinion at the beginning of the present century was that true chronological history of India dates back only to about 1,200 B.C., the date given by Max Muller for the oldest of the Vedas. However, excavations carried out in the Indus Valley in 1921 revealed the existence of a highly developed civilization there about the time of Abraham, and further excavations carried out since in the same valley at Harappa and Mohenjodaro showed that there had been a still earlier civilization corresponding to the Sumerian civilization in Mesopotamia.

Mr. Leonard Cottrell in *Lost Cities* (London, 1957) gives 1,500 B.C. as the date of the Aryan invasion of the Indus Valley, and about 2,500 B.C. as the date of the foundation of Harappa and the other cities already existing at the time of the invasion (pp. 120, 122). Dr. Albright in *From the Stone Age to Christianity* says:

> This early civilisation of India was no less dependent on the West than was the later Aryan culture, since there is close general parallelism and there are many specific points of identity between it and the contemporary culture of Mesopotamia and Susiana. (p. 30).

The conclusion to be drawn from the latest investigation of the Indus Valley, the oldest in India, is that members of the human race had not reached there before the great Mesopotamian flood.

Did the Waters of the Deluge Reach India and China?

Even if we had no direct evidence of a transgression of the sea in India and China in comparatively recent times, we would have to conclude that the waters that covered Mesopotamia to such a great depth that they reached the Plateau of Iran and extended to Siberia, must have covered the plains of India and China also. But we are not depending on indirect evidence; several geologists who have visited India have given direct evidence on the point.

Dr. G. F. Wright, the well-known American geologist who visited Asia in 1900, on his return wrote a series of papers on "Geological Confirmations of the Noachian Deluge" in which he gave evidence of a widespread inundation there. He said that the plains of China and of Northern Asia must have been submerged to a depth of 2,000 to 3,000 feet in comparatively recent times. Col. Davies F.G.S., who studied the same problem, comes to the same conclusion for India as Dr. G. F. Wright had come to for China and Northern Asia. In his lecture on the Deluge at The Victorian Institute of London, he gives the following quotation from an article published by Dr. Wright in an American Geological Bulletin in 1902:

> It is in place to point to the indubitable evidence of the *recent existence* of an inland sea as large as the Mediterranean over the area of the Gobi Desert. . . .
>
> The existence of this internal sea of Central Asia is attested by abundant sedimentary deposits along its margin. . .and also by the Chinese historical references to it as the "Great Han Hai" or Interior Sea. A general depression of Central Asia must have occurred to account for the phenomena we have presented, distributing the loess in the peculiar manner indicated, and filling the central depression of Mongolia with an Inland Sea. (G. F. Wright Bull, Geol. Soc. Amer. Vol. 13, 1902).

And he quotes R. C. Andrews as saying: "Since the end of the Ice Age, the drying up of the plateau has been rapid." (*On The Trail of Ancient Man,* 1926, p. 296).

Australia and Indonesia

No serious claim has been made for the existence of man in Australia at a date prior to the Mesopotamian flood. The claim for the existence of a race of ape-men in Java half-a-million years ago has been dealt with in "The Origin of Man" and has been proved to be without foundation.

North and South America

The common opinion at present is that the Red Indians were the first inhabitants of America, and that it is less than 10,000 years since their arrival there. However, some authorities such as G. F. Wright (see *The Origin and Antiquity of Man*) believe that there is sufficient evidence for the presence of man in North America during the last Glacial Period, long before the arrival of the Indians.

Contrary to the general impression, there was no obstacle to prevent man from passing from Asia to Alaska during the Last Glacial Period, for the icecap that covered the Scandanavian countries and North America to a depth of from one to two miles did not extend to either Siberia or Alaska, for the reason that there is not sufficient fall of snow in these countries to form an icecap. The Last Glacial Period ended about 7,000 B.C., but the ice had been melting for thousands of years before that, and the valleys of North America must have been free from ice long before the end of the Glacial Period.

Only one doubtful trace of man who would be prior to the Indians has been found in South America. This was in Curzo in Peru, where human fossils consisting of portions of skulls and bones were discovered. An account of these was published in *The American Journal of Science* in April, 1912, in which it was stated that "these skulls and bones correspond in all essential respects with those of normal adult Peruvians."

In North America, both human fossils and artifacts have been found which are regarded by G. F. Wright and other authorities as belonging to a period before the arrival of the Indians.

The claim for the great antiquity of the Calaveras skull, which was found in 1866, is now generally rejected, but G. F. Wright, in his book entitled *The Origin and Antiquity of Man* gives half-a-dozen other cases of human fossils and artifacts found in the valleys of North America which he believes to have belonged to people who preceded the Indians. If this be true it is quite certain that these had become extinct before the arrival of the Indians.

Did the Waters of the Deluge Reach America?

On this question there is a difference of opinion among geologists. Those who hold the theory that there were four glacial periods attribute all the deposits in the valleys of North America and the surface disturbances in the sides of the mountains to the action of the glaciers, but those geologists like Howorth who reject the theory that there were four glacial periods, while admitting that the deposits of what is known as the Terrace Epoch were certainly due to the melting of the ice of the Last Glacial Period, point out that the other deposits and disturbances attributed by some authorities to the other three disputed periods could not have been caused by the action of the glaciers, but must be attributed to a great flood such as the Deluge.

Howorth, who was one of the greatest authorities on the Glacial Periods and the Flood and who has written five large volumes of about 500 pages each on the Glacial Periods and on the Deluge, gives strong evidence to prove that a great part of North America 1) sank several hundred feet and 2) that it was covered with water to the same depth at the end of the Last Glacial Period, about 7,000 B.C., when according to the best authorities the Deluge occurred.

Chapter 12

EVIDENCE OF A DELUGE FROM GEOLOGY: CONCLUSIONS

The Geological Evidence for the Submergence Of Europe at the End of the Last Glacial Period

The evidence for the sudden disappearance of man from Europe and North Africa already has been given under the heading "Evidence from Paleontology," and reference has been made to the common opinion in France and Germany at the beginning of the last century that both these countries were under the waters of the Deluge. We give here the evidence from Geology which shows that all Europe was submerged toward the end of the Glacial Period. Only a brief summary can be given here, for it would take a whole book to give the evidence in full, but we will allow a well-known geologist, Lieut. Col. L. M. Davies, D.Sc., Ph.D., F.R.S.E., F.G.S., to make the summary for us from books by famous geologists. The following quotations are taken from his lecture delivered at the Victoria Institute, London, on January 20, 1930:[1]

> The kind of evidence to which Prestwich appealed is very different from that found in Northern Asia, which we have just been considering. Here, in Western Europe, we have not to do with a violent onset of a flood, but with its violent termination; the evidence consisting of masses of local and unrolled debris, which have apparently been swept with considerable violence into local pockets or catchment areas, without regard to the present drainage system.
>
> There is a singular absence, in these deposits, of anything like complete skeletons. Bones, indeed, abound in them; but,

1. Published with the kind permission of the Victoria Institute, London.

although often crowded together, and sometimes so associated as to imply that occasional complete limbs were buried, these bones seem for the most part to have been detached and swept into heterogeneous collections, regardless of species or individuals, before being buried. Yet they always appear to be fresh, and unrolled; and although they are nearly always broken, and often practically pulverized, yet they show *no signs of gnawing or of weathering.* The bones of carnivora are mixed indiscriminately with those of their natural prey; and the remains are most crowded either on higher ground, or where floods descending from higher ground might deposit part of their loads in hollows or other collecting places passed in transit.

Here, there is no such clear proof of exact contemporaneity as we found when considering the deposits in Northern Asia. Instantaneous, widespread, and lasting frost did not set in, in these regions, to preserve the soft parts of the victims of the occasion, and compel our recognition of the fact that the various sediments containing them must have been laid down at one and the same time. Consequently, as Prestwich remarked, many different explanations had been invented to account separately for the many different local collections and forms of these deposits.

One has only to read the discussion on his papers, too, in order to see how determined some of Prestwich's critics were to continue to regard these deposits as disassociated in time and cause, although they seem to have offered no reason for doing so. The determination often appears to exist independently of particular reasons.

The temporary, yet violent, nature of the action which formed these deposits is shown by the size of the *unrolled* and *local* rocks often found in them. For many of these boulders are of great weight, and have obviously been projected with considerable force well beyond the positions at which they would have come to rest if collecting under the mere influence of gravity, as part of a local scree or talus formation. The angle of deposition, too, of the sediments in general, where formed under cliffs, etc., is far lower than the normal angle of rest which they would have assumed as a simple talus; so here again we have evidence that these sediments were laid down in a violent manner under the influence of a powerfully projecting force, such as could only have been afforded by a great mass of waters in rapid motion.

How vast this volume of water was, and how great its lateral extent, we find indicated (where deposition occurred along a former coastline) by the disregard shown by the sediments for local depressions of the old cliffs, which would have localized lesser floods sweeping over the land. Another equally significant fact is that the masses of water seem to have been sufficiently great and enveloping to sweep down on *all sides* of isolated hills, independently of the local river systems. This is exactly what one would expect if the land were emerging from a state of *complete envelopment* by water; but it is singularly hard to explain on any other theory.

According to Prestwich, the evidence indicates that the land probably sank under the waters after a slow and gradual fashion; for there appears to be little trace left of the onset of the flood. Animals would seem, however, to have been driven before the advancing waters, and compelled to collect in heterogeneous crowds on such higher grounds as seemed to afford the best local chances of safety. Here, as the waters continued to rise, they were overwhelmed and drowned. Finally, after an interval of time which seems to have been sufficient to allow of the carcasses largely decomposing, the evidence indicates that the land emerged again from the waters by a succession of spasmodic upward movements, each of which produced its own wave of translation of waters off the land, bringing more similar material over the last, shifting the local boulders further, continuing the pounding action which broke the animal bones, and sweeping the land clear, over its smoother surfaces, of debris for which lodgment could not locally be found.

It seems clear that such an inundation as this would, by the mildness of its onset and the violence of its termination, leave only *scattered and local* traces. The comparatively *short duration* of the submergence would present the formation of marine deposits over the land, such as would inevitably have marked a prolonged submergence. And the violent action of the waters, on the emerging again of the land, would tend to sweep the surface clear of all traces of the disaster, except where the local pockets, old beaches, or newly opened fissures, offered lodgment for the same.

So much for the general character of these deposits, and the theory which accounts for them; we should now, perhaps, briefly explain the terms "Rubble-drift," "Head," and "Ossiferous Fissures" as used in this connection. The first term,

"Rubble-drift," refers to sediment in general; the peculiar and often massive collections of angular, unrolled and local materials tumultuously deposited in local pockets and catchment areas, and generally full of shattered Pleistocene bones, which compelled Prestwich to postulate a vast inundation of the land as the only means of accounting for them. "Head" is a term appled to this Rubble-drift where it masks an old raised beach. For this land often stood lower, in Pleistocene times, than it does now, and raised beaches at various heights above the present sea level are now found all over Western Europe and the Mediterranean, and are clearly of Pleistocene age, since the shells on them are all of recent species. When the Rubble-drift was being swept off the surface of the land by the retiring waters, it was poured over the tops of the old cliffs onto these former sea beaches, often covering the latter up entirely, and forming a gradual slope from the clifftops down to the sea, far beyond the locations of the old shorelines. The very existence of the old beaches was thus often concealed, until rivers, etc., cutting through the sediments, exposed sections of them and their overlying "head."

The "Ossiferous Fissures" are peculiarly interesting, since they seem to represent catchment areas which did not preexist the catastrophe, but were formed at the time of the catastrophe itself. The great strains to which the land was subjected, while rising again from the waters, seem to have caused the opening of local rents and fissures in the surface rocks. Some of these are of considerable size, and many are very deep. Their contemporaneity with the deposition of the Rubble-drift is shown by the fact that they are full of it (with its characteristic unrolled sediments and broken bones), and not of other types of deposits.

Indeed, it is probably due to the fact that they were filled with this drift as soon as they formed, that they did not close up again.

The bones in these fissures cannot be of animals which fell in alive, for no skeleton is complete. They cannot have been brought by beasts of prey, for none are gnawed. They were not brought by streams, for none are rolled; nor are they accompanied by rolled, or any but purely local materials. The bones could not have lain exposed for long, for none are weathered. They were not covered up normally, for they were broken by the violence of their deposition together with the associated rocks. That water had to do with their deposition is indicated (here as with other forms of the Rubble-drift) by the very general cementing together of the deposits by calcite. The formation of these Fissures in so many places, at the precise time of the formation of the Rubble-drift (proved by their filling to the top with that peculiar kind of drift *and no other deposit*), seems to confirm the belief that the Rubble-drift itself did not owe its origin to normal causes, but to something catastrophic in the nature of *earth movements*.

Prestwich also points out that these Ossiferous Fissures are often found upon *isolated hills* of considerable height. Such are the very localities where animals would naturally gather for safety in times of flood, and where (owing to the limited catchment areas found on the hills themselves) only a general inundation, covering the whole surrounding country to a great depth, could bring powerful water action to bear. A classical example of such an isolated hill is the "Montagne de Santenay," a flat-topped hill 1,640 feet high, and rising 1,030 feet above the surrounding plains, near Châlons-sur-Saône in Burgundy.

A fissure near the top of the hill is crowded with animal remains of a typical Rubble-drift type. No skeleton is entire; very few of the bones are in their proper relative positions; yet none of the bones have been gnawed. The bones are fractured, but unweathered; mixed together, but unrolled. As Gaudry remarked: "Why did so many wolves, bears, horses, and oxen scale a mountain isolated on all sides, and whence came the vast body of water necessary to wash them into the crevice, and to deposit the carbonate of lime with which they are surrounded?" All theories of glacial floods, as Prestwich and Howorth point out, break down here, and a general deluge can alone meet the case.

The Channel Islands were regarded by Prestwich as affording a "crucial test" of the accuracy of his views. Thus both Jersey and Guernsey are surrounded by fragments of raised beaches, which are covered by a "head," 10 to 30 feet in thickness, composed of fragments of local rock in a matrix of brick-earth or loess. The distances to which many of the larger blocks in this "head" were carried, witness to the violence with which it was deposited. Prestwich points out that the rapid emergence of the Islands from a totally-enveloping flood would alone explain the existence of this "head" *on all sides* of the Islands, and supply the necessary force for its deposition; for no theory of local streams would ever do so. . . .

Further evidence of extensive submergence (though probably representing a later stage in the retreat of the waters from some parts of the land) is afforded by Dr. Wright's discovery of a shoreline deposit of gravel at a height of 750 feet above the sea, at Trebizond, on the Black Sea. Corresponding shorelines, as he points out, have been reported at Sondak, on the south shore of the Crimea, nearly opposite Trebizond; also near Samsun, a hundred miles further west, on the south side of the Black Sea; while at Baku, on the west side of the Caspian Sea, stands yet another post-Tertiary shoreline at a height of 600 feet above sea level. Water standing at this level would, as Wright goes on to remark, submerge, with the exception of the Ural Mountains, "Northern Germany, all Russia, the Aral-Caspian basin, and all Central and Western Siberia." (*Origin and Antiquity of Man,* pp. 472-473).

That this submergence took place *since* man appeared in these parts, and apparently at the end of the Pleistocene (i.e., at the same geological period as the immersion spoken of by Howorth and Prestwich) is shown, as Wright points out, by Professor Armachevsky's discovery of Kief on the Dnieper, which is one of the largest tributaries of the Black Sea, of numerous remains of flint implements, also heaps of flint cores, associated with a large number of mammoth bones, with charred wood, broken and partially burnt bones, etc., at a depth of 53 feet below the undisturbed surface of the loess which covers the region. Similar discoveries of flint implements, charcoal, and mammoth bones, associated together and buried under the loess, were also made by Professor Armachevsky in five other places in European Russia; and Wright compares these facts with the similar discovery in Siberia, by Professor Kaschenko in 1896, of deeply buried mammoth remains associated with flint knives and scrapers, etc. (*op. cit.,* pp. 313, 314).

Now the European loess was definitely regarded by Prestwich (*pace* Richtofen) as one of the forms of his "Rubble-drift"; and he pointed out that analysis had shown that "in certain districts in Belgium the loess is largely impregnated with salt. . . "In general" (he adds) "the loess is so permeable that the rainwater would remove any salt that there might have been left in it, but in some instances the loess is sufficiently argillaceous to. . .favour the retention of the salt." The presence of this salt seems to be worth noting, for, according to

Professor Sollas (an eminent supporter of the aeolian theory), the loess was blown onto its present position by winds driving outwards from ice sheets, during periods of glacial accumulation, and such winds would hardly bring salt with them. Surely the presence of the salt supports those who attribute the distribution of the loess to the action of *marine waters* rather than continental winds.

The submergence hypothesis, as Prestwich remarked, alone accounts for all the facts.

How Loess Was Deposited

Loess, to which reference is made in the above quotation, is a well-known kind of soil that was formed from the glaciers during the Ice Age. It is found unevenly distributed over wide areas, hundreds of miles away from the nearest place that was covered with ice, sometimes spread in thin layers over the ground, and sometimes in deep pockets or fissures covered with earth.

How was it carried hundreds of miles away from the nearest glaciers? There are two theories: the one, called the aeolian theory, explains its presence so far away from its source by saying that it was carried as dust by the wind, the second theory—which is the only one that can explain its presence in deep pockets covered over with earth or debris—explains its presence by saying that it was laid down in water and by water. All evolutionists and all those who deny that the Deluge occurred adopt the aeolian theory, and they use it as an argument for the great antiquity of fossils or artifacts found in it, on the grounds that a deep layer of loess would take a very long time to deposit. The pockets, however, containing deep layers of loess, with layers of sand or gravel beneath them, indicate clearly that these layers must have been laid down by water. The argument therefore for the antiquity of the fossils found in them collapses, and instead, we have an argument for the Deluge.

As we shall see in the section on "The Antiquity of Man," the presence of deep layers of loess associated with the tools of the Old Stone Age or with human fossils in the Somme

Valley and at Heidelberg is used by both Professor Zeuner and Abbé Breuil as an argument for the great antiquity of man in Europe.

The mandible that has given its name to the Heidelberg Man was found in a layer of sand covered over with several layers of loess, and was 72 feet below the surface. Zeuner claims an antiquity of 450,000 years for the fossil, basing his claim on the depth of the layers of loess found over it; the claim is absurd and is now rejected. Men like Professor Zeuner, who use the presence of loess in association with fossils as a proof of their antiquity, wrongly assume that the loess has been deposited by the wind, and make no reference to the true explanation that it has been deposited by water.

Layers of loess, besides being found in Europe, have been found in all countries affected by the Ice Age, and are an indication that the places in which they are found have been covered with water.

Col. Davies gives the following information about the loess of India in the lecture referred to:

> The present writer (Col. Davies) has seen vast sheets of sediment, often of great thickness, spread over tracts in North-western India....In many places these deposits seem to be impregnated with salt; surface pools are brackish, and the whole ground is often white with saline efflorescence after rain. In his opinion these broad sheets of sediment....can only have been laid down by water, and in water; the latter being probably saline. They are utterly unlike windborne deposits, which now exist over large parts of the same area, but are quite distinct, and also later in character.

Conclusions

The following are the principal questions regarding the Deluge which have been discussed in the preceding pages, with their respective answers:

1) How are the statements in the Bible with regard to the universality of the Deluge to be interpreted?

The meaning of the word "all" in the Bible (as in most books) has to be determined either from the context or from the parallel passages. Both the context, which is the punishment of the sins of the human race, and the parallel passages which make no mention of the animals but insist that all men except those in the Ark perished, indicate that the meaning of *Genesis* is that all men except those in the Ark perished. This is the interpretation of the fathers.

2) What is the relation between the biblical account, and the earliest account from profane sources that has come down to us?

The very detailed and dogmatic account of *Genesis* could not have been derived from any, or all of the accounts in profane literature. It appears, however, to be certain that the Sumerian account, which is the earliest that has come down to us, refers to the same flood or disaster as that described in *Genesis*.

3) How far did the waters of the Deluge extend?

The waters of the Deluge covered all of Europe that was free of ice, at least all Northern Africa, all the plains of Asia and, probably, the plains of North America east of the Rocky Mountains.

4) What countries had members of the human race reached before the Deluge?

All Asia west of the Himalaya Mountains, but not beyond them; all Africa, and all of Europe that was free from ice. They had not reached India, China or Australia; probably they had reached North America, but not South America.

5) Did the whole human race, except those in the Ark, perish?

The evidence from geology and paleontology shows that the human race disappeared suddenly from Europe and Africa between the periods known as the Mousterian and the Aurignacian, while the evidence from archaeology shows that the whole population of Mesopotamia and the surrounding countries perished in a flood which must have occurred about the same time. The Bible, and all the earliest books or records of the human race, tell us that all men except those in the Ark perished.

6) Did all the animals not in the Ark perish?

It is now generally accepted that all the animals outside the Ark did not perish.

7) What was the date of the Deluge?

The date fixed by paleontologists is the end of the Mousterian period before the *hiatus;* the date fixed by geologists is the end of the Last Glacial Period; the actual date of the Deluge, which is based on the calculations of Baron de Geer and the evidence from Siberia is about 7,000 B.C.

8) Was the great historic flood of Mesopotamia part of the Deluge of Noe?

The answer to that question depends principally on whether we can fix the date of the Mesopotamian flood as early as 7,000 B.C. If that flood occurred sometime about 4,000 B.C. and covered only the plain of Mesopotamia, as writers such as Millar Burrows and Werner Keller say, then it was neither the Deluge of Noe, nor the flood of which both paleontologists and geologists give evidence; but the results of excavations carried out during the last few years in the Middle East show that 4,000 B.C. as the date of the Mesopotamian flood is much too late. Besides, the best authorities on archaeology admit that it is not possible to fix the date of that flood by the evidence of the excavations alone. As the date is certainly much earlier than 4,000 B.C. and as there is no evidence of two great floods in Mesopotamia, it is reasonable to conclude that the historic flood of Mesopotamia was part of the Deluge of Noe.

Part IV

The Antiquity of Man

THE ANTIQUITY OF MAN

Introductory

In the last section on the Deluge, evidence was given to show that the whole human race, with the exception of a small remnant, perished in a flood at the end of the last Glacial Period, which Baron de Geer and others date about 7,000 B.C. That brings us back to the beginning of the Aurignacian Period and to the end of the Upper Paleolithic Age. It only remains for us to calculate the length of the Lower Paleolithic Age, which was the age of the Neanderthal Man and of his predecessor, the recently discovered Fontéchevade Man. This should be a comparatively easy task, for recent excavations, especially those carried out at Jericho (for a description of which we refer our readers back to the last section), furnish us with new information on the life of earliest man and indications of his moderate antiquity, but the intense and aggressive propaganda of recent years in favor of the fantastic estimate of over half-a-million years' antiquity for men has been so successful, that this estimate, although devoid of real scientific foundation, is found in almost all recent books that deal directly or indirectly with the problem of the antiquity of man in the world.

This section will, therefore, be largely taken up with refuting the arguments put forward in favor of the half-a-million years' antiquity theory, and removing prejudices created against the common-sense traditional opinion.

It will be necessary for us to go back again to the period after the Deluge 1) to settle the question of the date of the great Mesopotamian flood which Miller Burrows and some others say was 4,000 B.C., and 2) to use the chronological information gained from the excavation of the ancient post-

Flood cities and from the history of the (post-Flood) Sumerian Empire as a sort of measuring rod by which to calculate the length of the pre-Flood period, for which we have no written records.

For a refutation of the arguments for the great antiquity of the human race based on the theory of human evolution and on the genuineness of the Peking Man, Java Man, etc., we refer the reader back to the section on the Origin of Man.

Some Extravagant Estimates Abandoned

The memory of the discovery of the Piltdown forgery is still fresh in the minds of us all. The Piltdown skull, a few thousand years old at most, and a fresh ape jawbone substituted for the original one, had been doing propaganda work for 40 years in favor of two theories closely allied: the theory of man's ape or lemur descent, and the theory that man's antiquity dates back to at least half a million years ago.

A test by the flourine method, which was afterwards proved to have been badly carried out, reduced the 500,000 years claim to 50,000, but left the man-from-ape claim untouched. A test by the carbon 14 method applied three years later revealed that the ape jawbone was a fresh specimen and that the skull was only a few thousand years old. The carbon test was then applied to the Galley Hill skull, for which Sir Arthur Keith had claimed an antiquity of 200,000 years, and showed that its antiquity was only about the same as that of the Piltdown skull.

More important perhaps still is the fact that the carbon 14 method applied to fossils in North and South America showed that 10,000 years was the outside figure for the existence of man in these countries, and thus put the two Americas out of the picture so far as claiming to be able to produce a "missing link" or a human fossil of respectable antiquity.

The propaganda for man's animal origin and the propaganda for an antiquity of man in the world or from half-a-million to a million years have gone hand in hand since the beginning of the present century. At first, Catholic writers, including those who had adopted the evolutionary theory, refused to accept the half million to a million years estimate, but they have practically all succumbed to the propaganda.

Sir Bertram Windle in *The Church and Science,* published in 1918, quotes Abbé Breuil as dating man's antiquity on earth at about 20,000 years (p. 269). Abbé Breuil has since then abandoned his safe position, and in his articles in *Anthropus* between 1940 and 1945 endeavored to show by reasons, which now no one would accept, that the arrival of man in the world must be put back to 600,000 years ago.

Not only do all evolutionists accept this figure as a minimum, but even theologians who reject completely the theory of human evolution think themselves compelled to accept a very long period.

Fr. Sagues S.J. in his chapter on the origin of man in *Sacrae Theologiae Summa* published in 1952, in which he rejected the theory of human evolution, gives estimates ranging from 35,000 to Abbé Breuil's estimate of 550,000—600,000 years.

However, evidence will be given in this book to show that the date can be put back to under 20,000 years, where geologists such as Prestwich and Wright had it in 1918.

The Factors that Make Up the Half-A-Million Years Estimate

The first and most important factor that goes to make up this half-a-million to a million-year period is the time necessary to allow man to evolve from a brute beast to a rational creature; for most of those who demand such a long period of time are propagandists for the theory of human evolution. Of these Sir Bertram writes in *The Church and Science* as follows:

> It may be remarked that, almost without exception, the more extravagant demands for time will be found to be made by anthropologists and not by geologists. The underlying reason for this is that most anthropologists believe that the body of man was evolved from some lower animal, and moreover believe that the process of evolution occurred by small variations taking place over a vast extent of time. They therefore postulate that vast extent of time.

The second factor that goes to make up "this vast extent of time" is akin to the first. Those who postulate the half-a-million to a million years assume that the Piltdown Man, the Peking Man, the Java Man and the Australopithecinae of Drs. Dart and Broom are human beings in the process of evolution.

Since the Neanderthal Man has been dropped as a candidate for the "missing link," the above are now the only candidates in the field, but the fossils on which the claim for each one of them is based have all been proved to be the fossils of apes or monkeys, as has been shown in the preceding chapters. They cannot therefore justly be used as arguments to prove the great antiquity of man. However, readers will find the fossils of the above "Men" (which are in reality fossils of apes or monkeys) given in standard works on human chronology as evidence for man's great antiquity. For instance, Professor Zeuner (who is a strong advocate of the theory of human evolution) on page 274 of his book entitled *Dating the Past* (1952 edition) makes a claim of 500,000 years antiquity for the Peking Man; on page 278, he claims 400,000 years for the Java Man, and on page 418, relying on the opinion of Le Gros Clerk, he claims more than a million years for the Australopithecinae of South Africa. It has been already stated that Dr. S. Zuckerman, in his chapter in *Evolution as a Process* edited by Sir Julian Huxley, proves conclusively that none of the Australopithecinae has any claim to be regarded as a creature in the process of evolution.

These extravagant estimates for man's antiquity given by Professor Zeuner and others are quoted in many books as if they were established facts. However, it is beginning to be recognized that they are altogether excessive. As they are based chiefly on the assumption that the fossils of the Peking Man, the Java Man and the Australopithecinae are the fossils of man and not of apes or monkeys, they can be rejected entirely.

A third factor in the formation of the half-a-million years claim for man's antiquity is the absurd estimate of from a quarter to a half million years for the length of the Old Stone Age. Sir Bertram Windle writes in *The Church and Science* (p. 268) as follows:

> The Mousterian Man (Neanderthal) was in every sense of the word a man and a capable man too. He had more difficulties to contend with than we have and had fewer advantages, but there is no reason to suppose that his intellectual potentialities were any less than ours today.
>
> What was this highly capable Mousterian Man doing, still more what were the undoubtedly talented Aurignacian and Solutreans doing that they made so little progress in such a vast extent of time?

The archeologists referred to in the last chapter who during the past 25 years have unearthed tools of the Old Stone Age associated with hand-made pottery at the lowest levels of the cities of Mesopotamia and Syria, which indicate that these tools were the work of men who were contemporaries of the Neanderthal Man, claim only a period of about 2,000 years (which is probably much too short) to account for the progress that had been made in Mesopotamia from the time of the earliest dwellers up to the invention of writing, which is the beginning of the historic period.

The paleontologists working in Europe, however, want a period of from 250,000 to 500,000 years to account for the progress made by the early dwellers in Europe in the art of making stone instruments. There is a complete lack of coordination between the estimates of the archaeologists who have carried out their excavations, unburdened by any theory, and the paleontologists who appear to have lost their way in search of "missing links."

Chapter 1

THREE MODERN METHODS FOR MEASURING TIME

The Radioactivity Method

The radioactivity method is used for calculating the length of long periods of millions of years, such as the geological periods, but is of no assistance in determining the antiquity of man. It is based on the discovery that radioactive substances, such as uranium containing radium, radiate their radium content at a regular rate until the radium is exhausted. In doing so they leave behind two products, lead and helium, the age of which can be determined by measuring the length of time it took for the radium content to disintegrate. One gram of radium will diminish by half in 1,590 years; this 1/2 gram will diminish by half in another 1,590 years; this 1/4 gram will become 1/8 gram in another 1,590 years and so on. This radioactivity method applied to the dating of the geological periods gives us 520 million years as the date of the beginning of the Cambrian Period, when life first appeared on our earth. As already mentioned, it cannot be used to determine the antiquity of the fossil remains of the vegetable or animal kingdoms. The modern methods employed in dating these are the Carbon 14 and fluorine methods.

The Carbon 14 or Radiocarbon Method

This method of dating was developed by Dr. W. F. Libby, a member of the United States Atomic Energy Commission, and a number of collaborators. These men discovered that the radioactive carbon (called carbon 14, because each of its atoms is composed of 14 nucleons) is produced high up in the earth's atmosphere by cosmic rays coming from outer space. It descends to lower levels of the atmosphere as a component of carbon dioxide, which is absorbed by plants in their growing process, and from plants it is absorbed by animals and human beings, all of which draw their nourishment from products of the vegetable kingdom. Carbon 14 is constantly being absorbed and radiated at a regular rate by plants and animals in such a way that the amount remains the same as long as the plants and animals are living, but as soon as they die, the absorption of further carbon 14 ceases, but the radiation continues until the whole amount of this substance contained in the plant or animal has disappeared. The rate at which carbon 14 disintegrates is known. It diminishes by half in a period of 5,700 years, and by half again in another period of the same length and so on. After 33,000 years only 1/64 of the original amount is left; but even this can be measured if conditions are ideal. As the amount decreases the rate of radiation decreases also in the same proportion.

That is the theory of the carbon 14 method, but practical results cannot be obtained from all kinds of fossils. Results cannot be obtained from fossil bones alone, if they are of considerable antiquity, because they do not contain a sufficient amount of carbon 14. The method works best when used on wood or animal bones which have been charred by fire, or on charcoal.

There are many difficulties inherent in the method. In the first place, a considerable amount of carbon is required for a single test, and several tests must be made to be reasonably sure of the result. The quantity required for two tests varies from 60 grams for charcoal to four or five lbs. for charred bone. Then the specimens tested must have been preserved under dry conditions, and not in open sites or in damp caves.

Tests were carried out by Libby and others on samples the age of which was already known approximately. The results obtained by the carbon 14 method for three specimens of wood of estimated ages of 1,372 $\pm$ 50,; 2,624 $\pm$ 50; and 3,792 $\pm$ 50 years, were 1,100 $\pm$ 150, 2,600 $\pm$ 150 and 3,700 $\pm$ 400 years respectively. It is possible, of course, that the estimated ages of these three specimens were not accurate; however, Libby and the others were satisfied that for specimens preserved under favorable conditions, the method gave results that were accurate to within a few hundred years for periods up to 4,000 years or so. When, therefore we hear of an age of 10,000 years being assigned to fossils by the carbon 14 method, we are to understand it as the extreme limit; the actual age may be several thousand years less.

The Fluorine Method of Dating Fossils

The fluorine method dates back to 1892 when Carnot, a French mineralogist, discovered that bones of animals and human beings, which contain no fluorine while life exists, begin to absorb it from the soil as soon as they are buried, and that the process of absorbing goes on indefinitely, and can be used to determine the relative ages of fossils found in the same place. If the fossils in a given place are found to contain the same proportion of fluorine they may be presumed to belong to the same time, hence this method can be used to find out whether separate fossils found in the same locality but some distance apart might have belonged to the same individual or not. In the case of the Piltdown skull and ape jawbone, the 1950 test, which was proved to have been faulty, indicated that they might have belonged to the same individual, but the 1953 test proved conclusively that such was impossible. When the test is applied to prove or disprove the theory of evolution, there is the temptation to find results in support of the theory held by the person making the test. It is alleged that the fluorine test had been applied to the disputed human thighbones and the ape-like skullcap of the Java Man which were found some distance apart, and that they contained the same proportion of fluorine; but even if this were true, it would not prove that they belonged to the same individual.

Other Methods of Calculating the Antiquity of Objects

There is the varve-analysis method, which has already been described in the chapter on the Deluge: there is the pollen-analysis method which has been used to check the results arrived at by Baron de Geer; there is the tree ring analysis method which has been used to determine the length of short periods; but none of these gives any help in calculating the length of time man existed before the Deluge. The carbon 14 method in theory should solve the problem, but the practical difficulties in its application are such that it cannot be counted on to give a complete solution. Its application in the cases of the Piltdown and Galley Hill fossils, when estimates for 500,000 and 200,000 years respectively were reduced to a few thousand years, has resulted in a drastic reduction of estimates for the antiquity of man in the world, and though in its present state of development it does not solve the problem completely, it gives substantial help.

Chapter 2

THE FOUR GLACIAL PERIODS

Great Antiquity of Man

One of the principal arguments used by the authors who claim an antiquity of half-a-million years or more for man in the world is his alleged presence in Europe during the warm intervals between the Four Glacial Periods said to have existed. This argument presupposes two things 1) that there were really four Glacial Periods in Europe and 2) that man existed in Europe during the alleged warm intervals between them.

Let us examine both these claims:

Many of the best authorities on the Glacial Periods hold 1) that there was only one Glacial Period (called the Wurm in Europe and the Wisconsin in America), and 2) that there are no certain indications of man's existence in Europe or anywhere else before this period. If therefore there was really only one Glacial Period, the argument for the great antiquity of man which is based on his existence during the three periods which are alleged to have preceded it collapses, and even if it could be proved that there were three such periods, it would still have to be proved that man existed during them.

However, readers will find it stated dogmatically in books by writers who hold the theory of human evolution, 1) that there were four Glacial Periods with three warm Interglacial Periods between them, 2) that the total length of these four periods was nearly a million years, 3) that man existed in Europe during the warm Interglacial Periods, and 4) that his existence in Europe goes back to about 600,000 B.C. Up to recently man's supposed existence in Europe during the Interglacial Periods was the chief argument used to prove his great antiquity. However, in the most recent books by evolutionists such as those by Dr. Albright, the 600,000 years claim has been reduced to 100,000 years, and by non-evolutionists to very much less. Let us therefore examine the arguments put forward for and against the existence of the Four Periods.

The Names of the Four Periods

Different terminology is used to denote these alleged Glacial Periods in different places. In Europe the names generally used are: The Wurm (fourth and last), the Riss (third), the Mindel (second), and the Gunz (first). The three Interglacial Periods are called: Riss-Wurm (third and latest), the Mindel-Riss (second), and the Gunz-Mindel (the first and most remote). In the Scandanavian countries the three disputed Periods are called: the Weichel (third), the Saal (second) and the Elster (first). In America the names used are: the Wisconsin (fourth and last), the Illinoian (third), the Kansan (second) and the Nebraskan (first); while the Interglacial periods are called: the Sangamon (third and last), the Yarmouth (second), and the Aftonean (first).

The Wurm (or Wisconsin) Glacial Period

All geologists are agreed about the existence of the Wurm Glacial Period, and about the extent of territory covered by the ice in both Europe and America. The limits of this Glacial Period are clearly defined by a line of terminal moraines (huge heaps of boulder clay, rocks and debris deposited where the glaciers melted), eskers (ridges of sand or gravel) and marks on the sides of the mountains made by the glaciers as they hurtled down. In Europe, these terminal moraines and other marks stretch across the south of Ireland to the Ural mountains; they run through England from the Bristol Channel to the mouth of the Thames, then over to the mouth of the Rhine, across Holland, Germany and Russia as far as the Ural mountains.

As already stated, Baron de Geer for Sweden and Sauramo for Finland, with teams of collaborators, counted the varves or yearly deposits left behind as the ice melted, and arrived at substantially the same conclusions, which show that this last period ended about 7,000 B.C.

The Three Disputed Periods

There are no such clear indications of the three Periods which are alleged to have preceded this last one: there are no terminal moraines to mark the places where the glaciers are supposed to have melted; the only indications given are great stones or boulders carried from a distance, which however could have been carried by water, and strata of boulder clay supposed to have been deposited during these three periods, which also could have been laid down by water.

The chief authorities quoted in favor of the theory of the Four Glacial Periods are Professor Geikie who, in a book published in 1871, claimed to have found indications of two Glacial Periods in Scotland; Professor Penck of Germany, who wrote various books and articles between 1882 and the end of the century, and claimed to have found traces of four Glacial Periods in different places in Europe; and Professor Brückner, also of Germany, who, in a book published in 1907 supported Professor Penck's theory. Their views were adopted by two American geologists, Chamberlain and Salsbury, who claimed to have found indications of five or six Glacial Periods in North America, but Howorth and Wright give convincing evidence which shows that there was only one Glacial Period in North America.

The arguments advanced in favor of the Four Glacial Periods theory have been examined in great detail by Sir Henry Howorth, who has written five large volumes on the question of the Glacial Periods; the first two of these were published in 1893 under the title *The Glacial Nightmare and the Flood;* the other three were published in 1905 under the title *Ice or Water.*

The following are a few quotations from these books in which he argues against the existence of more than one Glacial Period. In *The Glacial Nightmare* he writes:

> The best barometer we can use to test the character of a climate is the fauna and flora which lived while it prevailed. This is virtually the only barometer available when we inquire into the climate of past geological ages.

> Other evidence can be due to different causes: Boulders can be rolled by the sea. . . .but the biological evidence is unmistakable. Cold-blooded reptiles cannot live in icy water, semi-tropical plants or plants of temperate zones cannot ripen their seeds or sow themselves in arctic conditions. When, therefore, the so-called Glacial Periods are said to be a recurrent phenomenon, we should find evidence in the palaeontological record; if not, the theory collapses.
>
> As a matter of fact such evidence is virtually wanting. We may examine the whole series of geological horizons from the earliest palaeozoic beds down to the so-called glacial beds, and we find, as far as I know, no adequate evidence of discontinuous and alternating climates, no evidence whatever of the existence of periods of intense cold intervening between warm periods, but just the contrary. Not only that, but we shall find that the differentiation of the earth's climate into tropical and arctic zones is comparatively modern, and that in past ages not only were the climates more uniform, but more uniformly distributed over the whole world. (*Op. cit.*, p. 427).

Howorth—having remarked that there are no great terminal moraines to mark the limits of the alleged three Glacial Periods preceding the Wurm Period, but only rocks or boulders which show signs of having been carried by a great flood, and that the drift of boulder clay, referred to by Penck as being due to the melting of the glaciers during the alleged early Glacial Periods, differs from the boulder clay of the terminal moraines in that it is sifted, with the result that the clay is on top and the sand beneath, as in the case of deposits laid down by a flood—goes on to examine in detail the various places in Europe and America where, according to Penck and others, boulder clay belonging to alleged early Glacial periods has been found, and in each case gives reasons to show that the boulder clay or drift in question could not have been deposited by melting glaciers. He then gives the general conclusions from the book as follows:

> The distribution of drift (boulder clay) can only be explained by invoking a great diluvial catastrophe.
>
> In invoking a flood to explain the drift, we are appealing to a cause whose reasonableness and necessity has been established by biological and archaeological arguments.

> 1) The drift beds are the results of one great movement, and not separable into various horizons working different periods. [*Here he quotes the names of six eminent geologists—French, English and American—who support him*].
>
> 2) Continuous blankets of drift over wide areas with a soft rolling surface mark the operations of water moving on a wide scale.
>
> 3) The irregular margin of drift points to the same cause. The spread of the drift, irrespective of surface contour, also indicates the same cause; so does the distribution of the drift. The alternation of rough gravel and fine beds and the existence of gravel terraces are evidence of a flood.
>
> 4) The eskers are also evidence of a flood. The occurrence of boulders without sand and their gradual displacement by sand as we go south are also evidence of a flood.
>
> 5) A great flood would account for the transport of the chalk masses at Cromer and other places, for the arranging of the blocks in diverging lines, for their being massed in some places and absent in others, and for their being transported uphill and over heights.
>
> Many eminent geologists, such as Andrews, Hildyard and Murchison are of the opinion that there was a great flood.

The same signs of a great flood are found in North America and Canada. Professor Dana of the United States writes:

> The fact that a flood vast beyond conception was the final event in the history of the glaciers is manifest in the peculiar stratification of flood-made deposits, and in the spread of the stratified drift down southward along the Mississippi valley to the Gulf, at first made known by Hildyard. Only under the rapid contribution of immense amounts of sand and gravel and of water from so unlimited a source could such deposits have accumulated.

Astronomical Methods of Dating

Attempts have been made to confirm the Penck and Brückner theory of the Four Glacial Periods by appeal to other theories which are supposed to explain the origin of the Glacial Periods and to calculate their duration. According to one of these theories, the intensity of the sun's radiation has varied in cycles of low and high radiation, the dates of which can be calculated. The claim has been made by adherents of the theory such as Abbé Breuil, that each of the alleged Four Glacial Periods occurred during times of low solar radiation, and that the three warm inter-glacial periods occurred during times of high radiation.

In the first place, this theory has never been proved, and even if it had been proved, it could not account for the Glacial Periods, for heat as well as cold is required to form a Glacial Period. Great heat is required to produce the abnormal evaporation of water from the oceans that lowered their level by several hundred feet, and great cold is required to turn this vapor into snow and ice. If cold alone could produce an icecap, there should have been an icecap several thousand feet in depth over Siberia and Western Alaska, but there was no icecap at all. No geologist of any standing can be quoted in favor of this theory.

Another theory which has been advanced to explain the origin of the alleged Four Glacial Periods is that there have been at different times changes in the obliquity of the earth's axis so that the North Pole was deflected further away from the sun, thus increasing the area of the Arctic regions. This theory is absurd, as will be seen from the following considerations.

The earth's equator is surrounded by an immense bulge which is 25,000 miles in length, 6,000 miles in depth and 13-1/4 miles (about 70,000 feet) in height. This bulge around the earth has existed from the earliest geological period; revolving at the rate of more than a thousand miles an hour, it keeps the motion of the earth steady. No influence known to geologists would be capable of deflecting the earth's axis more than a couple of degrees, which would not affect the temperature of the Northern Region to any appreciable extent.

The same may be said about the theory which attributes the origin of the Glacial Periods to variations in the eccentricity of the earth's orbit. The earth revolves around the sun, not in a circle but in an ellipse, its greatest distance from the sun (which is in summer) being 93,750,000 miles, and its smallest distance (which is in winter) being 90,257,000 miles. Now Herschill calculated that a variation of the eccentricity as great as a fourth of the major axis would not raise the mean temperature more than three percent, and Dr. Croll is of the same opinion.

In giving his general conclusion about the various astronomical causes appealed to in order to explain the origin of the Glacial Period or Periods, Howorth quotes Dr. Croll as saying: "Under no circumstances known to us could astronomical causes produce a Glacial Period."

Abbé Breuil on the Antiquity of Man in the World

Abbé Breuil's opinion of the Antiquity of Man in the world has been frequently quoted in recent books dealing with this subject, the implication being that he is a great authority on the question. As a young man back in 1920, his opinion was that 20,000 years were quite sufficient to account for man's activities in the world, as then known. Since then he has changed his opinion and is now a supporter of the theory held by most evolutionists, that man's existence in the world goes back about 600,000 years. Though frequently quoted on this subject, Abbé Breuil himself does not pose as an authority on it; in fact he devotes only a few pages to it in his writings on the fossil remains and the artifacts of the men of the Old Stone Age. He wrote a series of articles on the men of the Old Stone Age in *ANTHROPOS* between 1945 and 1950. These were published in book form in 1951 under the title: *Les Hommes de La Pierre Ancienne.* In this book of 334 pages, he devotes only about five pages to the question of the antiquity of man. He based his opinion about the great antiquity of man on his supposed existence during the three disputed Interglacial Periods and does not seem to be aware that the very existence of these periods is at best extremely doubtful. He quotes the theory of the variation of the intensity of the sun's radiation in support of the theory of the Four Periods. In the book, he accepts the Piltdown Man as a genuine case of human evolution; he accepts also the Peking Man against Marcellin Boule, one of the greatest authorities of his time on human fossils; he accepts also the Australopithecinae of South Africa as beings in the process of evolution toward man, although they have been rejected by men like Professor Zuckerman. Besides, the 600,000-year estimate for the existence of the men of the Old Stone Age is regarded as absurd even by writers like Dr. Albright, who hold the theory of human evolution.

The use of the words: Riss-Wurm, Mindel-Riss and Gunz-Mindel after the names of fossils to denote an antiquity of about 100,000, 350,000 and 600,000 years respectively may therefore be taken as an indication that the writer who uses them is ignorant of the fact that the very existence of these periods is disputed and that the best authorities on the Glacial Periods give convincing reasons to show that there was only one Glacial Period; and of the fact that there is no real indication that man existed in any part of the world before the beginning of the last (Wurm) Glacial Period.

The claim that man existed in Europe during the alleged warm intervals between these four Glacial Periods can very easily be disproved by another argument. The boundaries of the last Glacial Period running across Europe are well-known, and about them there is neither doubt nor controversy. No fossil remains of man or pre-*hiatus* artifacts have ever been found inside the boundary line anywhere in the Scandanavian peninsula or in the part of Russia that was covered with ice. If, as is alleged, man had existed in Europe during the warm intervals half-a-million years ago, surely some fossil remains or some artifacts would have been found inside the boundary line of the last Glacial Period, but no claim for finding such has ever been made.

There is therefore no real foundation for the estimates of from half-a-million to a million years antiquity for man in Europe made by Abbé Breuil and others who hold the theory of the evolution of man and endeavor to make it appear plausible by providing the time which they admit is necessary to account for his supposed evolution.

Chapter 3

THE ORIGINAL HOME OF THE HUMAN RACE AND THE EARLIEST FIXED DATE

The Original Home of the Human Race

One of the first questions to be settled in order to estimate the antiquity of the human race is the location of the place where man first appeared. With the two Americas, Australia, Indonesia, China and India out of the picture, the choice is narrowed down to Mesopotamia, Iran, Egypt and Europe. Of these Europe may first be counted out, for no one, even among those who claim an antiquity of half-a-million years for the existence of man in Europe, would seriously say that the cradle of the human race is to be found there. No remains of prehistoric cities, or even of towns of considerable size have ever been found in Europe, except in Crete, which derived its civilization from Egypt.

For the site of the cradle of the human race the choice lies between Egypt and Mesopotamia. Of these two, modern archaeologists are unanimous in the choice of Mesopotamia. In forming their opinion on the site of the most ancient civilization in the world, archaeologists have been influenced solely by the evidence furnished by excavations; they appear to be totally unaware of the fact that they were confirming the account given by Moses in Chapter 2 of *Genesis,* which says that the Garden of Eden was watered by the Phison, the Gehon, the Tigris and the Euphrates. The Tigris and the Euphrates still retain their ancient names and are sufficient indication that, according to the biblical account, the Garden of Eden was situated somewhere in Mesopotamia. At the present day, there are no rivers in Mesopotamia called the Phison and the Gehon, but they have been identified by biblical commentators with the Phase and the Oukon (now called the Kerka), two rivers which flow through Mesopotamia.

There is no valid reason for rejecting the Mosaic account of the location of the Garden of Eden. Even if it were true, as evolutionists allege, that man's antiquity in the world goes back half-a-million years or more, and that, therefore, it would have been impossible to preserve the tradition about the Garden of Even from the time of Adam to Moses, yet Moses could have got his information by direct revelation from God, and probably did. Besides, we shall see that there is no solid scientific foundation for the claim of evolutionists that man's antiquity goes back half-a-million years. According to the latest evidence from all sources, 20,000 years are quite sufficient to account for all that happened since the time of Adam and Eve.

The Bible tells us that Adam and Eve were driven out of the Garden of Eden, which was situated in the plain of Mesopotamia, and which may have included the whole of that comparatively small plain. There is an ancient tradition that they went to Palestine after they had fallen, and that they were buried at Calvary. This tradition is supported by private revelation. There is nothing improbable in it, for archaeologists, in recent excavations in Palestine, have found the stone instruments of the Lower (earliest) Paleolithic Age all over Palestine, as well as the fossil remains of the Neanderthal Man, in addition to those of a mixed race that existed in Palestine before the Deluge. Besides, the excavations carried out at Jericho by Garstang have revealed the fact that this city rivals in antiquity the oldest pre-Flood cities of Mesopotamia, and that the early inhabitants lived in isolation from the people in Mesopotamia, up to the Flood. The results obtained from the most recent excavations carried out there under the direction of Dr. Kenyon confirm this view. (See Part I on the Deluge, Chapter 7).

The Earliest Fixed Date

The Findings of Archaeologists on the Chronology of Ancient Egypt and Mesopotamia.

Both pre-Flood and post-Flood civilizations of Mesopotamia are older than those of Egypt.

There is general agreement among archaeologists that while accurate dating can be pushed back further in Egypt than in Mesopotamia, there is no doubt about the fact that the pre-Flood civilization of Mesopotamia is older than that of Egypt; they are agreed also that the post-Flood civilization of Egypt of the Pharaohs was borrowed from Mesopotamia.

In estimating the antiquity of man in the world from the historic evidence available, archeologists divide the evidence into strictly historic evidence, by which dates can be fixed, and the prehistoric evidence afforded by the excavations of ancient sites on which estimates or guesses can be based. The first thing to be be done is to get the earliest certain fixed date. It is not an easy task to fix this date, for authorities are not agreed upon it. They are, however, agreed that accurate dating for Egypt goes back further than for Mesopotamia, although Mesopotamia has the older civilization.

The Earliest Fixed Date for Egypt

Egyptian chronology before 800 B.C. is based chiefly on the lists of the Pharaos given by Manetho, an Egyptian priest, who lived in the third century B.C. during the reign of Ptolemy Philadelphus and wrote a history of Egypt in Greek. This history has been lost, but the lists were copied by Josephus and are preserved in three other works of the early Christian era. The information contained in these lists has been checked by the evidence afforded by the excavations of the tombs of the Pharaohs and of ancient sites. Dr. Petrie, one of the best authorities on the chronology of Egypt, made a further check on the date arrived at from the lists of Pharaohs given by Manetho. In his book entitled *Origin and Antiquity of Man,* the author, G. F. Wright, says:

> Astronomical data also furnish us with important evidence of Egyptian antiquity.
>
> The Egyptians did not observe leap-year, hence, in every 1,460 years there occurred a complete shift of the nominal months. But the actual progress of the seasons always conformed to the progress of the sun in the eliptic. The inundation of the Nile began with the visible rising of the dog star (Sirius,

> or Sothis in Egyptian). The revolution of the nominal year occurred once in 1,460 natural years, and was called a Sothic year. One of these periods began in A.D. 139. This enables us to reckon back to the recorded beginning of a Sothic year in the reign of Merenptah, and through other Sothic years to earlier dynasties. From these astronomical data Petrie fixed the commencement of the First Dynasty at 4,777 B.C. (p. 51).

Contemporary authorities, however, basing their calculations on the lists of Manetho and the evidence of the monuments, fixed the date of the First Dynasty at 4,400 B.C. Besides, a papyrus discovered in 1847 by a Frenchman named Prisse contained evidence that it dated back to the last Pharaoh of the Third Dynasty, and, according to experts, the date was 4,450 B.C.

However, during the present century, these dates have been revised, and what is called "the short chronology" has been adopted by some authorities, but rejected by others. According to this system of dating, the beginning of the First Dynasty is placed at 3,400 B.C. This appears to be too late for the following reasons:

(*a*) The art of writing was known in Egypt at the time of the First Dynasty. It appeared suddenly in a developed form, and was evidently borrowed from Mesopotamia, where a long process of development can be traced during the reigns of the post-Flood Sumerian kings.

(*b*) In the chapter on the Deluge we have seen that there was undoubted evidence of the *hiatus* there when a fertile region among the upper reaches of the Nile was turned into the Sahara desert and the total population disappeared. What was the length of time that elapsed between the *hiatus* and the beginning of the First Dynasty? It must have been a long time, for the new race must have come from Mesopotamia or Iran. Time must be allowed both for the multiplication of the descendants of Noe and the development of the art of writing. Modern authorities such as Professor Albright will allow only about 600 years, but this is evidently altogether too short.

The date 4,440 for the First Dynasty appears, therefore, to be the more probable.

Earliest Fixed Date for Mesopotamia

After the great historic flood of Mesopotamia, which was almost certainly the Flood of Noe, there existed a Sumerian empire with a long list of kings which attained to a very high degree of civilization. During the time this empire existed, the art of writing was developed, a code of laws much more perfect than the code of Hammurabi was gradually elaborated, and the army was highly organized and had its war chariots. When the power of this empire declined, a conqueror from the North named Sargon I invaded it and became its first Babylonian king. The son of Sargon I, named Naram-Sin, built a temple at Ur of the Chaldees and placed clay tablets in the foundations, on which there were long inscriptions giving his name and particulars of his reign. This temple fell into ruins and was rebuilt by Nabonidus, the last Babylonian king. When preparing the foundations, Nabonidus found these inscriptions, replaced them and added an inscription of his own which stated that he was the first Babylonian king to gaze on this inscription of Naram-Sin after the lapse of 3,200 years. The reign of Nabonidus began in 550 B.C. This would leave the beginning of the reign of Naram-Sin in 3,750, and of Sargon I in 3,800.

When Sir Leonard Woolley excavated this temple built by Narbonidus at Ur of the Chaldees, he actually found these tablets. (See *Ur of the Chaldees* by Sir Leonard Woolley, 1950 ed., p. 138).

In spite of this evidence, Professor Wincler brought down the date of Sargon I to 3,000 B.C. and Professor Scheil of Paris, who was the first to publish the code of Hammurabi, brought it down to 2,460 B.C.

G. F. Wright, who gives their estimates, believes that neither Wincler nor Scheil was justified in changing Petrie's dates. (See *Origin and Antiquity of Man,* p. 499).

However, Professor Albright of the United States adopts the

shorter chronology, but admits that it is not accepted by all authorities. The evidence from the excavations carried out in recent years in the Middle East supports the older and better system of chronology. There is, therefore, a very wide gap in the figures given by "experts" for the earliest so-called fixed dates, and before these "fixed dates" we have only estimates or guesses, not real dates.

As there was a Sumerian empire in existence for several thousand years before the time of Sargon I or the First Dynasty of Egypt, it is absurd to speak of the date 4,000 B.C. as the date fixed by "the experts" for the historic flood of Mesopotamia. The date of that flood cannot be fixed either from the evidence from Mesopotamia or Egypt. The only way of fixing it is by the date of a flood that occurred about the same time in other places. As we have seen, there is evidence from paleontologists of a *hiatus* at the end of the Mousterian Period, and there is evidence from both geologists and authorities on the Ice Age of a flood at the end of the Ice Age, the date of which Baron de Geer fixes at about 7,000 B.C., as was shown in the section on the Deluge.

The nearest approach, therefore, to the earliest fixed date is the date of the great Flood at the end of the Ice Age, which may be safely regarded as the Deluge of Noe. This date is about 7,000 B.C., or probably a little before it.

Chapter 4

METHOD OF CALCULATING STRATIFIED SETTLEMENTS

Though accurate dating was not possible before the invention of the art of writing, the whole history of man right up to the earliest times can be traced by digging through the various strata of the ancient towns built in Mesopotamia along the Tigris and Euphrates, and in Palestine, Egypt and the Plateau of Iran.

How the Strata of the Ancient Sites Were Formed

In his book *Digging Up the Past,* Sir Leonard Woolley describes in detail how these strata have been formed. The following is a brief summary: In early prehistoric times, some of the inhabitants of Mesopotamia and the adjoining countries selected suitable sites near the Tigris, Euphrates and other rivers and built settlements on them, which they usually surrounded with ramparts. The earliest buildings were constructed of mud and wattle. The first occupation may have lasted a hundred or perhaps several hundred years, during which the houses may have been rebuilt several times. Then some disaster happened, and the settlement was destroyed and the place remained unoccupied for an indefinite period, during which the walls of the old houses crumbled away. After a few years or perhaps a few hundred years, new settlers came and built another town over the first one, and again as the result of war or some other calamity the second town was destroyed and abandoned. As the site was originally well-chosen, and as it was now raised above the level of the plain by the debris of two occupations, it was occupied a third time—and a third time destroyed and left unoccupied for an indefinite period. Where the site was eminently suitable, such as those near

Nineveh, Babylon, Susa, Jericho etc., the process of building and rebuilding towns went on, not for centuries but for milleniums. Then came the great flood in Mesopotamia (which almost certainly was the Deluge), and all the towns in Mesopotamia, great and small, and even the towns on the high plateau of Iran and of the whole country at least as far as Egypt, were destroyed. Then there must have been a long interval before the pre-Flood sites were reoccupied. All the sites, however, were not reoccupied. It was the most suitable sites that were chosen—those that had been built upon most often before the flood and which were raised highest above the plain by the accumulation of debris.

Many pre-Flood sites, such as those at 'Al Ubaid, 'Al Halaf and Arpachiyah (already described in the preceding section), were never built upon again, even to the present day. Some new sites not built on before the Flood were chosen for post-Flood settlements, such as Jemdet Nasr in the north of Mesopotamia. At the principal sites such as Nineveh, Babylon, Susa and Ur, the accumulation of debris raised the mounds to a height of from 60 to about 100 feet above the level of the plain. The mound at Tepe Gawra, near Nineveh, rose to a height of 92 feet and contained 26 occupational levels. Most of those levels had been built on several times before the town was destroyed and abandoned. As already stated, between the foundation of each of these settlements, there was an interval which might be a few years or a few hundred years.

In each stratum, which represents a settlement lasting for an unknown period during which houses were often rebuilt several times, the excavators found the tools and household utensils of thc period, which, as already described, consisted of stone instruments, pottery and finally hammered copper utensils just before the Flood; and after the Flood, of cast copper and other metal utensils, pottery made on the potter's wheel, and stone instruments which increased in perfection with time.

The strata belonging to the golden ages of Sumeria, Babylon and Assyria contained valuable objects made of gold, silver and precious stones, besides objects of art such as statues, which the museums of the world were eager to purchase and for which they were willing to pay high prices. The strata above the Flood level were therefore thoroughly searched and investigated, but the strata below the Flood level, though they held valuable information about the earliest history of mankind, contained very little of intrinsic value, and therefore very little to tempt the excavators to search them. Besides, they were buried beneath hundreds of thousands of tons of debris, to remove which would be an impossible task for any ordinary explorer. However, shafts have been dug through the pre-Flood strata right down to virgin soil at Tepe Gawra near Nineveh, at Kish near Babylon and at other places, and information about the pre-Flood cities has been obtained.

Sites of settlements such as 'Al Ubaid, Halaf and Arpachiyah, which have been recognized as pre-Flood by comparing the tools and utensils found in them with those found in the pre-Flood levels of Tepe Gawra, Kish and Susa, and which have never been reoccupied after the Flood, have been excavated and investigated.

Now in sites such as Tepe Gawra, Kish and Susa, which have been occupied both before the Flood and after it, there is no controversy about the order of the settlements; they are there one over the other, the settlement at the lowest level being necessarily the oldest. At both Kish and Tepe Gawra, the lowest levels were found to have been mere camping grounds with some primitive stone instruments and primitive unpainted pottery.

There can therefore be no doubt about the order of the settlements at Tepe Gawra, Kish, Ur, etc., which the excavations have revealed, but the following further important question remains to be settled: Have we any means of calculating the length of time that the various prehistoric settlements represented by the different strata lasted? We shall ask Sir Leonard Woolley, one of the best authorities on the excavations in Mesopotamia, to give the answer. In his book *Digging Up the Past* (Pelican ed.), when discussing the probable date of the post-Flood settlement of Jemdet Nasr, 18 miles from Kish, he warned the reader that no definite dates can be given for prehistoric settlements.

> I have talked of the date of Jemdet Nasr; it was a loose expression and perhaps I ought to withdraw it, certainly I ought not to let it pass without a warning. The archaeologist can re-create a great deal of human history; he can bear witness to its vicissitudes, but, in the absence of written records, he cannot fix dates.
>
> The stratification of the soil on an ancient site does not go by mathematical progression; if each of the first three feet represents 100 years, it does not follow that ten feet equal a thousand; they may stand for 400 or 3,000 years. (pp. 78, 79).

So therefore, if in any book we find the statement that experts are agreed in fixing the date of the great flood in Mesopotamia at 4,000 B.C., we may be quite sure that there is not and cannot be any such agreement. At Tepe Gawra there were not less than 26 strata, or occupational levels, only five of which come within the historic period, and these five bring us to about 3,000 B.C.; what are we to say about the remaining 21 occupational levels?

About these we are not altogether in the dark, for the excavations have revealed that before the foundation of the Babylonian empire there was a great Sumerian empire, the civilization of which bears somewhat the same relation to that of Babylon as the civilization of Crete and Mycenae bears to that of Greece, and that the Sumerian scribes have left us a written history of the empire.

The Sumerian Empire

About the Sumerian empire practically nothing was known until the beginning of the present century, and even still Scripture commentators have very inadequate ideas both of the length of time this empire lasted and the height of civilization that was attained in it. It was during the lifetime of this empire that the art of writing was discovered. The Sumerian historians of the Larsa Dynasty (which was the last) have left us a detailed history of lower Mesopotamia which goes back to the Great Flood, the history of which they relate, and from the Great Flood back to the time of the creation of the first man and woman.

For the period before the Flood there are three different lists of kings, two of which are practically identical. The first is the list of Berosus, a Babylonian priest of the time of Alexander the Great, who wrote a history of Babylonia in Greek in 250 B.C. Only a few fragments of this history are extant, and these have been preserved by Eusebius and some others of the Fathers. For the period before the Deluge, Berosus gives a list of 10 kings who reigned for a total of 120 sars, which is equal to 432,000 years, if 3,600 years are allowed for one sar—which is by no means certain.

The other two lists which are of Sumerian origin were published by Professor Langdon in 1924. One of these corresponds closely to the list of Berosus. It contains the names of 10 kings who reigned for a total of 126 sars and four ner, which by the same calculation as that applied to the list of Berosus equals 456,000 years. The other list contains the names of only eight kings who reigned for 66 sar and four ner, or 241,200 years, by the same calculation.

Some authorities believe that a sar is a period of 10 years. A year of 12 lunar months has 360 days, therefore 10 lunar years would equal 3,600 days. Calculating by that method, the figures given in the lists of Berosus and of the first list of Langdon would equal about 1,266 years, which is not far from the number of years (1,307) given in the Samaritan version of the Bible.

The Period After the Flood

For the period between the Flood and the foundation of the Babylonian empire, the Larsa list gives 19 Sumerian dynasties with 163 kings or rulers. Five of these dynasties with 41 kings or rulers belong to the period after the accession of Sargon I, the founder of the Babylonian empire. That still leaves 14 Sumerian Dynasties with 120 kings or rulers between the time of Sargon I and the Flood.

The first dynasty after the Flood was that of Kish, near the site of Babylon. For this dynasty the Larsa list gives 23 kings, who reigned for a total of 24,000 years, three months and 3-1/2 days. One of these kings is said to have ruled 1,500 years and two others 1,200 years each. These figures are evidently greatly exaggerated, but Sir Leonard Woolley believes that at least they convey the idea that there was a long period of peace after the Flood, and that at the time the Larsa list of Kings was written down (about 2,000 B.C.) the great Mesopotamian flood was regarded as an event that happened in the remote past.

The second Sumerian dynasty in order of time was that of Uruk (Arach of *Genesis* 10:10). For this dynasty the Larsa list contains 12 kings who reigned a total of 2,310 years. It has not been possible so far at least to check either the names of these kings or the length of their reigns.

The Historic Period: The First Dynasty of Ur

For Mesopotamia the historic period may be reckoned either from the beginning of the reign of Sargon I, which, according to the short chronology, was in 2,360 B.C. or from the beginning of the First Dynasty of Ur which, if fixed by the same system of chronology would be in 3,100 B.C.

The First Dynasty of Ur was the third Sumerian Dynasty.

If we reckon by the older system of chronology according to which the reign of Sargon I began in 3,800 B.C., we would have to add 1,460 years to this 3,100, which would give 4,560 B.C. as the date of the beginning of the First Dynasty of Ur.

Between this date, whether we make it 3,100 B.C. or 4,540 B.C. and the great Mesopotamian Flood, there were two Sumerian dynasties with 34 kings who, according to the Larsa figures, reigned for 27,820 years. No one accepts these figures as meaning anything more than that a long time elapsed between the flood and the beginning of the historic period. That the period was a very long one is proved by the evidence from the excavations at Ur itself. These excavations show that at the time of the First Dynasty of Ur (3,100 B.C. according to the shorter system of chronology, but 4,540 B.C. according to the old system) the art of writing was well-developed, that the science of metallurgy was far advanced, that armies were well-trained and well-equipped with metal weapons, that chariots were used in warfare, but perhaps most important of all, that there existed at that early time a highly developed social system with good humane laws, well-administered through law courts.

It was from these Sumerian laws that Hammurabi of Babylon borrowed his famous code. Sargon I, the founder of the Babylonian Empire, was a man of lowly origin, being according to tradition a cupbearer in the palace of the local king of Agade. He afterward became a great conqueror like Tamerlane, and subdued the whole country as far as the Mediterranean on the west and Assyria in the north, before he turned his arms against the Sumerians and conquered them. Subsequent kings adopted the Sumerian laws and customs, codified them and developed them on their own lines.

It was from the Sumerians that the Egyptians borrowed their civilization and their system of writing. The Egyptian civilization penetrated into Crete and Mycenae, and when these were conquered by the ancestors of the Greeks, the conquerors adopted the Mycenaean civilization and transformed it into the Grecian, in which modern civilization is chiefly based. Thus the whole world is indebted to the Sumerians, who developed the teaching which they inherited from Noe into a humane system of laws.

The following conclusions may be drawn from a comparison of the results obtained from the excavations of: (*a*) the post-Flood strata of ancient sites, and (*b*) the pre-Flood strata:

1) The post-Flood strata show the development of the small remnant of the population left after the Flood into several nations that built great cities in Egypt and Mesopotamia and then spread into India, China and America.

2) The strata of the same period reveal a gradual development of the arts of peace and war, first in Mesopotamia and Egypt, and then in all parts of the world. Later on, these arts of peace and war developed further and reached a high degree of perfection before the beginning of the Christian era. This whole period from the Flood to the time of Christ lasted only 7,000 years.

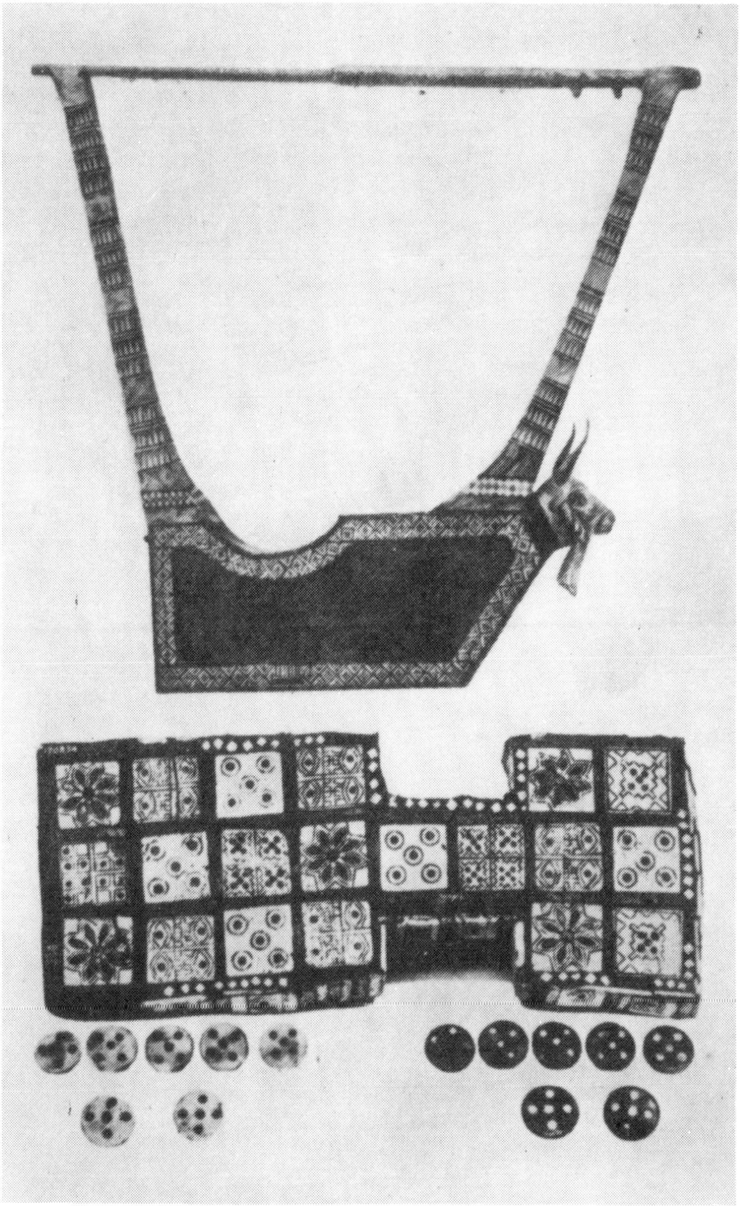

Top—A decorated lyre from the royal tombs.
Bottom—An inlaid gaming board with its "men."
These are specimens of Sumerian art of about 3,000 years after the Deluge.

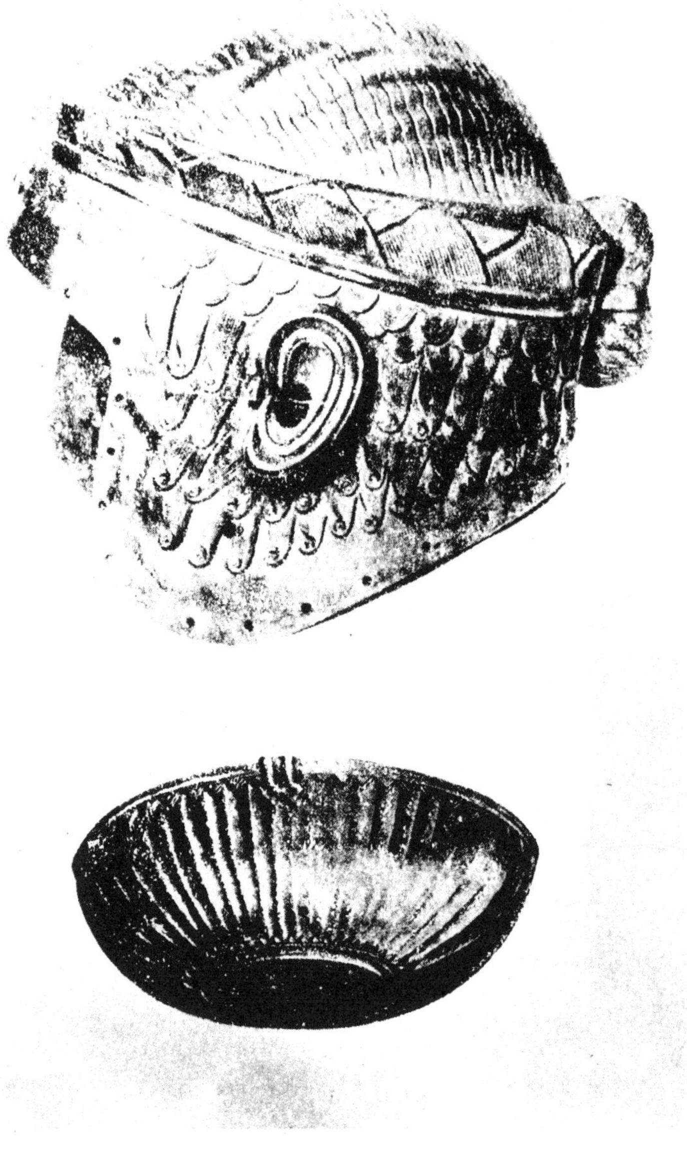

Top—The Gold Helmet of Mes-Kalam-Dug.
Bottom—A Gold Bowl from Queen Shub-Ad's tomb.
These are specimens of Sumerian art of about 3,000 years after the Deluge.

3) The pre-Flood strata of the ancient sites of Mesopotamia, Iran, Palestine and Egypt reveal the fact that the human race lived a normal life in these countries; that they tilled the ground and kept domestic animals from the earliest times, while Asia beyond the Himalayas was closed, and Europe and Africa were used merely as hunting grounds for adventurers and outlaws.

The pre-Flood population of the relatively small area under cultivation and of the hunters in Europe and Africa would represent only a small fraction of the population that was in the world at the time of Christ, and although they left undoubted proofs of natural ability and natural skill, as great, if not greater, than that of the peoples of the post-Flood period, they had only succeeded in making flint instruments, handmade pottery and a little hammered copper.

If the teeming populations and the high degree of civilization of the great empires of Sumeria, Babylonia, Egypt, Greece and Rome took only 7,000 years for their development, a very much less period should suffice for the development of the comparatively small population of the pre-Flood period, and for the development of the primitive instruments and culture. In the light of this comparison the biblical figures appear reasonable, while the estimates of the evolutionists are just a clumsy attempt to bolster up the fantastic theory that man with his glorious faculties and free will has been evolved from a brute beast.

4) (*a*) The evidence given above from the history of Sumeria is sufficient to prove that the date 4,000 B.C. given by Millar Burrows and the other writers as the date of the Flood is altogether too late.

(*b*) The Sumerian account of man before the Flood corresponds closely with the biblical account. If we interpret the word "sar" as a period of 10 years of 12 lunar months (each making 3,600 days instead of 3,600 years), the figures given in this history do not differ substantially from those in the Samaritan version of the Bible.

Chapter 5

THE PERIOD BETWEEN ADAM AND EVE AND THE DELUGE

Sufficient evidence has been given to show that the Deluge of the Bible and the great flood in Mesopotamia occurred at the same time and that the latter flood was part of the Deluge. It has been pointed out that the date 4,000 B.C. given by Millar Burrows and others for the Mesopotamian flood is much too low, and that the real date is about 7,000 B.C.

There are several sources of information from which estimates of the length of the period between the Deluge and the creation of Adam may be formed. The chief of these are: 1) the Biblical list of the Patriarchs with their respective ages; 2) the Sumerian list of the antediluvian dynasties; 3) the figures based on the investigations of ancient sites by the archaeologists; 4) the figures based on the researches of the paleontologists; and 5) the figures based on the tests made by the carbon 14 method. (The figures based on the investigations of the Glacial Periods by Baron de Geer and others help to fix the date of the Deluge, but tell us nothing about the period before it.).

The Evidence from the Bible

In assessing the value of the evidence from the Bible there are two extremes to be avoided: the first is to look to the Bible for complete, ready-made information on the antiquity of man in the world, and the second is to reject the information given in the Bible on this subject as being of no value. The Church has never made a pronouncement on the question of the antiquity of man in the world, or ever given anyone permission to reject the information contained in the Bible about it.

It was the Protestant Bishop Ussher who, in 1636, gave the figure 4,004 years for the whole period from the creation of the world to the birth of Christ. This figure is based on the Massoretic version of the Bible. Most of the Fathers adopted the figures from the Septuagint version, which would give 3,389 years for the period between Adam and the call of Abraham. If we add 2,000 years for the period between Abraham and Christ to this, we get 5,389 for the period between Adam and the birth of Christ. If we make allowance for gaps on the biblical list of the Patriarchs we will find that an estimate based on the biblical figures is not very far removed from the estimates given by modern archaeologists based on the short chronology. There is however an abyss that cannot be bridged between even the most generous estimate based on the Bible and the estimates, or rather the guesses of present-day paleontologists, who are practically all evolutionists.

The Biblical Figures

The three different versions of the Bible, the Hebrew, the Samaritan and the Septuagint, give three accounts of the ages of the Patriarchs and of the dates of the birth of their sons, which differ in important details, and give substantially different results. The Hebrew and the Septuagint agree completely about the ages of all the Patriarchs before the Flood, except Lamech, but differ about the times when their sons were born. The Samaritan version agrees with the other two about the ages of seven of the antediluvian Patriarchs but differs about the ages of Jared, Mathusalem and Lamech, for whom it gives 847, 720 and 653 years, instead of 962, 969 and 777 years.

The following are the three different totals for the periods before the Deluge and after the Deluge until Abraham:

	Hebrew	Samaritan	Septuagint
From Adam to Noe:	1,656 years	1,307 years	2,242 years
From Noe to the call of Abraham:	367 years	1,017 years	1,147 years
Total	2,035 years	2,324 years	3,389 years

There is evidence from both the Old and the New Testaments, though not in *Genesis* itself, that there are gaps in the genealogical lists of the Patriarchs between Noe and Abraham. Though there is no similar evidence for gaps in the list of 10 Patriarchs from Adam to Noe, modern writers think that there probably are gaps, and that the object of the genealogies is to give the line of descent, rather than a complete list of the Patriarchs from Adam to Noe.

There is a difference of opinion among modern scholars about the interpretation of the long ages of the Patriarchs, especially of those from Adam to Noe. Some scholars think that, as a span of nearly a thousand years seems to be an impossible age for a human being, the names given should be interpreted as the names of dynasties or tribes rather than the names of individuals. That is merely an opinion, for which no evidence is available. The only evidence that modern science affords on that question is that the earliest fossil bones of man discovered show that early man was of stronger build, that the vital parts in the chest and head were better protected, that the various diseases which shorten human life had not yet developed and that, all told, early man, living a normal life, had a better chance of a long life than modern man. Besides, if it was the will of God to keep a certain number of chosen men in the world for nearly a thousand years, He certainly had the power to do so. It is a less wonder to find men living a thousand years by a special providence of God, than to find people, like some of the stigmatists, living up to 20 and 30 years without earthly food, being nourished by the Blessed Sacrament alone. If it be objected that the average age of the Neanderthal men in Europe was less than that of modern man, it can be pointed out that all these were nomadic hunters, that they lived in altogether abnormal circumstances without the staple food provided by agriculture, and that the older men may have returned to warm climates according as they grew too old for the strenuous life of a hunter.

General Conclusions About the Antiquity of Man From the Information Contained in the Bible

The Catholic Church has never taught that the Bible furnishes us with complete information about the duration of man's existence in the world. However, up to modern times it has been the accepted belief among both the rulers of the Church and the faithful that the period of time between Adam and Christ was a comparatively short one, and that is still the general opinion.

The Evidence From Sumerian Lists Of Pre-Flood Dynasties

The figures based on the three different lists of pre-Flood dynasties have already been given. As it is impossible to settle the length of a sar, no definite conclusion can be based on these figures. The fact that the figure 10, used in two of the lists to indicate the number of dynasties, corresponds with the number of the pre-Flood Patriarchs given in the Bible, offers some support to the biblical account so far as the number of Patriarchs is concerned.

The Sumerian History and the Biblical Account

If we accept 3,600 days as the length of a sar when calculating the length of the pre-Flood and post-Flood periods, the Sumerian account is substantially the same as the biblical. The same towns are mentioned in both accounts, the only difference being that, in the Sumerian account, the Sumerian names of the towns are used, while in the biblical, the Babylonian names are substituted for some of them.

There is no reason to suppose that the biblical account was borrowed from the Sumerian. As in the case of the two accounts of the Flood, the biblical and the Sumerian, it is fair to presume that both are founded on the same facts.

Neither can the question of the number of years which elapsed between the First Dynasty of Ur (3,100 B.C. or 4,500 B.C.) and the Flood be settled. In giving a guess (or estimate) it is to be borne in mind that the descendants of Noe did not go down immediately after the Flood into the plains of Mesopotamia; they probably remained for hundreds of years in the higher regions where the Ark had settled.

Taking everything into account, a period of 2,500 years would not appear to be excessive to account for the development of the human race in Mesopotamia and Iran between the great Flood and the First Dynasty of Ur; if we accept 4,500 B.C. as the date of the beginning of the First Dynasty of Ur, that would give us 7,000 B.C. as the date of the Deluge.

The Period Before the Hiatus in Egypt

In the very same region in which the wonderful civilization of Egypt of the Pharaohs was developed, the instruments of the Old Stone Age have been found associated with pottery which, from primitive beginnings, reached a high standard of perfection just before the *hiatus.* The stone instruments, which also are in various stages of development, correspond with the stone instruments of the Old Stone Age found in Europe, with the difference, however, that the development of the pottery in Egypt before the *hiatus* went hand-in-hand with the development of the stone instruments, and finally hammered copper tools in small quantity made their apearance just before the *hiatus*.

What Length of Time Is To Be Allowed For the Development of the Stone Instruments in Egypt Before the Hiatus?

For an answer to that question, the archaeologists hand us over to the paleontologists. At the beginning of the century, the best authorities on paleontology were very conservative in their estimates. G. W. Wright, who spent 40 years investigating the glacial problems, writes in *The Origin and Antiquity of Man* (U.S.A. 1912) as follows:

> While the period of man's habitation on earth cannot be less than 10,000 years, it need not be more than 15,000. Eight thousand years of prehistoric time is ample to account for all the known facts of his development.

Wright's conservative estimate was supported by such a weighty authority as Sollas. If the results arrived at by the carbon 14 method of dating are accepted as accurate, Wright's figures might have to be increased a little, but it is evidently absurd to allow a period of from 4,000 to 7,000 years to account for all the events that took place between the great historic flood in Mesopotamia and the beginning of the Christian era, and to demand a period of 500,000 years or more to account for the slight improvement in the instruments of the Old Stone Age.

The idea, which is of comparatively recent origin, that man spent hundreds of thousands of years depending on stone instruments alone, that he then discovered the art of making pottery, and that only in comparatively recent times he began to use metals, has been proved to be completely erroneous by the results of recent excavations in the Middle East.

Mesopotamia

It has already been proved by quotations from Sir Leonard Woolley and others that what are given as dates for prehistoric events by writers such as Millar Burrows are not dates at all, but estimates or guesses. They are, however, important because they show the amount of time that experts who have examined the various strata of pre-Flood sites are willing to allow for the development of material civilization from primitive stone instruments to those of the Iron Age.

The round number of 4,000 B.C. used to be given for the age of strata just above the deposit left by the Mesopotamian flood, and about 1,000 years is all that used to be allowed for the 10 or more pre-Flood strata at such places as Kish and Tepe Gawra. However, the evidence furnished by the most recent excavations in Syria, Palestine, Mesopotamia and Iran has forced archaeologists to increase the estimates by several thousand years.

In his book *Twenty-five Years of Mesopotamian Discovery* (already referred to), M. E. Mallowan, who agrees with Woolley that it is impossible to fix dates for prehistoric events, gives as his opinion that the earliest pre-Flood strata in Mesopotamia, where he superintended excavations, go back to 6,000 or 7,000 B.C. Even this estimate (which makes no allowance for the break in the civilization at the Flood) is altogether too low to account for the 26 occupational levels at Tepe Gawra, 21 of which are prehistoric.

The estimate based on the old system of chronology (which has not been disproved) that places the Mesopotamian flood (and the Deluge of Noe) at about 7,000 B.C. and adds at least 3,000 years for the break in continuity and the 10 pre-Flood strata is far closer to the truth.

As no fixed settlements were built by the hunters in Europe, who were content to use caves, we have no stratified cities there. The most we have in any single cave is three or four strata, and if all the strata representing the different divisions of the Stone Ages were put one over the other in the same place, they would not amount to more than 20. If, therefore, the archaeologists who are not willing to allow more than 6,000 years for 26 occupational levels of the ancient cities, which represented great progress in civilization, were given the task of making out an estimate for a smaller number of occupational levels which represented merely an improvement in the method of flaking stone, they would be compelled to give a correspondingly smaller estimate.

To What Period of the Stone Age Do the Earliest Pre-Flood Strata Belong?

Readers will find it commonly stated in books on the excavations in Mesopotamia that the earliest stratum at such places as Kish and Tepe Gawra belongs to the Neolithic Age, and that before the time represented by the earliest stratum in these places man existed for tens of thousands of years of the Mesolithic and Paleolithic Ages. Now the stone instruments of the early Paleolithic hunters have been found in abundance in all the countries surrounding Mesopotamia—in Iran, Palestine, Syria and Egypt—the question naturally arises, were there no inhabitants in fertile Mesopotamia at the time that the hunters of Palestine used the caves of Mount Carmel as temporary shelters?

The statement commonly found in books that the earliest stratum of the pre-Flood cities of Mesopotamia only goes back to the Neolithic Age is based on several false assumptions. The first false assumption is that early man was a primitive savage, who after being evolved from an animal, spent tens of thousands of years as a hunter living in caves before any city was built. It is assumed that man depended solely on stone instruments for tens of thousands of years and that the art of making pottery was not discovered till the Neolithic Age. It is assumed also that the Stone, Copper, Bronze and Iron Ages of Europe corresponded with those of Asia.

The most recent excavations in Mesopotamia and Iran, as well as the most recent investigations in Europe, have shown that these assumptions are groundless. The biblical account of early man tells us that Cain was a husbandman who tilled the ground, and therefore must have had tools, and that Abel was a shepherd and must have had domestic animals.

The archaeologists corroborate this account, for they tell us that the stone instruments found in the lowest pre-Flood strata at 'Al Ubaid near Ur, at Arpachiyah near Nineveh, at Jericho in Palestine and at Siyalk in Iran were mostly agricultural instruments and primitive unbaked pottery. At Arpachiah, an early pre-Flood town, hundreds of flint sickle blades together with grain jars and samples of cereals, which have been identified as emmer, wheat and barley, have been found. (See *Twenty-five Years of Mesopotamian Discovery,* p. 5). Evidence has been found in Palestine that agriculture was carried on there among the Natufians as early as 7,000 or 8,000 B.C. Henry Field tells in *The Track of Man* (p. 171) that he found a jar containing barley below the Flood deposit at Kish. The best indication of the manner of life of earliest man—that he tilled the ground and kept domestic animals such as the cow, the goat and the sheep—is furnished by the artifacts found in the lowest pre-Flood strata at Jericho during the most recent excavations. (See "The Deluge," Chapter 7).

The results of a recent attempt at fixing the dates of the

Stone Ages in Europe are given in *Les Hommes Fossiles* by Boule and Vallois (p. 355). They are: 3,000 B.C. for the beginning of the Neolithic Age; 5,000 B.C. to 8,300 for the Mesolithic, up to the end of the Paleolithic. A period of 5,300 years for the Mesolithic Age appears to be altogether too long. However, 8,300 B.C. is a very moderate estimate for the end of the Paleolithic Age compared to the estimates found in most books, and would place the pre-Flood strata of the ancient settlements in the Paleolithic Age.

It is safe, therefore, to conclude that the agricultural stone instruments and primitive pottery found at the lowest levels of the pre-Flood towns in Asia belong to the lower Paleolithic Age.

The Estimates of the Paleontologists For the Antiquity of Man in Europe

Before giving any figures, certain facts that have been brought to light in recent years must be noticed.

The general impression conveyed by most paleontologists about prehistoric Europe is that it was a place where man dwelt for tens if not hundreds of thousands of years, where he gradually developed the instruments of the Old, Middle and New Stone Ages, and then pottery, agriculture and metallurgy. Excavations in Egypt and more recently in Palestine have shown that the tools of the Old Stone Age (the Chellean, Tayacian, Acheulean and Mousterian Periods) have been found in abundance in both Egypt and Palestine.

It may be regarded as certain, therefore, that it was in Africa and Asia that material civilization, from the most primitive stone instruments to the tools of the Iron Age, was first developed and then exported to Europe.

A second important fact to be noted is that there is no indication of permanent settlements in Europe in either the Paleolithic or the Mesolithic Ages. Europe was simply the hunting ground for the inhabitants of Asia and Africa. Wave after wave of hunters with the distinctive hunting weapons of their tribe arrived in Europe, most probably from Africa.

During the Paleolithic Age they built no settlements; they were contented with the shelter afforded by the caves in the various places and, as these were very limited in number, the same caves were occupied by wave after wave of migrants from Asia. An examination of 187 human fossils of ancient hunters revealed the fact that only three of them passed the age of 50, and that most of the children died in infancy. One of two conclusions must be drawn from this fact: either the men returned to the warmer climates as they grew old, or that the life of a hunter, without fixed habitation or the staple food of life provided by agriculture, was so unhealthy that nearly all the children died, and that those who survived had a very short life.

A third fact to be noted is that agriculture and the keeping of domestic animals such as the cow, the horse, the sheep, etc., were not introduced into northern Europe until about 2,000 B.C., and that when these were introduced they were brought from Egypt by new settlers. (See *Testimony of the Spade,* Chap. 27, by G. Bibby, London, 1957).

The Figures Given by the Paleontologists

The figures given by Paleontologists for the antiquity of man may be divided into three classes: To the first class belong the figures of the first quarter of the present century, when we had estimates by scientists without theories, such as the estimates by G. F. Wright and Windle ranging from 15,000 to 25,000 years; and estimates by evolutionists such as Penck, Keith and Geikie, ranging from half-a-million to a million years.

To the second class belong the figures of the second quarter of the century when the moderates had died and the field was left to the evolutionists. These latter figures are given by F. E. Zeuner in *Dating the Past* as follows:

For the Java Man, the Peking Man and the Australopithecinae of South Africa he allows 400,000, 500,000 and 1,000,000 years respectively. For the various divisions of the Old Stone Age he gives the following figures:

Industry	Earliest Date	Duration
Chellean	540,000	60,000
Clactonian	540,000	300,000
Acheulian	430,000	300,000
Levalloisian	250,000	180,000
Mousterian	140,000	70,000
	Hiatus	
Aurignacian	100,000	50,000
Magdalenian	50,000	40,000
Mesolithic	20,000	15,000

(See Zeuner, *op. cit.*, p. 292).

To the third class belong the present-day figures. About these there is no general agreement, except on one point, namely, that the figures quoted above from Zeuner for the various divisions of the Old Stone Age and for their duration are evidently absurd in the light of modern discoveries.

In his *From Stone Age to Christianity,* M. F. Albright attempts to give a system of chronology based on modern discoveries. On page 128 he says, "Thanks to the extraordinary progress of our knowledge of the Stone Age in the Near East, we can now present a *correct* chronological outline of the succession of human types and cultures." He begins by pointing out that the earliest cultures of the Old Stone Age had their origin in Palestine and Egypt and that the actual workshops have been found along the Nile. He then appears to have become confused, for he correlates the periods of the Old Stone Age with the Interglacial Periods of Penck and Brückner, and should therefore get the same results as Zeuner—but he actually reduces them to less than one-fifth. His figures are as follows:

Chellean Age	about 100,000 years ago
Acheulean Age	about 60,000 years ago
Levalloiso-Mousterian Age	about 30,000 years ago
Mesolithic Age	10,000 to 6,000 years ago

Albright can hardly be regarded as an authority on the chronology of the Old Stone Age, but his figures are interesting because they show that a believer in the theory of evolution and in the genuineness of the Peking Man, the Java Man, etc., sees himself compelled by modern discoveries to reduce the figures of Zeuner and Abbé Breuil to less than one-fifth. However, they are still altogether too high, and are out of proportion with his short chronology for Egypt and Mesopotamia, in which he allows only about 5,000 years for all the developments from the earliest pre-Flood strata in Mesopotamia and Iran to the time of the birth of Christ.

The Figures of Boule and Vallois

Marcellin Boule and Henri V. Vallois rank as two of the best authorities in the world on human paleontology. Their book, *Les Hommes Fossiles,* was originally written by Boule, and after his death was twice revised by Dr. Vallois: in 1946 and again in 1952. It is from the latest (1952) edition that the following information is taken.

Both Boule and Vallois were at least nominal adherents to the theory of human evolution, but they were careful not to allow the theory to spoil the scientific value of this standard work of reference. They give the views of contemporary authorities and allow their readers to make their choice. For the Old Stone Age, Vallois gives no figures in the 1952 edition, but he examines the various methods used by those who demand half-a-million to a million years antiquity of man to prove their contention and finds them wanting. Toward the end of the book he gives the following figures for the Neolithic and Mesolithic Ages and the end of the Paleolithic, which are based partly on an essay on the subject by J. Clarke:

Neolithic		3,000 B.C.	
Mesolithic	Upper	3,000 B.C.	5,000 B.C.
	Middle	5,000 B.C.	6,800 B.C.
	Lower	6,800 B.C.	8,300 B.C.
End of Paleolithic		8,300 B.C.	

(See p. 355, *op. cit.).*

Results Obtained from the Fluorine And Carbon 14 Methods

As already mentioned, the carbon 14 method can rarely be used to test fossil bones directly; they must have been preserved in a dry place or charred if results are to be obtained. Even then, there are other conditions necessary for an accurate test, which is seldom fulfilled. The test is usually applied to charcoal or some other object containing carbon which has been found near the fossils, in which case there is an element of doubt whether the object containing carbon and the fossils are of the same age.

The fluorine method cannot give the age; it can only be used to determine whether objects found in the same place contain the same proportion of fluorine; if so, they are presumed to be of the same age. Even in this case there is an element of doubt.

The Piltdown Forgery Case

The carbon 14 method usually gets the credit for discovering the Piltdown forgery, but the fact is, as J. S. Weiner admits in his book, *The Piltdown Forgery,* that the answer to the problem was already known from evidence of people who were cognizant of the fraud, and then other tests were applied, such as drilling the skull and mandible to give ocular demonstration that these were of different ages and that the mandible had been stained to give it the appearance of antiquity.

The results of the various tests was that the skull and mandible, which for 40 years had been doing propaganda work for the theory of human evolution and for an antiquity of 500,000, were proved to belong to different individuals, the mandible being that of an ape that had recently died, and the skull being only a few thousand years, instead of being half-a-million.

Results Obtained in Australia

An attempt was made by E. D. Gill to date the Keiler skull, which is reputed to be the oldest fossil in Australia. The carbon

14 method gave no direct result. By the fluorine method it was found to contain about the same proportion as the deposit in the local Maribyrnong River, which the carbon 14 method dated at 9,000 years (7,000 B.C.). There is no certainty about this date; the age of the skull is probably much less.

America

At Folsom, in New Mexico, the remains of a camp was found where the Indians had roasted camel and bison meat. Among the bones of these animals, stone instruments were found which got the name of "Folsom points." No human bones were found, but the presence of the stone instruments and the remains of the charcoal from the fire provide more than sufficient evidence of the presence of man. In 1953 the charcoal was tested by the carbon 14 method and gave the age of 9,883 years, plus or minus 350 (which is the equivalent of 7,575 or 8,275 B.C.).

In a Chilean cave in South America organic remains associated with human artifacts were tested by the carbon 14 method, which gave the age of 8,639 years ± 450 (which is the equivalent of 7,131 B.C. or 6,231 B.C.). (See *The National Geographical Magazine,* December, 1955, pp. 781-805). Claims have been made in the above numbers for the existence of man in America 20,000 years ago, but it has been established that it was by the Bering Straits that the Indians entered America, less than 10,000 years ago.

Mesopotamia and Iran

Agricultural produce found at Jarmo, Mesopotamia, was dated at 6707 ± 320 years by the carbon 14 test. Charred bones found at Belt Cave, in Iran, were tested three times and gave three different results: 8,004 ± 900 years; 10,560 ± 1,200 years and 8,004 ± 1,400 years.

France

Charred bones and charcoal found at La Garenne, that were supposed to be contemporary, gave three different results, which are as follows: 11,109 ± 480, 15,847 ± 1,200 and 12,986 ± 560 years.

The Age of the Paintings in the Lascaux Cave, France

A number of caves with colored paintings of various animals were discovered in the North of Spain and the South of France during the last half-century. The most famous of these is the Lascaux Cave which contains no less than 400 paintings of various animals and some human figures. A selection of these paintings (in black, white and red) can be seen in the 1948 December issue of *The National Geographical Magazine.*

An attempt to date them was made by testing charcoal found in the cave by the carbon 14 method. The result obtained from one test was 15,516 ± 900 years. The round figure of 15,000 years is now given in books instead of the 30,000 years that was formerly claimed. As only one test was made, the date is by no means certain; it may not be more than half of 15,000 years. Neither is it certain whether the paintings belong to the period before or after the *hiatus,* as no fossils have been found in the caves. Stone instruments which have been identified as belonging to the post-*hiatus* period have been found in them but it is possible that the caves, like many other ones, were occupied both before and after the *hiatus,* and that the charcoal belongs to the pre-*hiatus* period and the flint instruments to the post-*hiatus*.

At the time that these paintings were discovered, the fact that men of the Old Stone Age, who were supposed to be savages in the process of evolution, were able to produce them caused great surprise. However, as has already been pointed out, the art of painting goes back to the earliest prehistoric times and was in a high state of development at the time of the Deluge. The art seems to have been lost, and it was not until a long time after it that it was developed again. Accordingly, these paintings belong either to the period immediately before the Deluge or to a period long after it.

Cyrenaica

In *Nature,* 1953, a claim of 32,000 years (the limit for the carbon 14 test) was made for a Neanderthal fossil bone found at Hara Fteah in Cyrenaica. The claim need not be taken seriously, for as we have already seen, direct results can but rarely be obtained from fossil bones only a few thousand years old, not to speak of 32,000 years.

Even if this claim be granted, it still means that the age of the Neanderthal fossils has been brought down from quarter of a million years to a mere 32,000.

These are some of the results obtained from tests by the carbon 14 method, carried out on fossils or carbon more than 5,000 years old. These results already have had the effect of forcing a drastic reduction to be made in the estimates for the length of the Old Stone Age, and therefore for the length of man's existence in the world, because the flint instruments of the Old Stone Age were the tools of earliest man, and these neither rust nor decay. As already mentioned, Dr. Albright has brought down the estimate of the Old Stone Age from half a million to one hundred thousand years, and even this estimate cannot be maintained in face of the results obtained from the carbon 14 tests.

Chapter 6

REPLIES TO THE ARGUMENTS USED IN FAVOR OF THE HALF-A-MILLION YEARS' ANTIQUITY THEORY

The following replies to the arguments put forward by advocates of the theory that man's antiquity in the world dates back at least half-a-million years are taken chiefly from the latest edition of Les Hommes Fossiles, *published originally by Marcellin Boule in 1923, and brought up-to-date in 1952 by Henri Vallois, who is a recognized authority on paleontology and was formerly an advocate of the half-a-million years' antiquity theory but, as the following quotations show, found that the arguments on which the theory is based are not valid.* (See *Les Hommes Fossils*, H. V. Vallois, 1952 ed., pp. 33-45).

Analysis of the Arguments For the Great Antiquity of Man

Vallois passes over the argument from evolution, which assumes that man has been evolved from a brute beast and that his evolution from beast to man required hundreds of thousands of years. He does so wisely for, as we have seen, the argument for human evolution is based almost entirely on paleontology, and among the candidates put forward for the position of "missing links" all have been found wanting. The Neanderthal Man has been proved to be a civilized man; the other candidates—the Peking, Java and Piltdown Men—have been found to be forgeries, and the Australopithecinae just ordinary apes.

The First Argument

The first argument for the great antiquity of man, which is also the principal one, is that man existed in Europe during the warm Interglacial Periods mentioned by Penck and Brückner, and that the earliest of these periods (the Gunz-Mindel) dates back to between 500,000 and 600,000 years ago. Vallois admits that he was one of those who adopted that argument 50 years ago, but he has come to the conclusion that it is no longer tenable, or in other words, that the argument is out of date.

The question of the Glacial Periods has been discussed at length in Chapter 2 of this Part. There, readers will find very strong evidence that there was only one Glacial Period. Hence the argument based on the existence of four Glacial Periods, and the supposed presence of man in Europe during the warm intervals between them, collapses.

Then there is wide difference of opinion about the length of the Glacial Period or Periods—differences ranging from 40,000 to 600,000 years. The only certain information that we have on the length of the Period is that provided by Baron de Geer, which is, that it is less than 20,000 years to the peak of the last Glacial Period, and that the Post-Glacial Period began less than 9,000 years ago.

No Connection Between the Glacial Periods Or the Astronomical Theory and the Antiquity of Man in the World

Attempts have been made to show that man existed in Europe during the alleged Interglacial Periods, but no solid argument can be advanced. The common argument used is that the stone instruments of the earliest (Chellean) Period have been found, not in caves, but in the open, and that they have been found associated with tropical fauna.

Abbé Breuil and Zeuner claim that the Chellean Period dates back to about 540,000 B.C. and that it lasted 60,000 years. They say that the next period, the Acheulian, dates back 430,000 years and that it lasted 300,000 years.

According to these two writers, therefore, early man remained for 360,000 years, depending on roughly shaped hand axes. This absurd claim has been abandoned even by evolutionists such as W. F. Albright, who allows 100,000 years for the whole Old Stone Age. Besides, it has been known for the last 50 years that these stone industries (the Chellean and Acheulean) did not arise in Europe at all, but most probably in Egypt.

The Chellean and Acheulean stone axes have been found all over Palestine, Egypt and even in South Africa. Actual flint shops where they were manufactured have been found in the Sahara Desert; and down in Tanganyika, a series of stratified deposits, 300 feet in thickness, have been found in the Olduvai Gorge. These deposits show that the Chellean and Acheulean stone instruments were manufactured *at the same time*. Professor Leakey, the author of *Adam's Ancestors,* who is an extreme supporter of the theory of man's evolution, examined these deposits in the Olduvai Gorge and gives as his opinion that the division of the hand axe culture into the Chellean and the Acheulian is an arbitrary one. The claims, therefore, of those who say that the Chellean hand-axe industry existed 60,000 years before Acheulean industry began, is absurd in the extreme. (See *Adam's Ancestors,* p. 75).

Arguments from River Terraces And Layers of Loess

As the result of floods due to the melting of the glaciers, to torrential rains and to ingressions of the sea, deposits have been left behind in the valleys forming terraces along the rivers. In these terraces fossils of animals and man-made stone instruments have been found, and attempts have been made to date the stone instruments from the position of these stone instruments and of the fossils with which they are associated.

Boule and Vallois discuss this question in *Les Hommes Fossiles* (1952 ed., pp. 29-33), and come to the conclusion that river terraces, for various reasons which they give, do not provide a reliable chronometer.

The River Terraces at St. Acheul, Amiens And at Heidelberg, in Germany

The two river terraces on which the estimate of our 500,000 years for the beginning of the Old Stone Age in Europe is based chiefly are the river terraces at St. Acheul on the Somme which were examined by Abbé Breuil, and the terraces at Heidelberg in the valley of the Neckar which have been studied by F. E. Zeuner. There is a great similarity between the deposits in the two places. In both cases the deposits are covered with deep layers of loess on the top, and sand under it; and in both cases attempts have been made by Abbé Breuil and F. E. Zeuner to correlate the layers of loess with the different Interglacial Periods of Penck and Brückner and to date them accordingly. Now in the first place, it is an evident impossibility to identify and distinguish the loess of the various periods (the existence of which is denied by many authorities) for it is all composed of the same material, which is the dust of the glaciers carried by the winds, or by water for them. In the next place, no length of time could account for the position of the layers of loess and sand and for their great thickness; for at both St. Acheul and Heidelberg all the layers of loess are on top and the layer of sand is at the bottom, and at both places the layers are very thick. Only a great flood could account for the thickness of the layers and for their relative position. In any flood the sand and gravel carried by the water sink down to the bottom and are deposited first, while the earth, which is lighter, sinks more slowly and gradually. The deposits of loess and sand in the valleys and the deep deposits found in the caves on higher ground can all be explained by the great transgression of the sea which, according to geologists, covered all Europe, and which was almost certainly the Flood of Noe. It is a remarkable fact that, in the valley of the Somme, only the stone instruments of the Lower (earliest) Paleolithic Age have been found and, at Heidelberg, the Mauer jawbone that has been found at the bottom of the deep deposit is regarded by all as belonging also to the Lower Paleolithic Age. Instead of providing an argument for the great antiquity of man in Europe, the various layers of loess and sand in the Somme Valley and at Heidelberg provide an argument for the major transgression of the sea in Europe that caused the *hiatus* at the end of the Lower Paleolithic Age, and for the minor transgressions of which paleontologists tell us.

The first major transgression of the sea would account for the lower portion of the deposits on the Somme, at Heidelberg and in the caves, which is of the greatest depth, while the subsequent minor transgressions would explain the smaller deposits on the top. At any rate, the claim to be able to identify the various layers of loess in the Somme Valley and at Heidelberg, and to assign them to different glacial periods differing in date by hundreds of thousands of years, is evidently absurd.

Association of Artifacts and Fossils With Extinct Fauna of Warm and Cold Climates

The bones of various animals of both warm and cold climates which have become extinct in prehistoric times have been found in association with both the stone tools and the human fossils of the Paleolithic Age. This fact has been used as an argument for the antiquity of the artifacts and fossils, but the antiquity that it argues is by no means as great as the claim made.

The Fauna of the Cold Climates

The fauna of the Arctic regions were forced to migrate southward during the Glacial Periods because the whole Arctic region and the territory for hundreds of miles south of it became covered with ice. They were compelled to remain in the ice-free parts of southern Europe until the ice receded. As we have seen, the Scandinavian countries, northern Germany and northern Russia did not become free of ice until 7,000 B.C. No argument for great antiquity, then, can be based on fossils of Arctic animals, such as the mammoth, the woolly rhinocerous, the lemming or the reindeer, found in association with the instruments of the Old Stone Age or with the fossil remains of man.

The Predmost Hunting Cap

Predmost occupies a strategic position in central Moravia at a gap in the Sudetan Mountains and is the natural gateway between the Danube Valley and the northern European plain. During the Glacial Period it was in an ice-free corridor between the ice-covered region of northern Russia and the district of the Alpine glaciers.

The animals from the Arctic regions had to pass through this gap on their way to and from summer pastures of southern Europe. Prehistoric man of the Aurignacian (post-*hiatus*) period took advantage of this fact and set up a hunting camp there. The site of the camp has been excavated and the bones of more than 900 mammoths, for the most part calves and half-grown specimens, together with the bones of other Arctic animals have been unearthed. Besides, a large grave covered over with large stones, containing the skeletons of 20 human beings, was found in 1894 when the excavation of the place, which had begun as early as 1850, was nearly completed.

The skulls found were of the Cro-Magnon type, and the flint instruments, of which there were 25,000, belonged to the Aurignacian Period, which is the Period after the *hiatus* or flood. Geoffrey Bibby, who gives a very good description of the find in *The Testimony of the Spade*, thinks that this hunting camp might date back 20,000 years, but most probably that figure should be about 8,000 (i.e., to about 6,000 B.C.). *At any rate we have definite proof that the mammoth did not become extinct until comparatively recent times, and hence mammoth bones found in association with human fossils or artifacts cannot be used as an argument for great antiquity.*

The Fauna of the Tropical Climate

The fauna of warm climates have been found in the river terraces of the Somme Valley in association with the stone instruments of the Chellean and Acheulian periods, but no human fossils have been found with them. They have been found also in association with the Mauer jawbone, with the skulls of the pre-Neanderthal race (resembling those of modern man) found at Ehrignsdorf (1925), Steenheim (1933), Swanscombe (1933-37) and Fontéchevade (1947).

They have been found also in association with the two skulls discovered in 1929 and 1935 at Saccopastore, near Rome, which combine the characteristics of the Neanderthal Man and modern man.

As the fauna of the warm climates became extinct in Europe long before those of the cold climates, their association with human fossils or artifacts is proof that these fossils are older than those associated with the fauna of cold climates. It is a very remarkable fact that in Europe they are found only in association with the fossils of prehistoric men of the Fontéchevade type, and not in association with the fossils of the Neanderthal Man. It was the discovery of these skulls, especially the discovery of the Fontéchavade skulls in 1947, that decided the question whether the Neanderthal Man afforded any proof of human evolution, by showing that a race of men, in every respect the equal of modern man, existed before the Neanderthal Man.

Before these skulls were discovered, it used to be confidently asserted by supporters of the theory of evolution and of the great antiquity of man, that the presence of the fauna of warm climates in the valley of the Somme, along with the stone instruments of the Chellean and Acheulean Periods, was proof that man existed in Europe during the (alleged) warm Interglacial Periods. That assertion has been repeated again and again by evolutionists since the days of Boucher de Perthes more than a century ago.

The claim has been dropped in practice by those modern writers such as Albright, who reduces the date of the Old Stone Age given by Abbé Breuil and Zeuner from more than half-a-million years to a mere hundred thousand.

No proof has ever been brought forward to show that man existed during the alleged warm Interglacial Periods, and no answer has ever been given to the insuperable objection against the theory, namely, that no human fossils or artifacts of the Old Stone Age have been found in the Scandinavian countries or in those parts of Germany, Russia, etc., which were covered by the ice of the last Glacial Period.

There is no need to have recourse to the theory of Interglacial

Periods, during which man is supposed to have existed, in order to explain the fossils of animals of warm climates found in Europe in association with the fossils or artifacts of prehistoric man; for geologists tell us that there were land bridges from Africa to Europe across the Mediterranean at Sicily and Gibraltar until the last Glacial period, over which African fauna could pass freely to Europe. Those that were caught in Europe at the time of the last Glacial Period probably lingered on and were exterminated by the hunters who manufactured the stone instruments of the Aurignacian and Magdalanian Periods, or gradually perished by the cold.

Summary by Vallois

After discussing the various arguments brought forward by Lartet, de Mortellet, Breuil, etc., for the great antiquity of man, Vallois sums up as follows in *Les Hommes Fossiles* (1952 ed., p. 45):

> Each method then has its good qualities and its defects, and each of them taken by itself, is insufficient. Certain classifications established by pure geologists incur the grave reproach of not taking palaeontological or archaeological facts into consideration, and of endeavoring to explain everything by one physical phenomenon about which we know little, whether it be a glacial or a marine phenomenon. Classification based on fossils can serve only for the great divisions and should vary for the different regions of the globe.
>
> By invoking only archaeological facts (the various kinds of stone instruments), prehistorians succeed in making a great many divisions in the Stone Age and in establishing a rather detailed chronology. Unfortunately the classifications of this kind instituted and perfected by Lartet, de Mortillet, Piette, Cartailhac, Breuil, etc., can only be applied *â priori* to restricted portions of our own Continent alone.

Chapter 7

CONCLUSIONS

1) The opinion which says that man has existed in the world for 500,000 years or more is untenable, because (i) it had never any real scientific foundation and (ii) because the assumptions on which it was based have been proved to be false. These assumptions were: (*a*) that man's body has been evolved from an animal, (*b*) that the fossils of the Piltdown Man, the Peking Man etc., represented beings in process of evolution, (*c*) that there were four Glacial Periods with three warm intervals between them, during which man existed in Europe, and (*d*) that the Old Stone Age lasted about half-a-million years.

2) The opinion of Dr. Albright which says that the Old Stone Age lasted 100,000 years, and that man existed on earth at least that long, has been rendered untenable by the results obtained from carbon 14 tests on fossils etc., and by recent discoveries made in the excavations at Jericho and at other ancient sites.

3) The third conclusion is taken from the last chapter on the Deluge (q.v.). It is, that there is sufficient evidence to show that (*a*) the end of the Last Glacial Period, (*b*) the *hiatus* at the end of the Mousterian Period, (*c*) the destruction of the ancient settlements of Jericho in Palestine, of Ur, Kish, Tepe Gawra etc., of Mesopotamia, and of the early settlements of Iran, and (*d*) the Deluge, all occurred at the same time, which was about 7,000 B.C.; and that this date can be regarded as a landmark, scientifically established, from which to begin the calculation of the length of the period from the Deluge to the creation of Adam and Eve.

4) In estimating the antiquity of man for the period between Adam and the Deluge we have (i) the information given

in the Bible to guide us; we have (ii) the evidence gathered by paleontologists and archaeologists in this century of investigation which shows that man never passed the barriers of the ice-capped Himalayas until the ice of the last Glacial Period melted, less than 10,000 years ago; we have (iii) the evidence of the archaeologist who excavated dozens of pre-Flood towns and cities in the Middle East, which shows that, while nomadic tribes like the Neanderthal were hunting wild animals in Europe and Africa and living in caves, the main portion of the human race led a normal life in the Middle East, tilling the ground, building towns and cities, and manufacturing implements and utensils suitable for agriculture and domestic uses. For further proof of this assertion, we refer our readers to Chapter 5 of the previous Part on the Deluge.

5) With regard to the estimates for the period between Adam and the Deluge derived from the Bible—1,656, 1,307 and 2,242 years of the Hebrew, Samaritan and Septuagint versions, respectively—we are not sure that the list of the Patriarchs is complete and that the period may not therefore have been longer, but even the estimate from the Samaritan version, which is the lowest, is sufficient to account for the progress made by man in manufacturing tools and utensils, for we are bound to accept the common teaching of the Church based on *Genesis* that Adam was created in the state of original justice and that he had sufficient knowledge of both spiritual and temporal things to fit him for the position of head of the human race.

6) In 1912, G. F. Wright wrote in *The Origin and Antiquity of Man* (Oberlin, Ohio):

> While the antiquity of man in the world cannot be less than 10,000 years, it need not be more than 15,000. Eight thousand years of prehistoric time is ample to account for all the known facts relating to his development.

Sir Bertram Windle, his contemporary, is in substantial agreement with him, while Sollas would increase the estimate to about 25,000 years.

These men were real scientists capable of weighing evidence; they had before them the same evidence on the Glacial

Periods and the alleged Interglacial warm periods on which Zeuner and Abbé Breuil based their chief argument for the antiquity of man, but they rejected it as being devoid of proof. In doing so they had the support of their contemporary, Sir Henry Howorth, one of the greatest authorities on the Glacial Periods.

If we follow the second method of calculating the antiquity of man, which takes no account of the Deluge, and if we accept only scientific conclusions (rejecting mere theories) as evidence, we shall arrive at substantially the same results.

Clarke's estimate for the beginning of the New Stone Age in Europe, already quoted, is 3,000 B.C. The most recent estimates of the age of the earliest fixed settlements founded by man, in and around Mesopotamia, is about 7,000 B.C., which places them well within the Old Stone Age. The earliest stone instruments of the Chellean and Acheulian periods, which are presumed to be buried beneath the flood deposit in the low-lying plains of Mesopotamia, are found in abundance in the hills of Palestine and in the Sahara Desert. As already stated, the cradle of the human race is certainly to be found in Mesopotamia or the area surrounding it.

In that area, there was no break in the development of civilization between the Deluge and the time of Adam, hence 8,000 or 10,000 years at most is more than sufficient to account for the development of the human race between the time of the earliest fixed settlement in Mesopotamia and the creation of Adam and Eve.

These two periods added together do not amount to 20,000 years.

The scientific evidence from carbon 14 tests, etc., available for calculating the length of the period before the Deluge requires further checking; as it is, if we reject the estimates which have not been confirmed, such as the estimate of 15,000 years for the age of the Lascaux caves, it would permit the fixing of the minimum length at about 5,000 years (or even less), while the maximum estimate need not exceed 15,000 years before the Deluge.

BIBLIOGRAPHY

Anderez, Fr. S.J., *Hacia el Origen del Hombre.* Fr. Ezpondaburu, S.J., Editor. Santander, Spain. 1956.

Anderez, S.J., Fr. *L'Origini Dell' Uomo.* Milan. 1954.

Barclay, Vera. *Challenge to Darwinians.* 1951.

Barclay, Vera. *Darwin Is Not for Children.* 1950.

Begoeun, Comte. *Quelques Souvenirs sur le Mouvement des Idées Transformists.* Paris. 1945.

Bergounioux et Glory. *Les Premiers Hommes.* 1952.

Boule, Marcellin. *Les Hommes Fossiles.* Paris. 1923.

Broom and Robinson, Drs. *A New Type of Fossil Man.* 1949.

Carter, G. S. *A Hundred Years of Evolution.* Sidgwick and Jackson. 1958.

A Catholic Commentary on Holy Scripture. London. 1953.

The Catholic Encyclopedia. The Encyclopedia Press, Inc. New York. 1908.

Charlier, Dom Celestin. *La Lecture Chretienne de la Bible.* Paris. 1949.

The Christian Approach to the Bible. English translation of *La Lecture Chretienne de La Bible.* London. 1958.

Collin, Remy, M.D. *L'Evolution: Hypotheses et Problemes.* Paris. 1958.

Corte, Nicholas. *Les Origines de L'Homme.* Paris. 1957.

Cotter, A. C., S.J. *Natural Species.* 1947.

Darwin, Charles. *The Descent of Man.* London. 1874.

Darwin, Charles. *The Origin of Species.* Introduction by Dr. W. R. Thompson, F.R.S. Everyman's Library. 1959.

de Bivort, Jacques, Editor. *God, Man and the Universe.* London. 1954.

de Chardin, Fr. Teilhard. *Early Man in China.* Peking. 1941.

Dewar, Douglas. *A Challenge to Evolutionists.*

Dewar, Douglas. *Man a Special Creation.* 1946.

Dietz, Henry W. *The Story of Science.* Cleveland.

Dorlodot, Canon. *Darwinism and Catholic Thought.* London. 1922.

Gerard, F., S.J. *Evolutionary Philosophy.* 1904.

Grison, Fr. M. *Problemes d'Origines.* Paris. 1954.

Guide to the Bible. Frs. Robert and Tricot, Editors. Paris, Tournai, Rome and New York. 1955.

El Hombre Prehistorico y los Origines de la Humanidad. Madrid. 1944.

Evolution as a Process. Edited by Sir Julian Huxley, A. C. Hardy and E. B. Ford. 1954.

Fothergill, Philip G. *Historical Aspects of Organic Evolution.* London. 1952.

Gerard, Fr., S.J. *Evolutionary Philosophy.* 1904.

Gregorianum. Rome. 1948-1958.

Grison, Fr. M. *Problemes d' Origines.* Paris. 1954.

Hauret, Fr. Charles. *Origines* (Genèse: Chaps. I-III). Paris. 1953.

Höpfel, H., O.S.B., edited by Leloir, Ludovicus, O.S.B. *Introductio Generalis In Sacram Scripturam.* Naples and Rome. 1958.

Hoyle, Fred. *The Nature of the Universe.* London. 1953.

Huxley, Sir Julian. *Evolution in Action.* 1953.

Huxley, T. V. *Man's Place in Nature.* London. 1863.

Introduction a la Bible: Introduction Générale Ancien Testament. Frs. Robert and Feuillet, Editors. Desclée & Cie. 1957.

"Is Evolution Proved?" A debate between Douglas Dewar and H. S. Shelton. London. 1947.

Johnson, Fr. Humphrey. *The Bible and the Early History of Man.* London. 1947.

Keith, Sir Arthur. *A New Theory of Human Evolution.* London. 1949.

Keller, Werner. *The Bible as History.* English translation. London. 1956.

Knowles, F. G. W. *Biology and Man.* London. 1950.

La Sainte Bible. Commentary by Pirot, Fr. Louis and Canon Clamer. Paris. 1953.

Le Gros Clark, W. E. *The Fossil Evidence for Human Evolution.* Chicago. 1955.

Leakey, L. S. B. *Adam's Ancestors.* 1953.

Les Hommes Fossiles. Marcellin Boule. Paris. 1923.

Les Hommes Fossiles. Boule and Vallois. Paris. 1952.

Lunn, Arnold. *The Revolt Against Reason.* 1949.

Marcozzi, Fr., S.J. *L'Origini Dell' Uomo.* Milan. 1954.

Marcozzi, Fr., S.J. *L'Uomo Nello Spazio e nel Tempo.* Milan. 1953.

Mariani, Fr. Bonaventura. *Introductio in Libros Sacros Veteris Testamenti.* Rome. 1958.

McKenzie. The Rev. J. L., S.J. *Two-Edged Sword: An Interpretation of the Old Testament.* Bruce Publishing Co. 1955.

McLoughlin, Rev. Patrick J. *The Church and Modern Science.* Dublin. 1959.

Messenger, Dr. *Evolution and Theology.* London. 1931.

Messenger, Dr. *Theology and Evolution.* London. 1949.

Monroe, Margaret T. *Thinking About Genesis.* London. 1953.

Murray, Desmond, O.P. *Species Revalued.* London. 1955.

Obermaier. *El Hombre Fosil.* 1925.

Oevres de Pierre Teilhard de Chardin, S.J.: L'Apparition de L'Homme. Paris. 1957.

Philips and Cox. *A Second Book of Biology.* London. 1940.

On an Adolescent Skull of Sinanthropus, Pekinensis, Palaeontoligia Sinica. Peking. 1931.

Rome and the Study of Scriptures: A collection of Papal enactments on the study of the Scriptures, together with the decisions of the Biblical Commission.

Romer, A. S. *Man and the Vertebrates.* 2 Vols. Penguin Ed. 1954.

Ruffini, Cardinal Ernesto. *The Theory of Evolution Judged by Reason and Faith.* New York. 1959.

Sacrae Theologiae Summa. Spanish Jesuit Fathers. Madrid. 1952.

Sheehan the Most Rev. M., D.D. *Apologetics and Catholic Doctrine* and *The Origin of Life.* Dublin. 1950.

Short, Rendle A. *Modern Discovery and the Bible.* London. 1953.

Steinmueller, Mgr. John E., D.D., L.S.S. *Problems of the Old Testament.* Bruce Publishing Co. 1936.

Van Imshoot, the Rev. P. *Theologie de L'Ancien Testament: L'Homme.* Paris. 1956.

Vawter, Fr. Bruce. *A Path Through Genesis* and *God's Story of Creation.* London and Dublin. 1957.

Vere, Francis. *Lessons of Piltdown.* London. 1959.

Vere, Francis. *The Piltdown Fantasy.* London. 1955.

Vialleton, Louis. *L'Origine des Êtres Vivants: L'Illusion Transformiste* (15th ed.). Paris. 1930.

Walter and Sayles. *Biology of the Vertebrates.* New York. 1954.

Ward. H. *Evolution for John.* London. 1926.

Wasmann, The Rev. E., S.J. *Modern Biology and the Theory of Evolution.* English translation by A. U. Buchanan. London. 1910.

Weidenreich. *On the Earliest Representatives of Modern Mankind Discovered on the Soil of East Asia.* Peking Nat. His. Bull. 1939.

Weidenreich, F. *Apes, Giants and Men.* Chicago. 1945.

Weiner, J. S. *The Piltdown Forgery.* Oxford. 1955.

Windle, Sir Bertram. *The Church and Science.* London. 1918.

Zahm, The Rev. J. A. *The Bible, Science and Faith.* U.S.A. 1895.

Zimmerman, Walter. *Evolution: Geschichte Ihrer Probleme und Erkenntisse.* Munich. 1953.